Assessment Sensitivity

Context and Content

Series editor: François Recanati, Institut Nicod

Assessment Sensitivity

Relative Truth and its Applications

John MacFarlane

OXFORD
UNIVERSITY PRESS

OXFORD
UNIVERSITY PRESS

Great Clarendon Street, Oxford, OX2 6DP,
United Kingdom

Oxford University Press is a department of the University of Oxford.
It furthers the University's objective of excellence in research, scholarship,
and education by publishing worldwide. Oxford is a registered trade mark of
Oxford University Press in the UK and in certain other countries

Published in the United States of America by Oxford University Press
198 Madison Avenue, New York, NY 10016, United States of America

British Library Cataloguing in Publication Data
Data available

Library of Congress Control Number: 2001012345

ISBN 978–0–19–968275–1

As printed and bound by
CPI Group (UK) Ltd, Croydon, CR0 4YY

PREFACE

This book is about how we might make sense of the idea that truth is relative, and how we might use this idea to give satisfying accounts of parts of our thought and talk that have resisted traditional methods of analysis. Although there is a substantial philosophical literature on relativism about truth, going back to Plato's *Theaetetus*, this literature (both pro and con) has tended to focus on refutations of the doctrine, or refutations of these refutations, at the expense of saying clearly what the doctrine *is*. The approach here will be to start by giving a clear account of the view, and then to use the view to solve some problems that have concerned philosophers and semanticists. The main aim is to put relativist solutions to these problems on the table, so that they may be compared with non-relativist solutions and accepted or rejected on their merits. Comparatively little space will be devoted to blanket objections to the coherence of relativism, because these will largely be dispelled by a clear statement of the view.

When I finished graduate school, I would never have guessed that my first book would be a defense of relative truth. To proclaim oneself a relativist about truth, I assumed, was to ally oneself with the kind of postmodernist scepticism about the objectivity of science that the physicist Alan Sokal lampooned in his famous hoax article for *Social Text* (Sokal 1996b; Sokal 1996a). I regarded relativism about truth as hopelessly confused, easily refuted, and a sure sign of deficient intellectual character. And I was not alone in this: I did not know of a single prominent analytic philosopher who espoused relativism about truth, or even took it seriously enough to spend more than a few pages on it.

What happened? I have not changed my view that there is an objective world, or we can come to know about it using the methods of science. And I still think that most talk of relative truth has been hopelessly muddled. But I have become convinced that relativism about truth can be made philosophically intelligible, even to hard-headed scientific realists, and that it is a good tool for understanding parts of our thought and talk that fall short of being fully objective.

My own path to relativism began not with the usual worries about taste and morality, but with reflections on the semantics of contingent statements about the future, inspired mainly by Belnap and Green (1994). By June of 2002, I had concluded that the natural setting for a Belnap/Green-style approach to future contingents was a framework in which truth was relativized to both a context of use and a context of assessment. I presented this idea at ECAP IV in Lund, Sweden, where I found a fellow traveler: Max Kölbel, who had just finished *Truth Without Objectivity* (2002). By the end of August, 2002, I had written a manuscript "Three Grades of Truth Relativity," which was the germ of the present book. (Though this paper was never published, a self-standing treatment of future contingents was published as MacFarlane 2003.)

At this time, the philosophical literature was full of discussions of various forms of contextualism, and I could see that the relative-truth framework I had applied in "Three Grades" to future contingents, accommodation, and evaluative relativism had applications in these areas as well. I worked out two of these—to knowledge-attributing sentences and to epistemic modals—in summer 2003, and presented them as talks at Stanford, Utah, and Yale. (These became MacFarlane 2005a and MacFarlane 2011a.) Conversations with Jeff King and Jason Stanley spurred me to think more about how one might do relativist semantics in a propositional (rather than a sentential) framework, and the result was my Aristotelian Society paper "Making Sense of Relative Truth" (MacFarlane 2005c).

Others had been working independently along parallel lines. Andy Egan, John Hawthorne, and Brian Weatherson came out with their own relativist treatment of epistemic modals (Egan, Hawthorne, and Weatherson 2005). Mark Richard noticed the applications to knowledge attributions and accommodation (Richard 2004). And the linguist Peter Lasersohn, working at first in isolation from the emerging literature in philosophy, wrote an influential paper arguing for a relativist treatment of predicates of personal taste, employing a modification of Kaplan's semantics for indexicals that was very similar to my own approach in "Three Grades" (Lasersohn 2005). In September, 2005, LOGOS sponsored a well-attended conference on relativist semantics in Barcelona.

What continued to distinguish my work from others' was the notion of a *context of assessment*. Others had made the move of relativizing propositional truth to parameters other than worlds, such as judges, perspectives, or standards of taste. But I had argued in MacFarlane (2005c) that this alone was not enough to make one a relativist about truth in the most philosophically interesting sense. The interesting divide, I argued, is between views that allow truth to vary with the context of assessment and those that do not. My next batch of papers (2007a, 2009, 2008) was devoted to making this point in more detail, and to fleshing out the distinction between "nonindexical contextualist" views, which relativize propositional truth to nonstandard parameters but do not posit assessment sensitivity, and genuinely "relativist" views.

In Spring 2007 I sat in on my colleague Niko Kolodny's seminar on reasons and rationality, and this led to a fruitful and ongoing collaboration. Niko helped me bring my semantic ideas into contact with important debates in the literature on practical reasoning. Our joint paper (Kolodny and MacFarlane 2010) applied relativist ideas to the semantics of deontic modals and indicative conditionals.

This is a large project, with many interconnecting parts, and journal papers have not been the ideal medium for presenting it. Without the applications, the foundational ideas appear abstract and sterile; but the applications cannot be adequately explained without the foundational ideas. Moreover, because it would not be rational to make significant changes in one's semantic framework just to handle one recalcitrant construction, it is important to see that there are many systematically related applications of the proposed framework. Hence I have always envisioned a book-length treatment covering foundations and applications in a unified way. Though the present book draws on earlier articles, with a few exceptions I have written everything afresh, removing inconsistencies, improving explanations, and responding to criticism that has appeared in the literature.

Analytic philosophers are now considerably more open to relativism about truth than they were when I began this project. My initial aim was merely to place relativist views on the table as real options. Many of those who initially accused these views of incoherence have come around to regarding them as merely empirically false. I am grateful for the company, and I hope that the book is still timely.

J. M.
Berkeley

ACKNOWLEDGEMENTS

I began this book while on leave in 2003–4, thanks to a Berkeley Humanities Research Fellowship and an ACLS/Andrew W. Mellon Fellowship for Junior Faculty. An additional semester of leave in fall 2008, supplemented again by a Berkeley Humanities Research Fellowship, allowed me to make considerable progress on the manuscript.

Many of the ideas herein were first worked out in journal articles. Chapters 3–5 draw on MacFarlane (2003), MacFarlane (2005c), MacFarlane (2009), MacFarlane (2008), and MacFarlane (2011b). Chapter 6 draws on MacFarlane (2007a). Chapter 9 draws on MacFarlane (2003) and MacFarlane (2008). Chapter 8 draws on MacFarlane (2005a), MacFarlane (2005b), MacFarlane (2009), and MacFarlane (2007a). Chapters 10 and 11 draw on MacFarlane (2011a) and Kolodny and MacFarlane (2010). Some passages in Chapter 5 are reprinted verbatim from MacFarlane (2005c), by courtesty of the Editor of the Aristotelian Society. Thanks also to Oxford University Press for allowing me to use some material from MacFarlane (2011b), MacFarlane (2008), and MacFarlane (2011a) in Chapters 5, 9, and 10, respectively.

In developing my ideas, I have been greatly helped by students in two graduate seminars at Berkeley (Spring 2005 and Spring 2008), especially Michael Caie, Stanley Chen, Fabrizio Cariani, Kenny Easwaran, Michael Rieppel, and Skip Schmall. Joe Karbowski did excellent work as my research assistant in 2004, as did Michael Rieppel in 2009 and 2011, and Ian Boon and Sophie Dandelet in 2012. I benefited immensely from intensive seminars on the first six chapters of the book given for the LOGOS group in Barcelona in March 2009, the Cogito group in Bologna in June 2010, and the Institut Jean Nicod in Paris in October 2010, and I thank Manuel García-Carpintero, Paolo Leonardi, and François Recanati, for making these possible. In March 2012, I had the opportunity to present some material from the book in three lectures at Princeton as Whitney J. Oates Fellow in the Humanities Council. I am grateful to Princeton's Humanities Council for the opportunity, and to the philosophers there for lively discussion. I have also benefited from questions from audiences at talks in Berkeley, Bristol, Buenos Aires, Chicago, Connecticut, Davis, Dublin, Guangzhou, Harvard, Irvine, Las Vegas, London, Los

Angeles, MIT, Mexico City, Michigan, Minneapolis, New York, Notre Dame, Oslo, Oxford, Paris, Pittsburgh, Portland, Providence, Princeton, Riverside, Rutgers, San Diego, Santa Barbara, Santa Cruz, San Francisco, St Andrews, Stanford, Toronto, Tucson, Utah, and Yale; and from conversations (both in person and over e-mail) with a large number of philosophers and linguists, including Kent Bach, Chris Barker, Nuel Belnap, Matthew Benton, Andrea Bianchi, Paul Boghossian, John Campbell, Joe Camp, Richard Dietz, Cian Dorr, Andy Egan, Iris Einheuser, Delia Graff Fara, Hartry Field, Branden Fitelson, Kit Fine, Manuel García-Carpintero, Hannah Ginsborg, David Hunter, Peter Hanks, Benj Hellie, Dirk Kindermann, Niko Kolodny, Max Kölbel, Jeff King,, Peter Lasersohn, Elijah Millgram, Friederike Moltmann, Sebastiano Moruzzi, Thomas Müller, Stephen Neale, Ram Neta, Eva Picardi, Stefano Predelli, Graham Priest, François Recanati, Tobias Rosenfeldt (and his graduate seminar at the Humboldt University of Berlin), Sven Rosenkrantz, Daniel Lopez de Sa, Karl Schafer, Jonathan Schaffer, Lionel Shapiro, Mark Schroeder, Barry Smith, Jason Stanley, Isidora Stojanovic, Zoltán Gendler Szabó, Ken Taylor, Paul Teller, Giorgio Volpe, Lee Walters, Jacek Wawer, Brian Weatherson, Matthew Weiner, Dag Westerståhl, Crispin Wright, Seth Yalcin, and Aaron Zimmerman. Throughout the process, my editor Peter Momtchiloff provided patient encouragement and advice. I am also grateful to two anonymous referees from Oxford University Press, who provided helpful feedback on a penultimate draft.

I owe larger intellectual debts to my teachers, Bob Brandom, Nuel Belnap, and Joe Camp. They planted the seeds that grew into the present manuscript, which they may regard as an exotic weed.

The book has taken a long time to write. It might have been done sooner had it not been for my wife Colleen Boyle and our daughter Claire, who have made the "real world" as enchanting as the world of ideas.

CONTENTS

1

A TASTE OF RELATIVISM

You bite into a fresh apple. It is the tart kind that you particularly like, and it is perfectly ripe. "Tasty," you say, without a moment's hesitation. But what did you *mean* by that? What, exactly, are you saying about the apple?

I have found that people tend to give one of three kinds of answers:

Objectivism I am saying that the apple has an objective property, the property of being tasty, that I can detect perceptually. This is the same property others attribute when they use the word "tasty." Whether the apple has this property is a simple matter of fact, independent of perspective.

Contextualism I am saying that the apple strikes me in a certain way, or is pleasing to my tastes, or to the tastes of a group with which I identify. The word "tasty" is contextually sensitive, so that my use of it ascribes the property of being pleasing to me or my tastes, while your use of the same word would ascribe a different property: the property of being pleasing to *you* or your tastes.

Expressivism I am not asserting anything at all about the apple. I am just expressing my liking of its flavor—something I could have done nonverbally by smiling and licking my lips. This is different from *saying* that I like its flavor.

I think that there is something right about each of these answers: each captures something about the use of "tasty." But there is also something wrong about each of them. It is as if all three have part of the truth; we just need to synthesize them into a view that has all of their advantages and none of their disadvantages. The task of this book is to make such a view available, not just to illuminate our puzzle about "tasty," but to make sense of our thought and talk about what people know, what will happen tomorrow, what might be the case, and what we ought to do.

Before we get out of the rabbit-hole, we need to fall into it. Let us begin, then, by looking at what is unsatisfactory about the usual answers to our question about the meaning of "tasty."

1.1   Objectivism

Objectivism, as we will understand it here, is the view that

(a) "tasty" is true of some things, false of others, and

(b) whether "tasty" is true or false of a thing, on a particular occasion of use, does not depend on the idiosyncratic tastes of the speaker, assessor, or anyone else.

According to objectivism, "tasty" is much like the other predicates we use to describe the world—"red," "deciduous," "acidic." These words are used to characterize objects independently of their relation to the speaker (or other salient individual).

So understood, objectivism is compatible with the view that tastiness is defined in relation to humans. An objectivist might hold, for example, that to be tasty is to have a flavor that is pleasing to the tongue of a normal human being in normal conditions for tasting. On this view, tastiness would be a perfectly objective property, though perhaps not one of much interest to non-humans.[1] Alternatively, an objectivist might hold that "tasty," as used by a member of species S, expresses the property of being pleasing to the tongue of a normal member of S in normal conditions for tasting. On such a view, the extension of "tasty" would be contextually sensitive, but still independent of individual idiosyncracies of taste.[2] It would also be consistent with objectivism to allow that "tasty" is contextually sensitive in the familiar way that all gradable adjectives are. Just how red, tall, or flat something has to be in order to count as "red," "tall," or "flat" plausibly varies with context. An objectivist can allow that the threshold for counting as "tasty" is contextually sensitive, as long as the underlying relation "is tastier than" is fixed independently of any individual's subjective tastes.

If you like, think of objectivism as the view that "tasty" is no less objective than "red." How red something needs to be to count as "red" simpliciter can vary with the context—as can which parts of it need to be red, and in which shades. A fire engine the color of a red grapefruit might not be considered red. Moreover, on many philosophers' views, redness cannot be defined without reference to humans; it is a dispositional property to affect human visual perception in certain ways. All of this is compatible with objectivism in the

---

[1]If this view were correct, then a chimpanzee could learn the meaning of "tasty," but the word could not have the same role in the chimp's life that it has in human life.

[2]For a similar notion of objectivism, see Wollheim (1980: 232).

broad sense at issue here. What would *not* be compatible with objectivism is a view on which the extension of "red" varied with idiosyncracies of the speaker's perceptual system. But it is widely agreed that this is not the case. Though a color-blind person may be disposed to use the word "red" to describe certain green fruits, we have no temptation to say that "red," as that person is using it, is *true* of the green fruits. The color-blind person is simply getting it wrong—speaking falsely. "Red" does not mean "disposed to produce certain visual sensations in *me*".

Although I have known some objectivists about "tasty," most people seem to recoil from the view. They do not think that there is a "fact of the matter" about whether a thing is tasty in the way that there is a fact of the matter about whether it is red or deciduous or acidic. What underlies this intuition, I suggest, is a realization that if "tasty," like "red," expresses an objective property of things, then our ordinary methods for deciding which things to call "tasty" are radically defective.

What methods are these? To a pretty good first approximation, we call a food "tasty" when we find its taste pleasing, and "not tasty" when we do not. A few qualifications are needed. We don't think we're warranted in calling something "tasty" just because it tastes good to us after we have eaten *Synsepalum dulcificum* (a berry that increases the perceived sweetness of foods, to the point of making lemons taste sweet) or in calling it "not tasty" just because it tastes bad to us just after brushing our teeth, or when we have a cold. Plausibly, this is because we think that in these conditions, tasting the food does not give us accurate knowledge of its taste. So, our rule must be restricted to cases in which we have knowledge of how the food tastes.

Indeed, it seems that first-hand knowledge is required. Suppose a food critic that we trust has written that fried rattlesnake tastes just like fried chicken. We might regard this as giving us (testimonial) knowledge of how fried rattlesnake tastes, but even if we like the taste of fried chicken, it would be odd to say on the basis of the critic's testimony alone that fried rattlesnake is "tasty." "Tasty" thus seems to have an evidential aspect, which we can capture by restricting our rule to cases in which we have first-hand knowledge of the flavor of a food.[3]

Taking these qualifications into account, we get the following rule:

---

[3]This evidential aspect is not peculiar to "tasty," but seems to affect all terms of aesthetic appraisal (Wollheim 1980: 233).

TP. *If you know first-hand how something tastes, call it "tasty" just in case its flavor is pleasing to you, and "not tasty" just in case its flavor is not pleasing to you.*

If you are skeptical that *TP* guides our use of "tasty," consider how odd it would sound to say:

(1) I'm not sure whether espresso is tasty, but I hate how it tastes.

(2) I've never been able to stand the taste of durian. Might it be tasty?

(3) I love orange juice and hate tomato juice. But who knows? Perhaps tomato juice is tastier.

These speeches sound bizarre. In each case there is a strong tension between the definiteness of the affective reaction and the unwillingness to make a tastiness judgment. But to reject *TP* is to allow that claims like these can be warranted.

Indeed, it is not clear that our practices in using "tasty" could change in such a way that (1)–(3) became natural, without losing their point and purpose entirely. We classify things as tasty or not tasty in order to help guide our gustatory deliberations. We eat things we regard as tasty because we expect them to taste good to us. Conversely, we may avoid eating things we don't know are tasty, because they might taste bad to us. But these explanations presuppose something like *TP*.

By itself, *TP* is not inconsistent with a robust objectivism about "tasty." If all of us took pleasure in the same foods (in normal conditions), then it would not be unreasonable to regard this pleasure as a natural indicator of some shared objective property of the foods. But in fact, there are large differences in the foods different people find pleasant tasting. A strongly spiced pickle that delights the taste of an Indian may be disgusting to an Eskimo, while the Eskimo's favored breakfast of raw whale blubber may be disgusting to the Indian. Nor do we need to cut across cultures to find examples: even siblings brought up in the same way can find different foods pleasant. We are all well aware of these facts. So if we take "tasty" to express an objective property, we must regard *TP* as a very unreliable principle for applying it.

Perhaps, the objectivist might reply, each of us believes that our own propensities to take pleasure in food are sensitive to the property of tastiness, even if others' are not. We all think we have won the lottery and acquired a sense of taste that tracks objective tastiness. That would explain our adherence to *TP* in the face of widespread and evident disagreement in taste. But to say this would be to attribute an unreflective chauvinism to every competent speaker. What basis do we have for taking our own gustatory pleasure to be better correlated with tastiness than anyone else's?

It is useful to compare "tasty" to color words like "red" and non-evaluative flavor words like "salty." We do not universally agree in our judgments about what is red or salty. But when there is disagreement, we do not blithely continue to maintain our own views without hesitation. The fact that others report seeing red where you saw green, or tasting saltiness where you tasted none, makes you less confident in your own color or flavor judgments. It makes you suspect that the lighting is funny, or that you are ill or under the influence of a drug, or that your perceptual equipment is defective (as it is in color-blind people). To insist without further investigation that your own judgment is right, and that the other's is wrong, would be rash and unwarranted.[4] But when it comes to disagreement about whether something is "tasty," we find no comparable hesitation. Why should speakers be chauvinistic in one case but not in the other?[5]

Perhaps there is something the objectivist can say here. Psychologists have shown that those who have low levels of skill in an area significantly overestimate their own abilities (Kruger and Dunning 1999). In one study, students were given a test of standard English grammar and asked to estimate their percentile rank among the other students taking the test. Students scoring in the bottom quartile on the test rated themselves, on average, in the sixtieth percentile. This overestimation persisted, and even increased, after the students became aware of the discrepancies between their answers and their peers' (1126–7). The researchers explained this by positing that "the same knowledge that underlies the ability to produce correct judgment is also the knowledge that underlies the ability to recognize correct judgment" (1122). Interestingly, an earlier version of the study had subjects making judgments about how funny different jokes were. After observing results similar to the ones described above, the researchers speculated that ". . . it may have been

---

[4]This point about perceptual judgments is granted even by those who reject the general claim that we should give the considered views of our epistemic peers equal weight with our own (Kelly 2010: 150–1).

[5]Of course, one can be taste-blind in just the way one can be color-blind, by being unable to discriminate tastes that ordinary people can discriminate. Someone who can taste bitterness but not saltiness, for example, might refrain from calling things "tasty" on the grounds that she is ignorant of how they really taste. But this is not what is normally happening in disagreements about whether a food is "tasty."

the tendency to define humor idiosyncratically, and in ways favorable to one's tastes and sensibilities, that produced the miscalibration we observed—not the tendency of the incompetent to miss their own failings" (Kruger and Dunning 1999: 1124). The fact that the same results can be obtained in the paradigmatically objective domain of mathematics is striking.

Perhaps, then, we are all chauvinistic when it comes to taste because we are all very bad at recognizing when something is tasty. Our lack of ability makes us overconfident in our own judgments, even in the face of disagreement with our peers. The question would remain why people who are bad at recognizing colors—color-blind people—do not exhibit a similar overconfidence. But perhaps it is because they routinely receive negative feedback that helps even those with low ability calibrate their own accuracy (Kruger and Dunning 1999: 1131), whereas it is rare for people to chastise others for their judgments of tastiness.

However, the package deal the objectivism is now offering—wholesale attribution of chauvinism, made more palatable by wholesale attribution of cluelessness—is rather hard to swallow. First, it is hard to accept the idea that most of us are highly unreliable in our judgments of tastiness. We all learned the concept *tasty*, I suppose, by being exposed to foods that caused pleasure and having mom or dad say "tasty!" It is difficult to believe that the concept we acquired through this procedure expresses an obscure property that we are not very reliable in picking out. How did our word get the meaning the objectivist says it has?

Second, it is hard to see why reflection on the extent of our disagreements about which foods are tasty, and on the similarities in our respective trainings with "tasty," shouldn't make at least some of us less chauvinistic. If objectivism were correct, then, we should expect to find some people suspending judgment about which foods are "tasty" in the way exhibited in (1)–(3). But we do not. And if we did, we would, I think, question these speakers' competence with "tasty."

Finally, we seem to use "tasty" in conformance with *TP* even when we expect our tastes to become better educated. Having grown up tasting only grocery-store Red Delicious apples, Sam enrolls in an apple tasting course. During the four-week course, the students will taste heirloom apples from all over the country. Sam is assured by the instructor that by the end of the course, his tastes in apples will be completely changed. On the first day, the instructor gives Sam four apples to try and asks him which is tastiest. Will he shrug his shoulders and remain agnostic? That would be bizarre. More likely, he will answer confidently, on the basis of his present tastes. But if we explain his confidence by supposing that he thinks his tastes already track objective tastiness, then what is his motive for taking the course?

1.2 Contextualism

Short of positing chauvinism, how might we explain why speakers think that liking the taste of something is sufficient grounds for calling it "tasty"? A natural explanation is that "tasty," as used by a speaker *S*, is true of just those things whose flavor *S* likes.

According to a plausible version of contextualism, "tasty," while monadic on the surface, actually expresses a relation with two argument places: one for a food, the other for a taste or perhaps an experiencer. Sometimes, the extra argument place is made explicit, as when we say that Tim's lasagna is tasty *to Fatma*, but not to most people. But when it is not explicitly filled or bound by a quantifier, it is given a value by context.

This kind of contextualism takes "tasty" to work like "local," "ready," and "tall." The same bar can be local to Berkeley but not local to San Diego. Alice can be ready to run a mile but not ready to go fishing or take her exam. Sam can be tall for a graduate student but not tall for a basketball player. When one says simply that a bar is "local," or that Alice is "ready," or that Sam is "tall," one intends to ascribe one of these more determinate properties.[6]

Is "tasty" context-sensitive in the same sense?[7] Are utterances of "This is

[6]This much, I think, is uncontroversial, though there is a lot of controversy about just how to explain what is happening with "bare" uses of "local," "ready," or "tall." (See for example Stanley 2007, Cappelen and Lepore 2005, and the essays in Preyer and Peter 2007.) Some writers hold that such words are associated with variables in the logical form that, when not bound by quantifiers or supplied a value explicitly, are given values by context. Some hold that the completion or enrichment does not require any syntactic trigger. Some hold that these words express simple, nonrelational properties, but that the full communicative content of a speech act is richer and more determinate than the minimal "official" content of its sentential vehicle. We will not need to sort out these issues about semantic content here. It is common ground between all of these writers that in saying "Alice is ready," one is asserting that she is ready for *X*, for some *X*. In this sense, at least, words like "ready" are clearly context-sensitive.

[7]As we have already observed, there may be other respects in which "tasty" is contextually sensitive. Because "tasty" is a gradable adjective, one would expect it to be contextually sensitive at least with respect to the threshold: how high on the tastiness scale something has to be in order to count as "tasty" (see Glanzberg 2007: 8–9; drawing on Kennedy 2007). This kind of contextual variation, however, is not going to help vindicate *TP*, and does not require positing contextual sensitivity to a standard of taste or experiencer.

tasty" generally understood as assertions that the demonstrated food tastes good to the speaker? In favor of this hypothesis, it might be noted that "tasty," like "local" and "ready," can occur in explicitly relativized form. I can characterize a food as "tasty for teenagers" or as "tasty for me." These forms are easy to explain on the contextualist view, which posits an extra argument place in the relation expressed. By contrast, as Lasersohn (2005: 656) points out, it is difficult to see how the objectivist can explain the explicitly relativized forms. With paradigm objective predicates, like "five feet tall," we have no similar explicitly relativized forms; we do not say that someone is "five feet tall to me," or "five feet tall for a teenager."[8] If we take the explicitly relativized forms of "tasty" to indicate the presence of an extra argument place for a taste or taster, then it is a short step to the conclusion that, when no argument is provided explicitly, an argument is supplied by context.

However, contextualism about "tasty" faces two serious problems: it cannot account for agreement and disagreement about what is "tasty," and it cannot explain why speakers are willing to retract earlier assertions made using "tasty" when their tastes have changed.

1.2.1 *Agreement and disagreement*

If the truth of my claim that a food is "tasty" depends on how it strikes *me*, while the truth of your claim that the same food is "not tasty" depends on how it strikes *you*, then our claims are compatible, and we do not disagree in making them. But it seems that we *do* disagree—even if we are aware that the source of our disagreement is our differing tastes. The following dialogue sounds terrible:

(4) A: It's tasty, isn't it?
     B: #I agree, but it's not tasty to me.

Whereas this one sounds fine:

(5) A: It's tasty, isn't it?
     B: I disagree—though it may be tasty to you.

Here we do see a clear difference between "tasty" and our paradigm context-sensitive words. If Abe says that Sarah's favorite bar is a local bar (meaning

---

[8] A color-blind person might say "These socks look red to me," but "to me" goes with "look" here, not with "red." If he were to say, "These socks are red to me," we would be at a loss as to what he meant, if not that the socks *look* red to him.

local to Anchorage), and Sam says that her favorite bar is not a local bar (meaning local to Savannah), there is no real disagreement between them. This dialogue is fine:

(6) ABE: Sarah's favorite bar is a local bar.
SAM: I agree, but it isn't local to me.

Whereas this one sounds bad, unless we think that Sam has misunderstood Abe:

(7) ABE: Sarah's favorite bar is a local bar.
SAM: #I disagree—though it may be local to you.

The contextualist might resist the intuition that when I say the food is "tasty" and you that it is "not tasty," we are really disagreeing. Don't we say, after all, that "there's no disputing taste"? So it is worth recounting some reasons for thinking that there really is disagreement in such cases, and considering some ways in which the data might be reinterpreted.

First, it is natural to use explicit marks of disagreement, such as "No," "I disagree," "you're mistaken," or "that's false." These responses would be inappropriate if the two parties were simply making claims about what tastes good to *them*:

(8) A: Licorice is tasty.[9]
B: No/I disagree/You're mistaken/That's false, it's not tasty.

(9) A: Licorice tastes good to me.
B: #No/I disagree/You're mistaken/That's false, it doesn't taste good to me.

Faced with this argument, contextualists sometimes note that words like "No," "You're mistaken," and "That's false" can target something other than the

---

[9]Note that this sentence is a generic, like "Dogs have four legs" and "Sharks attack bathers." The truth conditions of generics are poorly understood (for an introduction to the topic, see Leslie 2012). For example, "Sharks attack bathers" seems true and "Dogs have three legs" false, even though the percentage of sharks that attack bathers is less than the percentage of dogs that have three legs. For this reason, Cappelen and Hawthorne (2009) note that we should be cautious about relying solely on examples using generics in arguing against contextualist theories. While caution is certainly in order, I think that the patterns of use I will discuss in this chapter hold for both generic and non-generic "tasty" claims, and I see no hope of explaining these patterns in terms of known features of generics. The reader who is bothered by the use of a generic here may substitute "This piece of licorice is tasty."

asserted proposition. For example, they can target the content of the reported speech or attitude:

(10)   A: Sahin said that you had a car.
       B: No/That's false. I don't have a car.

They can also target a presupposition:

(11)   A: Your wife is very beautiful.
       B: No/You're mistaken. We're not married.

Grice (1989: 64–5) observes that disagreement markers can also target the result of "factoring out" a shared assumption from the asserted content. He gives this nice example:

(12)   A: Either Wilson or Heath will be the next Prime Minister.
       B: I disagree, it will be either Wilson or Thorpe.

Here there is disagreement even though the two disjunctions are compatible. The explanation is that it is "accepted as common ground that Wilson is a serious possibility" (65). So what is being rejected is just that Heath is the other serious contender.

But it is difficult to see how any of these models would apply to the contextualist's proposal about "tasty." Moreover, a striking difference between (8) and (10)–(11) is that in (8) the asserted proposition is explicitly negated in the reply. So the real parallels would be these:

(10′)   A: Sahin said that you had a car.
        B: No/That's false. He didn't say that I had a car.

(11′)   A: Your wife is very beautiful.
        B: No/You're mistaken. She's not very beautiful.

And here "No," "You're mistaken," and "That's false" clearly target the whole asserted proposition.[10]

The contextualist might try claiming that the marks of disagreement express attitudes towards the *words* used, not the propositions they express. So,

---

[10](12) is trickier. Here it seems okay for the objector to say: "I disagree, it's not the case that Wilson or Heath will be the next Prime Minister," but only if some emphasis is given to "Heath." The fact that special emphasis is needed suggests that this is a case of *metalinguistic negation* (Horn 1989: ch. 6), as does the fact that the negation cannot be incorporated into the disjunction: "#I disagree, neither Wilson nor Heath will be the next Prime Minister" (Horn 1989: §6.4.1).

"No" in (8) would mean: "No, I wouldn't use that sentence to make an assertion." And "That's false" would mean "That sentence, as used by me now, would express a falsehood."[11] But, in the absence of data supporting these alternative uses of "No" and "That's false" in other contexts, this just seems like special pleading. Moreover, the contextualist would have to hold that in disputes of this kind, "No" and "That's false" *always* get the nonstandard reading. Otherwise there ought to be a reading of the following dialogue in which *B* is not contradicting herself:

(13) A: Apples are tasty.
      B: That's not true. But apples are tasty.

The contextualist needs to explain why such readings are unavailable.

Note, also, that the phenomenon persists even when the demonstrative "That" is replaced with a term that explicitly denotes the proposition expressed. In (8), instead of saying "That's false," *B* might have said (somewhat pedantically) "The proposition you expressed is false" or "What you asserted is false." Here the nonstandard reading is explicitly blocked.

A second indication that we take ourselves to be disagreeing about matters of tastiness, besides the explicit disagreement markers, is that we sometimes *argue* about them: "Brussels sprouts, tasty? They taste like grass! Do you also say that grass is tasty? Doesn't their bitterness completely overwhelm other flavors?" We do not generally argue with others' claims about what tastes good to *them*, so the fact that we argue about what is "tasty" speaks against the contextualist analysis.

It is open to the contextualist to say that our tendency to argue about claims of taste, and our perception that we are disagreeing with each other in making them, is just a delusion. But if the contextualist is willing to attribute this much systematic error to speakers, it is unclear what reason remains to prefer contextualism to a simple objectivist view. After all, what seemed unattractive about objectivism was precisely that it forced us to attribute systematic error to speakers. Indeed, it seems that the contextualist will have to attribute the same kind of chauvinism that the objectivist does, *plus* a semantic error that the objectivist does not attribute. For in order to explain why we take ourselves to be disagreeing in our claims of taste, the contextualist will have to take us to have an inchoate objectivist theory of the semantics of these

---

[11]I have not seen this argument in print, but I have heard it in conversation, and Kölbel (2002: 39) finds it worth criticizing.

statements. But if that is how we think of them, then our habits of asserting that things are tasty on the basis of our own affective reactions, in the face of abundant evidence of the diversity of such reactions, must be explained by the same unreflective chauvinism we found objectionable in our discussion of objectivism.

The contextualist might alternatively accept that there is disagreement, and try to explain it by taking the argument place for an experiencer (or taste) to be filled, not by the speaker herself (or her own idiosyncratic taste), but by a group including the speaker and her audience (or a standard of taste that is somehow shared by them). If in (8) *A* is asserting that licorice does not taste good to the whole group—to *A*, *B*, and other relevant participants in the conversation—then we can readily understand *B* as joining issue with what *A* said. *B* knows that licorice does not taste good to *him*, and that is good grounds for disagreeing with the claim that licorice tastes good to the whole group.

The problem with this move is that it loses *TP*. If claims about what is "tasty" are often claims about what is tasty to a group, then it is unclear why finding the food pleasing oneself should be sufficient warrant for claiming that it is "tasty." There might, admittedly, be some cases where one has good grounds for thinking that others' tastes are relevantly similar to one's own. But since that is often not the case, we should expect there to be many cases where *TP* fails, and sentences like (1)–(3) sound okay. I submit that there are not. Even when I know that some of the people I am talking to do not like the taste of orange juice, it would be bizarre for me to deny that orange juice (which I like a lot) is tasty, or to express skepticism about whether it is tasty.

Further, if we explain the disagreement in (8) in this way, we should expect that *A* would immediately retract her claim on finding that *B* does not like licorice. For on this view, *A* has asserted that everyone in the group likes the taste of licorice, and *B* has revealed that he does not. But it would not be strange for *A* to continue to maintain that licorice is "tasty," even after learning that *B* does not like it. Indeed, disagreements about what is tasty often take this shape.[12]

---

[12] For similar objections, see Lasersohn (2005: 651–2). Note that the same objection applies to the view that there is a shared standard of taste that speakers try to change through accommodation (in the sense of Lewis 1979b). When there is continued, clear-eyed disagreement about what is "tasty," these views predict that both parties should see that no shared standard has been established, leaving all predications of "tasty" without a truth value. In that case it would not

One of the attractive features of contextualism was that it promised to vindicate *TP*. But it now appears that vindicating the *TP* requires that the extra argument place be filled solipsistically, while explaining disagreement requires that it be filled collectively. There would be no problem for the contextualist if some uses of "tasty" were governed by *TP*, but were not targets of disagreement, while others were targets of disagreement, but were not governed by *TP*. For in principle, different uses of "tasty" can have different contextual completions. The problem is that the very *same* uses of "tasty" that seem governed by *TP* seem to be legitimate targets for disagreement, and this contextualists cannot explain.

We have focused here on disagreement, but the analogous points can be made about *agreement*. Suppose both Sam and Sal like the taste of raisins. Both might say,

(14)   Raisins are tasty,

and we will naturally report them as having agreed:

(15)   Sal and Sam agree that raisins are tasty.

On the contextualist analysis, (15) must be interpreted as

(15a) Sal and Sam agree that raisins are tasty to Sal, or

(15b) Sal and Sam agree that raisins are tasty to Sam, or

(15c) Sal and Sam agree that raisins are tasty to Sam and Sal both.

But we can easily construct a case in which (15) seems true while (15a–c) are all false. Just imagine that Sam and Sal both like the taste of raisins, but neither thinks the other does. They seem to agree, not about whether raisins taste good to some person or persons, but about whether they are tasty—where that is something different.

1.2.2   *Retraction*

When our own tastes change, so that a food we used to find pleasant to the taste now tastes bad, we may say that we were mistaken in saying that the food was "tasty." When I was a kid, I once told my mother, "Fish sticks are tasty." Now that I have exposed my palate to a broader range of tastes, I think

be rational to continue to make assertions about what is "tasty." See Lasersohn (2005: 659–662), de Sa (2008: 302–3), and Sundell (2011: §§3.5, 4) for relevant discussion.

I was wrong about that; I've changed my mind about the tastiness of fish sticks. So, if someone said, "But you said years ago that fish sticks were tasty," I would retract the earlier assertion. I wouldn't say, "They were tasty then, but they aren't tasty any more," since that would imply that their taste changed. Nor would I say, "When I said that, I only meant that they were tasty to me then." I *didn't* mean that. At the time I took myself to be disagreeing with adults who claimed that fish sticks weren't tasty.

The contextualist cannot easily explain why I would retract my earlier assertion. On the contextualist account, the content I expressed then by "fish sticks are tasty" is perfectly compatible with the content I express now by "fish sticks are not tasty." So retraction should not be required. Indeed, it should seem as odd as it does in this conversation:

(16)   SAM: [*in Phoenix*] You can get a swamp cooler at any local hardware store.

SAM: [*the next day, in Boston*] Nobody sells swamp coolers around here.

JANE: But you said you can get one at any local hardware store!

SAM: I take that back.

The contextualist might try to explain retraction by moving towards a less subjective form of contextualism—for example, by construing taste claims as claims about what would be pleasing to a suitably idealized version of the agent.[13] If, in saying that fish sticks are tasty, I was predicting that they would be pleasing to my more educated palate, then I ought to retract my claim in light of what my more educated palate tells me.

But is it really plausible that in calling things "tasty," we are making claims about how they will strike idealized versions of ourselves? Consider the story of Sam and the apple tasting course, recounted in §1.1. On the first day, the instructor gives Sam four apples to try and asks him which is tastiest. If he were really being asked to say which would best please his future, more educated palate, shouldn't he shrug his shoulders and remain agnostic? But that is not how we use the word "tasty." He will answer confidently, despite his belief that within a month his tastes may be very different.

Like objectivism, then, contextualism fails to capture what is distinctive about words like "tasty." To be sure, there is something that seems right about

---

[13] For the idealization move, see Egan (2010).

it. It can vindicate the idea—enshrined in *TP*—that the proper criterion for applying "tasty" is one's own affective reactions. But it can only do so at the cost of making disagreement about what is "tasty," and retraction of early claims about what is "tasty," unintelligible.

1.3 Expressivism

Given the failure of objectivism and contextualism to account for the facts about our use of "tasty," it is natural to question what both take for granted: that in deploying "tasty" we are making genuine assertions, taking a stand on how things are. Consider what A. J. Ayer says about moral vocabulary:

> The presence of an ethical symbol in a proposition adds nothing to its factual content. Thus if I say to someone, 'You acted wrongly in stealing that money,' I am not stating anything more than if I had simply said, 'You stole that money.' In adding that this action is wrong I am not making any further statement about it. I am simply evincing my moral disapproval of it. It is as if I had said, 'You stole that money,' in a peculiar tone of horror, or written it with the addition of some special exclamation marks. (Ayer 1959: 107)

Applying Ayer's thought to "tasty," we get what I will call *classical expressivism*: the view that in saying "It's tasty" one is not making an assertion, but simply expressing one's liking for a food.

It is crucial to mark the distinction between *expressing* one's liking for a food and *asserting* that one likes the food. One does the former, but not the latter, when one smacks one's lips in delight after a good meal. One does the latter, but perhaps not the former, when one tells one's host, with an unconcealed expression of dutiful weariness, that one liked her cooking.[14]

The classical expressivist agrees with the objectivist, against the contextualist, that in saying "That's tasty" one is not asserting that the food tastes pleasant to one (or to a larger group). But that is because, unlike the objectivist, the expressivist doesn't think one is asserting anything at all. For the expressivist, saying "That's tasty" is just a verbal way of smacking one's lips,

[14] According to some speech-act theorists, assertion is the expression of belief (for discussion, see MacFarlane 2011b). The expressivist who takes this view of assertion can still draw a principled line between assertions and the expression of "non-cognitive" attitudes like desires and preferences. However, she must tread delicately in saying what it is to express an attitude. As Jackson and Pettit (1998) note, one might naturally take "That's good" to express not just the speaker's approval, but also her *belief* that she has this attitude, in the absence of which she would not have uttered the sentence. The expressivist will need to explicate "express an attitude" in a way that distinguishes between the first-order attitude of approval and the second-order belief about this attitude.

just as "Drat!" is a verbal way of expressing disappointment. In this way, the expressivist avoids the fundamental problem facing objectivism: explaining how we can persist in making assertions that (unless we are chauvinistic) we can only regard as highly prone to be mistaken. One makes no mistake (except, occasionally, a mistake of etiquette) in expressing one's liking for a food.

1.3.1 Disagreement and retraction

The objectivist might legitimately wonder, though, whether the expressivist does any better than the contextualist in accounting for the apparent *disagreement* we express using "tasty." Ayer himself notes that expressivism vindicates disagreement only in a relatively weak sense:

Another man may disagree with me about the wrongness of stealing, in the sense that he may not have the same feeling about stealing as I have, and he may quarrel with me on account of my moral sentiments. But he cannot, strictly speaking, contradict me. For in saying that a certain type of action is right or wrong, I am not making any factual statement, not even a statement about my own state of mind. I am merely expressing certain moral sentiments. And the man who is ostensibly contradicting me is merely expressing his moral sentiments. (Ayer 1959: 107)

Although Ayer concluded that an expressivist account of aesthetic terms implies that there is "no possibility of arguing about questions of value in aesthetics" (1959: 113), Stevenson (1963: ch. 1) proposed that the kind of *disagreement in attitude* that expressivists accept is enough to make such arguments intelligible. Suppose Lizzie likes Sam, while Sal hates him. Lizzie and Sal might try to induce each other to share their attitude towards Sam, and they might do so by offering considerations and counter-considerations, in just the way we do when we are arguing about the truth of a proposition. The fact that in this case the dispute does not concern any particular fact about Sam does not prevent it from having the shape of an argument.

   Even if this were a successful strategy for defending expressivism, it would leave us without a clear reason for preferring expressivism to contextualism, since contextualists can also appeal to disagreement in attitude (Jackson and Pettit 1998: 251 and Dreier 1999: 569). However, there is good reason to think that disagreements involving "tasty" go beyond mere disagreement in attitude. For one thing, it seems appropriate to express disagreement about what is "tasty" by saying, "That's false" or "You're wrong."[15] Even if Sal and Lizzie disagree in their attitudes about Sam, they wouldn't express it this way:

(17)   LIZZIE: I like Sam!
      SAL: # You're wrong, I hate him.

Moreover, mere disagreement in attitude would not motivate retraction. On becoming convinced through experience that peaty whiskeys are tasty, one might say:

(18)   Last year I said that they weren't very tasty, but I take that back. I was wrong.

An assertion can be retracted, but it doesn't make much sense to "take back" or retract the expression of an attitude. Imagine a dirty old man attempting to "take back" a lecherous leer, on finding that its object is an employee of his.[16]

It is not clear, then, that expressivism does better than contextualism in explaining disagreement about taste. On the other hand, it faces a number of difficult problems that contextualism avoids. These will occupy us for the rest of the chapter.

1.3.2   *Force and content*

Frege taught us to analyze speech acts by factoring them into two components—*force* and *content*. Consider, for example, Tom's assertion that there is fresh powder in the mountains. Its content—what he has asserted—is that there is fresh powder in the mountains. Its force is that of an assertion. He could have asserted that there is black ice in the mountains; in that case, his speech act would have had the same force but different content. Or he could have asked whether there is fresh powder in the mountains; in that case, his speech act would have had a different force but the same content. The same distinction can be applied to mental states. Wondering whether there is fresh powder in the mountains and desiring that there be fresh powder in the mountains share a content but differ in force; believing that

---

[15]This is how Schroeder (2008: 17) distinguishes the "shallow" disagreement problem for expressivism, which can be met by invoking disagreement in attitude, from the "deep" problem.

[16]Several people have objected that one can retract an apology, which seems to be an expression of an attitude. I agree that one can retract an apology, but that just shows that there is more to making an apology than simply expressing contrition. One can, after all, express contrition without apologizing.

there is fresh powder in the mountains and believing that there is black ice in the mountains share a force but differ in content.

The force/content analysis makes the study of language and thought more systematic. One part of our study can concern itself with the possible contents of thoughts and speech acts, and another with the possible forces. Combining these, we can account for the significance of acts with any of these possible contents and possible forces.

Classical expressivism gives up the force/content analysis in the domains to which it applies. It denies that there are propositions characterizing foods as tasty. (If there were, the job of "That's tasty" would presumably be to assert such propositions, and we wouldn't need to talk separately of expressing attitudes.) Instead of letting the significance of utterances of "That's tasty" emerge from separate accounts of assertoric force and the content of tastiness-ascribing propositions, the expressivist explains their significance *directly*, by saying what speech acts they are used to perform, or what mental states they express. And that is problematic for at least four reasons.

Non-declaratives   The first reason is that "tasty" occurs not just in declarative sentences like "That's tasty," but in interrogative, imperative, and optative ones:

(19)   Is that tasty?

(20)   Make it tasty!

(21)   If only that were tasty!

None of these sentences are used to express the speaker's liking for the demonstrated food. So even if we accept the expressivist's account of the meaning of "That's tasty," we are left without any account of the meaning of very similar non-declarative sentences.

On a truth-conditional approach, by contrast, we need only give an account of the propositional content expressed by "That is tasty" (at a context), and our existing accounts of interrogative, imperative, and optative force will combine with this to give us an account of the meanings of these sentences.[17]

---

[17] The classic modern version of this can be found in John Searle's work on speech-act theory (Searle 1969; Searle 1979). Searle's account may need some adjustment to account for the phenomena—for example, most linguists now take the contents of questions to be something other than propositions (Hamblin 1973; Karttunen 1977; Groenendijk and Stokhof 1997)—but virtually everyone who does systematic semantics accepts some version of the force/content distinction.

Mental attitudes   Second, in addition to *saying* "That's tasty," we can also *think* it. One can believe that a certain food is tasty, suppose that it is tasty, wonder whether it is tasty, and desire that it be tasty. In so doing, one is not expressing an attitude, because one need not be expressing anything at all. One might just keep one's thoughts to oneself. So the classical expressivist account does not extend in any obvious way to an account of these attitudes. But it does rule out the standard kind of account in terms of content and attitudinal force, because it denies that there *is* a content of the sort that would be needed (the proposition that *that is tasty*).

A hard-line expressivist response would bite the bullet and deny that there are genuine attitudes of believing that a food is tasty, or wondering whether a food is tasty. This bullet-biting response would have to be coupled with an expressivist account of what we are doing when we say, for example,

(22)   He believes that licorice is tasty.

(23)   He wishes that licorice were tasty.

Presumably, these sentences are used to attribute to the subject the attitude of liking licorice, and (less plausibly) of wishing he liked licorice.

Propositional anaphora   A third problem is that it is natural to use propositional anaphora in connection with uses of "tasty":

(24)   This fish is tasty!

(25)   a.   Yes, that's true.

     b.   No, that's not true.

     c.   Sam said that too.

     d.   That's just what Sarah promised.

The uses of "that" in (25a)–(25d) are most naturally understood as pronouns referring back to the proposition expressed by (24). But the classical expressivist can't explain them this way, having denied that (24) *does* express a proposition. And it is unclear how the classical expressivist *can* explain them. Presumably (25a) will be understood as an expression of agreement in attitude with the first speaker, and (25b) as an expression of disagreement in attitude. But the fact that expressions of agreement and disagreement should take this form—with the surface appearance of propositional anaphora—needs explaining. Surely the simplest hypothesis is that there really is propositional anaphora in these cases.

The problem is amplified by the need to make sense of simple inferences like

(26) Sam believes that this fish is tasty.
      Sally believes that too.
      So, there is something that Sam and Sally both believe.

It is easy to see why this inference is valid, if "that" in the second premise refers to the proposition denoted by "that this fish is tasty" in the first premise. The classical expressivist owes an alternative account.

Embeddings A more general problem for classical expressivism is how to extend its account of standalone sentences predicating "tasty" of some subject to an account of *arbitrary* sentences involving "tasty," including, for example,

(27) If that's tasty, he'll eat it.

(28) It will be tasty or the cook will give you your money back.

(29) That might be tasty.

(30) There are no tasty cookies in that jar.

All of these sentences employ "tasty" as a predicate, but in none of them is anything being *called* "tasty." What classical expressivists have done is to give an account of what one is doing in *calling* something "tasty." But this account does not extend to the uses of "tasty" in (27)–(30), in which nothing is being called "tasty," and in which the speaker need not be expressing liking for anything at all.

The point is made forcefully by Geach (1960), who accuses expressivists of losing sight of Frege's distinction between *predicating F* of *a* and *asserting F* of *a*:

In order that the use of a sentence in which "P" is predicated of a thing may count as an act of *calling* the thing "P," the sentence must be used assertively; and this is something quite distinct from the predication, for, as we have remarked, "P" may still be predicated of the thing even in a sentence used nonassertively as a clause within another sentence. Hence, calling a thing "P" has to be explained in terms of predicating "P" of the thing, not the other way round. (Geach 1960: 223; see also Geach 1965; Searle 1962; and Searle 1969: §6.2)

As Geach observes, the expressivist cannot meet the objection by saying that merely predicative uses of "tasty" have a different meaning than assertive uses, for then simple instances of modus ponens will be guilty of equivocation:

(31) If that is tasty$_{predicative}$, he will eat it.
      That is tasty$_{assertive}$.
      So, he will eat it.

The solution, Geach thinks, is to recognize that the two occurrences of "that is tasty" have a common *content* (the same truth conditions), though only the first is put forth with assertoric force. But that solution is not available to the expressivist, who does not think that "that is tasty" *has* a content or truth conditions.

Expressivists have shown considerable ingenuity in the last fifty years trying to find ways to reply to Geach's objection.[18] But all of the difficulties would vanish if we could treat "that is tasty" as expressing a content and having truth conditions. For then we would get, *for free*, an understanding of non-declarative sentences involving "tasty," of various mental attitudes that would be reported using "tasty," and of propositional anaphora. And we could appeal to existing truth-conditional accounts of disjunction, negation, conditionals, tenses, modals, quantifiers, and other forms of combination to understand the contribution "tasty" makes to the meaning of sentences in which it occurs embedded.

Expressivists are right about one thing: standard paradigms for doing truth-conditional semantics lack the resources for dealing adequately with "tasty." But the solution, I will urge, is not to abandon the whole project of truth-conditional semantics, but to broaden it.

1.4 A relativist approach

Our discussion so far suggests the following desiderata for a satisfactory account of the meaning of "tasty":

1. *Generality.* Our account should explain the contribution "tasty" makes, not just to simple sentences, but to all of the sentences in which it can occur.

2. *Assertion conditions.* Our account should explain why speakers who know first-hand how something tastes are warranted in calling something tasty just in case its flavor is pleasing to them (*TP*).

---

[18]See, for example, Hare (1970), Blackburn (1984, 1988), Gibbard (1990, 2003), Price (1994), Horwich (2005), Schroeder (2008), and Richard (2008). We will look more closely at some of these in §7.3.

3. *Retraction conditions.* Our account should explain why speakers will retract (rather than stand by) an earlier assertion that something was tasty, if the flavor the thing had at the time of the assertion is not pleasing to their *present* tastes—even if it was pleasing to the tastes they had then.

4. *Disagreement.* Our account should explain how there can be genuine disagreements about whether something is tasty, even when both parties have first-hand knowledge of its flavor and know that its flavor is pleasing to one of them but not the other.

5. *Expression of attitude.* Our account should explain why, in calling something tasty, one expresses one's liking for its flavor.

As we have seen, each of the three standard views about "tasty" meets some of these desiderata, but none meets them all. Expressivists have trouble with *Disagreement, Retraction conditions,* and *Generality.*[19] Objectivists have trouble with *Assertion conditions* and *Expression of attitude.* Contextualists can pick their poison, depending on how they set the contextual parameter for an experiencer or taste for a given occurence of "tasty." If they set it narrowly—to an individual or idiosyncratic taste—they can meet *Assertion conditions* and *Expression of attitude* but have trouble with *Disagreement* and *Retraction conditions.* If they set it broadly—to a group or shared taste—they can do better with *Disagreement* and *Retraction conditions,* but they fail to meet *Assertion conditions* or *Expression of attitude.*

It is natural to think at this point that our menu of options is incomplete. In considering the options for contextualism, we have been tacitly assuming that a particular occurrence of "tasty," used in a particular context, has its extension absolutely. This makes it impossible to jointly satisfy *Assertion conditions* and *Retraction conditions,* which seem to put incompatible constraints on this extension: the former requires it to depend on the speaker's tastes at the time the assertion is made, while the latter requires it to depend on the speaker's tastes at the time retraction is being considered. What if we say, instead, that assigning an extension to an occurrence of "tasty" requires not just fixing the facts about the context in which it is *used*, but also fixing the facts about the context in which it is being *assessed*? We could then say that a single occurrence of "This is tasty," used by a particular speaker in relation to

---

[19] At least classical expressivists do. In §§7.3 and 10.6 we will consider whether expressivists can meet *Generality* by using the same sort of compositional semantics a relativist would use, and what substantive differences remain between this sort of expressivism and relativism.

a particular food, is true as assessed from the context in which it is used, but false as assessed from a later context (after the speaker's tastes have changed). And that would open up space to say that the assertion conditions of "This is tasty" are keyed to the speaker's tastes at the time the assertion is made, while the retraction conditions of an earlier assertion of "This is tasty" are keyed to the speaker's *current* tastes, even if they have changed since she made the assertion.

Such a move would allow us to satisfy the first three desiderata, and would afford good prospects for satisfying the other two as well. Such a view would not regard claims of taste as equivalent to claims about what one finds pleasing: although the assertion conditions are the same, the retraction conditions are not. Yet claims of taste could be said to *express* one's liking for a food, since in performing a speech act that is warranted only when one likes a food, one gives others a reason to take one to like it, and in that sense expresses one's liking for it. So the fifth desideratum, *Expression of attitude*, could be met. In addition, we would be able to say that two parties who dispute whether a food is tasty genuinely disagree, in the sense that both parties occupy a perspective from which the other's assertion is untrue. In this way, the fourth desideratum, *Disagreement*, could be met.

Thus, by relaxing our tacit assumption that occurrences of "tasty" have their extensions determined by facts about the contexts in which they are used, and letting them depend also on the context in which they are assessed, we can meet all of our desiderata and give an account of "tasty" that saves what seems right about each of the standard accounts, while avoiding their limitations. "Tasty," on this view, would be an *assessment-sensitive* predicate.

A nice story, to be sure—but does it make any *sense* to talk of truth relative to a context of assessment? Answering that question is the main task of Part I of this book. Relativism about truth has a bad reputation among analytic philosophers, in part because of the sloppiness with which it has been formulated, and in part because of the widespread view that it is subject to some simple knock-down objections. In Chapter 2, I consider the standard objections to relativism about truth. We will see that they are far from being knock-down objections, though they do raise some useful questions that any relativist view must answer.

The aim of the next three chapters is to state the truth relativist's position clearly enough that all of these questions, and more, can be answered. In Chapter 3, I argue that relativism about truth should be understood as the view that truth is *assessment-sensitive*. Assessment sensitivity is understood by analogy with ordinary context sensitivity, or, as I call it, *use-sensitivity*. Just as the truth of uses of ordinary context-sensitive sentences depends on features of the context in which they are used, so the truth of uses of assessment-sensitive sentences depends on features of the context in which they are assessed. Building on ideas of David Lewis and David Kaplan, I develop a framework that makes room for assessment-sensitivity.

In Chapter 4, I show how propositions can fit into this framework, and I extend the notion of assessment sensitivity from sentences to propositions. This allows us to draw an important distinction between relativism about truth (which involves a commitment to assessment sensitivity) and nonindexical contextualism (which does not), and shows that taking propositional truth to be relevant to parameters besides possible worlds (and perhaps times) is neither necessary nor sufficient for relativism about truth, in the sense articulated here.

In Chapter 5, I address the substantive philosophical question that remains: what does it *mean* to talk of truth relative to a context of assessment? I do this by explaining the theoretical role of assessment-relative truth in a larger account of language use. The combined theory of Chapters 3–5 allows us to see the *practical* difference between asserting assessment-sensitive and non-assessment-sensitive propositions, and so tells us just what to look for in adjudicating between relativist and nonrelativist accounts. This suffices, I think, to "make sense of relative truth" and ward off a priori objections to its intelligibility.

Chapter 6 is devoted to the concept of disagreement, which plays a central role in debates between relativists, contextualists, and objectivists. I distinguish several varieties or "levels" of disagreement and show how the issue between these views can be reduced to an issue about what kind of disagreement there is in the domain in question.

Once the framework of Chapters 3–6 is in place, it becomes a broadly empirical question whether any of our thought and talk is best understood in terms of a relativist semantics. In Part II of the book, I make a case for an affirmative answer through five case studies.

Chapter 7 returns to our opening question about the meaning of "tasty," developing a relativist semantics that preserves what is right in objectivism, contextualism, and classical expressivism while avoiding the problems they face. The view has some affinities to the sophisticated version of expressivism developed by Allan Gibbard, so I spend some time looking at that view and how it differs from the sort of view advocated here.

In Chapter 8, I consider how a relativist account of knowledge attributions might steer a middle course between contextualist and invariantist accounts.

In Chapter 9, I argue that a relativist account of our future-directed talk is needed if such talk is to be compatible with the objective openness of the future.

In Chapter 10, I make a case for a relativist treatment of epistemic modal claims, like *Joe might be in Boston*, over the standard contextualist and expressivist alternatives.

Finally, in Chapter 11, I argue that a relativist treatment of deontic modal claims, like *Sam ought to flag down the approaching car*, can avoid the need for the problematic distinction, common in the ethics literature, between objective and subjective uses of "ought."

Chapters 3–6 tell us what the practical difference is between assessment-sensitive and non-assessment-sensitive discourse, and Chapters 7–11 offer reasons to think *that* some of our thought and talk is assessment-sensitive. One might still wonder, though, *why* it is. How can it be rational to assert something one expects to have to retract at some point in the future, because one will then occupy a perspective relative to which it is false? And why should we have evolved practices that allow us to do this without censure? In Chapter 12, I sketch a tentative answer: given our purposes in using these expressions, and given some assumptions about engineering constraints, it is better that they be assessment-sensitive. If these considerations are sound, they vindicate the rationality of assessment sensitivity and suggest a kind of teleological explanation of its existence.

PART I

FOUNDATIONS

2

THE STANDARD OBJECTIONS

The consensus among analytic philosophers is that relativism about truth is incoherent, or, at best, hopelessly confused. Here is a representative sampling of attitudes:

That (total) relativism is inconsistent is a truism among philosophers. After all, is it not *obviously* contradictory to *hold* a point of view while at the same time holding that *no* point of view is more justified or right than any other? (Putnam 1981: 119)

The label 'relativistic' is widely regarded as pejorative, and few philosophers have been willing to mount an explicit defense of relativism. (Swoyer 1982: 84)

Of all the conceptual options that have ever crossed the mind of the philosophical tribe, none has attracted quite the scorn and ridicule of the relativist. (Margolis 1991: xiv)

Relativism is even sillier than it at first appears. Indeed, if relativism were not so popular, it wouldn't be worth discussing at all. And even given its popularity, it isn't worth discussing for long. (Whyte 1993: 112)

The contemporary consensus among analytic philosophers is that relativism is not just wrong, but too confused a position to be worth taking seriously. (Bennigson 1999: 211)

Even Richard Rorty, who is often taken by analytic philosophers to be a relativist about truth, repudiates the doctrine:

Truth is, to be sure, an absolute notion, in the following sense: 'true for me but not for you' and 'true in my culture but not in yours' are weird, pointless locutions. So is 'true then, but not now.' Whereas we often say 'good for this purpose, but not for that' and 'right in this situation, but not in that,' it seems pointlessly paradoxical to relativize truth to purposes or situations. (Rorty 1998: 2)

I think that this consensus is mistaken. In the pages that follow, I will argue that we can make clear philosophical sense of a form of relativism about truth; that the view, properly understood, is neither incoherent nor inconsistent; and that we need it to make good sense of our thought and talk about the future, about what is tasty, about what people know, about what might be the case, and about what we ought to do.

It will take a good deal of concept-mongering to get where we are going, and most of this book will be devoted to that constructive task. Let us start, though, by looking at some of the reasons philosophers have given for dismissing truth relativism out of hand, with an eye to establishing criteria of adequacy for a defensible relativism about truth.

2.1 Self-refutation

The most famous charge against relativism about truth is that it is self-refuting. This charge is leveled against a very strong kind of global relativism: the view that *all* truths are true merely relatively, and that nothing is true absolutely. In its simplest form, the refutation takes the form of a dilemma. If the global relativist says that relativism is true for everyone, then she is acknowledging that there is at least one non-relative truth, and this contradicts her thesis of global relativism. On the other hand, if she concedes that relativism is not true for everyone (or equivalently that absolutism is true for someone), then . . .

Then what? It is usually conceded that there is no real contradiction in the relativist's holding that relativism is not true for everyone. Plato's Socrates is sometimes read as finding a real contradiction in a relativist position he attributes to Protagoras in the *Theaetetus*, but if so his argument cheats by dropping the crucial "for *x*" qualifiers at the final stage.[1] Hales (1997a) shows that global relativism is self-refuting if we assume that

(1)   If it is relatively true (true for someone) that it is absolutely true that p, then it is absolutely true that p.[2]

But it is not clear why the global relativist should accept (1).[3] For this reason,

---

[1] See Burnyeat (1976b: 174–5), who cites Grote, Runciman, Sayre, and Vlastos for the charge. Burnyeat tries ingeniously to find a more subtle argument in the text, but Fine (1983) is probably right that Plato, like Sextus and all other ancient commentators (cf. Burnyeat 1976a), takes Protagoras to be a subjectivist rather than a relativist. Subjectivism, the view that everything that appears to be the case is true (absolutely), is just the sort of view that would require the radical Heraclitean metaphysics of temporary person-relative appearance-objects attributed to Protagoras in the first part of the dialogue. And it is cogently refuted by the Socratic argument that seems feeble as a response to relativism.

[2] This is analogous to the S5 axiom of modal logic, which says that if it is possible that it is necessary that p, then it is necessary that p.

[3] See Shogenji (1997) for this criticism and Hales (1997b) for a reply. Bennigson (1999) defends the consistency of global relativism by describing a model in which relative truth is truth in some accessible framework, absolute truth is truth in every accessible framework, and the absolutist's framework is accessible from the relativist's framework, but not vice versa. This amounts to a rejection of Hales' S5-like premise, since the S5 axiom requires that accessibility be transitive.

most commentators have taken the problem with the second horn of the relativist's dilemma to be something other than outright inconsistency.

2.1.1 *Pragmatic inconsistency?*

Although the sentence "I am not asserting anything" is not inconsistent, it cannot be correctly asserted. We might say that it is *pragmatically self-refuting*. It is often suggested that the global relativist's thesis is self-refuting in something like the same way. For example, John Passmore says:

even if we can make some sense of the description of *p* as 'being true for *x*' . . . Protagoras is still asserting that '*p* is true for *x*' and '*p* is not true for *y*'; these propositions he is taking to be true. It has to be true not only for *x* but for everybody that '*p* is true for *x*' since this is exactly what is involved in asserting that 'man is the measure of all things.'

The fundamental criticism of Protagoras can now be put thus: to engage in discourse at all he has to assert that something is the case. (Passmore 1961: 67)

Passmore's idea is that to assert something is to put it forward as true, not just for oneself, but for everyone—true absolutely. So, while the relativist's thesis entails that it is not true absolutely, in asserting it the relativist is putting it forward as true absolutely. The very act of asserting the thesis presupposes its falsity, and in that sense it is pragmatically self-refuting. As Myles Burnyeat puts the point: "No amount of maneuvering with his relativizing qualifiers will extricate Protagoras from the commitment to truth absolute which is bound up with the very act of assertion" (Burnyeat 1976b: 195).

But why should the relativist concede that an assertion is a "commitment to truth absolute"? Why can't the relativist say that in asserting that *p*, one is putting forward *p* as *relatively* true—perhaps as true in one's own perspective?[4] These are hard questions, to be sure. It is not clear what it could mean to put forward *p* as true relative to one's own perspective, if this is not the same as putting it forward as true absolutely that *p* is true relative to one's own perspective. So there is a job of work for the relativist to do. But it is certainly not obvious that it is an impossible one.

---

[4]Cf. Kölbel (2002: 123): "The relativist might concede that asserting something does constitute certain commitments, such as the obligation to state reasons for what one has asserted if asked to do so, to defend what one has asserted if challenged, and to retract one's assertion if one is unable to defend it against challenge. But he or she will deny that commitment to the absolute truth of what has been asserted is among the commitments constituted by an assertion."

2.1.2   *Regress of formulation?*

Indeed, many who pursue a self-refutation argument have conceded that it must take a more subtle form (Burnyeat 1976b: 192–3; Putnam 1981: 120–1; Vallicella 1984: 462–3; Lockie 2003: 331; Boghossian 2006: 54). The real problem, they think, is that the relativist faces a kind of regress in formulating her own position. When the relativist says,

>   (2)   I'm only putting my thesis forward as true *for me*,

the objector can ask whether *this* claim is being put forward as true absolutely. If the relativist says yes, then she has conceded that there is at least one absolute truth, and stands refuted. If she says no,

>   (3)   I'm only putting (2) forward as true *for me*,

then the procedure can be iterated, and so on indefinitely. And this is supposed to spell doom for the relativist's position. As Putnam explains:

A *total* relativist would have to say that whether or not X is true *relative* to P is *itself* relative. At this point our grasp on what the position even means begins to wobble, as Plato observed. (Putnam 1981: 121)

But what, exactly, is problematic about the relativist's willingness to say of *all* of her assertions—even metatheoretic ones like (2)—that she is only putting them forth as true for herself, or true relative to her own framework or perspective?

　　Burnyeat (1976b: 193) suggests that the problem lies in the complexity of the propositions to which we will be led if we iterate the move from (2) to (3):

Protagoras, as Socrates keeps saying, is a clever fellow, but he is not so clever that there is no limit to the complexity of the propositions he can understand and so judge to be true. Therefore, the relativist prefix 'It is true for Protagoras that . . .,' unlike the absolute prefix, admits of only limited reiteration.

But it is hard to see how this objection hits home. The relativist need only move from stage k of the regress to stage $k + 1$ if an intelligible question has been raised about whether stage k has been put forth as true absolutely or merely as true relatively. But surely this question is intelligible if and only if its possible answers are; they are of equal complexity. So, if stage $k + 1$ is unintelligible because of its complexity, so is the question that would require the relativist to produce it, and we can rest content at stage k (cf. Bennigson 1999: 224–6).

　　Boghossian (2006: 56) gives a somewhat different diagnosis. According to Boghossian, the relativist holds that if our factual judgements are to have any prospect of being true, we must not construe utterances of the form

"*p*"

as expressing the claim

p

but rather as expressing the claim

According to a theory, T, that we accept, p. (52)

But of course it would be odd for the relativist to hold that there are absolute facts about what theories say (and hence, presumably, about the contents of minds), but about nothing else. So claims about what theories say also have to be understood as merely claims about what theories say, and a regress ensues:

The upshot is that the fact-relativist is committed to the view that the only facts there are, are infinitary facts of the form:

According to a theory that we accept, there is a theory that we accept and according to this latter theory, there is a theory we accept and . . . there have been dinosaurs.

But it is absurd to propose that, in order for our utterances to have any prospect of being true, what we must mean by them are infinitary propositions that we could neither express nor understand. (56)

This is indeed absurd, but Boghossian's argument that the relativist is committed to it depends on a tendentious characterization of the relativist's position. Boghossian's relativist takes a speaker who utters "snow is white" to have asserted that according to her world-theory, snow is white.[5] But the relativist need not, and should not, hold that to put *p* forward as true for oneself is to put forward the claim *that p is true for oneself*. The point of "for oneself" is not to characterize the *content* that is asserted, but to characterize what the relativist is *doing* in making her assertion: putting its content forward as *true for herself*.

[5]Boghossian models his version of truth relativism on Gilbert Harman's version of moral relativism (Harman 1975), which is essentially a form of contextualism about terms of moral evaluation. As Kölbel (2002: 119) observes, "It can be shown that no global relativist can accept Harman's view that relativity is always a matter of logical form and empty argument places. For if he accepted that, any predicate would have an indefinite number of argument places. . . . So, global relativists must have a different view of what is involved in being relative to some parameter whether some *x* is *F*." See also Wright (2008).

2.1.3   *Belief and the possibility of error*

Putnam (1981) sees that the infinite regress argument cannot bear much weight (120), but he thinks that Plato's argument points dimly towards an argument he finds in Wittgenstein:

> The argument is that the relativist cannot, in the end, make any sense of the distinction between *being right* and *thinking he is right*; and that means that there is, in the end, no difference between *asserting* or *thinking*, on the one hand, and *making noises (or producing mental images)* on the other. But this means that (on this conception) I am not a *thinker* at all but a *mere* animal. To hold such a view is to commit a sort of mental suicide. (122)

But this argument works only against an extreme subjectivist relativist: one who holds that "*p* is true for *X*" is equivalent to "*X* believes that *p*." If *X* can be wrong about what is true for *X*—if it can be false for *X* that *p* is true for *X*, even though *X* believes *p*—then we *do* have a distinction between *X*'s being right and *X*'s thinking she is right.

   Although Putnam's criticism is too narrowly focused to cause much trouble for a truth relativist, it reminds us that the questions the relativist must answer about assertion can also be raised about belief. According to the relativist, I can believe that *p* even if I think that *p* is not true for you. Believing that *p* is not a matter of taking *p* to be true absolutely. What is the difference, then, between my believing that *p* and my believing that *p* is true for me? There had better be a difference, or we face Boghossian's regress. But it isn't clear what the difference is supposed to be.

2.1.4   *Is local relativism immune?*

A common relativist response to the self-refutation argument is to point out that it targets only a radical *global* relativism according to which nothing is true absolutely—even the relativist thesis itself (Nozick 2001: 15; MacFarlane 2005c: 338 n. 19). It seems inapplicable to a *local* relativism, according to which only certain kinds of claims—for example, claims of taste—have truth values relatively. The local relativist can simply say that she is putting her thesis forward as true absolutely, grasping the horn of the dilemma that was not available to the global relativist. There is no inconsistency or pragmatic incoherence in saying, for example, that it is absolutely true that claims of taste are true only relative to judges or standards of taste. For this claim is presumably not itself a claim of taste.

   However, even if local relativism is not self-refuting, it would be a mistake for the local relativist to be too complacent. For the real problem the self-refutation argument raises for the global relativist—explaining how we can make sense of assertion, if not as putting forward a content as true absolutely—is equally pressing for the local relativist. The local relativist could say that there are two kinds of assertion—putting forward as absolutely true and putting foward as relatively true—and that the relativist thesis itself is being asserted in the first way. But something would still need to be said about the second kind of assertion. A more appealing approach would be to give a uniform account of assertion that does not assume that asserted contents are put forward as true absolutely. The relativist could then say that the thesis of relativism is being asserted in the very same sense as, say, claims of taste.

Although none of the "self-refutation" arguments against global relativism are compelling, then, they do raise questions that any relativist (global or local) must answer. What is it, exactly, to assert something if one is not putting it forward as true absolutely? What is it to believe something one does not take to be true absolutely? These are important questions, but the objections have given no principled reason to think that the relativist cannot answer them satisfactorily. We will take them up in Chapter 5.

2.2 Disagreement

A related objection to truth relativism concerns the possibility of disagreement. In his unpublished manuscript "Logic," Frege writes:

If something were true only for him who held it to be true, there would be no contradiction between the opinions of different people. So to be consistent, any person holding this view would have no right whatever to contradict the opposite view, he would have to espouse the principle: *non disputandum est*. He would not be able to assert anything at all in the normal sense, and even if his utterances had the form of assertions, they would only have the status of interjections—of expressions of mental states or processes, between which and such states or processes in another person there could be no contradiction. (Frege 1979: 233)

Moltmann (2010: 213) spells out the worry in a more contemporary setting:

If a speaker utters *chocolate tastes good* then, knowing the truth-relative semantics of the sentence, the speaker should know that the content of his truth-directed attitude or act would be true just relative to his own context. From his point of view, no considerations need to be made that the content of his utterance also target the context of the addressee. Of course, the speaker may know that the addressee will evaluate the utterance at his context. But why should he be bothered about that and why should it lead to possible disagreement? The addressee, in turn, given his knowledge of the relativist semantics of the sentence uttered should know that too. It thus remains a mystery why the situation should give rise to disagreement. The situation appears entirely undistinguishable from the one where the speaker expresses or upholds his own subjective opinion without targeting the addressee's parameters of evaluation in any way, that is, the situation made explicit by attitude reports like *I consider chocolate tasty*.

Does relativism about truth make it possible to understand how there can be disagreements of taste, as we suggested in Chapter 1? Or does it make this impossible, as Frege and Moltmann argue? In order to get clearer about this, we need to ask what disagreement amounts to, and we need to understand in what sense, precisely, there can be disagreement about contents whose truth is perspectival. We will return to this issue in Chapter 6, after we have clarified what truth relativism amounts to.

2.3   What are the bearers of relative truth?

The relativist holds that the truth of *something* is relative: but what? Newton-Smith (1981: 35) argues that there is no good answer. For the thesis that a *sentence* could be true in one social group or theory Ψ and false in another Θ is trivial, since the sentence could have different meanings in Ψ and Θ. Nobody would deny that sentences with different meanings can have different truth values. An interesting relativism, then, must "focus not on sentences but on what is expressed by a sentence"—a *proposition*. But the thesis that a single proposition can be true in Ψ and false in Θ is incoherent:[6]

Let p be the proposition expressed by sentence 'S_1' in Ψ and by sentence 'S_2' in Θ. Could it be the case that p is true in Ψ and false in Θ? No, for it is a necessary condition for the sentence 'S_1' to express the same proposition as the sentence 'S_2' that the sentences have the same truth-conditions. To specify the truth-conditions of a sentence is to specify what would make it true and to specify what would make it false. If in fact 'S_1' and 'S_2' differ in truth-value, their truth-conditions must be different. If their truth-conditions differ they say different things—they say that different conditions obtain—and hence they do not express the same proposition. Thus if we focus on propositions we cannot find a proposition expressed by a sentence 'S_1' in Θ and by a sentence 'S_2' in Ψ which is true in the one case and false in the other.[7] (Newton-Smith 1981: 35)

---

[6]For similar arguments, see also Husserl (2001: 79), Burke (1979: 204), Newton-Smith (1982: 107–8), Swoyer (1982: 105), Stevenson (1988: 282–3). For critical discussion, see White (1986: 332), Hales (1997a: 39), and Kölbel (2002: 119–122).

[7]Newton-Smith seems to have inadvertently reversed "Θ" and "Ψ" here.

This argument has some surface plausibility, and it may have led some relativists to put their position as a thesis about the truth of *utterances* or *assertions* (construed as acts) rather than propositions. This, I think, is misguided (as I will argue in Chapter 3). It is also unnecessary, because the argument trades on a failure to distinguish different senses of "truth-conditions" and "in Θ"—but a proper discussion will have to wait until we are in a position to make those distinctions ourselves (§4.9).

2.4 The equivalence schema

It is sometimes argued that relativism about truth is incompatible with the

Equivalence Schema. *The proposition that φ is true iff φ.*

For example, in his posthumously published article "The Nature of Truth" (2001), Frank Ramsey criticizes philosophers who "produce definitions of truth according to which the earth can be round without its being true that it is round" (441). He notes that ". . . according to William James a pragmatist could think both that Shakespeare's plays were written by Bacon and that someone else's opinion that Shakespeare wrote them might be perfectly true 'for him.' " (445–5 n. 12, citing James 1909: 274 = James 1978: 313).

Although the Equivalence Schema is implicated in the Liar Paradox, and may need to be qualified or restricted in some way, it is generally regarded as fundamental to our use of the truth predicate. The point can be made intuitively: it would be incoherent to say, for example, that it is true that dogs bark, while denying that dogs bark, or to say that dogs bark while denying that it is true that they do. But the Equivalence Schema can also be motivated on logical and expressive grounds. English and other natural languages do not allow quantification into sentence position: the grammatical position occupied by 'φ' in the Equivalence Schema. So, we cannot express our agreement with everything Billy asserted by saying,

(4) For all *P*, if Billy asserted that *P*, *P*.
 # If Billy asserted something, then it.[8]

---

[8]Some philosophers have claimed that English *does* contain propositional quantifiers, and that (4) is expressed as "If Billy asserted something, it is true," where the phrase "it is true" functions as a bindable "prosentence," and not a sentence constructed of independently significant components "it," "is," and "true" (Grover 1979; Grover, Camp, and Belnap 1975). I think that this view will have difficulty making sense of sentences like "If Billy asserted something, it is both true and well supported." Künne (2003: §6.2.1) suggests that we might express (4) without using a truth

Natural languages get around this apparent limitation in expressive power by providing a way to simulate quantification into sentence position using ordinary quantification over objects:

(5)   For all propositions x, if Billy asserted x, x is true
       If Billy asserted something, it is true.

But if (5) is to do the work that (4) would do, we must be able to move from (5) and

(6)   Billy asserted that snow is white

to

(7)   Snow is white.

And what we need for that is precisely an instance of the Equivalence Schema:

(8)   The proposition that snow is white is true iff snow is white.

So the Equivalence Schema underlies the essential expressive function of the truth predicate.

   Although some relativists about truth have conceded that their view is incompatible with the equivalence schema (Nozick 2001: 41), it is open to a relativist to promote the theoretical utility of a relativized (dyadic) truth predicate, while acknowledging that the truth predicate used in ordinary talk is a monadic predicate for which the Equivalence Schema holds (cf. Unwin 1987: 304–5; Kölbel 2008b). On this view, if

(9)   Licorice is tasty

is true relative to some perspectives and false relative to others, then so is

(10)   The proposition that licorice is tasty is true.

A relativist who says this can hold on to the Equivalence Schema, taking its instances to be true relative to every perspective.

   However, this strategy raises serious questions about how the monadic truth predicate and the dyadic truth predicate are related, and why the latter

predicate, as "However things may be said to be, if Billy asserted that things are that way, then things are that way," where "things are that way" functions as a prosentence. If this is right, then the idea that the truth predicate is needed to compensate for an expressive limitation is undercut. But nothing below hinges on that claim; all we really need is that (5) can do the work that (4) would do, not that it is the only sentence that can do this work.

deserves to be called a truth predicate at all. Suppose we use "true" to express the monadic property which obeys the Equivalence Schema and "True for x" to express the relativist's relational property. Then, as Fox (1994: 73) notes, either the Equivalence Schema holds for "True for x" no matter what the value of x, or it does not. If it does—that is, if

(11) $\forall x$(the proposition that ϕ is True for x iff ϕ)

is a valid schema, then the relativization to x looks like an idle wheel. But if it does not, "the most cogent of arguments that Truth needs relativizing could not carry over to an argument that truth does."

Thus it is crucial for the relativist to give an adequate account of the relation between her relativized notion of truth and the monadic predicate we use in ordinary talk. We will return to this issue in §4.8.

2.5 What does it mean?

Perhaps the most pressing worry about relativism about truth is that it is not clear what it *means* to call a proposition "true for Sal" or "true relative to Sal's tastes."

The problem is not that "true for x" doesn't have a use in non-philosophical English. It is often used to specify the domain for which a generalization holds. For example:

(12) While the doors to high civil, military and academic office have been opened to merit for members of other communities, this has not been *true for Muslims*. (Shissler 2003: 153)

is used to say that the generalization

(13) The doors to high civil, military and academic office have been opened to merit for members of their communities.

holds of non-Muslims, but not of Muslims. This is not "relative truth" in any very interesting sense.[9] Here are some further examples of the same phenomenon:

[9]The demonstrative "this" in (12) denotes not the proposition expressed immediately before it, (*) *that the doors to high civil, military and academic office have been opened to merit for members of other [than Muslim] communities*, but rather a property abstracted from it. This abstraction must be triggered by the predicate "true for Muslims," since if we substituted (say) "widely recognized," "this" would naturally be taken to denote the proposition (*).

(14)   It is well known that certain human subjects are especially resistant to the gas and I have frequently found this to be *true for dogs*. (Jackson 1917: 70)

(15)   "The pianos used by Mozart, Beethoven or Chopin were radically different from the large, loud black instruments found in all modern concert halls," Moroney said. "The same is *true for violins*." (Maclay 2001)

(16)   Not only was it useless to try to derive the satisfaction she needed from another individual through subordinating her needs to that person's, but even attempting to do so was destroying her. Generalizing her insights, she concluded that what was *true for her* was *true for all people*. (Fellman 2008: 62)

"True for" also seems to have what we might call an *intentional* use: to call something "true for *x*" is sometimes just to say that *x* *takes* it to be true, or that it is "true in *x*'s book." The work here is being done by "for," not "true," since in a similar spirit we can say

(17)   For Sarah (the creationist), that fossil is less than 5000 years old.

(18)   For John (the color-blind man), those socks are the same color.

(19)   For Elroy (the imaginative child), ant mounds are space stations.

This use of "true for" is no help to the relativist, as Meiland and Krausz observe:

If all that were meant by saying a belief is true for Jones is that Jones holds that belief, then every belief that Jones holds would be true for Jones. But the relativist rejects this notion of relative truth; he or she takes the notion of relative truth more seriously than this. "Relative truth" is a form of truth; the expression "relative truth" is not a name for something bearing little relation to our ordinary conception of truth. And just as our ordinary conception of truth allows a person to hold beliefs which are false, so too the notion of relative truth must allow an individual to hold beliefs which are false *for him* or *her*. If it were not possible for a person to hold beliefs which were false for him or her, then the notion of relative truth would be superfluous . . . (Meiland and Krausz 1982: 4; cf. Fox 1994: 70–1; Vallicella 1984: 454; Swoyer 1982: 94)

Thus the relativist cannot claim to be explicating a relational truth locution that is already in use in natural speech. If she uses a relativized truth predicate, she must explain what it means. And she must do so in a way that makes it clear why the relativized predicate she is explaining is a relativized *truth* predicate, and not something else entirely. This is, I think, the *principal* challenge for truth relativism, and the one that the existing literature has made least progress in answering.

Extant answers typically start with one of the traditional "theories of truth": correspondence, pragmatic, or epistemic. (Deflationary theories, according to which there is nothing to be said about truth beyond the Equivalence Schema, are no help to the relativist, since the Equivalence Schema essentially involves a *monadic* truth predicate.) They then attempt to show that these theories, when properly understood, lead to the idea that truth is a relative property. The point is perhaps easiest to see with a pragmatic theory of truth. If truth is, as James says, "only the expedient in the way of our thinking" (James 1978: 106), then relativism about truth is just the plausible thesis that what is expedient for one person to think need not be expedient for another.[10] James seems to accept this thesis: "in any concrete account of what is denoted by 'truth' in human life, the word can only be used relatively to some particular trower" (James 1978: 313).

Epistemic theories of truth, which call true what a community of idealized enquirers would be justified in believing, also give a clear sense to the idea that truth might be relative. Bennigson (1999: 213) motivates his relativism in this way:

Begin with an epistemic account of truth as some sort of idealization of rational acceptability: true sentences are those which disinterested inquirers would assent to under ideal conditions, or at some idealized 'limit of inquiry.' The relativist simply adds that different communities of inquirers, starting from different sets of assumptions about what is plausible, noteworthy, explanatory, etc., might approach different limits. Thus, on the appropriate epistemic conception of truth, conflicting conclusions could be true for different communities.

Even if we suppose (rather implausibly) that any two communities of idealized enquirers would have access to the same observations and experimental results, an epistemic conception of truth tends toward relativism. Most philosophers have abandoned Carnap's idea that the relation *evidence e confirms proposition p* can be spelled out in formal logical terms. Whether a given

---

[10]How plausible this is will depend on how, exactly, one spells out the pragmatist's slogan. James himself does not limit the kinds of expediency that might be at issue (he says "Expedient in almost any fashion"), and he acknowledges that idiosyncrasies of taste may play a role: "Truth in science is what gives us the maximum possible sum of satisfactions, taste included, but consistency both with previous truth and with novel fact is always the most imperious claimant" (104).

proposition is supported by a given body of evidence, and how strongly, depends on facts about the background of inquiry—for Goodman (1979), the relative "entrenchment" of predicates; for Bayesians, prior probabilities and a background corpus.[11] If two communities of idealized enquirers differed in these factors, then even if they went on to have all the same observations and perform all the same experiments, they might diverge in their justified beliefs at "the end of inquiry."

The problem with making sense of relative truth in these ways is that pragmatic and epistemic theories of truth are not very plausible. Surely it is coherent to suppose that there are truths that even idealized enquirers could not come to know, and truths that it would not be expedient to believe.[12] Moreover, pragmatic and epistemic theories would support a diffuse *global* relativism, not the kind of targeted local relativism we might use to explain the characteristic features of certain kinds of discourse.

It is not surprising, then, that some relativists have sought to make sense of their doctrine in the framework of a correspondence theory of truth. Jack Meiland proposes that "ϕ is true for Jones" means "ϕ corresponds to reality for Jones." To the obvious objection—what does "corresponds to reality for Jones" mean?—Meiland has this reply:

Although this question is embarrassing in the sense that it is difficult for the relativist to give any useful answer to it, nevertheless the relativist is in no worse a position than the absolutist at this point. . . . relativism is not to be faulted for being unable to give an account of that which the absolutist cannot give an account of in his own position either. (Meiland 1977: 580)

Meiland is right to insist that the relativist not be held to a higher standard in explicating truth than the absolutist. And he is right that "corresponds to reality for Jones" is no less intelligible than "corresponds to reality" (assuming nothing more is said to explicate *that*). However, to say that truth is "correspondence to the facts" is, at best, only to give the schema for an explication of truth. By itself it provides no illumination. And neither does saying that truth for Jones is correspondence to reality for Jones.

Though Meiland's specific account is unilluminating, I think the strategy he pursues is a promising one: look at the best non-relativist explication of truth, and explicate relative truth in a similar way, using similar materials. We will return to this project in Chapter 5.

---

[11] See Fitelson (2005) for a useful survey.

[12] For an in-depth discussion, see Künne (2003: ch. 7).

2.6 Conclusion

Under closer examination, none of the standard objections to truth relativism look like knock-down arguments. Still, they point to real problems that a relativist must address. The relativist needs an account of propositions that allows them to be "merely relatively true." She needs to explain what it is to assert a proposition, if not to put it forward as true absolutely, and what it is to believe a proposition, if not to take it to be true absolutely. She needs to explain how disagreement about relatively true propositions is possible. She needs to explain how the ordinary monadic truth predicate is related to her relativized truth predicate. And she needs to say more about what her relativized "true for" or "true at" *means*.

The aim of the next four chapters is to state the truth relativist's position clearly enough that all of these questions, and more, can be answered.

3

ASSESSMENT SENSITIVITY

Most of the literature on truth relativism concerns either motivations for relativizing truth or arguments against the coherence of truth relativism. Comparatively little attention has been given to saying with precision what it *is* to be a truth relativist. The aim of this chapter is to say precisely what kinds of views count as forms of truth relativism. As Meiland (1977: 568) rightly says:

Perhaps truth is relative; perhaps not. But I think that we cannot decide whether or not truth is relative until we first determine what "relative truth" might be.

The characterization of truth relativism proferred below will count as relativist some views that others would not, and fail to count as relativist some views that others would. The project is not to give a general account of the meaning of "relative truth" as that phrase is used in philosophical discourse. It is used in many ways. Nor is it to insist that there is only one legitimate or useful thing to mean by this phrase. Rather, the characterization is offered as an *explication* (in Rudolf Carnap's sense) of philosophical talk of "relative truth." If, after my explication, some readers prefer to continue using the phrase "relative truth" in some other way, that is fine. Not much hangs on the words, so long as the concept to which I would prefer to attach them—assessment sensitivity—is clearly grasped.

3.1 Characterizing relativism

One might think that being a relativist about truth is just a matter of relativizing truth to some parameter. But it is not that simple. Many relativizations of truth are entirely orthodox.

3.1.1 *Sentences*

Considered by itself, in abstraction from any particular context of use, the sentence

(1)   I have been to China.

cannot be said to be true or false. It can be used to say something with either truth value. For certain purposes, we might find it useful to assign (1) truth values relative to possible *contexts of use*, which determine a denotation for "I" (the speaker) and a reference time (the time of use). This way of relativizing truth is familiar from David Kaplan's pioneering work on indexicals (Kaplan 1989). But nobody would say that Kaplan is a "relativist about truth" in any philosophically interesting sense. This relativization simply registers a fact obvious to everyone—that in general, whether sentences express truths or falsehoods depends on the settings in which they are used.

Other orthodox relativizations of sentence truth have technical motivations. Consider the problem of giving systematic truth conditions for quantified sentences, like

(2)   For all integers x, there exists an integer y such that $x + y = 0$.

If we think of this sentence in the standard way, as the result of combining a quantifier "For all integers x" with an open sentence

(3)   there exists an integer y such that $x + y = 0$,

then a compositional semantics ought to give truth conditions for (2) as a function of the truth conditions of (3). But there are no "conditions" under which (3) is true simpliciter, only conditions under which it is true for some value of x or another. Tarski's solution to this problem was to recursively define *truth on an assignment of values to the variables* rather than truth simpliciter (Tarski 1935; Tarski 1983).[1] Thus, for example, the clause governing the universal quantifier looks like this:

(4) $\ulcorner \forall \alpha \phi \urcorner$ is true on assignment a iff for every assignment a' that differs from a at most in the value it gives to α, ϕ is true on a'.

Note that even the clauses for the truth-functional connectives must be stated in terms of truth on an assignment:

(5) $\ulcorner \neg \phi \urcorner$ is true on assignment a iff ϕ is not true on a.

For these connectives may operate on open formulas, as is the case in

(6) $\forall x \neg (x < 0)$.

---

[1] Tarski encoded his assignments as infinite sequences of values, and so talked of "truth on a sequence," but the decision to use a sequence rather than a function is just a technical one.

So truth is relativized to assignments for all formulas. But nobody would call Tarski a "relativist about truth" on this account.

Why aren't these relativizations of truth philosophically problematic? For relativization to an assignment, the answer is clear: this relativization is just a technical device, not something we need to make sense of independently of its role in systematizing absolute truth values. At the end of the day, what we care about is truth, not truth on an assignment. So our recursive definition of truth on an assignment for arbitrary formulas is of interest to us only because truth simpliciter can be defined in terms of truth on an assignment:

(7)   If ϕ is a sentence, then ϕ is true iff ϕ is true on every assignment.[2]

Because the role played by truth on an assignment is a purely technical one, we could use different terminology without changing the theory in any important way. Instead of talking of "truth on an assignment," for example, we could define a valuation function v that maps sentence/assignment pairs to 0 or 1:

(4′)

$$v(\ulcorner \forall \alpha \phi \urcorner, a) = \begin{cases} 1 \text{ if for every assignment } a' \text{ that differs from} \\ \quad a \text{ at most in the value it gives to } \alpha, \\ \quad v(\phi, a') = 1 \\ 0 \text{ otherwise} \end{cases}$$

(5′)

$$v(\ulcorner \neg \phi \urcorner, a) = \begin{cases} 1 \text{ if } v(\phi, a) = 0 \\ 0 \text{ otherwise} \end{cases}$$

And then, at the end:

(7′)   If ϕ is a sentence, then ϕ is true iff for every assignment a, $v(\phi, a) = 1$.

The recursive definition of v does exactly the same work as the recursive definition of truth on an assignment. Talk of truth relative to an assignment, then, is consistent with holding that truth in the philosophically interesting sense is absolute.

What about truth relative to a context of use? One might try a parallel strategy here, arguing that we talk of truth at a context for sentences only as a

----

[2] Equivalently, "on *some* assignment," or even "on assignment a_0," since a sentence—a formula with no free variables—will have the same truth value on every assignment.

technical device for systematizing truth simpliciter for *utterances*—particular acts of uttering or using sentences.[3] If we assume that for each utterance there is a unique context at which it occurs, we can define utterance truth in terms of sentence truth at a context:

(8)   An utterance u is true iff the sentence of which u is an utterance is true at the context in which u occurs.

Utterance truth, so defined, is "absolute."

3.1.2   *Utterances*

This suggests that we might characterize truth relativism as the view that *utterance truth* is relative: one and the same utterance (of a declarative sentence) can be true, relative to X, and false, relative to Y. This is in the right ballpark, I think.[4] But there are some reasons to be dissatisfied with it as a characterization of truth relativism.

First, it is linguistically odd to talk of utterances—in the sense of utterance *acts*, not the things uttered (sentences)—as being true or false. In general, we characterize actions as correct or incorrect, but not as true or false. It might be suggested that although "true" and "false" do not apply to all kinds of actions, they do apply to certain speech acts. However, it sounds strange to say "That speech act was true" or "What he did in asserting that sentence was true." This suggests that when we say "His assertion was false" or "That was a true utterance," we are using "assertion" and "utterance" to refer to what is asserted, and not to the *act* of asserting it (Strawson 1950: 130; Bar-Hillel 1973: 304).

---

[3]Sometimes it is thought that although truth for sentence *types* is context-relative, truth for sentence *tokens*—particular sounds or acoustic blasts—is absolute. But even a sentence *token* can have different truth values on different occasions of use. When I leave my office for a quick errand, I put an old yellow post-it note with a token of "I'll be back in a minute" on my door. Sometimes this sentence token expresses a truth, sometimes a falsehood. For relevant discussion, see Percival (1994: 204–5), Perry (2001: 37–9).

Can similar worries be raised about utterances, construed as acts? Zimmerman (2007: 315–16) gives an example in which a single utterance of the words "He got plastered" is meant in two senses, describing someone whose buddies covered him in plaster after he became intoxicated. This shows, Zimmerman thinks, that a single utterance can have different truth values under different construals. But if what is uttered is a sentence type, not an orthographic type, then in Zimmerman's case we have a single talking act counting as two distinct utterance acts, of the sentences "He got plastered$_1$" and "He got plastered$_2$" respectively.

[4]In MacFarlane (2003), I characterize the relativist as someone who rejects the Absoluteness of Utterance Truth.

By itself, this may not be a compelling reason for rejecting talk of utterance truth in a theoretical context. Donald Davidson, acknowledging the oddity of characterizing utterance acts as true, says: "Verbal felicity apart, there is no reason not to call the utterance of a sentence, under conditions that make the sentence true, a true utterance" (Davidson 1990: 310).

But even if we look past verbal infelicity, talk of utterances does not seem sufficiently fundamental. If utterances of sentences have truth values, they presumably have them in virtue of expressing propositions that have truth values. So the claim that utterance truth is relative immediately raises questions about the truth of propositions. Suppose Jim asserts that p by uttering sentence S at context c, and suppose that his utterance is true relative to X but false relative to Y. Is this relativity attributable to a relativity of the truth of p? If so, what is this relativity, and why can't relativism about truth be characterized directly in terms of it? If not, how can an utterance expressing a proposition whose truth is not relative to X and Y have truth values only relative to X and Y?[5]

Moreover, as David Kaplan points out, the notion of an "utterance" is not proper to semantics:

It is important to distinguish an *utterance* from a *sentence-in-context*. The former notion is from the theory of speech acts, the latter from semantics. Utterances take time, and utterances of distinct sentences cannot be simultaneous (i.e., in the same context). But to develop a logic of demonstratives it seems most natural to be able to evaluate several premises and a conclusion all in the same context. Thus the notion of ϕ *being true in c and* $\mathfrak{A}$ does not require an utterance of ϕ. In particular, c_A need not be uttering ϕ in c_W at c_T. (Kaplan 1989: 563)

It would be odd if whether a view counted as a form of truth relativism could only be discerned from within the theory of speech acts. One might expect there to be a *semantic* difference between relativist and nonrelativist views.

Finally, the assumption on which (8) depends—that each utterance occurs at a unique context—is not one that everyone will grant. For example, many people hold that an utterance is a concrete event, that a concrete event can belong to multiple possible worlds, and that a context determines a unique possible world. But on these assumptions, an utterance will not determine a unique context, and cannot be assigned an absolute truth value in the manner of (8) (de Sa 2009). We would not want to class everyone with this

---

[5] *Exercise to the reader:* Return to these questions after reading Chapter 4.

combination of metaphysical views as a truth relativist, or worse, deny that they can understand what it is to be a truth relativist.

3.1.3 *Propositions*

All of this suggests that the relativist doctrine should be stated not as a claim about the truth of assert*ings*, but as a claim about the things that are assert*ed*, which, following tradition, I will call *propositions*.[6] Propositions are usually thought of as the "primary bearers of truth value." What this means is that other things that have truth values (sentences, beliefs, assertions, etc.) have them by virtue of standing in an appropriate relation to propositions that have those truth values. It is natural to think, then, that if all of these other things have their truth values only relatively, it is because propositions do.

Accordingly, Max Kölbel has characterized "non-tame" relativism about truth as the view that "the truth of propositions (or contents) of some kind can be relative" (Kölbel 2002: 119). By this criterion, though, just about everyone who uses propositions in formal semantics would count as a non-tame relativist. For it is orthodox practice to relativize truth of propositions to possible worlds—and in some frameworks worlds and times.[7] For example, the proposition that dodos are extinct in 2004 is true in the actual world, but there are possible worlds relative to which the very same proposition is false. Surely this much relativism does not constitute "relativism about truth" in the sense we are trying to capture. It can be motivated by considerations that have nothing to do with deficient objectivity, and it is perfectly compatible with the idea that particular assertions can be assigned absolute truth values. We only need to add that an assertion that p is true (or false) simpliciter just in case p is true (or false) at the actual world.

Faced with this fact, most writers who seek to characterize truth relativism at the propositional level resort to discrimination. Relativizing propositional truth to possible worlds, they say, is just a formal way of registering the fact that the truth of a proposition depends on how things are. It is relativizing propositional truth to factors *beyond* just worlds that makes one a relativist about truth (Nozick 2001: 19; Stanley 2005b: 137; Zimmerman 2007: 316; Kölbel 2008a: 4).

---

[6] For some arguments for the theoretical utility of propositions, and the point that propositions are not to be identified with sentence meanings, see Cartwright (1962).

[7] See, for example, Stalnaker (1987), Kripke (1972), Lewis (1986), and Kaplan (1989).

This characterization is problematic. It casts *temporalism*—the view that propositions have truth values relative to times, in addition to possible worlds—as a kind of truth relativism. And this seems to put the line between relativist and nonrelativist views in the wrong place. Every reason against letting relativization of propositional truth to possible worlds count as "truth relativism" applies also to relativization of propositional truth to times.

First, doing so would class a number of orthodox thinkers as relativists about truth. Prior (1957, 2003) and Kaplan (1989: 502–9) have taken propositions to have truth values relative to (worlds and) times.[8]

Second, the debates between temporalists and eternalists turn on ordinary practices of reporting that two people "believe the same thing" and on technical issues concerning tense and semantic value.[9] They do not seem to turn on any of the issues that are at stake in traditional debates about relative truth.

Third, and most important, both relativizations are consistent with the absoluteness of utterance truth. Just as the eternalist will say that an assertion that *p* is true simpliciter if *p* is true at the actual world, so the temporalist will say that an assertion that *p* is true simpliciter if *p* is true at the actual world and the time at which the assertion occurs. The temporalist and the eternalist will agree on all questions about the truth of particular utterances, and they will take all such questions to have "absolute" answers. If the eternalists' commitment to the absoluteness of utterance truth is what keeps them from being counted as truth relativists, temporalists should not be counted as truth relativists either.

It is not important here whether one accepts or rejects temporalism. The question is whether the temporalist position—even if it is wrong or misguided—should count as a form of relativism about truth. What I am

---

[8]Kaplan talks of "contents," not "propositions," and notes that his notion of content departs from "the traditional notion of a proposition" in virtue of this time-relativity (503 n. 28; cf. 546). However, he explicitly identifies the content of a declarative sentence with "what is said" by an utterance of it, and notes that "the content of a sentence in a given context is what has traditionally been called a proposition" (500). Moreover, his reservations about calling his contents "propositions" are not very substantial, since the "tradition" of taking propositions to have their truth values eternally is actually quite recent. The view that propositional truth is time-relative was widespread in ancient, medieval, and modern philosophy, and only began to wane in the twentieth century (for an illuminating account of the history, see Prior 1957: Appendix A). Since Kaplan assigns his contents roles traditionally played by propositions, I will treat his views about the contents of declarative sentences as views about propositions.

[9]For relevant discussion, see Richard (1980, 1982, 2003), Salmon (1986, 2003), King (2003), and especially Kaplan (1989: 503 n. 28).

arguing is that there is no good reason to count it as relativist that would not apply equally to eternalism.

One might try saying that one is a relativist about truth if one relativizes propositional truth to something besides worlds and times. But now the characterization begins to look unprincipled. Are worlds and times the only innocuous parameters? What about the proposal—also considered by Kaplan—to countenance "locationally neutral" propositions, like the proposition *that it is raining*, that have truth values relative to worlds, times, and *locations* (Kaplan 1989: 504)? This proposal does not seem different in kind from the proposal to relativize propositional truth to times. Again, there may be reasons for countenancing temporally neutral propositions but not locationally neutral ones, but the question here is whether a commitment to locationally neutral propositions makes one a relativist about truth, and if so why. By what general principle do we decide whether relativizing truth to a parameter X makes one a relativist about truth?[10]

Putting aside worries about the unprincipled nature of the division between "innocuous" and "suspicious" parameters of propositional truth, there is a more serious problem with the proposed characterization of relativism. The problem is that one can describe views that make utterance truth relative without countenancing any nonstandard parameters of propositional truth at all. We can describe a simple example using the temporalist's tensed (time-relative) propositions. Reasonable temporalists, like Kaplan, will say that an assertion of a tensed proposition is true just in case the proposition is true at the (world and) time of utterance. So, if at 2 p.m. I assert that Socrates is sitting, then my utterance is true just in case the proposition I have asserted—*that Socrates is sitting*—is true at 2 p.m. But instead of taking this reasonable view, one could instead say that such an utterance has no truth value simpliciter, but only time-relative truth values: as assessed from time t_1, an assertion of p at t_0 is true just in case p is true at (the world of utterance and) t_1.[11] On this view, one evaluates the truth or correctness of an earlier assertion by asking whether its content is true at the current time. This means, for example, that if it is 3 p.m. and Socrates is now standing, we should deny that our assertion

---

[10]Nozick (2001: 307 n. 7) admits (and regrets) that he has no principled basis for demarcating "the harmless factors, relativity to which does not constitute relativism, from the factors that make for relativism."

[11]This is essentially the view (6) criticized by Evans (1985: 347), substituting utterance truth for "correctness."

at 2 p.m. was true—even if Socrates was, in fact, sitting at 2 p.m. Such a view would be silly, of course, but the question is whether it should count as a form of relativism about truth. Presumably it should, since it denies that assertion-acts have absolute truth values. Despite that, it does not relativize propositional truth to any "nonstandard" parameters. So relativization to nonstandard parameters is not necessary for relativism about truth. (This point will be made more forcefully in Chapter 9, where we will examine a non-silly relativist view that relativizes propositional truth to nothing besides possible worlds.)

I will argue in Chapter 4 that relativization of propositional truth to nonstandard parameters is not *sufficient* for relativism about truth, either. As we will see, it is not the *kind* of parameters to which one relativizes propositional truth that makes one a relativist, but rather what one does with them.

3.2 Assessment Sensitivity

I am going to suggest that what makes one a relativist about truth is a commitment to the *assessment sensitivity* of some sentences or propositions. The primary task of this section, then, is to explain what assessment sensitivity is. For simplicity, I will work in a semantic framework, due to Lewis (1980), that works only with sentences (and open formulas), not propositions. In Chapter 4, we will see what assessment sensitivity looks like in a semantic framework, like that of Kaplan (1989), that makes use of the notion of a proposition.

3.2.1 *Truth at a context of use*

The goal of a semantic theory for a language L, as Lewis (1980) conceives it, is to define truth at a context of use for arbitrary sentences of L.[12] That is, given any sentence S of L, the semantic theory must tell us what a context must

---

[12] Although Lewis talks at first of defining "true-in-L" for a particular language L, say, English, he notes that for non-mathematical languages truth will depend on "features of the situation in which the words are said," so the target notion becomes "truth-in-English at a context." "To do their first job of determining whether truth-in-English would be achieved if a given sentence were uttered in a given context, the semantic values of sentences must provide information about the dependence of truth on context" (Lewis 1998: 31). In what follows, we will drop the qualifier "in-L." The qualifier is needed if we think of sentences as orthographic strings, so that the same sentence might be true-in-L_1 but not true-in-L_2. But if we think of sentences as essentially sentences of a language, we can drop the "in-L" and simply define "true," on a restricted domain consisting of the sentences of L. For this approach, see Neale (2001: 25).

be like in order for an utterance of S at that context to express a truth. For example, a semantic theory for English will tell us that

(9)   I am six feet tall

is true at a context if the agent of that context is six feet in height at the time and world of the context. It will tell us that

(10)   Snow is white and grass is green

is true at a context just in case snow is white and grass is green at the time and world of the context. And so on. In short, it will give us "truth conditions" for all the sentences in the language.

We will think of a context as a possible occasion of use of a sentence (Kaplan 1989: 494).[13] Formally, we might model a context as a sequence of parameters (agent, world, time, location, and so on) or as a "centered possible world" (a world with a designated time and location as "center"). We will assume that however a context is represented, it determines a unique agent, time, world, and location. By the "agent" of a context, I mean the user or potential user of the sentence. ("Speaker" is not general enough, since we might want to consider contexts at which the agent is not speaking.)[14]

Why is truth-at-a-context the target notion of a semantic theory? Because truth-at-a-context has direct pragmatic relevance. When we speak, in the normal case, we try to use sentences that are true at our contexts, and we expect others to do the same:

The foremost thing we do with words is to impart information, and this is how we do it. Suppose (1) that you do not know whether A or B or . . .; and (2) that I do know; and (3) that I want you to know; and (4) that no extraneous reasons much constrain my choice of words; and (5) that we both know that the conditions (1)–(5) obtain. Then I will be truthful and you will be trusting and thereby you will come to share my knowledge. I will find something to say that depends for its truth on whether A or B or . . . and that I take to be true. I will say it and you will hear it. You, trusting me to be

[13]This is an objective concept of context. Contrast Stalnaker (1978), who thinks of a context as the set of propositions that are taken for granted as common ground in a conversation.

[14]Even when sentences are spoken, the time, and location of the context of use can diverge from the time and location of speech. I might begin a story by saying, "It is 1976, and Ford is still President." Or I might leave an answering machine message beginning "I am not here now." Predelli (2005: ch. 2) argues, on the basis of cases like this, that we should drop the usual assumption that the agent of a context exists at the world and time of the context, and is at the location of the context at the time of the context (Lewis 1980: 28–9, Kaplan 1989: 512 n. 37).

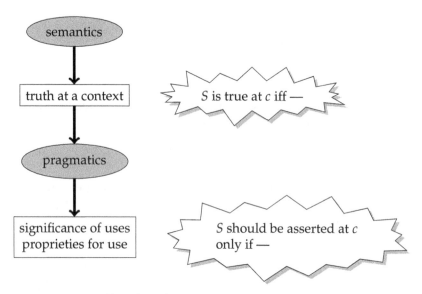

FIG. 3.1. Semantics and pragmatics

willing and able to tell the truth, will then be in a position to infer whether *A* or *B* or
... (Lewis 1998: 22; cf. Lewis 1983: §III)

So the central semantic fact we need to know if we are to *use* a sentence and
understand others' uses of it is the condition for its truth at a context.[15] Truth
at a context is the point at which semantics makes contact with pragmatics, in
the broad sense—the study of the use of language.

As a starting point, then, we might think of the study of meaning as having
two parts: *semantics*, which tells us the conditions under which sentences are
true at a context, and *pragmatics*, which tells us something about the use of
these sentences, given the conditions for their truth at a context (see Fig. 3.1).[16]
One simple form the pragmatics might take (following Lewis) is a specification
of the norms or conventions for using a sentence *S* to make a speech act of
type Φ, but this kind of account is more plausible for assertion than for other

---

[15] *Objection:* one can know that "$2 + 2 = 4$" is true at *every* context without having any idea
how to use it. *Reply:* To know that "$2 + 2 = 4$" is true at every context is not to know the *condition*
for it to be true at a context. To know this, one must know that the sentence is true at a context iff
the sum of 2 and 2 is 4 at the world of that context. It may be that this condition is satisfied by
every context, but the extra bit of mathematical knowledge it takes to see this is not part of the
condition itself.

[16] The word "pragmatics" is often used in a narrower sense, for the theory of implicatures. I
might have used the term "theory of speech acts" instead of "pragmatics."

types of speech acts, and might be rejected even for assertion. We will not presuppose that the pragmatics takes any particular form; the essential thing is that it relates the output of the semantic theory to the use of sentences.

3.2.2 *Truth at an index and context*

It is a simple enough matter to state the condition for a particular sentence to be true at a context. But a semantic theory for a language needs to encode truth conditions for *all* sentences of the language. Since natural languages (and most artificial ones) allow the formation of arbitrarily complex sentences, there will be infinitely many of them. Obviously, we can't just *list* them together with their truth conditions. We need some way of *computing* the truth conditions of a sentence from a structural description of it.

For some simple languages, we can do this by direct recursion. Suppose our language contains just two atomic sentences, "I am happy" and "Grass is green," together with a unary connective "It is not the case that" and a binary connective "and." Then we can specify truth conditions for all of its sentences with the following clauses:

(11) "I am happy" is true at c iff the agent of c is happy at the world of c.

(12) "Grass is green" is true at c iff grass is green at the world of c.

(13) ⌜It is not the case that ϕ⌝ is true at c iff ϕ is not true at c.

(14) ⌜ϕ and ψ⌝ is true at c iff ϕ is true at c and ψ is true at c.

The same technique will work for any language with a finite number of atomic sentences and truth-functional connectives. But it will not work for languages with quantifiers or non-truth-functional operators. We have already seen why it will not work for quantifiers: quantified sentences are constructed out of open formulas, and these do not have truth values at contexts (§3.1.1). To see why it won't work for non-truth-functional operators, suppose we add to our language a unary operator "It has always been the case that." One might try:

(15) ⌜It has always been the case that ϕ⌝ is true at c iff it has always been the case that ϕ is true at c.

But this doesn't give us what we want, because "true at c" is a timeless predicate. A context includes a time and a state of the world, so if ϕ is true at c, then it has always been and will always be true at c. For example, if c is a context occurring on a Monday, then it has always been the case that "it is Monday" is true at c. But "It has always been the case that it is Monday" (or more colloquially, "it has always been Monday") is not true at c. So (15) cannot be right.

A natural thought would be to evaluate the embedded sentence relative to all *earlier* contexts:

(16)   ⌜It has always been the case that ϕ⌝ is true at c iff for every context c' that differs from c at most in taking place at an earlier time, ϕ is true at c'.

But this won't work, either, for two reasons. The first problem is that if ϕ contains a time-sensitive indexical like "now" or "yesterday," its denotation will shift as we evaluate ϕ relative to the time-shifted contexts. And this will get the truth conditions wrong: "now" and "yesterday" should not shift their denotations when embedded under "it has always been the case that. . ." (Kamp 1971).[17] Thus, for example, (16) would class "It has always been the case that yesterday was the 15th of March" as false, even when uttered on the 16th of March.

The second problem is that if we look only at contexts that differ from c *only* in the time of the context—agreeing with c on the agent and world of the context—we won't be looking at *all* the times prior to the time of c. Since the agent (speaker) of a context must *exist* at the time and world of the context, we will not be looking at any times prior to the birth of the speaker of c in the world of c. There just *aren't* any possible contexts c' such that the agent of c' = the agent of c, the world of c' = the world of c, and the time of c' is earlier than the birth of the agent of c in the world of c. Surely, though, "It has always been the case that" must quantify over *all* times prior to the time of the context. Lewis summarizes the problem succinctly:

Unless our grammar explains away all seeming cases of shiftiness, we need to know what happens to the truth values of constituent sentences when one feature of context is shifted and the rest are held fixed. But features of context do not vary independently. No two contexts differ by only one feature. Shift one feature only, and the result of the shift is not a context at all. (Lewis 1998: 29; cf. Kaplan 1989: 509)[18]

---

[17]Kaplan (1989: 510–12) argues, further, that natural languages do not contain any operators that shift contexts, as "It has always been the case that" does on the semantics of (16). The claim has been widely accepted, though Schlenker (2003) has questioned it.

[18]Lewis might seem to be overstating things. Couldn't two contexts differ only in the time of the context? Certainly the agent and world of the context could be the same. But, as Lewis notes, there are "countless other features" of contexts that might, in theory, be semantically significant: for example, the temperature of the context, the conversationally salient objects of the context, and so on. In any case, the argument against (16) does not depend on the strong claim that *no*

The solution, Lewis suggests, is to relativize truth not just to contexts but to *indices*: "packages of features of context so combined that they *can* vary independently":

An index is an *n*-tuple of features of context of various sorts; call these features the *coordinates* of the index. We impose no requirement that the coordinates of an index should all be features of any one context. For instance, an index might have among its coordinates a speaker, a time before his birth, and a world where he never lived at all. Any *n*-tuple of things of the right kinds is an index. So, although we can never go from one context to another by shifting only one feature, we can always go from one index to another by shifting only one coordinate. (Lewis 1998: 29–30)

Instead of taking our operator "It has always been the case that" to shift the context, and evaluating the embedded sentence relative to earlier contexts, we can take it to shift the time coordinate of the index, which can vary independently of the time of the context. If our indices include times and worlds, then, we get the following semantic clause:

(17) ⌜It has always been the case that ϕ⌝ is true at $c, \langle w, t \rangle$ iff for every time $t' \leq t$, ϕ is true at $c, \langle w, t' \rangle$.

This definition avoids the problems we saw with (15) and (16), but it raises a new concern. We are now defining truth at a context and index, where the index includes a time coordinate that can be shifted independently of the time of the context.[19] At the end of the day, though, what we care about is truth at a context, since it is this notion, not the technical notion of truth at a context and an artifical sequence of coordinates, that has direct pragmatic relevance. How can we turn a definition of truth at a context and index into a definition of truth at a context?

In Lewis's framework the trick is easy. We have assumed that coordinates of indices will be "features of context." So a context determines a unique index, *the index of the context*, whose coordinates are set to (or *initialized by*) the corresponding features of the context.[20] In our example, the index of a context c would be $\langle w_c, t_c \rangle$, where w_c is the world of c and t_c is the time of c. We can then define truth at a context as follows:

---

two contexts differ in just the time of the context.

[19] The term *point of evaluation* is sometimes used for this package of context and index.

[20] The vocabulary of "initializing" comes from Belnap, Perloff, and Xu (2001: 148–9). In computer programming, variables are "initialized" with starting values which can then be shifted by other operations.

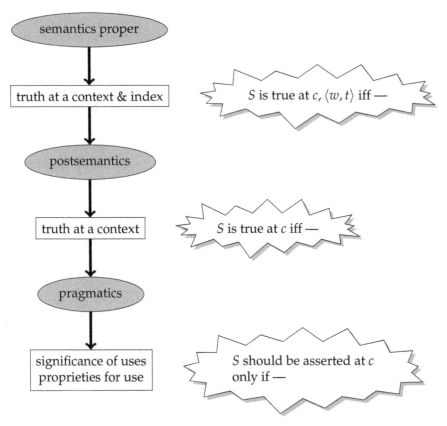

FIG. 3.2. Components of a theory of meaning

Let us say that sentence *s* is true at context *c* iff *s* is true at *c* at the index of the context *c*. (Lewis 1998: 31)

So, although we cannot define truth at a context directly, we can define it indirectly, by recursively defining truth at a context and index, and then defining truth at a context in terms of this more technical notion. In MacFarlane 2003: §V, I call the definition of truth at a context and index the *semantics proper* and the definition of truth at a context in terms of this the *postsemantics*, and I will sometimes use this terminology in what follows. The distinction gives us a slightly more complex picture of the components of a theory of meaning (see Fig. 3.2).

Although Lewis requires that each coordinate of the index be a "feature of context," this requirement can be relaxed. What is essential is that we have some way of moving from truth-at-a-context-and-index to truth-at-a-context.

Lewis's requirement gives us a particularly straightforward way of making this move, since it guarantees that the context of use will supply an initial value for every coordinate of the index: that is, for any coordinate X, we can always talk of "the X of the context." But the requirement does not make sense for some shiftable coordinates. Consider assignments of values to the variables, for example, which are shifted by quantifiers. Assignments are not features of contexts; contexts determine places, times, worlds, and many other things, but not assignments of values to variables (cf. Kaplan 1989: 592–3; Belnap, Perloff, and Xu 2001: 150–1).[21] Given that context does not initialize the assignment parameter, how do we eliminate the relativization to assignment in a definition of truth at a context? By quantifying over all assignments (7). We could do the same thing for any coordinate of the index that was not a "feature of context." For example, if we thought that possible worlds could overlap and then diverge, so that a possible context of use would pick out a set of overlapping worlds, not a single world,[22] then we could quantify over these worlds in our postsemantics:

(18)   A sentence S is true at context c iff for all indices $\langle w, t_c, a \rangle$, where w is one of the worlds overlapping at c, t_c is the time of c, and a is any assignment, S is true at c, $\langle w, t_c, a \rangle$.

It makes sense, then, to relax Lewis's requirement that indices be *features* of context, as long as we can still define truth at a context in terms of truth at a context and index. Doing this also allows us to think of the assignment as a coordinate of the index.

Let us take stock. Neither of the relativizations of truth we have considered so far involves us in any philosophically controversial kind of "relative truth." The relativization to contexts is required because the same sentence can be used to make true or false claims, depending on the context. The relativization to indices is required as a technical expedient for systematizing truth at a

---

[21] Although Lewis (1980) says nothing about assignments or quantifiers, Lewis (1970b) does talk of an assignment coordinate of indices. Perhaps Lewis (1980) would do semantics for quantified languages by relativizing truth to a context, an index, *and* an assignment. But there is no good reason, other than the requirement being discussed here, not to count the assignment as a coordinate of indices. The motivation for assignments is exactly the same as the motivation for other coordinates of indices: the proper treatment of shiftiness.

[22] For motivation, see the treatment of worlds in the semantics for future contingents in Chapter 9.

context. Since indices have no theoretical role beyond their role in defining truth at a context, the only motivation for positing a coordinate of indices is the presence of an operator that shifts it; conversely, the only grounds for objecting to a coordinate of indices is the absence of such operators. General considerations about truth and reality simply aren't relevant here.[23] So from a philosophical point of view, no eyebrows should be raised even at "wild" coordinates of indices like standards of precision or aesthetic standards. These are merely technical devices for systematizing truth at a context, to be justified (or not) on *linguistic* grounds. For example, if "strictly speaking" is best understood as a sentential operator that shifts standards of precision, we will need a standards-of-precision coordinate; if not, not. In any case the debate is not a distinctively philosophical one.

3.2.3   *Contexts of assessment*

I now want to suggest that the philosophically interesting line between truth absolutism and truth relativism is crossed when we relativize truth not just to a context of use and an index, but also to a *context of assessment*.

   We are already comfortable with the notion of a "context of use," understood as a possible situation in which a sentence might be used. So we ought to be able to make good sense of the notion of a "context of assessment"—a possible situation in which a use of a sentence might be *assessed*. There shouldn't be anything controversial about contexts of assessment: if there can be assessments of uses of sentences, then surely we can talk of the contexts in which these assessments would occur.

   To move from Lewis's framework to a framework in which relativist proposals can be described, we need only give contexts of assessment a role in our semantics parallel to that of contexts of use. Our target notion, then—the one with direct pragmatic relevance—will be not "true as used at c," but "true as used at c_1 and assessed from c_2" (see Fig. 3.3). (We will return to the question *how* this doubly-relativized truth predicate is pragmatically relevant in Chapter 5.)

   Ontologically speaking, contexts of use and contexts of assessment can be thought of as the same kind of thing. They might both, for example, be modeled as centered possible worlds (possible worlds with a designated time

---

[23]Indeed, as we have already observed for the special case of assignments (§3.1.1), we could dispense with talk of truth at a context and index in favor of a function from sentence, context, index triples onto $\{0, 1\}$, and then define truth at a context directly in terms of this function.

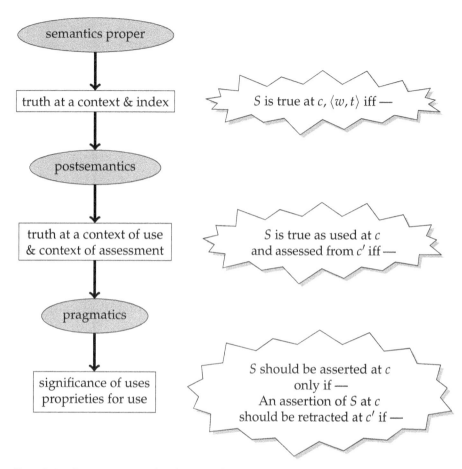

FIG. 3.3. Components of a theory of meaning, allowing for assessment sensitivity

and agent or location). The qualifiers "of use" and "of assessment" distinguish two different roles a context can play in semantics. We can think of a context as a possible situation of *use* of a sentence, or as a possible situation of *assessment* of a use of a sentence. In the former case, the agent of the context is the user of the sentence—the speaker, when the use is a speaking—while in the latter, the agent of the context is the assessor of a use of the sentence.

A particular use of a sentence may be assessed from indefinitely many possible contexts. Thus, although we may talk of "*the* context of use" for such a use, we may not talk in the same way of "*the* context of assessment." The definite article will be appropriate only when we have in mind not just a particular use, but a particular assessment. It is important that the context of assessment is not fixed in any way by facts about the context of use, including the speaker's intentions; there is no "correct" context from which to assess a particular speech act.[24]

How might a context of assessment enter into the semantics for an expression? In just the same ways as a context of use. In general, there are two ways for a feature of a context of use to be semantically relevant: it can be *locally* relevant, by playing a role in the semantics proper—that is, in the recursive clause for a particular linguistic construction—or it can be *globally* relevant, by playing a role in the postsemantics—the definition of truth at a context in terms of truth at a context and index. For example, in Kaplan's semantics for indexicals (Kaplan 1989), the time of the context of use (t_c) is locally relevant because of the role it plays in the clause for the operator *Now*:

(19) $\ulcorner Now\ \phi \urcorner$ is true at c, $\langle w, t, a \rangle$ iff ϕ is true at c, $\langle w, t_c, a \rangle$ (545, with notational changes)

and globally relevant through its role in the definition of truth at a context:

(20)   A sentence S is true at a context c iff for every assignment a, S is true at c, $\langle w_c, t_c, a \rangle$. (546, simplified with notational changes)

Some features of context are only locally relevant (for example, the agent of the context, which figures in the semantic clause for "I"). And in principle, a feature might be only globally relevant (as the world of the context would be in a language not containing an actuality operator).[25]

Features of contexts of assessment can likewise be semantically relevant either locally or globally. Imagine adding to English a word "noy" that works

[24]This distinguishes the proposal being made here from other proposals in the literature that bifurcate context. Predelli (1998) argues that in making a recorded utterance, e.g. "I am not here now" on an answering machine, the speaker may *have in mind* a "context of interpretation" relative to which some of the context-sensitive expressions ("here," "now"), but not others ("I") are to be evaluated. Schlenker (2004) proposes distinguishing "context of utterance" (controlling the interpretation of tense and person) and "context of thought" (controlling the interpretation of other indexicals) in order to make sense of free indirect discourse ("Tomorrow was Monday, Monday, the beginning of another school week!") and the historical present ("Fifty eight years ago to this day, on 22 January 1944, just as the Americans are about to invade Europe, the Germans attack Vercors"). A context of assessment, by contrast, has nothing to do with the speaker's (or author's) intentions, and is not fixed in any way (even "intentionally") by the context of use.

[25]As Kaplan (1989: 595) observes: "it may appear that for a modal language *without* indexicals, without expressions that require a parameter, the notion of a context of use has no bearing. This is not correct. Truth in every model means truth in the 'designated' world of every model. This 'designated' world, the world at which truth is assessed, plays the role of actual-world."

like "now," except that where "now" shifts the time of evaluation to the time of the context of use, "noy" shifts it to the time of the context of assessment.[26] To do semantics for a language containing "noy," we would need to recursively define truth relative to a *pair* of contexts (of use and assessment) and an index. Compare the recursive clauses for operators *Now* and *Noy*:

(21) $\ulcorner Now\ \phi \urcorner$ is true at $c_1, c_2, \langle w, t, a \rangle$ iff ϕ is true at $c_1, c_2, \langle w, t_{c_1}, a \rangle$.

(22) $\ulcorner Noy\ \phi \urcorner$ is true at $c_1, c_2, \langle w, t, a \rangle$ iff ϕ is true at $c_1, c_2, \langle w, t_{c_2}, a \rangle$.

Since the time of the context of assessment features directly in the semantic clause for *Noy*, it is locally relevant.

Admittedly, "noy" is a pretty silly word—one for which it is hard to find a use. But one can see how it differs from "now." Suppose, for example, that Jim is hungry at t_1, but not at t_2. An occurrence of "*Now* Jim is hungry" at t_1 will be true as assessed at either t_1 or t_2. Its truth depends only on whether Jim is hungry at the time the sentence is used (t_1). An occurrence of "*Noy* Jim is hungry" at t_1, by contrast, will be true as assessed at t_1 but false as assessed at t_2. Its truth depends on whether Jim is hungry at the time the sentence is assessed.

For an example of a globally relevant feature of contexts of assessment, suppose we replace (18) with

(23) A sentence S is true as used at context c_1 and assessed from (a later) context c_2 iff for all indices $\langle w, t_{c_1}, a \rangle$, where w is one of the worlds overlapping at c_2, t_{c_1} is the time of c_1, and a is any assignment, S is true at $c_1, \langle w, t_{c_1}, a \rangle$.[27]

---

[26]Kaplan (1989: 491 n. 12) reports Donnellan as having suggested something superficially similar: "if there were typically a significant lag between our production of speech and its audition (for example, if sound traveled very very slowly), our language might contain two forms of 'now': one for the time of production, another for the time of audition." Donnellan's second form of "now" is not the same as "noy," because audition is not the same as assessment: if one reassesses an assertion some time after first hearing it, the time of assessment is different, but the time of audition is the same.

[27]Here we are defining truth at a context of use and context of assessment in terms of truth at a context of use and an index. One might ask why we do not define it in terms of truth at a context of use *and context of assessment* and an index. The answer is that this is not necessary unless the language contains expressions, like "noy," that are *locally* sensitive to features of contexts of assessment. The present definition highlights the fact that the context of assessment is only *globally* relevant; there is no way it *could* be locally relevant, because the recursive clauses for individual expressions see only the context of use and index.

This definition draws on the context of use to tell us which time to look at, and on the context of assessment to tell us which *worlds* to look at (see §9.8.1). Even if the language does not contain any expression whose semantic clause makes reference to the context of assessment, the context of assessment is still semantically relevant through its role in the postsemantics—the definition of truth-at-contexts in terms of truth-at-contexts-and-an-index.

In a framework in which both context of use and context of assessment may be semantically relevant, context sensitivity comes in two flavors:

Use-sensitive. *An expression is* use-sensitive *if its extension (relative to a context of use and context of assessment) depends on features of the context of use.*

Assessment-sensitive. *An expression is* assessment-sensitive *if its extension (relative to a context of use and context of assessment) depends on features of the context of assessment.*

Note that every contingent sentence counts as use-sensitive on this definition, since its truth value depends on the world of the context of use.[28] It is useful, then, to parameterize the notions of use sensitivity and assessment sensitivity to indicate the *feature* of context on which an expression's extension depends:

F-use-sensitive. *An expression is* F-use-sensitive *if its extension (relative to a context of use and context of assessment) depends on the F of the context of use.*

F-assessment-sensitive. *An expression is* F-assessment-sensitive *if its extension (relative to a context of use and context of assessment) depends on the F of the context of assessment.*[29]

So, for example, "The US stock market plunged on 22 October 2008" is world-use-sensitive but not time-use-sensitive, and "Jim is sitting noy" is time-assessment-sensitive.

3.3 Truth relativism as assessment sensitivity

Using these concepts, we can say what it is to be a relativist about truth, in the serious and philosophically nontrivial sense we have been seeking.

---

[28]This is what David Lewis was getting at when he said that "contingency is a kind of indexicality," (Lewis 1998: 25); for further discussion, see MacFarlane 2009: §3.

[29]Note that "depends" in these definitions has causal/explanatory force. To show that the truth value of S depends on feature F, it is not enough just to find two contexts that differ with respect to F and relative to which S has different truth values. For the difference in truth values may be due to other differences between these contexts. As we have noted, it is generally not possible to find pairs of contexts that differ in some respect F without differing in many other ways as well.

Relativism about truth. *To be a* relativist about truth *is to hold that languages with assessment-sensitive expressions are at least conceptually possible.*

This is a position one might endorse or reject on nonempirical, philosophical grounds; what it requires is that one come to understand *what it would be* for an expression's extension to depend on features of the context of assessment. By contrast, relativism about truth in English is at least partly an empirical thesis:

Relativism about truth in English. *To be a* relativist about truth in English *(or some other natural language) is to hold that some expressions of English are assessment-sensitive.*

It is coherent to hold that, although we can understand what it would be for an expression to be assessment-sensitive, assessment-sensitive expressions are not found in natural languages.

This characterization of truth relativism fits naturally with the idea (explored in §3.1.2) that a truth relativist is a relativist about the truth of *utterances* or *assertions* (conceived as acts). Even if an utterance of a sentence determines a unique context of use—the context in which the utterance occurs—it does not determine a unique relevant context of assessment. So utterances of assessment-sensitive sentences can be assigned truth values (if at all) only relative to a context of assessment. However, our characterization of truth relativism in terms of assessment sensitivity avoids all the liabilities of defining relativism in terms of utterance truth. It avoids a linguistically odd application of a truth predicate to *acts*. It is a purely semantic characterization, not one that requires notions from pragmatics or the theory of speech acts. And it does not depend on controversial assumptions about the metaphysics of utterances or contexts.

Most importantly, it distinguishes clearly between three ways in which the truth of a sentence might be relative to some feature F:

1. The sentence's truth might vary with the F coordinate of the index.
2. The sentence might be F-use-sensitive.
3. The sentence might be F-assessment-sensitive.

Some examples may help to make these distinctions concrete. Assume for concreteness that we're working in a framework with temporal operators, so that indices include both a time and a world. Then

(24)   Socrates is sitting

is time-use-sensitive, but not time-assessment-sensitive, and its truth varies with the time coordinate of the index.

(25)   Socrates is sitting now

is time-use-sensitive, but not time-assessment-sensitive, and its truth does not vary with the time coordinate of the index, because "now" forces evaluation at the time of the context of use.

(26)   Socrates is sitting noy

is time-assessment-sensitive but not time-use-sensitive, and its truth does not vary with the time coordinate of the index. Finally,

(27)   Everyone who is now sitting is sitting

is neither use-sensitive nor assessment-sensitive, since it is true at every context of use and context of assessment. However, its truth is sensitive to the time of the index, as can be seen by embedding it under an operator that shifts this time:

(28)   Next year it will be the case that everyone who is now sitting is sitting.

As these examples reveal, it is not the *kind* of thing to which truth is relativized that makes a position "seriously relativist," but the *way* in which truth is relativized to it. Examples (24)–(28) all involve some kind of relativization of truth to times, but only (26) is "seriously relativist."

To see this even more clearly, imagine a language with aesthetic terms ("beautiful," "ugly") and a sentential operator *By any aesthetic standard*. Put aside worries about whether "by any aesthetic standard" is best treated as a sentential operator in English; just stipulate that the language we are dealing with has a sentential operator with this meaning. An operator needs a coordinate of the index to shift, so we will need an "aesthetic standard" coordinate in our indices. Whether a sentence like "That painting is beautiful" is true at a context and index will depend in part on the aesthetic standard coordinate of the index. The operator *By any aesthetic standard* can then be treated as follows:

(29) $\ulcorner$*By any aesthetic standard* $\phi\urcorner$ is true at c, $\langle w, s \rangle$ iff for all aesthetic standards s', ϕ is true at c, $\langle w, s' \rangle$.

In doing this much, have we committed ourselves to any serious kind of relativism about truth? Plainly not. For we might define truth at a context in the following way:

Absolutist postsemantics. *A sentence S is true at a context c iff S is true at*
c, $\langle w_c, s_G \rangle$, where w_c is the world of c and s_G is God's aesthetic standard.

On this semantics, the truth of aesthetic sentences would be completely insensitive to the aesthetic standards of the speaker or the assessor. The relativization to aesthetic standards in the index would have a merely technical role,
for systematizing the truth conditions of sentences containing the operator
By any aesthetic standard.

Alternatively, we might define truth at a context as follows:

Contextualist postsemantics. *A sentence S is true at a context c iff S is true at*
c, $\langle w_c, s_c \rangle$, where w_c is the world of c and s_c is the aesthetic standard of the agent of
c.

On this semantics, the truth of aesthetic sentences would depend on the
speaker's aesthetic standards, but would be completely independent of the
assessor's standards. Utterances of aesthetic sentences could be assigned
absolute truth values.

The threshold of relative truth is only crossed when we give a semantically
significant role to the context of assessment:

Relativist postsemantics. *A sentence S is true as used at a context c_1 and assessed*
from a context c_2 iff S is true at c_1, $\langle w_{c_1}, s_{c_2} \rangle$, where w_{c_1} is the world of c_1 and s_{c_2} is
the aesthetic standard of the agent of c_2.

This semantics does not allow us to assign absolute truth values to utterances
of "That painting is beautiful." It holds that aesthetic sentences can be assigned
truth values only relative to the aesthetic standard of the assessor. It is only
at this point—at which assessment sensitivity is countenanced—that we run
into *philosophical* issues concerning truth.

The relativization of truth to aesthetic standards in the *Absolutist postse-*
mantics is just a technical device, like relativization of truth to an assignment.
It is justified, if at all, by the technical requirements of the project of defining
truth at a context, and if it is justified in that way, it requires no further defense. The relativity of truth to the aesthetic standards of the speaker in the
Contextualist postsemantics is of the same character as the relativity of truth
of sentences containing "here" to the location of the speaker. It is justified, if
at all, by the sorts of considerations that normally support positing context
sensitivity, and if it is justified in that way, it raises no philosophical problems
not already raised by "here" and the like. But with the relativization of truth

to the aesthetic standards of the assessor in the *Relativist postsemantics*, we find something genuinely new—something that needs philosophical clarification and justification. We will turn to that task in Chapter 5.

3.4 Generalizing the logical notions

In the logic of indexicals (Kaplan 1989: 522–3), logical truth and consequence are defined as truth and truth preservation at every context:[30]

Logical truth. *A sentence S is* logically true *iff for all contexts c, S is true at c.*

Logical consequence. *A sentence S is a* logical consequence *of a set Γ of sentences iff for all contexts c, if every member of Γ is true at c, then S is true at c.*

Logical equivalence. *Two sentences S and T are* logically equivalent *iff for every context c, S is true at c iff T is true at c.*

Kaplan emphasizes the importance of distinguishing these notions from notions we can define by quantifying over points of evaluation—context/index pairs—rather than contexts:[31]

Logical necessity. *A formula φ is* logically necessary *iff for every point of evaluation (context and index) e, φ is true at e.*

Logical implication. *A formula φ is* logically implied *by a set Γ of formulas iff for every point of evaluation e, if every member of Γ is true at e, then φ is true at e.*

Strict equivalence. *Two formulas φ and ψ are* strictly equivalent *iff for every point of evaluation e, φ is true at e iff ψ is true at e.*

In many familiar semantic frameworks, a sentence is logically true iff it is logically necessary, and a sentence is a logical consequence of a set of sentences

---

[30]Kaplan's definitions include an additional quantification over *structures*, which define a set of possible contexts, a set of indices, a set of individuals, and an interpretation of the language's nonlogical expressions. Logical truth, for example, is truth in every possible context in every structure. The quantification over structures is needed if we are to avoid making "If something is water, it is H_2O" and like sentences into logical truths. I leave the quantification over structures implicit here for the sake of a simpler presentation, and because the treatment of structures is not affected by the addition of contexts of assessment. Note that in the chapters that follow, I will treat the expressions of interest ("tasty," "knows," temporal modifiers, epistemic and deontic modals, and indicative conditionals) as logical expressions, whose interpretations do not vary across structures.

[31]On the need for these two distinct notions, see Thomason (1970: 273), Kaplan (1989: 548–50), and Belnap, Perloff, and Xu (2001: 236–7). Note that while logical truth and consequence are defined only for sentences, logical necessity and implication are defined for all formulas, open and closed.

iff it is logically implied by this set of sentences. But as Kaplan shows, in languages containing certain kinds of context-sensitive expressions, these notions come apart, and it is possible for a sentence to be logically true without being logically necessary, or to be a logical consequence of a set of sentences without being logically implied by them. For example, in Kaplan's logic of indexicals,

(30)   *Actually Now P*

is a logical consequence of

(31)   *P*

even though (30) is not logically implied by (31). And

(32)   I am here now

is a logical truth—since there is no context of use at which it is false—even though it is not logically necessary.

How can we generalize these notions when truth is relativized not just to a context of use, but to a context of assessment? Logical necessity and implication can stay as they are, but there are two ways in which logical truth and consequence might be generalized. We might, first, quantify independently over contexts of use and assessment:

Absolute logical truth.   *A sentence S is* absolutely logically true *iff for all contexts c_1, c_2, S is true as used at c_1 and assessed from c_2.*

Absolute logical consequence.   *A sentence S is an* absolute logical consequence *of a set Γ of sentences iff for all contexts c_1, c_2, if every member of Γ is true as used at c_1 and assessed from c_2, then S is true as used at c_1 and assessed from c_2.*

Absolute logical equivalence.   *Two sentences S and T are* absolutely logically equivalent *iff for all contexts c_1, c_2, S is true as used at c_1 and assessed from c_2 iff T is true as used at c_1 and assessed from c_2.*

Alternatively, we can restrict ourselves to cases where the context of use and context of assessment are the same:

Diagonal logical truth.   *A sentence S is* diagonally logically true *iff for all contexts c, S is true as used at c and assessed from c.*

Diagonal logical consequence.   *A sentence S is a* diagonal logical consequence *of a set Γ of sentences iff for all contexts c, if every member of Γ is true as used at c and assessed from c, then S is true as used at c and assessed from c.*

Diagonal logical equivalence. *Two sentences S and T are diagonally logically equivalent iff for every context c, S is true as used at c and assessed from c iff T is true as used at c and assessed from c.*

There is no need to choose between these notions, just as there was no need to choose between logical truth and logical necessity. Both notions have their uses. An absolute logical truth is a sentence one can count on to be true even if one does not know relevant details about the context in which the sentence was used or the context in which it is being assessed. However, when one is considering whether to assert or believe something, one is focused on its truth as used at *and* assessed from one's current context. For such purposes, diagonal logical truth and consequence are important properties.

We gain clarity by distinguishing between these concepts. We will see some examples in Part II of this book, but, to anticipate, a relativist will be able to say that

(33)   If this is tasty to me, it's tasty

is a diagonal logical truth, but not an absolute logical truth. (That is, it can only be false when the context of assessment is different from the context of use.) In a framework that does not countenance assessment sensitivity, and thus does not distinguish between diagonal and absolute validity, this difference cannot be split, and our recognition that (33) has a special logical status pulls us towards a crude contextualism, which would make

(34)   It's tasty

and

(35)   It's tasty to me

logically equivalent.

4

PROPOSITIONS

In §3.2, we defined assessment sensitivity for sentences and other linguistic expressions. But we assert and believe propositions, not sentences; and sentences are true or false because they express propositions that are true or false. Thus, anyone who countenances assessment sensitivity in sentences faces a host of questions about propositions. Do assessment-sensitive sentences express propositions? Must we take them to express different propositions relative to different contexts of assessment? If not, what must we say about the propositions they express? What could it mean to say that a *proposition* is assessment-sensitive? This chapter is devoted to answering these questions.

4.1   What are propositions?

I will use the term "proposition" in what I take to be its historically most central sense. Propositions, as I understand them, are the contents of assertions and beliefs, and the things we call "true" or "false" in ordinary discourse. Consider the following dialogue:

> ANNE: The president should get out of Afghanistan.
> BILL: That is true.
> CYNTHIA: François believes that too.

The word "that" in Bill's and Cynthia's claims does not refer to Anne's mental state or to the sentence she used to express it, but to *what Anne believes* (Cartwright 1962). What she believes—the content of her belief—is the proposition that the president should get out of Afghanistan. Propositions, so understood, are neither mental entities nor the meanings of sentences; they are abstract objects we use to characterize speech acts or mental states, much as we use numbers to characterize weights and lengths (Churchland 1979: 105; Stalnaker 1987: 8).

I take this core conception to be a common starting point from which one might defend other claims about the nature of propositions: for example, that propositions have, or do not have, a quasi-linguistic structure; that they are, or

are not, made up of objects and properties; that they are, or are not, meanings
of declarative sentences; that they are, or are not, the "primary bearers of truth
values"; that they do, or do not, have possible-worlds intensions; that they
are, or are not, "information contents." I take all of these further claims to be
substantive claims about propositions, not matters of definitional stipulation.[1]

In what follows, I will try to remain neutral on all issues about the nature
of propositions that I am not forced to take a stand on. Thus, in particular,
I will remain neutral about whether propositions are structured or unstruc-
tured, and on whether they are individuated conceptually (in a Fregean vein)
or objectually (in a Russellian vein). I will also remain neutral on whether
propositions should be the semantic values of sentences in a compositional
semantics. Even if, like Lewis (1980: §§9–12), one thinks that propositions do
not have a central role to play in semantic theory, one may have need of them
elsewhere: for instance, in the philosophy of mind, the theory of speech acts,
or the semantics of attitude reports or truth ascriptions.

4.2 Content relativism

Let's start with an example of a putatively assessment-sensitive sentence:

(1)   Licorice is tasty.

Suppose we say that the truth of this sentence, as used at some context c
and assessed from another context c', depends on the tastes of the assessor
at c'—so that, if Yum likes the taste of licorice and Yuk is disgusted by it, (1)
is true as used by Yum and assessed by Yum, but false as used by Yum and
assessed by Yuk.

Now suppose that in context c_0, Yum utters (1) with the intention of
making an assertion. Assuming that the assessment-sensitive semantics is
correct, then Yum will correctly take herself to have uttered a sentence that
is true (as used at c_0), while Yuk will correctly take Yum to have uttered a
sentence that is false (as used at c_0). Yum is not speaking ironically or using
figurative language, so both parties know that if (1) is true (as used at c_0),

---

[1]One could choose to use the word "proposition" differently—say, defining a proposition as a
set of possible worlds. Relative to that stipulation, the claim that propositions are the contents of
beliefs would be a substantive claim. Thus, Lewis (1979a), who takes propositions to be essentially
sets of possible worlds, concludes that the content of beliefs are not propositions, but *properties*,
which have truth values relative to worlds, times, and agents; whereas I would take his argument
to show something about the nature of propositions. Nothing of substance hangs on these verbal
issues.

then the proposition that Yum asserts is true, and if (1) is false (as used at c_0), then the proposition that she asserts is false. So Yum will correctly take herself to have asserted a true proposition, and Yuk will correctly take Yum to have asserted a false proposition.

There are two ways to make this supposition coherent. The first is to make sense of the idea that propositions, as well as sentences, can vary in truth value from one context of assessment to another. Call that view *truth-value relativism*. According to truth-value relativism, there is no absolute fact of the matter about whether a proposition, as used at a particular context, is true; it can be true as assessed from one context and false as assessed from another.

The second approach is to reject the idea that the proposition Yum correctly takes himself to have asserted is the same as the proposition Yuk correctly takes Yum to have asserted. According to *content relativism*,[2] there is no absolute fact of the matter about the propositional content of a given assertion or belief. In the case at hand, we might say that as assessed from Yum's context, the proposition Yum asserted is *that licorice is pleasing to Yum's tastes*; but as assessed from Yuk's context, the proposition Yum asserted is *that licorice is pleasing to Yuk's tastes*.

The second approach may seem more parsimonious, because it seems not to require us to say anything new about propositions. Relativism about which proposition is asserted is compatible with absolutism about the truth of these propositions. In fact, though, it is difficult to make sense of content relativism without countenancing truth-value relativism as well. For suppose Yum says:

(2)   I asserted that licorice is pleasing to my tastes.[3]

According to the content relativist, Yum should take herself to have asserted something true in uttering (2), while Yuk should take Yum to have asserted something false. So again we face a choice between saying that it is an assessment-relative matter which proposition Yum asserted in uttering (2), or saying that the proposition Yum asserted is itself assessment-sensitive. To take the latter option is to embrace truth-value relativism. But the former option is hard to make sense of. What proposition shall we say that (2) expresses,

---

[2] This term comes from Egan, Hawthorne, and Weatherson (2005). Note that MacFarlane (2005c) uses "expressive relativism" for this, and "propositional relativism" for what Egan, Hawthorne, and Weatherson call "truth-value relativism." I now prefer, and use, their terminology. For a similar distinction, see Percival (1994: 192–3).

[3] Or, alternatively: I asserted a proposition that is true if and only if licorice is pleasing to my tastes.

as assessed from Yuk's context? Surely it would not be plausible to say that "my tastes," as used by Yum and assessed by Yuk, refers to Yuk's tastes. That is just not how the word "my" works in English. It seems, then, that we can make sense of content relativism only if we can also make sense of truth-value relativism.

Moreover, content relativism seems to get the phenomena wrong. If Yuk were to claim that Yum had asserted that licorice is pleasing to Yuk's tastes, Yum would simply deny this, and ordinarily this denial would be taken to be authoritative. (When there is doubt about what speakers have asserted, we can ask them to clarify, and barring worries about sincerity, we take them at their word.) In support of his claim, Yum could point out that her basis for making the assertion was that licorice tasted good to *her*, and that she was aware of the deep differences between her tastes and Yuk's. So it would have been completely irrational for her to assert that licorice is pleasing to Yuk's tastes.[4]

One can easily lose sight of how bizarre and radical this kind of content relativism is if one confuses it with a much more plausible *pluralism*—the view that one can, with a single utterance act, assert many distinct propositions. A marine drill sergeant might say to one hundred assembled recruits:

(3)   If your mother knew the pain I am going to put you through, she would never have let you enlist.

The pronoun "you" here must be singular, since the recruits have different mothers. But the sergeant is talking to all the recruits, so we must take him to have asserted one hundred propositions, one for each recruit. Cappelen (2008b) describes such cases as examples of content relativism, but they are not (cf. Egan 2009: 270, 277 n. 26). Each recruit can agree that the sergeant asserted one hundred propositions, and can agree about what they are. Only one of these is "directed to" any one recruit, but they are all asserted, and the sergeant is responsible for all of them. So these cases give us no reason to relativize assertoric content to contexts of assessment, and they do not pose the problems we saw above in connection with Yum and Yuk.

Cappelen (2008a) suggests that content relativism is implicit in our practices in reporting others' assertions. Suppose Andrew says:

[4]Weatherson (2009: 343–4) acknowledges the force of an objection like this, but argues that his content relativism about indicative conditionals can evade it because of special features of the case.

(4) At around 11 p.m., I put on a white shirt, a blue suit, dark socks and my brown Bruno Magli shoes, I then got into a waiting limousine and drove off into heavy traffic to the airport, where I just made my midnight flight to Chicago.

Depending on the context, we might report his assertion in a variety of different, and non-equivalent ways, for example:

(5) Andrew said that he put on a white shirt.

(6) Andrew said that he dressed around 11 p.m., went to the airport and took the midnight flight to Chicago.

(7) Andrew said that he put on some really fancy shoes before he went to the airport.

Not only can we imagine contexts in which all of these reports would be used, we can also imagine contexts in which at least some of them would be contested. ("Wait, did he really assert that he put on *really fancy* shoes? He has much fancier ones, and wouldn't have described Bruno Maglis that way.") If we think of these reports as complete and precise descriptions of the content of Andrew's assertion, then contextual variability in the truth of the reports would imply content relativism.[5]

More plausibly, though, the variation in reports reflects a certain looseness in our reporting practices. We report only the parts of the discourse that are relevant to present concerns, and we describe them in ways that makes their relevance clear. In this way our reports of speech are no different from our reports of anything else: in describing the weather, for instance, we use round numbers for temperatures and leave out much of the detail. When challenged, though, we are ready to retreat from the loose descriptions to tighter ones. For example, if Andrew objects:

(8) I didn't call the shoes fancy—that was your contribution.

then we would be prepared to retract (7) and retreat to saying that he said he put on Bruno Maglis. This suggests that the phenomenon at issue is one of looseness rather than relativism.

[5]What Cappelen says is this: "if what speakers say is closely related to true indirect reports of what they say (and how could it not be?) and if the latter varies across contexts of interpretation, then what speakers say varies across contexts of interpretation as well." He does not officially endorse this argument for "strong content relativism," but he seems to accept its premises.

Once content relativism is distinguished from pluralism and looseness, we can see that it is pretty bizarre. It would be good, then, if a commitment to assessment sensitivity did not require content relativism. In the remainder of this chapter, we will see what it would take to make sense of truth-value relativism, the view that assessment-sensitive sentences express propositions that are themselves assessment-sensitive.

4.3   Context and circumstance

We will start with a fairly standard story about propositional truth, from Kaplan (1989), and see what needs to change if we are to talk sensibly of propositions being assessment-sensitive. On Kaplan's view, contents have extensions only relative to *circumstances of evaluation*:

By ["circumstances"] I mean both actual and counterfactual situations with respect to which it is appropriate to ask for the extensions of a given well-formed expression. A circumstance will usually include a possible state or history of the world, a time, and perhaps other features as well. (Kaplan 1989: 502)

Take, for example, the content of the word "human," which for Kaplan is the property of being human. It makes sense to ask about the extension of "human"—the set of objects that have the property of being human—only relative to a possible state of the world and time. (At the beginning of the Jurassic period, it applied to nothing; now it applies to billions of things.) Similarly, it makes sense to ask about the extension of the sentence "There exists at least one human"—that is, its truth value—only relative to a possible state of the world and time. So Kaplan takes the content of this sentence—the proposition it expresses[6]—to have truth values only relative to worlds and times. A circumstance, then, comprises at least a world and a time.[7]

In the passage quoted above, Kaplan suggests that we might need other coordinates of circumstances beyond world and time—for example, location. Other philosophers have argued that circumstances should not even include

---

[6]See ch. 3 n. 8, this volume.

[7]Despite the superficial similarity in names, circumstances of evaluation should not be confused with contexts of assessment. In Chapter 3 terms, a circumstance of evaluation is much more like an index than a context of assessment. In Kaplan's system, contents have truth values relative to circumstances of evaluation, but there is no assessment sensitivity: every sentence has an absolute truth value at a context of use. Contexts and circumstances play fundamentally different roles in Kaplan-style systems, and contexts of assessment, while different from contexts of use, play a context-like role. We will see more clearly in §4.7 how variation in truth across circumstances of evaluation relates to variation in truth across contexts of assessment.

times, and that contents should be conceived as including all the time determinations relevant to their extensions (Richard 1980; King 2003). We will soon ask how such questions about the coordinates of circumstances are to be resolved, but our immediate concern here is how truth at a circumstance relates to truth at a context of use.

Like Lewis, Kaplan defines truth at a context of use for sentences. On Kaplan's view, a sentence is true at a context if its content is true at "the circumstance of the context":

If c is a context, then an occurrence of [a sentence] ϕ in c is true iff the content expressed by ϕ in this context is true when evaluated with respect to the circumstance of the context. (Kaplan 1989: 522; cf. the formal version on 547)

Kaplan is entitled to talk of "*the* circumstance of the context," because his circumstances of evaluation are composed of a world and a time, and he thinks of a context of use as determining a unique world and time. But in the interest of full generality, we should not assume that context will always pick out a unique circumstance of evaluation. For example, in a framework with *overlapping* worlds or histories, a possible occasion of utterance will be contained in multiple overlapping worlds, so there will be no unique "world of the context of use." For this reason, I prefer to talk of "all circumstances of evaluation compatible with the context" rather than "the circumstance of the context." Thus:

(9) A sentence S is true at context c iff the proposition expressed by S in c is true at all circumstances of evaluation compatible with c.[8]

Or with more generality:

(10) An expression E has extension x at context c iff E has extension x at every circumstance of evaluation compatible with c.

What "compatibility" amounts to must be worked out in detail for each semantic theory. In Kaplan's system, a circumstance $\langle w, t \rangle$ will be compatible with a context c just in case w is the world of c and t is the time of c.

Although Kaplan only defines truth at a context for *sentences*, the definition can be extended in a natural way to propositions (and contents in general):

---

[8]Kaplan suggests in a footnote that it "seems necessary for the definition of truth" that "a circumstance is an aspect of the context" (Kaplan 1989: 511 n. 35). The definition given here shows that this is not so. Compare our earlier discussion of Lewis on "the index of the context" (§3.2.2).

(11) A proposition p is true at a context of use c iff p is true at all circumstances of evaluation compatible with c.

(12) A content κ has extension x at context of use c iff the extension of κ is x at every circumstance of evaluation compatible with c.

We can now rephrase our definition of sentence truth at a context (and more generally, expression extension at a context) as follows:

(13) A sentence S is true at context c iff the proposition expressed by S in c is true at c.

(14) An expression E has extension x at context c iff the content of E in c has extension x at c.

It may seem strange to talk of a proposition being true at a context of use, because a proposition is not "used" in the way that a sentence is.[9] But the definition suffices to give the notion a clear sense. We can ask about the truth of propositions relative to contexts at which *sentences* might be used.[10] And, in an extended sense, we can think of assertions or beliefs as "uses" of the propositions asserted or believed. Having a notion of context-relative truth for propositions will be useful when we connect our semantics with a theory of assertion, since it is propositions, not sentences, that are asserted.

4.4 Two kinds of context sensitivity

It should be clear from (9) and (13) that the context of use plays two distinct roles in the definition of sentence truth at a context. It plays a *content-determining* role, since a sentence will express different propositions at different contexts. And it plays a *circumstance-determining* role, selecting the

[9]The worry is not that we cannot use abstract objects at all. I might use the Compactness Theorem to prove that there are nonstandard models of arithmetic, or use a particular musical phrase in playing the Orange Blossom Special. But it would be odd to say that in playing the Orange Blossom Special, I am using the Orange Blossom Special; and in the same way it would be odd to say that in asserting that p, I am using the proposition that p. The proposition is *what I am asserting*, not something I am using to assert it. For this reason, it might be better to talk of the "context of the act" rather than the "context of use," but I have opted to stick with the more familiar terminology, as nothing substantive turns on it.

[10]Even in the case of sentences, talk of S being true at context c carries no commitment to there being an actual *use* or *utterance* of S at c. See Kaplan (1989: 522).

circumstances of evaluation that are relevant to the truth of an occurrence of a sentence at the context.[11]

What this means is that there are two distinct ways in which an expression can be context-sensitive. Its extension can depend on a feature of context because that feature plays a content-determining role or because that feature plays a circumstance-determining role. To see this point is to see that use sensitivity and use indexicality come apart:

Use-sensitive. *An expression (or content) is* use-sensitive *iff its extension (relative to a context of use and context of assessment) depends on features of the context of use.*

Use-indexical. *An expression is* use-indexical *iff it expresses different contents at different contexts of use.*[12]

F-use-sensitive. *An expression (or content) is* F-use-sensitive *iff its extension (relative to a context of use and context of assessment) depends on the F of the context of use.*

F-use-indexical. *An expression is* F-use-indexical *iff the content it expresses at a context depends on the F of that context.*

"I am over five feet tall" is use-indexical; it expresses different propositions at different contexts of use. (To be precise, it is *agent*-use-indexical, because the content it expresses depends on the agent of the context; and on some views, it is also *time*-use-indexical.) It is also use-sensitive; it has different truth values at different contexts of use. But a sentence can be use-indexical without being use-sensitive, and even *F*-use-indexical without being *F*-use-sensitive. The sentence

(15)   If it is raining now, it is raining.

is true at every context of use (and thus not use-sensitive). But because it contains the indexical expression "now," it is (time-)use-indexical. This basic point is well known from Kaplan (1989), who argues that certain sentences

---

[11]For the point, see Belnap, Perloff, and Xu (2001: 148–9), MacFarlane (2005c: 326–7), Lasersohn (2005: 663).

[12]The sense of "indexical" defined by *Use-indexical* is quite broad. It does not distinguish between different mechanisms by which an expression might express different contents at different contexts. Sometimes "indexicality" is used in a narrower sense to cover just some of these mechanisms Stanley (2000: 411). If you like, call the sense defined by *Use-indexical* "broad indexicality."

containing indexicals, like "I am here now," can be logically true, or true at every context of use.

Less well known is that the converse point also holds. A sentence can be use-sensitive without being use-indexical, and a sentence can be *F*-use-sensitive without being *F*-use-indexical. That is, its truth value can depend on a feature of the context of use even though its content does not depend on this feature. Consider a contingent sentence like

(16)   Barack Obama was inaugurated on 20 January 2009.

Sentence (16) is not indexical; it expresses the same proposition at every context of use. But its truth value at a context of use depends on the world of the context, so it is (world)-use-sensitive. It is false as used at contexts in worlds where Obama lost the election, not because it expresses different contents at these contexts, but because the content it invariantly expresses is false at these worlds.[13]

Here's another example. Suppose we hold (with Kaplan 1989 and other *temporalists*) that the contents of sentences have truth values relative to worlds and times. Then we will naturally take

(17)   Socrates is sitting

to express, at every context of use, a time-neutral proposition—one that is true relative to some times of evaluation and false relative to others. Because we take (17) to express the same proposition at every context, we will not take it to be indexical. But we will still take it to be use-sensitive, since we take the truth of this sentence to depend on the time of the context. (9) shows how this is possible: the temporalist need only say that a circumstance of evaluation $\langle w, t \rangle$ is compatible with a context c just in case w is the world of c and t is the time of c, and the truth value of tensed sentences will depend on the time of the context of use, even if the content does not.[14]

Thus, for the temporalist, (17) will be use-sensitive (specifically *time*-use-sensitive), but not use-indexical. The temporalist and the eternalist can agree

---

[13]Compare David Lewis's remark, already noted in §3.2.3, that "contingency is a kind of indexicality" (1998: 25). Lewis was using the term "indexicality" to mean what we mean here by "use sensitivity."

[14]Compare Percival (1989: 193–5), defending the temporalist theory against Mellor's (1981) objection that if tensed sentence expressed the same proposition at every time, all actual occurrences of this sentence should have the same truth value, regardless of the context in which they occur.

that tensed sentences are use-sensitive—indeed, they can agree about what truth values such sentences have relative to every context of use—while disagreeing about whether this use sensitivity derives the dependence of the sentence's content on the context, or from the use sensitivity of the content itself.[15]

4.5 Coordinates of circumstances

Before considering what it could mean for a proposition to be *assessment-sensitive*, let us return to the question we set aside in §4.3: what are the coordinates of circumstances of evaluation? Some philosophers take circumstances to be possible worlds, but as we have seen, Kaplan himself takes a more permissive view: on his view, circumstances include not just a possible world but a time, and "perhaps other features as well":

> What sorts of intensional operators to admit seems to me largely a matter of language engineering. It is a question of which features of what we intuitively think of as possible circumstances can be sufficiently well defined and isolated. If we wish to isolate location and regard it as a feature of possible circumstances we can introduce locational operators: 'Two miles north it is the case that', etc. ... However, to make such operators interesting we must have contents which are locationally neutral. That is, it must be appropriate to ask if *what is said* would be true in Pakistan. (For example, 'It is raining' seems to be locationally as well as temporally and modally neutral.) (Kaplan 1989: 504)

How far can this permissiveness be pressed? Could one take the content of "tasty," for example, to have an extension only relative to a world, time, and taste—so that it is not only temporally and modally neutral, but *taste-neutral*? Could one take the proposition *that it is likely that it will rain tomorrow* to have a truth value only relative to a world, time, location, and information state? Such proposals would have to be justified by their utility in the web of theories that employ notions of content (such as propositional attitude psychology and the theory of speech acts). But are there any principled arguments that would rule them out of court altogether?

In this section, I consider two influential arguments that, if cogent, would impose serious constraints on the coordinates of circumstances. I will ar-

---

[15]Although many philosophers define "context-sensitive" the way I have defined "use-indexical" (Soames 2002: 245; Cappelen and Lepore 2005: 146; Stanley 2005b: 16), it seems to me that both use sensitivity and use indexicality are kinds of contextual sensitivity. It would be odd, anyway, for temporalists to deny that (17) is context-sensitive.

gue that neither argument gives us reason to avoid relativizing the truth of contents to parameters besides possible worlds.

4.5.1   *Operator arguments*

Kaplan himself takes questions about what coordinates to include in circumstances to be very closely tied to questions about what *sentential operators* a language contains (Kaplan 1989: 502, 504). This is very explicit in his discussion of times as coordinates of circumstances. Following the tense logic tradition, Kaplan treats tenses as intensional operators, analyzing "Joe will bake a cake" as "*Will* Joe bakes a cake." He understands these to be operators on contents (502); that is, as functions from contents to contents. Semantically, temporal operators shift the time of evaluation: "*Will* Joe bakes a cake" is true at t just in case the content of "Joe bakes a cake" is true at some t' later than t. As Kaplan observes, such operators make sense only if the contents to which they are applied have truth values relative to times:

> If *what is said* is thought of as incorporating reference to a specific time, or state of the world, or whatever, it is otiose to ask whether what is said would have been true at another time, in another state of the world, or whatever. Temporal operators applied to eternal sentences (those whose contents incorporate a specific time of evaluation) are redundant. (Kaplan 1989: 503)

Putting this all together, we get the following argument for relativizing the truth of contents to times:

Kaplan's operator argument.

K1   *Tenses in our language are best understood as sentential operators.*

K2   *Sentential operators operate on the contents of sentences.*

K3   *Semantically, temporal operators shift the time of evaluation; they are redundant unless they operate on something that can vary in truth value across times.*

K4   ∴ *The contents of sentences can vary in truth value across times.*

Kaplan's argument relies on two controversial premises, K1 and K2. Some eternalists have rejected the argument by rejecting K1, arguing that tenses in natural language are not best understood as operators (King 2003). Others have rejected K2, arguing that the compositional semantic values of sentences—the things on which sentential operators operate—need not be the same as the contents of beliefs and assertions (Lewis 1980; Richard 1980; Salmon 1986).[16]

---

[16]Of course, anyone who takes the semantic values of sentences to be non-propositional needs an extra step to identify the proposition that would be asserted by a sentence at a context. But the

Whatever one thinks of K1 and K2, it is important to recognize that Kaplan's argument only purports to give a *sufficient* condition for time-neutral contents, not a *necessary* condition. If it is cogent, it shows that a time-shifting operator requires a time coordinate of circumstances, not that a time coordinate of circumstances requires a time-shifting operator. To establish the converse, one would need the additional premise that nothing else besides operators can motivate countenancing a coordinate of circumstances. And such a premise would be hard to support, since there are plenty of other considerations that bear on the nature of contents. To give just two examples: Lewis (1979a) argues that we need contents that are temporally neutral if we are to understand, for example, how an amnesiac named Lingens in a library might know when Lingens got lost without knowing when *he* got lost, and Recanati (2007) argues that we need such contents if we are to understand episodic memory. These arguments are independent of issues concerning operators, and (if cogent) might motivate coordinates of circumstances even if there are no operators that shift them.[17]

One might argue that, if there *were* a time coordinate of circumstances, languages would have operators that shift it; so that the lack of such an operator is evidence that there is no such coordinate. But why accept the premise of this argument? It does not seem to be true, in general, that languages abhor an expressive vacuum. It is orthodox to relativize truth of contents to possible worlds, but as Hazen (1976) points out, there are whole classes of operators on possible-worlds contents that we do not find in natural languages—operators that are sensitive to *how many* worlds the content is true at. Should we find it surprising that our language does not contain these operators? Should we take this as evidence against our theory of belief contents? That is far from clear.

Suppose we were studying speakers of a primitive language that does not yet contain modal operators, counterfactual conditionals, or other world-

---

step is an obvious one: we can get a proposition by saturating a temporally neutral sentential semantic value with the time of the context of use.

[17]Stanley (2005b: 150) argues, citing Lewis (1980), that "the difference between elements of the circumstance of evaluation and elements of the context of use is precisely that it is elements of the former that are shiftable by sentence operators." But Lewis is talking about indices, not circumstances of evaluation; indeed, a major point of his paper is that one need not have "contents" as intermediate semantic values in compositional semantics. What I am suggesting is that considerations that would tell decisively against inclusion of a coordinate in the Lewisian index need not settle the analogous issue about circumstances of evaluation.

shifting expressions. Would we take these speakers' lack of modal vocabulary to debar them from expressing the same kinds of propositions we express—for example, the proposition *that snow is white*?[18] And would we say that, after they have acquired modal vocabulary, the contents of *all* of their beliefs change, and come to be true or false relative to worlds when they were not before? From the perspective of a philosopher of mind or theorist of speech acts, the idea should seem bizarre. While some of the pressures on theories of propositions may come from semantics, there is no reason to think that all of them do.

In sum, it is not clear whether considerations about sentential operators are relevant at all to questions about the coordinates of circumstances, since one might reject Kaplan's view that the semantic values of sentences are propositions. But even if they are relevant, they are not the only relevant considerations. Showing that there is no plausible candidate for a "taste-shifting" operator, then, would not be enough by itself to rule out tastes as coordinates of circumstances.[19]

4.5.2   *Incompleteness*

Another common objection to time-neutral, location-neutral, and taste-neutral contents is that they are "incomplete" and so not suited to be the contents of assertions and beliefs. Those who make this objection sometimes appeal to this passage from Frege's unpublished article "Logic":

If someone wished to cite, say, 'The total number of inhabitants of the German Empire is 52 000 000', as a counter-example to the timelessness of thoughts, I should reply: This sentence is not a complete expression of a thought at all, since it lacks a time-determination. If we add such a determination, for example, 'at noon on 1 January 1897 by central European time', then the thought is either true, in which case it is always, or better, timelessly, true, or it is false and in that case it is false without qualification. (Frege 1979: 135)

---

[18] As Sellars (1948) argues, it may be a condition on our possession of concepts like *snow* and *white* that we be sensitive to subjunctive inferences involving them. But it would be a further step to say that we need to be able to make these inferences explicit in modal vocabulary.

[19] Kaplan tells me (p.c.) that although he is willing to consider times and locations as aspects of circumstances, he would himself draw the line at tastes and epistemic standards, on the grounds that these are too subjective and perspectival to be "features of what we intuitively think of as possible circumstances." Given Kaplan's linkage of questions about circumstances with the operators contained in a language, this restriction amounts to an a priori assumption that no language will contain an operator like "by any standard of taste."

By "thought" here, Frege means the sense of a declarative sentence, which he also takes to be the content of a propositional attitude—what we are calling a "proposition." So one might expect this passage to give aid and comfort to the modern opponent of time-neutral propositions. But in fact it does not.

The paragraph from which our passage is taken begins with the issue of whether the propositions themselves are abstract and unchanging or concrete and mutable:

Whereas ideas (in the psychological sense of the word) have no fixed boundaries, but are constantly changing and, Proteus-like, assume different forms, thoughts always remain the same. It is of the essence of a thought to be non-temporal and non-spatial.

And, after our passage, Frege returns to the theme of whether the propositions (thoughts) change. But this issue is orthogonal to the issue that concerns us—whether the truth of a proposition is relative to times. A temporalist can agree with Frege that propositions are abstract, timeless entities; that is perfectly compatible with their having different truth values at different times of evaluation. (Those who take Beethoven's Appassionata sonata to be an unchanging abstract object, defined by its score, need not deny that some notes in the sonata occur before others, and those who take mathematical functions to be unchanging abstract objects need not deny that a function from times to integers can have different values at different times.)

Was Frege simply confusing two different senses of timelessness, which we might call *nonrelativity* and *unchangingness*? One can rescue Frege from the charge of confusion if one takes him to be assuming that propositions (thoughts) have their truth values intrinsically. It would then follow that thoughts can have different truth values at different times only if they undergo temporal change in their intrinsic features.[20] An intelligible motivation for the assumption that thoughts have their truth values intrinsically might be extracted from Frege's general view that sense determines reference, and hence that thoughts determine truth values (which Frege takes to be the referents of sentences). On a strong reading of "determines," this implies that thoughts have their truth values intrinsically: one could not have the same thought with a different truth value.

But if this is the right way to read the passage, then it cannot be used to support a view on which propositional truth is relative to worlds but not times. On the strong reading, Frege's thesis of the determination of reference

---

[20] I am grateful to Giorgio Volpe for helpful discussion.

by sense rules out relativity to worlds just as much as relativity to times. Thus, either the passage embodies a confusion, or it is no help to someone who wishes to draw a line between relativity to worlds and relativity to times and other parameters.[21]

One might try to cash out an "incompleteness" worry in the following way. Propositions are supposed to be the contents of beliefs and other propositional attitudes. But if we specify the content of someone's belief in a way that does not settle what is relevant to the accuracy of the belief, we have not given its complete content. Thus, for example, if we don't know whether the accuracy of Sam's belief that it is 0° C depends on the temperature in London on Tuesday or the temperature in Paris on Wednesday, then we don't yet have the full story about what it is that Sam believes. Similarly, if we don't know whether the accuracy of Yuk's belief that licorice is tasty depends on how licorice affects Yuk or on how it affects Yum, then we don't yet know what it is that Yuk believes. A location-neutral, time-neutral, or taste-neutral content would only incompletely determine the conditions for an attitude to be accurate, and so could not be the complete content of the attitude.

But this line of thought proves too much. For surely the accuracy of *any* contingent belief depends on features of the world in which the believer is situated—the world of the context of use. Even if we specify the content of Sam's belief in a way that builds in time and place—*that it is 0° C at the base of the Eiffel Tower at noon local time on 22 February 2005*—it is still not determined whether the accuracy of his belief depends on the temperature in Paris in world w_1 or on the temperature in Paris in world w_2. To know that, we would have to know not just what Sam believes—the content of his belief—but in what context, and in particular in what world, the belief occurs.

One might respond to these considerations by bringing the world of the context of use into the *content* of Sam's thought, so that what he thinks is that it is 0° C at the base of the Eiffel Tower at noon local time on 22 February 2005, in *this* world (Schaffer 2012). Intuitively, though, Sam could have had a thought with the very same content even if the world had been very different. Our ordinary ways of individuating thought contents do not support making

---

[21]Of course, we can make Frege's determination thesis compatible with world-relativity by reading it as saying that a sense, *together with a possible world*, determines a referent. But a temporalist could similarly read it as saying that a sense, *together with a possible world and a time*, determines a referent. Perhaps there are reasons for choosing between these formulations, but the bare idea of determination of referent by sense does not favor one over the other.

the world of the context of use part of the content, except in exceptional circumstances. Moreover, bringing the world of the context into the content of Sam's thought would make this content a necessary truth about this possible world, rather than a contingent truth about the weather in Paris. We should not say, then, that Sam's thought is *about* the world of the context of use. It is not *about* any particular world. Acknowledging the fact that it depends for its correctness on the world of the context, we may adopt John Perry's terminology and say that it *concerns* the world of the context (Perry 1986). We will say that an assertion or belief-state *concerns* X if whether the belief-state is correct depends on how things are with X, and that it is *about* X if the truth of its content at an arbitrary circumstance of evaluation depends on how things are with X.

One might argue that the relativity to worlds is special, and does not imply incompleteness the way relativity to times would, because there is always a privileged world—the actual world—that alone matters in assessing the accuracy of a claim. The thought is that the relativity of propositional truth to worlds can always be eliminated, by plugging in the actual world; whereas with times and locations, there is no unique "default value," so the relativity is more thoroughgoing (Evans 1985: 351). In fact, however, the parallel between worlds and times is a good one, provided one accepts the indexical view of actuality (Lewis 1970a). According to the indexical view, "the actual world" denotes the world of the context of use. So, when a speaker in world w talks about what "actually" happened, she is talking about what happens in w, not what happens in the world *we* call "actual." "Actually" is thus the modal analogue of "now," and the actual world is privileged in no deeper sense than the current time: it is the world we are in.

It is sometimes thought that this conception of actuality makes sense only for modal realists, who take possible worlds to be concrete worlds like our own, and not for modal ersatzists, who take possible worlds to be abstract representations of alternative states of affairs. But it makes sense for anyone who thinks of possible worlds as aspects of context.[22] Arguably, we need the indexical view of "actually" in order to make sense of our judgments about counterfactual utterances. I said "It is actually raining," and it actually was raining at the time, so I spoke truly. But if I had said this when it hadn't been raining, I would have spoken falsely—even though in fact, it actually was

---

[22]Stalnaker (1987: 47–9) is one example of an ersatzist who accepts it.

raining. The truth-in-context of this counterfactual claim depends on how things are in the world where it is made, not in the world *we* call "actual."

The objection from "incompleteness" may be motivated, in part, by an appreciation of the fact that the truth predicate we use in ordinary speech is monadic. We don't characterize claims as "true-in-w," or as "true-in-w-at-t-on-s," but as "true" (simpliciter). But this no more shows that propositional truth is not relative to parameters than the fact that we normally say it's "3 p.m.," and not "3 p.m. Pacific Daylight Time," shows that the time of day is not relative to a time zone. (We will return in §4.8 to the proper treatment of the monadic predicate "true.")

Once we accept the relativity of propositional truth to worlds, we have accepted a kind of "incompleteness." We have accepted the idea that both the content of an assertion or belief and its context must be taken into account in assessing it for accuracy. The question is just *which* features of which contexts must be taken into account, and how. This is the topic of the next two sections.

4.6 Nonindexical contextualism

The upshot of the previous section is that there is no in-principle objection to including things like tastes or aesthetic standards as coordinates of circumstances of evaluation. But relativizing the truth of propositions to tastes or aesthetic standards in this way would not necessarily make one a truth relativist in the sense of Chapter 3. To say that a proposition has truth values relative to parameters besides worlds and times is not to say that it is assessment-sensitive.

For example, even if we hold that propositions have truth values relative to worlds and aesthetic standards, we need not say that sentences like "The *Mona Lisa* is beautiful" are assessment-sensitive. For, as in the case of temporalism, we could take the context of use to determine values for both parameters. We could say that a sentence is true at a context of use c just in case the proposition it expresses at c is true relative to the world of c and the aesthetic standard relevant at c. (In terms of (11), this would amount to saying that a circumstance $\langle w, s \rangle$ is compatible with a context of use c just in case w is the world of c and s is the aesthetic standard relevant at c.)

The resulting position would resemble contextualist approaches in taking the truth of sentences about what is "beautiful" to depend on the taste of the speaker. But, unlike standard forms of contextualism, it would not take the *content* of such sentences to depend on the taste of the speaker. Because this is a view on which such sentences are aesthetic-standard-use-sensitive but not aesthetic-standard-use-indexical, it is aptly characterized not as relativism but as a kind of *nonindexical contextualism*.[23] However, others have used the word "relativism" for this kind of position,[24] and I do not want to get too caught up in disputes about labeling. The important thing to see is that the position just described would have much in common with more standard forms of contextualism. To be sure, it would disagree with ordinary contextualism about the contents of aesthetic claims. But it would agree with ordinary contextualism on every question about the truth of sentences, and like standard contextualism it would give every use of a proposition an absolute truth value. It would remain on the safe side of the really interesting line—the line between use sensitivity and assessment sensitivity.

Even when we are talking about propositional truth, then, it is not just *what* propositional truth is relativized to—worlds, times, tastes, standards—that matters, but *how* it is relativized. It is therefore unfortunate that many recent critiques characterize truth relativism as the relativization of propositional truth to something besides possible worlds.[25] Granted, there are interesting issues raised by this kind of relativization. But if I am right, these issues are orthogonal to the issue of assessment sensitivity, since the relativity of propositional truth to things besides worlds is neither necessary nor sufficient for assessment sensitivity. It is not sufficient, because it is compatible with nonindexical contextualism, which does not countenance assessment sensitivity. It is also not necessary, because, as we will see in Chapter 9, one can

---

[23]See MacFarlane (2009) for a fuller discussion, with examples.

[24]The "moderate relativism" of Recanati (2007, 2008) is much closer to nonindexical contextualism than to what I have been calling "relativism." Some other self-proclaimed truth relativists relativize propositional truth to features other than worlds and times, but do not make explicit a commitment to assessment sensitivity, so that it is hard to tell whether they are relativists, in my sense, or nonindexical contextualists (Kölbel 2002; Richard 2004; Richard 2008; Egan, Hawthorne, and Weatherson 2005; Egan 2007). Lasersohn (2005) does not explicitly relativize truth to contexts of assessment, so it might appear that his view is nonindexical contextualist. However, that would be misleading. For Lasersohn, a "context of use" is not a concrete possible situation in which a sentence might be used, but an abstract sequence of parameters. How we should set these parameters in interpreting an utterance of "This is tasty" depends, Lasersohn holds, both on features of the concrete speech situation, which help determine the reference of "this" and the relevant world and time, and on features of the concrete assessment situation, which determine the "judge" of the context. So both the concrete use situation and the concrete assessment situation play a role, even though the distinction between them is not made notationally salient.

[25]See for example Zimmerman (2007: 316), Stanley (2005b: 137), Glanzberg (2007: 2), Cappelen and Hawthorne (2009).

describe a view on which even standard possible-worlds propositions are assessment-sensitive.

4.7   Truth-value relativism

Recall what we said in §4.3 about the relation between a content's truth (extension) at a circumstance and its truth (extension) at a context:

(11)   A proposition p is true at a context of use c iff p is true at all circumstances of evaluation compatible with c.

(12)   A content κ has extension x at context of use c iff the extension of κ is x at every circumstance of evaluation compatible with c.

To make room for contents that are assessment-sensitive, we need to modify these definitions as follows:

(18)   A proposition p is true at as used at c_1 and assessed from c_2 iff p is true at all circumstances of evaluation compatible with $\langle c_1, c_2 \rangle$.

(19)   A content κ has extension x as used at c_1 and assessed from c_2 iff the extension of κ is x at every circumstance of evaluation compatible with $\langle c_1, c_2 \rangle$.

The relation of "compatibility" now holds between circumstances and a *pair* of contexts—a context of use and context of assessment. Thus, for example, a relativist about aesthetic vocabulary who holds that circumstances of evaluation are world/aesthetic standard pairs might say that

(20)   A circumstance $\langle w, s \rangle$ is compatible with $\langle c_1, c_2 \rangle$ iff w is the world of c_1 and s is the aesthetic standard relevant at c_2.

On this account, uses of propositions cannot be assigned truth values absolutely, but only relative to contexts of assessment. When we assess an assertion, made yesterday by Ted, that the *Mona Lisa* is beautiful, what matters for its truth is not Ted's aesthetic standards but our own. So, we say that Ted has spoken truly if the *Mona Lisa* is beautiful by *our* standards.

Importantly, the formal relativization of propositional truth to contexts of assessment in (18) does not by itself commit one to assessment sensitivity. An aesthetic nonindexical contextualist, for example, could replace (20) with

(21)   A circumstance $\langle w, s \rangle$ is compatible with $\langle c_1, c_2 \rangle$ iff w is the world of c_1 and s is the aesthetic standard relevant at c_1.

On this view, aesthetic propositions would not be assessment-sensitive, since the truth of a proposition relative to a context of use and context of assessment would be entirely settled by the context of use. This view would be a form of nonindexical contextualism, not relativism.

Note that the relativist and the nonindexical contextualist would agree that propositions have truth values relative to worlds and aesthetic standards. Their conceptions of these propositions would differ, however, because they would have different conceptions of how the taste parameter relates to contexts. The nonindexical contextualist would take it that an assertion is correct if its content is true at the world and aesthetic standard relevant at the context of use. A relativist, by contrast, would say that there is an answer to the question whether an assertion is correct only relative to a context of assessment, and that it is the context of assessment, not the context of use, that fixes the relevant aesthetic standard.

If one wants a notion of sentence truth (or more generally, of extensions for expressions of all types), it can be defined in terms of the truth of contents in the obvious way:

(22) A sentence S is true as used at c_1 and assessed from c_2 iff the proposition expressed by S in c_1 (as assessed from c_2) is true as used at c_1 and assessed from c_2.

(23) An expression E has extension x as used at c_1 and assessed from c_2 iff the content of E in c_1 (as assessed from c_2) has extension x as used at c_1 and assessed from c_2.

Thus a relativist can accept the traditional view that propositions are the primary bearers of truth value, in the sense that sentences have the truth values they do (relative to a context of use and a context of assessment) because of the truth values (again doubly relativized) of the propositions they express.

One can see from (22) that there are two different ways in which a sentence might be assessment-sensitive. First, it might be assessment-sensitive because it is *assessment-indexical*:

Assessment-indexical. *An expression is* assessment-indexical *iff it expresses different contents relative to different contexts of assessment.*

F-assessment-indexical. *An expression is* F-assessment-indexical *iff the content it expresses as assessed from c depends on the F of c.*

We have already used the term "content relativism" to describe views that countenance assessment indexicality (§4.2). But, just as a sentence can be F-use-sensitive without being F-use-indexical, so a sentence can be F-assessment-sensitive without being F-assessment-indexical. It can do so by expressing a proposition that is itself F-assessment-sensitive:

Assessment-sensitive (contents). *A content is assessment-sensitive if its extension as used at c_1 and assessed from c_2 depends on features of c_2.*[26]

F-assessment-sensitive (contents). *A content is F-assessment-sensitive if its extension as used at c_1 and assessed from c_2 depends on the F of c_2.*

A plausible form of relativism about what is tasty would take this form. According to such a view, which we have called *truth-value relativism*, the sentence "licorice is tasty" expresses the same proposition relative to every context of use and context of assessment, but this proposition—the proposition that licorice is tasty—is itself (taste-)assessment-sensitive, since its truth value (relative to a context of assessment) depends on the assessor's tastes.

In §4.5.2, we introduced a distinction (due to Perry) between an assertion's or belief's being *about* some feature X and its *concerning* X. This distinction is useful for contrasting eternalism with temporalist, and more generally indexical with nonindexical forms of contextualism. Thus, the eternalist holds that tensed assertions are *about* a particular time, while the temporalist holds that they are not about any particular time (since their contents are time-neutral), but may *concern* a particular time. Similarly, an indexical contextualist about "tasty" may hold that assertions of "That's tasty" are (partly) about the speaker's tastes, while a nonindexical contextualist will say that they are not about any taste in particular (since their contents are taste-neutral), but *concern* the speaker's tastes, since it is this on which their correctness depends. On a relativist view of "tasty," however, assertions of "That's tasty" do not even *concern* a particular taste, since they are appropriately assessed for correctness, from different points of view, in light of many different tastes. In this sense, relativist views reject subjectivism more thoroughly than either sort of contextualist view.

---

[26]Recall that the extension of a proposition—the content of a sentence—is a truth value. So a proposition is assessment-sensitive if its truth value as used at c_1 and assessed from c_2 depends on features of c_2.

4.8   Monadic "true" and the Equivalence Schema

Relativism, as developed here, is the view that truth-conditional semantics should have as its output a definition of truth relative to a context of use and context of assessment. To resist relativism would be to defend the usual view that we need only truth relative to a context of use. But whichever view we take, the context-relativized truth predicate used in semantics is a technical term, which gets its meaning in part from an account of its pragmatic relevance (for example, in Lewis's theory, the view that speakers at c try to assert what is true at c, and trust others to be doing so). It is not the ordinary truth predicate used in everyday talk—a *monadic* predicate that applies to propositions, and is governed by the

Equivalence Schema.   *The proposition that* Φ *is true iff* Φ.

The relativist (or nonindexical contextualist) can treat the monadic predicate "true" as just another predicate of the object language—the language for which she is giving a semantics. The natural semantics for it is this:[27]

Semantics for monadic "true."   *"True" expresses the same property at every context of use—the property of* being true. *The extension of this property at a circumstance of evaluation e is the set of propositions that are true at e.*

Given this semantics for "true," every instance of the Equivalence Schema will be true at every circumstance of evaluation, and hence also at every context of use and context of assessment.[28] (Note that, if the language can express any assessment-sensitive propositions, "true" will also be assessment sensitive, since if p is assessment-sensitive, the proposition that p is true must be assessment-sensitive too. This shows what is wrong with the thought that relativism about truth amounts to nothing more than an ordinary contextualist semantics for "true." On such a view, "true" would be use-sensitive, not assessment-sensitive.)

As we saw in §2.4, some philosophers have thought that the Equivalence Schema is incompatible with relativism about truth. Since the relativist semantics for "true" fully vindicates the Equivalence Schema, this worry can be

---

[27]It is, of course, a naive semantics, in the sense that it provides no solution to the semantic paradoxes. I am assuming, perhaps rashly, that the issues raised by the paradoxes are orthogonal to those we are worried about here, and can be dealt with separately.

[28]To see this, note that whatever circumstance e we choose, the right and left hand sides of the biconditional will have the same truth value at e. I assume here that "the proposition that Φ" rigidly denotes a proposition.

dismissed. But there *is* a legitimate concern in the vicinity. Granted that our doubly relativized truth predicate is not the ordinary (monadic) truth predicate we use in ordinary speech, but a piece of *technical* vocabulary, we need to say something about how it is connected up with other parts of our theories of language and communication, so we can see the practical significance of going for a relativist semantic theory as opposed to a nonrelativist one. I want to emphasize, though, that this is a burden faced by nonrelativists, too—by anyone who uses "true at a context" in a truth-conditional semantic theory. (The point goes back at least to Dummett 1959.) We will return to this issue in Chapter 5.

4.9   Newton-Smith's argument

We are now in a position to revisit Newton-Smith's oft-cited objection to relative truth (§2.3). Here is the argument, as well as I can reconstruct it:

N1. Suppose, as the relativist holds, that there are sentences S_1 and S_2, a proposition p, and contexts Ψ and Θ such that:

   (a) S_1 is true in Ψ,
   (b) S_2 is not true in Θ.
   (c) p is expressed by S_1 in Ψ and by S_2 in Θ.

N2. If S_1 and S_2 express the same proposition, then they have the same truth-conditions. (premise)

N3. Hence S_1 and S_2 have the same truth-conditions. (by N2, N1c)

N4. If S_1 and S_2 have different truth values, then they have different truth-conditions. (premise)

N5. S_1 and S_2 have different truth values (by N1a and N1b).

N6. So S_1 and S_2 have different truth-conditions. (by N4, N5)

N7. This contradicts N3. So, by reductio, the clauses of N1 cannot all be true.

If the step to N3 is to be valid, we must understand N2 as

N2*. If S_1 expresses the same proposition in Ψ that S_2 expresses in Θ, then S_1 and S_2 have the same truth-conditions.

And if the step to N5 is to be valid, we must understand N4 as

N4*. If the truth value of S_1 in Ψ is different from the truth value of S_2 in Θ, then S_1 and S_2 have different truth-conditions.

These changes give us a valid argument. But is it sound?

First, consider N2*. In general, sentences have truth values only relative to contexts, so the only reasonable notion of truth-condition for a *sentence* is the condition a *context* (or contexts) must satisfy in order for the sentence to be true. In this sense of "truth-condition," the sentences "I am here now" and "He was there then" have different truth-conditions, but nonetheless it may be the case that the same proposition that is expressed by the former in one context is expressed by the latter in another context. So N2* would be rejected even by most non-relativists.

One might charitably read Newton-Smith as talking not about the truth-condition of a sentence-type, but about the truth-condition of an occurrence of the sentence in a context, which might be identified with an intension: a function from circumstances of evaluation to truth values.

N2†. If S_1 expresses the same proposition in Ψ that S_2 expresses in Θ, then S_1 has the same intension in Ψ that S_2 has in Θ.

On this reading, the premise would be true, since two occurrences of sentences in context that express the same proposition will have the same intension.

Before we can ask whether N4* is true, we need to decide what is meant by "in Ψ" and "in Θ." It is unclear whether Newton-Smith is thinking of relativity to a context of use or to a context of assessment, so let us consider both possibilities. We will interpret the talk of "truth-conditions" as talk of the intensions of occurrences of sentences in context, since that is the only interpretation on which N2 is plausible.

If "in Ψ" means "as used at Ψ," then we get

N4†. If the truth value of S_1 as used at Ψ is different from the truth value of S_2 as used at Θ, then S_1 has a different intension at Ψ than S_2 has at Θ.

But this should be rejected, as it ignores the circumstance-determining role of context (see §4.4).[29] It is possible for S_1 and S_2 to have the same intension at Ψ and Θ, but different truth values, if the circumstances compatible with Ψ are different from the circumstances compatible with Θ. For example, if S_1 and S_2 both express the tensed proposition *that Socrates is sitting*, and Socrates is sitting at the time of Ψ but not at the time of Θ, then S_1 will be true at Ψ while S_2 is false at Θ. Of course, Newton-Smith might reject temporalism, but he has given no independent reason for thinking it to be incoherent. And even

---

[29]In this respect Newton-Smith's argument has something in common with "context-shifting arguments" for contextualism: see MacFarlane 2007b for discussion.

an eternalist can find a counterexample to N4†, by letting Ψ and Θ occur at different possible worlds.

On the other hand, if "in Ψ" means "as assessed from Ψ," then we get

N4‡. If the truth value of S_1 as used at and assessed from Ψ is different from the truth value of S_2 as used at and assessed from Θ, then S_1 has a different intension at Ψ than S_2 has at Θ.

Like N4†, this ignores the circumstance-determining role of context (this time, of both the context of use and the context of assessment), so it is no more plausible than N4†.

Newton-Smith's argument exemplifies a deplorable general tendency in much of the literature on relative truth. Terms like "true in," "true for," and "truth-conditions" are deployed without any sensitivity to the various *kinds* of relativization of truth that are used in semantics. As we have seen, proper statement of a relativist position requires some care. A general argument against relative truth needs to take the same care.

5

MAKING SENSE OF RELATIVE TRUTH

In Chapters 3 and 4, I argued that relativism about truth is best understood as a commitment to the assessment sensitivity of some sentences or propositions. But do we really understand what this comes to? In order to understand what it would be for a sentence or proposition to be assessment-sensitive, we must understand what is meant by "true as used at c_1 and assessed from c_2." And it is not clear that we do. For it is not clear that the concept of truth *admits* of relativization to assessors. Meiland (1977) states the problem very clearly as a dilemma. If "true" as it occurs in "true for X" is just the ordinary, nonrelative truth predicate, then it is unclear what "for X" adds.[1] On the other hand, if the occurrence of "true" in "true for X" is like the "cat" in "cattle"—an orthographic, not a semantic, part—then the relativist needs to explain what "true-for-X" means and what it has to do with truth, as ordinarily conceived. Meiland's own solution—explicating "true for X" as "corresponds to reality for X"—just pushes the problem back a level. The absolutist can say: my understanding of "correspondence to reality" leaves no room for an added "for X," so the proposed explicans is just as mysterious as the explanandum.

This, I think, is the hardest question for the relativist. Is assessment sensitivity really intelligible? Do we have enough grip on the notion of assessment-sensitive truth to understand what relativist proposals in specific areas—say, predicates of personal taste or future contingents—amount to? Do we understand the practical difference between relativist and nonrelativist proposals sufficiently to tell what evidence would count in favor of each?

5.1 A strategy

Relativists commonly try to meet this challenge by giving a *definition* of truth that makes its assessment-relativity plain. If truth is idealized justification,

---

[1] As noted in §2.5, "true for X" can be used to specify the domain of a generalization or to say how things are "by X's lights," but neither of these uses captures what the truth relativist is aiming at.

then, as we observed in §2.5, it might reasonably be thought to be assessor-relative, since ideal reasoners with different beliefs, propensities, or prior probabilities might take the same ideal body of evidence to support different conclusions. Similarly, if truth is defined pragmatically, as what is good to believe, then it might also be assessor-relative, insofar as different things are good for different assessors to believe. But although these epistemic and pragmatic definitions of truth capture the "relative" part of "relative truth," I do not believe they capture the "truth" part. Like Davidson (1997), I doubt that the concept of truth can be usefully illuminated by a definition in terms of more primitive concepts.

Of course, the relativist semanticist can give a formal definition of "true as used at c_1 and assessed from c_2" that fixes its extension over a particular class of sentences and contexts. But such a definition would not answer the challenge, for reasons Michael Dummett made clear in his classic paper "Truth" (Dummett 1959). If our aim in giving a Tarskian truth definition is to explain the meanings of expressions by showing how they contribute to the truth conditions of sentences containing them, then we must have a grasp of the concept of truth that goes beyond what the Tarskian truth definition tells us. A recursive definition of "true in L" cannot simultaneously explain both the meanings of the expressions of L *and* the meaning of "true in L." It is only if we have some antecedent grasp of the significance of "true in L" that an assignment of truth-conditions can tell us something about the meanings of sentences and subsentential expressions.

Dummett illustrates his point by considering the concept of winning in a game—say, chess. Here is one kind of definition of "winning in chess":

(1)   White wins at chess just in case the current disposition of pieces on the board has been reached by a series of legal chess moves, with White and Black alternating, and Black's king is in checkmate.

   a.   Black's king is in checkmate iff Black's king is in check and Black has no legal move available that would result in Black's king not being in check.

   b.   Black's king is in check iff one of White's pieces could capture Black's king if it were White's move.

   c.   A chess move is legal iff . . .

Someone who knew this definition would be in a position to tell when White had won a game of chess. But if she had *only* this knowledge, she would be missing a crucial aspect of the concept of winning: that winning is what one conventionally aims at in playing a game.[2] One can imagine a Martian who knows which chess positions are "winning" ones but thinks that in playing chess one aims to *avoid* reaching a "winning" position. The Martian would have an extensionally correct definition of winning at chess, but would not grasp the concept.[3]

In the same way, Dummett suggests, someone who had an extensionally correct Tarskian truth definition for a language but did not understand the *significance* of characterizing sentences as true would not grasp the concept of truth. Imagine, again, a Martian who has a correct definition of truth at a context of use for a language but thinks that speakers conventionally try to *avoid* uttering true sentences, and take others to be doing the same. The Martian's knowledge of the truth-conditions of sentences would not enable it to use these sentences to say anything, or to understand others' uses.

Dummett summarizes the general point as follows:

> If it was to be possible to explain the notion of meaning in terms of that of truth, if the meaning of an expression was to be regarded as a principle governing the contribution that it made to determining the truth-conditions of sentences containing it, then it must be possible to say more about the concept of truth than under which conditions it applied to given sentences. Since meaning depends, ultimately and exhaustively, on use, what was required was a uniform means of characterising the use of a sentence, given its truth-conditions. (Dummett 1978: xxi)[4]

This "uniform means of characterising the use of a sentence, given its truth-conditions" would be an account of the various illocutionary forces (for example, assertoric force) with which we can put forth sentences: "corresponding to each different kind of force will be a different uniform pattern of derivation of the use of a sentence from its sense, considered as determined by its truth-conditions" (Dummett 1981: 361). Hence, "what has to be added to a truth-definition for the sentences of a language, if the notion of truth is to

---

[2]This does not imply that, when one intentionally throws the game in order to make one's opponent feel good, one is not really playing chess. For even in that case, one represents oneself as having the intention of winning (Dummett 1981: 301).

[3]One might object: isn't it at least conceivable that one day we should all begin to play games to lose? Dummett would say that we are really conceiving of a scenario in which (a) we have changed what counts as winning in all these games, so that what formerly counted as losing now counts as winning, and (b) we have started to use the word "lose" to mean what "win" used to mean. See Dummett (1981: 320).

[4]For similar points, see Wiggins (1980) and Davidson (1990: 300).

be explained, is a description of the linguistic activity of making assertions" Dummett (1978: 20). Although Dummett acknowledges that this task is one of "enormous complexity," he does propose, as one example of the shape such an account might take, that assertoric utterances are governed by the convention that one should intend to utter only true sentences.[5] (Had he been thinking of context-sensitive language, he might have said: "only sentences that are true at the context of utterance.") This is certainly a reasonable candidate for the knowledge that the Martian observer would need in order to use its correct specification of the truth conditions of English sentences to understand and speak to English speakers.

We will discuss this specific proposal in more detail shortly, but two general points are worth noting now. First, Dummett has given an example of an explication of "true" that does not take the form of a definition. Instead of defining "true," Dummett proposes to illuminate it by describing its role in a broader theory of language use—in particular, its connection to the speech act of assertion. As Davidson (1997) points out, most philosophically interesting concepts are not definable in simpler terms, but they can still be illuminated by articulating their theoretical connections to other concepts.

Second, if Dummett is right, then it is not just the relativist who owes an explication of the significance of her truth predicate. The absolutist owes one as well—at least if she is to use this predicate in semantics.[6] So although Percival (1994: 208) is quite correct to say of truth relativism that "in the absence of the clear statement of this doctrine's consequences for the evaluation of utterances, it is empty and worthless," the same could be said of *any* use of truth in giving a theory of meaning. It may be that the task is easier to discharge for the non-relativist, but the task is the same for both sides.

These two points suggest a strategy for the truth relativist. Start with an account of assertoric force that is acceptable to the nonrelativist. Such an account will explicate "true at c" by relating it to proprieties for assertion. Then extend this to an explication of "true as used at c_1 and assessed from c_2"

---

[5]Dummett (1981: 302); compare Lewis (1983: §III) and Lewis (1980: §2), discussed in §3.2.1.

[6]*Semantic deflationists* hold that there is nothing more to the concept of truth than its role as a device for semantic ascent—a role that is captured (for a given language) by a Tarskian truth definition. The Dummett argument, if it is correct, shows that semantic deflationists should not use truth definitions to give the meanings of expressions. Most deflationists have accepted this argument, and consequently favor inferentialist explications of meaning over truth-conditional ones (Brandom 1994; Field 1994; Horwich 1998). For a dissenting view, see Williams (1999); for a recent defense of the argument, see Patterson (2005).

by finding a natural role for contexts of assessment to play in the account of assertoric force. If this strategy is successful, the relativist should be able to say to the absolutist: "If you can make sense of your absolute truth predicate, you should be able to make sense of my relative one, too, and see why it deserves to be called a *truth* predicate."

5.2 The Truth Rule

Dummett's analogy with games suggests that the connection between truth and assertion is teleological: in making assertions, one represents oneself as aiming to put forward truths. No doubt there is something right about this, but it does not give us a distinguishing feature of *truth*. For, in making assertions, one also represents oneself as aiming to say things for which one has good evidence, and things that are relevant for the purposes of the conversation. Dummett himself notes that it is absurd to think that one could get a grip on the notion of truth simply by being told that it is the aim of assertion (Dummett 1978: 20; cf. Dummett 1981: 299–301).

A more plausible way of getting at the root idea is by giving a normative account of assertion. Instead of saying that assertion aims at the truth, we can say that assertion is constitutively governed by the

Truth Rule. *At a context c, assert that p only if p is true at c.*

To say that the Truth Rule is *constitutive* of assertion is to say that nothing that is not subject to this rule can count as an assertion. It is crucial here to distinguish between the "constitutive rules" that *define* the move of assertion and other kinds of norms that govern it. We can make such a distinction in the case of other game moves. For example, the rule of chess that says you can't castle if the king is in check is partially constitutive of the move of castling. A move that was not subject to this rule would not be castling.[7] Since castling is nothing more than a move in chess, one can say what castling is by articulating all of the constitutive rules for castling: castling is the move that is subject to these rules. Similarly, the thought goes, to give an account of assertion, it is sufficient to articulate its constitutive rules.

---

[7]This is different from saying that a move that does not *obey* this rule would not be castling. A move may be subject to a rule either by obeying it or by being in violation of it. One can castle incorrectly. If you are tempted to deny this, consider instead the move of *serving* in tennis. Clearly you can serve and violate the rules governing serving, even though being subject to these rules is what makes your movement a serve, and not just a racket-swing.

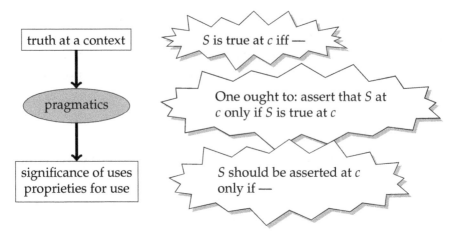

F<small>IG</small>. 5.1. Semantics and pragmatics

Of course, there are other norms governing assertion—for example, norms of politeness, evidence, prudence, and relevance. And these norms can sometimes override the Truth Rule in one's deliberations about what to assert. But one can recognize these things while still taking the Truth Rule to be the sole norm that is constitutive of assertion. Given that assertion is governed by the Truth Rule, and given other facts about our interests and purposes in engaging in conversation, one can explain why assertion is governed by these other norms as well. Asserting what is unjustified or irrelevant violates norms of cooperative conversation, but not the norms an act must be subject to in order to count as asserting, just as castling too late in the game violates norms of strategy, but not the norms a move must be subject to in order to count as castling.

The Truth Rule is a semantic-pragmatic bridge principle (Fig. 5.1). It connects a semantic theory—a theory whose output is a definition of truth at a context for arbitrary sentences of a language, and for the propositions they express—with norms for the use of these sentences and propositions. We need not think of either truth or assertion as more fundamental than the other; the bridge principle helps illuminate both.[8]

5.3   Relativism and the Truth Rule

Suppose we start with the Truth Rule, then, as our basic way of explicating "true (as used) at context c" by connecting it with the *use* of sentences. (Those

---

[8]Compare our discussion of Lewis in §3.2.1.

who still find the Knowledge Rule more plausible will be accommodated in §5.6.) Pursuing the strategy laid out in §5.1, let us ask whether this explication of "true as used at c" can be generalized in a natural way to an explication of "true as used at c_1 and assessed from c_2." How can we restate the Truth Rule using a truth predicate that is relativized to both contexts of use and contexts of assessment?

It seems that there are three basic options for dealing with the extra context parameter. First, we could *relativize the norm itself to contexts of assessment:*

Relativized Truth Rule. *Relative to context c_2, an agent is permitted to assert that p at c_1 only if p is true as used at c_1 and assessed from c_2.*

(Here we have stated the rule as a deontic principle rather than an imperative; this will make things easier later.) On this view, there is no "absolute" answer to the question "what is the norm governing assertion?", but only a perspective-relative answer. Second, we could *quantify over contexts of assessment:*

Quantified Truth Rule. *An agent is permitted to assert that p at context c_1 only if p is true as used at c_1 and assessed from* some/all/most *contexts.*

Finally, we could *privilege one context of assessment.* The only natural choice is the context occupied by the asserter in making the assertion:[9]

Reflexive Truth Rule. *An agent is permitted to assert that p at context c_1 only if p is true as used at c_1 and assessed from c_1.*

However, none of these options gives us what we are looking for: a practical grip on the doubly relativized predicate "true as used at c_1 and assessed from c_2." The Relativized Truth Rule just explains one mysterious relativization in terms of another. What is it for assertion to be governed by one constitutive rule from one context of assessment, and by another from another? We can readily make sense of game rules whose contents make reference to context— for example, "if you're on a corner square, do this; if not, do that"—but what is envisioned here is that it is a context-relative matter what the rule *is*. It is not helpful to be reminded that the rules for football are different in the US and

---

[9]In some cases, it may also make sense to privilege another context that the speaker has in mind, but quite often there will not be a unique such context, since the speaker will intend her assertion to be assessable from many different contexts. In any case, the objections in what follows to the Reflexive Truth Rule will apply equally to a proposal to fix the relevant context of assessment as the one the speaker has in mind.

in Australia; clearly, there are two different games here, "American football" and "Australian rules football." Any particular game is going to be subject to the rules of one or the other. To get an analogy with the Relativized Truth Rule, we'd need to imagine a pass in a single televised game that was legal as assessed from America but not as assessed from Australia. We could make sense of such a thing if we could understand what it was for the claim *that that particular pass was legal* to be true as assessed from one context, but not as assessed from another. But that is just what we are hoping that the Relativized Truth Rule would help illuminate. The rule presupposes, rather than provides, an understanding of assessment-relative truth.

The various versions of the Quantified Truth Rule are at least intelligible, but they will not serve the relativist's purposes. It is too easy to assert something that is true at *some* context of assessment, and if we require truth at *every* context of assessment, the resulting norm will forbid asserting anything assessment-sensitive. One might avoid these extremes by quantifying over *most* contexts of assessment, but the appeal to majority rule here seems arbitrary; nor is it clear what "most" means in this context, if, as seems likely, there are infinitely many possible contexts of assessment.[10]

The Reflexive Truth Rule seems most promising. It makes sense to privilege the context the asserter occupies when she makes the assertion as the one relative to which she should assert only truths.[11] But this option will not help us make sense of relative truth, for it leaves contexts of assessment without any *essential* role to play. Given any semantic theory T that posits assessment sensitivity, we can construct a rival theory $T*$ that does not posit assessment sensitivity, but has exactly the same consequences for the correctness of assertions, as far as the Reflexive Truth Rule goes:

Construction of $T*$. *For all sentences S and contexts c_1, c_2: S is $true_{T*}$ as used at c_1 and assessed from c_2 iff S is $true_T$ as used at c_1 and assessed from c_1.*

It is plain from the construction that $T*$ will always agree with T about when a sentence (and derivatively a content) is true as used at and assessed from a given context. So the two theories will agree, given the Reflexive Truth Rule, in their predictions about what may be asserted when, even though they

---

[10]All three proposals would also face the difficulty discussed below for the Reflexive Truth Rule—as would proposals that quantify over contexts of assessment that are related in some specific way to the context of use.

[11]See Kölbel (2002: 125), Egan, Hawthorne, and Weatherson (2005: 153).

disagree about whether sentences are assessment-sensitive. The relativity of truth to contexts of assessment threatens to be an idle wheel unless we can say something more about its significance.

The point is more easily appreciated with a concrete example. Suppose we accept the Reflexive Truth Rule as our basic account of how truth at a context of use and context of assessment relates to proprieties for language use. Let us now compare two theories, R and C. The two theories do not differ in the semantics proper (in the sense of §3.2.2). Both define truth relative to a context and an index consisting of a world and a taste, and both contain the following clause for the predicate "tasty":

(2) The extension of "tasty" at c_1, $\langle w, g \rangle$ is the set of things whose taste at w is good as evaluated by taste g.

Moreover, both theories take "tasty" to invariantly express a property, the property of being tasty, whose intension is a function from world/taste pairs to truth values. The two theories differ only in the postsemantics. R defines truth at a context of use and context of assessment as follows (cf. §4.7):

(3) A proposition p is true as used at c_1 and assessed from c_2 iff p is true at $\langle w_{c_1}, g_{c_2} \rangle$, where w_{c_1} is the world of c_1 and g_{c_2} is the taste of the agent of c_2.

According to R, "tasty" is assessment-sensitive. C defines truth at a context of use and context of assessment as follows (cf. §4.6):

(4) A proposition p is true as used at c_1 and assessed from c_2 iff p is true at $\langle w_{c_1}, g_{c_1} \rangle$, where w_{c_1} is the world of c_1 and g_{c_1} is the taste of the agent of c_1.

According to C, "tasty" is use-sensitive, but not assessment-sensitive.

We would like to see some difference in practice between the relativist theory R and the nonindexical contextualist theory C. But, as far as the Reflexive Truth Rule tells us, the two theories have exactly the same normative consequences. They both predict that agents should assert that a food is tasty only when that food tastes good to them. This is a problem for the relativist. The problem is not that the prediction is implausible, or one the relativist should reject. The problem is that, if the Reflexive Truth Rule is our sole point of connection between the semantic theory and facts (in this case, normative facts) about the use of language, then the relativist has not explained the practical difference between a relativist theory and a nonrelativist one.

Suppose there are three possible contexts: c_1, c_2, and c_3. The contexts all have the same agent but take place at different times (t_1, t_2, t_3). The agent likes licorice at t_1 and t_2, but not at t_3. Let p be the proposition that licorice is tasty.[12] We can compare R and C by looking at the truth values they assign to p at each possible combination of a context of use and context of assessment (see Tables 5.1 and 5.2).

TABLE 5.1. R (relativist)

	assessed		
	c_1	c_2	c_3
c_1	T	T	F
c_2	T	T	F
c_3	T	T	F

(used)

TABLE 5.2. C (contextualist)

	assessed		
	c_1	c_2	c_3
c_1	T	T	T
c_2	T	T	T
c_3	F	F	F

(used)

Note that the only cells of the table that matter to the propriety of assertions, as far as the Reflexive Truth Rule goes, are the shaded cells on the diagonal (where the context of assessment is the same as the context of use). Since R and C agree on these cells, the Reflexive Truth Rule does not help us to distinguish between them. They are "normatively equivalent" theories. Thus the antirelativist can say to the relativist:

What you call "truth as used at and assessed from c," and identify with the norm of assertion, is what I call "truth as used at c." At any rate, they are identical in their normative and empirical import. But you have done nothing to explain what "truth as used at c_1 and assessed from c_2" means, when $c_1 \neq c_2$. If you had, we would be able to see a difference in the consequences for language use between a relativist theory and a nonindexical contextualist theory that coincides with it "on the diagonal," as C coincides with R.

It might be protested that even if the difference between R and C does not manifest itself as a difference in the norms for asserting p, it manifests itself as a difference in the norms for asserting that particular assertions of p are "true." One might expect that the relativist and the nonindexical contextualist theories would disagree at least about this. It turns out, though, that they do not. Recall the natural semantics for "true" given in §4.8:

Semantics for monadic "true." *"True" expresses the same property at every context of use—the property of being true. The extension of this property at a circumstance of evaluation e is the set of propositions that are true at e.*

---

[12] If you like, you can add "throughout the period $t_1 \ldots t_3$": we will assume that the taste of licorice does not change during this period.

Suppose that Jake asserts p (the proposition that licorice is tasty) at c_1, and we are assessing his assertion from c_3. As we have already seen, R and C disagree about whether p is true as used at c_1 and assessed from c_3. But they do not disagree about whether the proposition expressed at c_3 by

(5)   What Jake said at t_1 is true.[13]

—call it $T(p)$—is true as used at and assessed from c_3. For, on both accounts, (5) will be true as used at and assessed from c_3 just in case $T(p)$ is true at $\langle w_{c_3}, g_{c_3} \rangle$, where w_{c_3} is the world of c_3 and g_{c_3} the taste of the agent at c_3. And, given our semantics for monadic "true," $T(p)$ will be true at $\langle w_{c_3}, g_{c_3} \rangle$ just in case p is true at $\langle w_{c_3}, g_{c_3} \rangle$. Since R and C agree that p is false at $\langle w_{c_3}, g_{c_3} \rangle$, they will agree that $T(p)$ is false as used at and assessed from c_3. And, given the Reflexive Truth Rule, they will agree that what Jake said cannot be correctly said at c_3 to be "true."

Granted, the two theories will make different predictions about whether an assessor at c_3 could correctly call Jake's *utterance* (in the "act" sense) "true." But, as noted in §3.1.2, the monadic predicate "true" in ordinary use is a predicate of propositions, not utterances. Perhaps we can understand utterance truth as a technical notion, by saying that an utterance at c_1 is true (as assessed from c_2) just in case the sentence uttered is true as used at c_1 and assessed from c_2. But precisely because utterance truth is a technical semantic notion, we should not expect to be able to adjudicate between two theories (R and C) by looking at their predictions about the use of sentences that characterize utterances as true. Theorists who accept R will apply "true" to utterances in one way; those who accept C will apply it in another way; and ordinary speakers will not apply "true" to utterances at all. Besides, what happens if the language we are studying does not contain "true" as a predicate of utterances? Do we then lose our grip on the significance of assessment-relative truth assignments?

We must conclude, then, that if the Reflexive Truth Rule is all we have to connect our truth-conditional semantic theory with proprieties for the use of language, we cannot make sense of assessment-relative truth. The point can be generalized: given only a principle governing when it is correct to make assertions (whether it be the Truth Rule, the Knowledge Rule, or anything similar), we cannot discern any practical difference between semantic theories

---

[13]Or "was true." Since in this example we are operating with eternalist propositions, whose truth values do not vary with time, there is no significant difference.

that posit assessment sensitivity and those that do not, since in the situation where an assertion is being made, the context of use and context of assessment coincide. Parallel considerations will rule out explaining the significance of relative truth by talking of truth as the norm of belief, rather than assertion. Some philosophers have concluded on this basis that relative truth talk is incoherent.[14]

5.4   Retraction

I want to suggest a less bleak diagnosis. The basic thought is that the pragmatic difference between R and C manifests itself in norms for the *retraction* of assertions rather than norms for the *making* of assertions. R predicts that an assertion of p at c_1 ought to be retracted by the asserter in c_3, while C predicts that it need not be retracted. Thus, the Reflexive Truth Rule is not so much wrong as incomplete. It needs to be supplemented by a constitutive norm for retraction:

Retraction Rule.   *An agent in context c_2 is required to retract an (unretracted) assertion of p made at c_1 if p is not true as used at c_1 and assessed from c_2.*

By "retraction," I mean the speech act one performs in saying "I take that back" or "I retract that."[15] The target of a retraction is another speech act, which may be an assertion, a question, a command, an offer, or a speech act of another kind. The effect of retracting a speech act is to "undo" the normative changes effected by the original speech act. So, for example, in retracting a question, one releases the audience from an obligation to answer it, and in retracting an offer, one withdraws a permission that one has extended. Similarly, in retracting an assertion, one disavows the assertoric commitment undertaken in the original assertion. This means, among other things, that one is no longer obliged to respond to challenges to the assertion (since one has already conceded, in effect), and that others are no longer entitled to rely on one's authority for the accuracy of this assertion. (One can, of course, still be held morally accountable if others relied on one's assertion before they knew that it was retracted.)

---

[14]In addition to Evans (1985), see the nuanced discussions in Percival (1994) and Campbell (1997: 165–6).

[15]Explicit retractions of assertions are relatively rare, because it is usually assumed that in acknowledging the inaccuracy of the original assertion, one implicitly retracts it. But this presumption can be defeated: I might say, for example, "I know that what I said was almost certainly false, but I'm standing by it and not retracting."

Note that the Retraction Rule *obliges* retraction under certain conditions, while the Reflexive Truth Rule *forbids* assertion under certain conditions. This is as it should be. In asserting, the fault lies in commission (asserting something untrue), while in retracting, the fault lies in omission (failing to retract something untrue). There is nothing inherently wrong with retracting an assertion one still thinks is true—one may not want others to rely on one's word in this matter, or one may not want to take on the obligation of defending the assertion—and doing so is not "insincere" in the way that asserting something one does not believe to be true is.[16]

Because retractions are always retractions of some specific speech act, there are always *two* relevant contexts: the context in which the retraction itself takes place and the context in which the original speech act took place. It is by exploiting this fact that the Retraction Rule gives a normative role to contexts of assessment. It requires retraction when the proposition asserted is untrue as used at the context of the original assertion and assessed from the context in which the retraction is being considered.

Together, the Reflexive Truth Rule and the Retraction Rule allow us to see the practical difference between semantic theories that posit assessment sensitivity (like R) and theories that do not (like C). An example will help show how. Let c_1 be a context centered on ten-year-old Joey, who loves fish sticks. According to both R and C, the proposition that fish sticks are tasty is true as used at and assessed from c_1. So the Reflexive Truth Rule tells us that Joey is permitted to assert that fish sticks are tasty. Let us suppose that he does. Now consider another context c_2 centered on Joey, ten years later. As a twenty-year old, Joey no longer likes the taste of fish sticks. Here R and C diverge. According to R, the proposition that fish sticks are tasty is false as used at c_1 and assessed from c_2, so by the Retraction Rule, Joey is now required to retract his earlier assertion. According to C, by contrast, the proposition that fish sticks are tasty is true as used at c_1 and assessed from c_2, and Joey need not retract.[17] The practical difference between C and R lies in

---

[16]This point is missed by one of the few explicit accounts of retractions in the literature on speech act theory. Bach and Harnish (1979: 43) say that "In uttering e, S retracts the claim that P if S expresses: i. that he no longer believes that P, contrary to what he previously indicated he believed, and ii. the intention that H [the hearer] not believe that P."

[17]Note that, if C is a nonindexical contextualist theory, it will predict that Joey should hold that *what he asserted earlier*—that fish sticks are tasty—is (and was) false. (See §4.8.) For the nonindexical contextualist, though, this is not sufficient grounds for Joey to retract his assertion. He would have such grounds only if he took what he asserted earlier to have been false by

what they imply about Joey's obligation to retract his earlier assertion.

As we can see from the example, the combination of the Reflexive Truth Rule and the Retraction Rule allow that someone who asserts that p in c_1 might be compelled to retract this assertion in a later context c_2, even though the assertion was permissible for her to make at c_1. (This will happen when p is true as used at and assessed from c_1, but not true as used at c_1 and assessed from c_2.) This may seem odd. Percival (1994: 209) asks, "How can I believe both that the aims given A, for him, by the language he employs were successfully pursued, and that I have every right to force him to withdraw his utterance?"

Here it is important to keep in mind that withdrawing an assertion (or other speech act) is not tantamount to conceding that one was at fault in making it. Suppose one's evidence strongly suggests that Uncle Jack is coming to lunch, and on the strength of that evidence you assert that Uncle Jack is coming. A bit later, Aunt Sally calls to say that Uncle Jack has broken his leg. This makes it quite unlikely that he is coming, so you retract your assertion. Nonetheless, you were perfectly reasonable in making it, and cannot be criticized for having done so. Retracting it is not admitting fault.

The case the relativist allows is similar, only the difference between the later context and the earlier one is not (just) a difference in the *evidence* one has for a claim, but a difference in the very *truth* of the claim. Perhaps there is something odd about this, but its oddity cannot consist in the fact that you are compelled to withdraw an assertion that you had every right to make, since we see that in the epistemic case as well.

5.5 Rejection

An alternative approach would be to countenance a speech act of *rejecting* another assertion, governed by the

Rejection Rule. *An agent in context c_2 is permitted to reject an assertion of p made at c_1 if p is not true as used at c_1 and assessed from c_2.*

Like retraction, rejection targets a speech act, and not its content. What is rejected is not *what Samantha asserted yesterday*, but Samantha's act of asserting it yesterday.

the standards of taste he had at the time. If this seems odd, compare the temporalist, who can coherently think that the content of an earlier assertion *that it is noon* is false, without being obliged to retract the assertion. She would be obliged to retract it only if its content *was* false at the time she made it.

Retraction can be thought of as a special case of rejection: to retract an assertion is to reject an assertion one has previously made. Even given this understanding of retraction, though, the Rejection Rule does not imply the Retraction Rule, since the former gives a sufficient condition for being *permitted* to reject, while the latter gives a sufficient condition for being *obliged* to retract. The Rejection Rule should therefore be seen as supplementing the Retraction Rule rather than replacing it.

We distinguished a relativist account of "tasty" from a nonindexical contextualist account by showing how they make different predictions about whether Joey is obliged to retract his earlier assertion that fish sticks are tasty. If we add the Rejection Rule, we can supplement this intrapersonal difference with an interpersonal one. The relativist account implies that Joey may reject Samantha's assertion that fish sticks are tasty, since *he* doesn't now like them, whereas the nonindexical contextualist does not.[18]

Though I am not opposed to this approach, I do not take it in this book.[19] It is clearer that there is a speech act of retraction than that there is a speech act of rejection. And, I think, the retraction norm is all we need to understand the difference between relativism and all forms of contextualism. Even the interpersonal relation of disagreement can be understood, as we will see in §6.6, in terms of norms for assertion and retraction.

5.6 Relativism and the Knowledge Rule

Timothy Williamson (1996; 2000: ch. 11) has argued that assertion is constitutively governed not by the Truth Rule but by the

Knowledge Rule. *At a context c, assert that p only if you know that p at c.*

Williamson gives three main arguments, but none of them are compelling.[20]

First, he claims, there are other speech acts, such as conjecturing, that are governed by a truth rule, so we cannot define assertion as the unique speech act type V whose constitutive rule is "V that p only if p is true." But this is far from clear. If conjecturing were governed by a truth rule, it would be irresponsible to make conjectures one did not have strong reasons to think

---

[18]The nonindexical contextualist will predict that Joey should regard what Samantha asserted as false—but on the nonindexical contextualist account, this is not grounds for rejecting her assertion. See n. 17, this chapter.

[19]In MacFarlane (2007a: §5.2), I presuppose a permissive norm for challenging others' assertions, similar to the Rejection Rule.

[20]The thesis and some of the arguments derive from Unger (1975: ch. VI).

were true—and it is not. Perhaps Williamson is moved by the fact that one must retract conjectures whose contents have been shown to be untrue. But does that entail that one must *make* conjectures only when their contents are true?

Second, Williamson argues, the Truth Rule cannot explain why we shouldn't assert of a randomly selected lottery ticket that it won't win. The assumption here is that, although we don't *know* that the ticket won't win, it is overwhelming likely to be *true* that it won't win. So we have excellent evidence that in asserting that the ticket won't win, we will satisfy the Truth Rule. Why, then, should it be wrong to assert this? The proponent of the Knowledge Rule has an easy answer, since the merely statistical evidence we have that the ticket won't win is not sufficient for knowledge.

But a proponent of the Truth Rule can also answer the question, by invoking a principle that Williamson himself should accept:

(6) One ought not believe that a lottery ticket will not win merely on the grounds that it is one of a very large number of tickets, only one of which will win.

This follows from another principle Williamson accepts, the knowledge norm for belief, together with the plausible claim that we are not in a position to *know* that a lottery ticket will not win, as long as it has a fair chance of winning, however small. But (6) is independently plausible. One might support it, for example, by noting that it does not seem irrational to buy a ticket in a fair lottery, but that it does seem irrational to buy a ticket one believes will not win.

Given (6), an agent playing a fair lottery should not believe that her ticket will not win, but only that her ticket has a low probability of winning. It follows that she should not believe that she would be satisfying the Truth Rule were she to assert that her ticket will not win. It does not follow that she ought not to assert that the ticket will not win, but only that she ought not believe that this assertion is permissible. But this weaker conclusion is enough to account for the intuition that there is something wrong with asserting, on her evidence, that the ticket will not win.

Williamson's third argument for the Knowledge Rule is that it can explain, as the Truth Rule cannot, why assertions can be challenged by asking "How do you know?" It does not seem appropriate to respond by saying, "I never said I *knew*," which suggests that in asserting anything, one is representing oneself as knowing it (Unger 1975: 263–4). Relatedly, it never seems appropriate to assert a proposition of the form

(7)   *P*, but I don't know that *P*

(Unger 1975: 258–60). This, too, is nicely explained if assertion is governed by the Knowledge Rule.

However, the Truth Rule can also explain these things, in combination with a knowledge norm for belief. If one should not believe what one does not know, then "How do you know?" is a way of challenging the asserter's entitlement to the belief that the assertion satisfies the Truth Rule. And, in asserting the second conjunct of (7), the speaker is conceding that either she does not believe the first conjunct, or she believes it impermissibly. In either case, the assertion is infelicitous.

Thus Williamson's arguments against the Truth Rule seem inconclusive. But even those who accept them can "make sense of relative truth," for the Knowledge Rule, like the Truth Rule, can be generalized to make room for assessment sensitivity.

This may seem surprising. It is sometimes argued that the factivity of knowledge precludes relativism. The thought is something like this: if it can be known that *p*, then *p* must be a fact, and hence true absolutely. Thus nothing that can be known can be assessment-sensitive. The Knowledge Rule would then imply that nothing assessment-sensitive can permissibly be asserted. Such an account would certainly not help to illuminate relative truth.

But the line of thought just scouted is faulty. What we can conclude from the factivity of "knows" is that if ϕ is assessment-sensitive, so is $\ulcorner \alpha$ knows that $\phi \urcorner$, and so is the predicate "knows" (since its extension varies as we shift the context of assessment). Thus the argument above relies on the tacit premise that "knows" is not assessment-sensitive. But it is question-begging to assume this in an argument that purports to rule out the possibility of assessment sensitivity.[21]

Let us then allow for the possibility that "knows" is assessment-sensitive. If we do that, then the Knowledge Rule needs to be restated in non-assessment-sensitive language. A reasonable candidate, following the pattern of the Reflexive Truth Rule, is

---

[21] Perhaps there are independent arguments that "knows" cannot be assessment-sensitive. I do not know of any. For independent arguments *for* the assessment sensitivity of "knows," see MacFarlane (2005a) and Chapter 8, this volume.

Reflexive Knowledge Rule. *An agent is permitted to assert that p (at a context c) only if the proposition* that she knows (at t_c) that p *is true as used at and assessed from c.*

Together with the Retraction Rule, the Reflexive Knowledge Rule would allow us to make sense of relative truth, by giving us a clear practical grip on the distinction between relativist and nonindexical contextualist theories.

In what follows, we will take the Reflexive Truth Rule and the Retraction Rule to be the fundamental norms connecting the semantic theory to the use of language. Readers who favor the Knowledge Rule over the Truth Rule, however, may simply substitute the Reflexive Knowledge Rule for the Reflexive Truth Rule, adjusting the arguments that follow to fit.

5.7 Believing relative truths

We have sought to understand what it is for truth to be assessment-relative by understanding the practical difference between *asserting* assessment-sensitive and assessment-invariant contents. One might wonder: why this focus on assertion? Why not make sense of relative truth by trying to understand what it is to *believe* an assessment-sensitive content? More generally, why should we focus on the significance of assessment sensitivity for speech acts rather than for mental attitudes?

The problem is not that we cannot make sense of beliefs with assessment-sensitive contents. Once we understand what it is to assert an assessment-sensitive proposition, there is no obstacle to countenancing beliefs with these propositions as their contents. The problem is, rather, that we cannot make sense of assessment sensitivity *by* understanding what it is to believe assessment-sensitive contents. To put it starkly: for creatures that were only believers, and did not also make assertions, we could not discern any practical difference between an assessment-sensitive and a non-assessment-sensitive semantic theory.

The reason is simple: there is nothing corresponding to the *retraction* of a belief. Recall that we could make sense of the distinction between an assessment-sensitive and an assessment-invariant theory that agreed on the intensions of propositions[22] only by considering norms for retraction (or commitments to retract). Retraction was the key to making sense of assessment sensitivity, because in retraction there are always two significant contexts: the

---

[22]That is, their truth values relative to circumstances of evaluation.

context in which the retraction is being considered and the context in which the assertion whose retraction is being contemplated was made. This gives both the context of assessment and the context of use a job to do in a norm for retraction.

Why is there nothing like retraction in the case of belief? Can't one give up a belief, just as one can retract an assertion? Here it is important to keep in mind a metaphysical difference between assertions and beliefs. An assertion is an *action*, and hence also an *event*, while a belief is not an action or event, but a *state* that an agent can be in over a period of time. The *inception* of a belief may be an event, but the belief itself is not. When one gives up a belief that p, one transitions from being in the state of believing that p to being in the state of not believing that p, but this transition is not directed towards any particular past event. Retraction, by contrast, is always retraction *of* some past speech act.[23]

Here is another way to see the point. Suppose that at t_0 we query Jim about tomatoes, and he asserts that tomatoes are vegetables. Then, at some later time t_1, we query him again, and—perhaps because he has come to doubt the grounds he had before—he refuses to assert that tomatoes are vegetables. This refusal to assert that tomatoes are vegetables is not itself a retraction of his earlier assertion that tomatoes are vegetables. Jim might *also* retract the earlier assertion, signaling that he is no longer committed to its truth, but if he does, that is a distinct act. It is an act he *ought* to perform if he wants to be coherent, but he might fail to perform it. We can distinguish, then, between no longer being willing to assert that tomatoes are vegetables and retracting an earlier assertion that tomatoes are vegetables. In the case of belief, though, there is no comparable distinction. We can certainly imagine Jim believing that tomatoes are vegetables at t_0 and then, in response to new evidence, ceasing believing that tomatoes are vegetables at t_1. But there is no further backwards-directed act he needs to perform in order to be coherent. Ceasing believing is all he needs to do; he need not somehow "undo" his earlier belief.

Consider this analogy. Two men, Alberto and Bernardo, are walking around an Italian garden. Alberto carries with him a supply of stakes with

---

[23]If we countenance mental acts of judgment, then we might try talking of retractions of such acts. This would open up the possibility of making sense of assessment sensitivity without assertions. However, it is not clear to me either that there are mental acts of judgment, or that there is anything corresponding to retraction of such acts. We should beware of carrying the analogy between thought and discourse too far.

flags on them. He stops periodically, drives a stake into the ground, and writes on the flag, "Viola is the loveliest woman on earth." Bernardo is also an admirer of Viola, but instead of planting flags in the ground, he simply *carries* his flag reading "Viola is the loveliest woman on earth." Halfway through the garden, Alberto and Bernardo both spot Cynthia and are immediately smitten. Alberto begins to plant flags reading "Cynthia is the loveliest woman on earth," and Bernardo repaints his flag to read the same. At this point, Alberto must go back and pick up all the flags declaring Viola to be the loveliest woman on earth. Bernardo faces no comparable task; it is enough for him simply to change his flag.

It is in the norms for retraction that we find an independent role for the notion of a context of assessment, so if there is nothing like retraction for beliefs, then it is not clear how we could distinguish between relativist and nonindexical contextualist theories just by looking at their predictions about when people should believe the propositions in question. The problem is not, as is sometimes supposed, that the relativist can't make sense of belief as "aiming at truth," or of norms for belief. To say that belief aims at truth is to say that a belief in context c succeeds in its aim if its propositional content is true as used at and assessed from c.[24] To say that truth is a norm for belief is to say that at a context c one ought to believe only propositions that are true as used at and assessed from c (cf. Kölbel 2002: 32, 91).[25] The problem, rather, is exactly the same as the problem about assertion we discussed in §5.3: saying these things isn't enough to distinguish relativist views from nonindexical contextualist variants of them that generate exactly the same normative predictions. The solution there was to bring in norms for retraction, but that solution is not available for belief.

What makes relative truth intelligible is the potential difference between the context at which an assertion is made and the contexts at which challenges to it will have to be met and retractions considered. Thus, even though

[24]Of course, beliefs don't literally "aim at" anything. For attempts to unpack the metaphor, see Velleman (2000) and Wedgwood (2002).

[25]Zimmerman (2007: 337) argues that a rational agent seeking to believe the truth will not clearheadedly "believe a proposition that is both relatively true and relatively false." But surely it is perfectly rational for an agent to believe, for example, that Dodos are extinct, even though this proposition is true at some circumstances of evaluation (worlds) and false at others. Similarly, temporalists will hold that it is rational to believe that it is raining, even though this (tensed) proposition is true at some times and false at others. What matters is whether the proposition at issue is true relative to the context the believer currently occupies.

assessment-sensitive propositions can be believed, judged, doubted, supposed, and so on, there would be no theoretical need for relative truth if we did not also make assertions.

5.8 Conclusion

In §2.1, we concluded that the solid core of the self-refutation objection was a challenge for the relativist. The relativist cannot understand asserting that p as putting p forward as absolutely true. But what is it to put p forward as true, but only relatively so?

In this chapter we have tried to meet this challenge head on, by showing how the assertion of assessment-sensitive contents can be rendered intelligible in the context of several different kinds of accounts of assertion. Given one of these accounts, we can say precisely what the difference in practice is between asserting an assessment-sensitive content and asserting an assessment-invariant one.

It is worth emphasizing that these accounts are *conservative*, in the following sense: if all contents are assessment-invariant, they agree in all of their normative predictions with the orthodox accounts from which they are derived. They are more open-minded than the orthodox accounts, since they make room for assessment sensitivity, but they do not settle the question of whether there *is* any assessment sensitivity in language. They thus provide a framework that both the relativist and the nonrelativist should be able to accept—a neutral framework that tells us what to look for in arguing for or against a relativist theory.

It is time to put to rest the common but unsupported view that relativism about truth is self-refuting or incoherent, and ask instead whether it is supported by the (broadly linguistic) evidence.

6

DISAGREEMENT

The Achilles' heel of contextualism is the problem of *lost disagreement*. If in saying "That's tasty" Yum is asserting that the food tastes good to her, and in saying "That's not tasty" Yuk is asserting that it doesn't taste good to him, then their claims are compatible and it is mysterious why they should regard themselves as disagreeing. Sophisticated contextualists attempt to regain the lost disagreement by taking "tasty" to express the property of tasting good to a contextually relevant *group*, or to a suitably idealized version of the speaker. But as we saw §1.2, such moves face a dilemma. If the group is kept small and surveyable, and the idealization mild, then it is always possible to find cases of apparent disagreement it will not explain. But if we expand the group (or idealization) far enough to capture all the apparent disagreement, we can no longer understand how speakers could regard themselves as suitably placed to make the relevant assertions in the first place. A primary selling point of relativist views against contextualist ones is that they purport to capture the subjectivity of claims of taste without losing the disagreement.

But this claim needs more scrutiny. Some critics have charged that relativists about truth are unable to account for disagreement at all. For example, Frege, who favors a contextualist account of taste predicates,[1] writes in his unpublished manuscript "Logic":

If something were true only for him who held it to be true, there would be no contradiction between the opinions of different people. So to be consistent, any person holding this view would have no right whatever to contradict the opposite view, he would have to espouse the principle: *non disputandum est*. (Frege 1979: 233)

Does relativism about truth make it possible to understand how there can be disagreements of taste? Or does it make this impossible, as Frege suggests?[2] In order to get clearer about this, we need to ask what disagreement amounts

---

[1] "As regards a sentence containing a judgement of taste like, 'This rose is beautiful', the identity of the speaker is essential to the sense, even though the word 'I' does not occur in it" (Frege 1979: 235).

[2] See Moltmann (2010: 213), quoted in §2.2, for an argument to this effect.

to. We need an account of disagreement that illuminates how it bears on the issues about truth and content that divide contextualists and relativists.

However, it is easy to ask the wrong question. If we ask, "What is *real* disagreement?", instead of "What kinds of disagreement are there?", our question is unfair to both the contextualist and the relativist. It is unfair to the contextualist because, even if there are kinds of disagreement that contextualist accounts do not capture, there may be other kinds that it does capture. And it is unfair to the relativist because it makes it look as if the relativist needs to vindicate the very same kind of disagreement that is secured by objectivist accounts. Even those who are sympathetic to relativism may feel that disagreement about matters of taste is, though genuine, not quite the same kind of thing as disagreement about the age of the earth.

Instead of arguing about what is "real" disagreement, then, our strategy will be to identify several varieties of disagreement. We can then ask, about each dialogue of interest, which of these kinds of disagreement can be found in it, and we can adjudicate between candidate theories of meaning by asking which theories predict the kinds of disagreement we find.

6.1 Clarifying the target

Cappelen and Hawthorne (2009: 60–1) point out that "agree" has both a state and an activity meaning. The same is true of "disagree." When we characterize two people as disagreeing, we sometimes mean that they are *having a disagreement*—engaging in a kind of activity—and sometimes just that they *are in disagreement*, which is a kind of state.

People can be *in disagreement* even if they do not know of each other. The ancient Greeks were in disagreement with the ancient Indians about whether the bodies of the dead should be burned or buried even before Herodotus and other travelers made this disagreement known to them. Whether two people are in disagreement is a function of their first-order attitudes, not of their attitudes towards each other.

Whether they are *having a disagreement*, by contrast, depends only on their attitudes and actions towards each other. Two people who agree about all the issues at stake can nonetheless be having a disagreement if, through some misunderstanding, they take their views to differ, or if one is playing devil's advocate. The question "Why are you disagreeing with me, if we agree about what is at issue?" is perfectly intelligible.

Here we will be primarily concerned with the state of being in disagreement, rather than the activity of having a disagreement. It seems plausible that any account of the activity will make reference to the state, since having a disagreement requires taking oneself to be in disagreement. If this is right, then the state sense of "disagree" is more fundamental.

What is the logical form of the relation we seek to explicate? We could take as our target the relation

(1) x is in disagreement with y.

But this concept is not sufficiently discriminating. Nobody agrees with anybody about *everything*, so this is a relation everyone will stand in to everyone else. We need a way of saying that Yum and Yuk disagree in some particular respect. So we might take our target to be the relation

(2) x is in disagreement with y about whether p.

But this target is not going to work with all of the varieties of disagreement we will be considering. Some kinds of disagreement involve attitudes without propositional content. In other cases, whether there is a disagreement depends not just on the contents of the relevant attitudes, but on the contexts in which they occur. So a more general target is

(3) x is in disagreement with y in virtue of y's ϕing-in-context-c.

where ϕ can be replaced by a verb phrase describing an attitude—for example, *believe that Mary is smart*, or *hate the taste of grape jelly*. Since a context includes the agent of the context, we can omit the reference to y:

(4) x is in disagreement with ϕing-in-context-c.

Disagreement, in this sense, is a relation between a person and a possible speech act or attitude in context.

We will consider some different ways of explicating this relation; all of them, I think, are genuine kinds of disagreement. Given this relation between a person and an attitude or speech act in context, we can presumably define a relation between a person and a person, and between a person, a person, and a proposition, in the special cases where this is appropriate. So we do not lose anything by focusing on this admittedly somewhat artificial relation.

6.2 Noncotenability

In one sense, I disagree with someone's attitude if I could not coherently adopt that same attitude (an attitude with the same content and force[3]) without changing my mind—that is, without dropping some of my current attitudes.[4] In other words, I disagree with attitudes that are not *cotenable* with my current attitudes.[5]

Many paradigm cases of disagreement are cases of noncotenability (in addition to being disagreements in other senses). For example, suppose George believes that all bankers are rich, while Sally believes that Vern is a poor banker. Sally's belief is not cotenable with George's attitudes, because George could not coherently come to believe what Sally does—that Vern is a poor banker—without giving up his existing belief that all bankers are rich.

Asked what disagreement is, I suspect many philosophers' first answer will be what we might call

The Simple View of Disagreement. *To disagree with someone's belief that p is to have beliefs whose contents are jointly incompatible with p.*[6]

---

[3]See §1.3.2.

[4]Fabrizio Cariani and Gerald Marsh independently noted that if I already have incoherent beliefs (perhaps about unrelated matters), then this definition counts me as disagreeing with *all* attitudes, since it is true of all attitudes that I could not adopt them and be in a coherent state without dropping some of my current attitudes. We could solve this problem if we had a notion of being "more incoherent," since we could then say that adopting the attitude would make me more incoherent. Cariani also points out that if I currently believe that I don't have any beliefs about California, then this definition counts me as disagreeing with anyone who believes anything about California, since if I came to have their beliefs about California, this would clash with my existing higher-order belief. Intuitively that is wrong. Perhaps this could be fixed by interpreting "incoherence" narrowly as inconsistency, so as to exclude the kind of incoherence we have in Moore's paradoxical cases. In the end, I am not so concerned about such counterexamples, since part of my point in what follows is that many cases of doxastic noncotenability do not seem like intuitive cases of disagreement.

[5]This notion can be extended from attitudes to claims: I disagree with someone's claim if I could not coherently make the same claim—a claim with the same content—without changing my mind or retracting one or more of my own claims. This extension might be useful in cases where the parties are playing devil's advocate or in some other way speaking against their own beliefs. If Lawyer *A* says "my client is innocent" and Lawyer *B* says, "no, he is guilty," then they have made noncotenable claims; no one person could make both claims without incoherence. But they may not have noncotenable beliefs, since both may believe that the client is guilty. Here there is a disagreement in claims, but not in beliefs.

[6]Of course, if contents are individuated coarsely—for example, as sets of possible worlds or Russellian propositions—more must be said. We might not want to say that Hammurabi

The notion of disagreement captured by the Simple View can be seen as a special case of noncotenability, considering only attitudes of full belief. But noncotenability yields interesting notions of disagreement when applied to other kinds of attitudes as well.

Ned, the weather reporter for Channel 4, has a credence of 0.7 that it will rain tomorrow. Ted, the weather reporter for Channel 5, has a credence of 0.8 that it will rain. Ned could not adopt Ted's attitude without change of mind, so we have a case of noncotenability, even though both Ned and Ted take it to be pretty likely that it will rain. This is a kind of disagreement, though it is not the first thing one thinks of when one thinks of disagreement. The disagreement between the atheist and the agnostic is also of this kind.

Or consider the following (Huvenes 2012: 171 n. 7):

(5)   Pierre: The hypothesis is false.
        Marie: I disagree, we need to do further testing.

Here Marie seems to be disagreeing with Pierre, even though what Pierre has said is not incompatible with anything she believes. (She may think Pierre's claim is more likely than not to be true.) We can understand the disagreement in terms of noncotenability. In asserting that the hypothesis is false, Pierre has expressed a high degree of confidence that it is false. This confidence is not cotenable with Marie's attitudes, which warrant a lower degree of confidence pending further tests.

We can also have noncotenability of nondoxastic attitudes, like desires, likings, or preferences. Suppose that Jane likes Bob, but Sarah hates him. In a perfectly respectable sense, Jane disagrees with Sarah, even if she believes all the same things about Bob. She does not disagree with Sarah about whether *p*, for any *p*, but she disagrees with Sarah *about Bob*, since Sarah's attitude towards Bob is not cotenable with hers. In this case, the incoherence that would result if she adopted it would not be inconsistency, but a kind of practical incoherence: the incoherence one suffers when one likes and hates the same thing. In the same sense, two kids might disagree about licorice, one wanting to eat it, the other being repulsed by it. There need not be any

disagrees with Sammurabi's belief that Hesperus is visible in virtue of believing that Phosphorus is not visible. One solution is to adopt a conception of contents, and of compatibility, on which *Hesperus is visible* is compatible with *Phosphorus is not visible*. Another is to require not just that the beliefs be incompatible, but that it be possible to come to know that they are so without further empirical investigation.

proposition they differ about for them to disagree about licorice. It is enough if they just have different attitudes towards licorice.

So, noncotenability is a kind of disagreement. As we will see, however, it is not the only kind of disagreement we can make sense of. And it is not the kind of disagreement that distinguishes relativism from contextualism.[7]

6.3   Preclusion of joint satisfaction

Does Jane and Sarah's difference in attitude towards Bob really amount to a disagreement? It does seem natural to say that they disagree in their attitude towards Bob. But perhaps that is rather thin. A disagreement, we might think, is a kind of conflict or dispute. To disagree with someone is not just to have a different attitude, but to be in a state of tension that can only be resolved by one or both parties *changing* their minds. Mere practical noncotenability does not always give us that. If Jane would rather be with Bob than with anyone else, and Bob would rather be with Jane than with anyone else, then their attitudes are not practically cotenable, but they seem to be in a happy state of concord.

We might, then, want to think about disagreement in attitude in a some-what different way, following C. L. Stevenson:

This occurs when Mr. A has a favorable attitude to something, when Mr. B has an unfavorable or less favorable attitude to it, and *when neither is content to let the other's attitude remain unchanged.* (Stevenson 1963: 1, emphasis added)

This won't quite do if we're trying to explicate the "state" sense of disagreement, which is not supposed to depend on the parties' attitudes towards each other. But Stevenson later recharacterizes "disagreement in attitude" in terms that are more suitable for our purposes:

The difference between the two senses of "disagreement" is essentially this: the first involves an opposition of beliefs, both of which cannot be true, and the second involves an opposition of attitudes, both of which cannot be satisfied. (2)

I disagree with someone's attitude, on this account, if its satisfaction precludes satisfaction of my own. Call this sense of disagreement *preclusion of joint satisfaction.*

---

[7] Kölbel (2004b: 305), defending a kind of truth relativism, says that two parties disagree if one could not rationally accept what the other says without changing her mind. If we understand "accept what the other says" as "come to believe what the other says," as seems natural, then this amounts to doxastic noncotenability. We will see below that there are certain contextualist positions that can secure disagreement in this sense, but fall short of securing the more robust kind of disagreement the relativist aims to capture.

Whether two attitudes are cotenable depends only on their forces and their contents. But whether they can both be satisfied depends also on the contexts in which they occur (for example, on who has them and when). As a result, preclusion of joint satisfaction and noncotenability can come apart.

Here is an example. There is a cupcake on the table. Alvin and Melvin both want to eat it. They both have a desire with the content *to eat that cupcake*. Their desires are the same in force and content, hence cotenable. Yet clearly they cannot be jointly satisfied; the cupcake can only be eaten by one of them.

Meg and Peg are also looking at the cupcake. Meg desires to eat the frosting only. Peg desires to eat the cake part only. Their desires have different contents and are not cotenable. (Desiring to eat the frosting only and to eat the cake part only is practically incoherent.) However, it is perfectly easy for both desires to be satisfied.

I have assumed here a certain view about the content of desires. Desires are naturally attributed with infinitival complements: one desires to ϕ, for some ϕ.[8] I take it, then, that the content of a desire is the kind of thing that is expressed by such a complement: presumably, a property, or perhaps a centered proposition (which has truth values relative to a world, a time, and an agent as "center").

If we said instead that, in the first example, the content of Alvin's desire is *that Alvin eat the cupcake* and the content of Melvin's is *that Melvin eat the cupcake*, then the example would no longer distinguish contenability from preclusion of joint satisfaction, because the two attitudes would not be cotenable. Similarly, if we said in the second example that the content of Meg's desire is *that Meg eat the frosting only* and the content of Peg's desire is *that Peg eat the cake part only*, then the two attitudes would be cotenable. So if one insisted that the contents of all desires are uncentered propositions, the distinction between practical noncotenability and preclusion of joint satisfaction would become purely notional, at least in the case of desirings-to-do. (It is far from clear how the strategy could be extended to attitudes like *preferring Jane's company to anyone else's*.)

This is not the place to settle a dispute about the contents of desires. But the controversy here provides no reason to resist distinguishing between practical noncotenability and preclusion of joint satisfaction. Even if it turns out that

---

[8]We can also say that someone desires an object—a cookie, a prize, an outcome, a person. I assume that these desire attributions are to be understood in terms of desire attributions with infinitival complements. To desire a cookie is to desire to eat it, or to have it.

the two notions are necessarily equivalent, so that the distinction between them is merely notional, that wouldn't show that the distinction is pointless.

6.4 Preclusion of joint accuracy

The point made in the last section can be generalized from the practical to the doxastic. As we saw, whether a desire is satisfied depends not just on its content but on its context (for example, on who has it and when). Similarly, whether a belief is accurate depends not just on its content but on its context.

The point can be seen easily if we countenance beliefs with centered propositions as their contents. A centered proposition, recall, is a proposition that has truth values relative to a world and a "center" (a distinguished point of view in the world, usually represented by a time and a location or individual). So, for example, there is a centered proposition *I am eating a sandwich* that is true at a world/time/individual triple $\langle w, t, i \rangle$ just in case i is eating a sandwich at t in w. Quite a few philosophers have suggested, for various purposes, that we broaden propositional attitude psychology to allow beliefs and other attitudes with centered propositions as their contents.[9]

Suppose, then, that Andy believes the centered proposition *I am eating a sandwich*, and that David believes its complement, the centered proposition *I am not eating a sandwich*. Clearly their beliefs are doxastically noncotenable; Andy could not come to have David's belief without giving up his own. But for all that, both of their beliefs might be accurate. For Andy's belief is accurate if Andy (the agent of its context) is eating a sandwich (at the time of its context), and David's is accurate if David is not eating a sandwich. If Andy but not David is eating a sandwich, then both beliefs are accurate.

That's a case where noncotenable beliefs are both accurate. It's also easy to imagine a case where cotenable beliefs preclude each others' accuracy. Suppose that at 2 p.m. Andy believes the centered proposition *I am eating a sandwich*, while at 3 p.m. David believes the centered proposition *Nobody was eating a sandwich an hour ago*. Clearly the accuracy of Andy's belief precludes the accuracy of David's, and vice versa. However, their beliefs are doxastically cotenable: David could coherently come to believe the centered proposition *I am eating a sandwich* without ceasing to believe *Nobody was eating a sandwich an hour ago*, and Andy could coherently believe *Nobody was eating a sandwich an hour ago* without ceasing to believe *I am eating a sandwich*.

---

[9]Lewis (1979a), who originated this approach, talks instead of beliefs as the self-ascriptions of properties, but the distinction seems mostly terminological. See ch. 4 n. 1, this volume.

Although we can concede that doxastic noncotenability is a kind of disagreement, we can now see that it is not going to give us everything we might have wanted in a notion of disagreement. For, in at least one sense of disagreement that we care deeply about, when two people disagree in virtue of having certain beliefs, those beliefs cannot both be accurate. If two people disagree, they can't both be right. Similarly, if they agree, it can't be that one's belief is accurate and the other's inaccurate.

We have, then, another variety of disagreement. To disagree with someone's attitude, in this sense, is to have attitudes the accuracy of which would preclude its accuracy.[10]

I am not going to try to spell out more precisely what I mean by "preclude"; instead, I'll rely on an intuitive grasp. Though it is initially tempting to give a modal analysis of "the accuracy of A precludes the accuracy of B"—perhaps as "it is impossible for B to be accurate if A is"—this will not work. For whenever it is impossible for B to be accurate, it will be true that it is impossible for B to be accurate if A is. But in such a case it would be wrong to say that the accuracy of A *precludes* the accuracy of B. Although it is difficult to say what preclusion amounts to in other terms, I think we have a tolerable grasp of the notion (otherwise we would not be so confident about the counterexamples we can easily construct to various modal explications).[11]

I have used "accuracy" in an informal way, but one can say precisely how it is related to the various relativized notions of truth we have looked at in Chapters 3–5. An attitude or speech act has a content, and this content can be properly said to be true or false. But the same content can be true relative to one circumstance of evaluation and false relative to another. To say that the attitude or speech act is accurate is, roughly, to say that it is true relative to the circumstance that matters. In the case of attitudes with centered contents, this is usually taken to be the world, time, and agent of the context. So although I now take the content believed by David yesterday— the centered proposition *I am eating a sandwich*—to be false, I take David's

[10]Note that the disagreement between the atheist and the agnostic cannot be understood in this way. Even if the atheist is right, that doesn't make the agnostic's suspension of belief inaccurate.

[11]Although it is difficult to define preclusion, one can begin to elucidate the notion through its formal properties, as Lee Walters suggested to me. Preclusion is anti-reflexive (A can't preclude itself), symmetric (if A precludes B, B precludes A), and monotonic (if A precludes B, then the combination of A and C precludes B). In addition, whether A precludes B seems to depend on what the *subject matter* of A and B is. Hence, in seeking a more precise account, one might look to theories of subject matters (for example, Lewis 1988).

belief yesterday to have been accurate, since its content is true at the triple ⟨actual world, yesterday, David⟩. In this case, to say that a belief or assertion is accurate is to say that its content is true relative to its context. More generally, allowing for assessment sensitivity:

Accuracy. *An attitude or speech act occurring at c_1 is* accurate, *as assessed from a context c_2, just in case its content is true as used at c_1 and assessed from c_2.*

The distinction between truth and accuracy doesn't matter much when we're considering whether to assert or believe something ourselves. For in that case it will be correct to judge the assertion or belief accurate just in case it is correct to judge its content true (in the monadic sense, §4.8). But the distinction matters a great deal when we are considering the speech acts and attitudes of others, or our own earlier speech acts and attitudes. A past assertion need not be retracted if it was accurate, even if its content is one we now take to be false. Conversely, it ought to be retracted if it was inaccurate, even if its content is one we now take to be true.

In prying apart doxastic noncotenability and preclusion of joint accuracy, I have appealed to examples involving nonstandard contents, like centered propositions. So someone who held to a steady diet of regular, non-centered, non-tensed propositions might question the need for distinguishing the two varieties of disagreement. To such a question, I would respond as before: even if the distinction is merely notional, it seems harmless to recognize it. What is more, failure to recognize it can lead to equivocation in arguments from premises about disagreement to conclusions about propositions. For example, Cappelen and Hawthorne (2009: 96–8) argue more or less as follows:[12]

(a) Two parties disagree if there is a proposition that one believes and the other disbelieves.

(b) Suppose that tensed propositions can be the contents of beliefs.

(c) Then it should follow that if Bill believed, two days ago, the tensed proposition *It is raining in Boston*, and Janet disbelieved the same tensed proposition two weeks ago, they disagreed.

(d) But this pattern of attitudes does not constitute disagreement.

(e) So, by reductio, tensed propositions cannot be the contents of beliefs.

Once we have distinguished between disagreement as doxastic noncotenability and disagreement as preclusion of joint accuracy, we can see that this

---

[12]I have modified the argument to concern disagreement rather than agreement.

argument has no force against the temporalist. If tensed propositions *can* be the contents of beliefs, then premise (a) is only true if "disagree" is taken in the first sense, while (d) is only true if "disagree" is taken in the second sense.

Arguably, a need for the distinction between doxastic noncotenability and preclusion of joint accuracy can be seen even if we countenance only eternalist propositions, which have truth values relative to possible worlds. Consider Jane, in this world (the one we call "actual"), and June, in another possible world. Jane believes that Mars has two moons, and June believes Mars has just one moon. Both of their beliefs are accurate, since in June's world Mars does have just one moon. Does Jane disagree with this belief of June's?

In a way, yes. Jane could not adopt the attitude June would have without giving up her own belief. But also, in a way, no. Borrowing some terminology from Perry (1986), we might say that although neither belief is *about* any particular world, Jane's belief *concerns* our world, while June's concerns hers, and both beliefs are accurate.[13] In at least one important sense of "disagree," two beliefs that are both accurate cannot be said to disagree. The situation here is analogous to the situation with centered propositions believed by different agents at different times.

One might worry that the argument here hinges on "realist" talk of worlds—talk that makes relations between possible situations look more like relations between times than perhaps they should. But perhaps we do not need the apparatus of worlds. We can ask directly whether June, believing what she actually does, is in disagreement with the belief state June *would have* been in in the imagined counterfactual situation. Note that the question is *not* whether Jane disagrees with what June would have believed.[14] That question concerns a relation between June and a content and force, but we can't settle questions of accuracy unless *contexts* are also in play. The question, then, is whether Jane disagrees with a counterfactual attitude-in-context June might have had—one that she acknowledges would have been accurate given its context.

It seems to me that the answer should be no (in at least one good sense of disagreement). I concede, though, that it is difficult to have any stable intuitions about the case, so I do not want to rest too much weight on this argument.

[13]See §4.5.2, this volume.

[14]I mistakenly put it this way in MacFarlane (2007a), and Cappelen and Hawthorne (2009: ch. 2, §17) rightly called me on it.

6.5   Preclusion of joint reflexive accuracy

There is still a further distinction to be made. In order to motivate it, though, we will need to review the difference between objectivist, nonindexical contextualist, and relativist accounts of taste propositions.

Unlike standard (indexical) contextualism, all three of these accounts are happy to countenance beliefs with the content *that licorice is tasty*—not *tasty to Yum*, or *to us*, or *to most people*, but just *tasty*. But they differ in what they say about the intension of this proposition, and about what it takes for a belief with this content to be accurate.

The objectivist says that the proposition has a standard possible-worlds intension. If we specify a state of the world, then there will be an answer to the question whether the proposition would be true were things that way. And a belief or assertion with this content is accurate just in case it takes place in a world relative to which the proposition is true.

The nonindexical contextualist and the relativist both say that the proposition has a non-standard intension: it has truth values relative to worlds and *tastes*. So even if we specify a state of the world, there is no saying whether the proposition is true until we specify the relevant taste.

The two views diverge, however, in what they say about the *accuracy* of beliefs and assertions with such contents. The nonindexical contextualist says that an assertion or belief occurring in a context c is accurate if its content is true relative to the world of c and the taste of the agent of c (the asserter or believer). So, Yum and Yuk may believe incompatible taste propositions, and both their beliefs may be accurate, because they have different tastes.

The relativist, on the other hand, denies that accuracy is an absolute matter. A belief or assertion in c can only be said to be accurate relative to a context of assessment: it is accurate, as assessed from a context c', just in case its content is true at the world of c and the taste of the agent of c' (the assessor). If Yum and Yuk believe incompatible taste propositions, then, there will be no context of assessment relative to which both beliefs are accurate.

Both the relativist and the objectivist, then, will say that disagreements about what is tasty involve preclusion of joint accuracy. At least this is so if by "preclusion of joint accuracy" we mean

Preclusion of joint accuracy.   *The accuracy of my attitudes (as assessed from any context) precludes the accuracy of your attitude or speech act (as assessed from that same context).*

However, there is another way in which we might generalize the notion of preclusion of joint accuracy, which distinguishes the relativist from the objectivist:

Preclusion of joint reflexive accuracy.   *The accuracy of my attitudes (as assesssed from my context) precludes the accuracy of your attitude or speech act (as assessed from your context).*

On a relativist account, when two people have incompatible beliefs about whether something is tasty, joint accuracy is precluded, but joint reflexive accuracy is not. Yum's belief may be accurate as assessed from her context, while Yuk's is accurate as assessed from his. For the relativist, then, preclusion of joint accuracy and preclusion of joint reflexive accuracy come apart. For the objectivist, by contrast, they coincide, because accuracy is absolute. A belief is accurate as assessed from one believer's context just in case it is accurate as assessed from the other's.

The relativist, then, need not claim to be vindicating disagreement in all the same senses as the objectivist is. She can acknowledge that, in some respects, disagreement about taste is less robust than paradigm objective disagreements, which do preclude joint reflexive accuracy.

6.6   Disagreement in disputes of taste

Enough distinguishing! Recall our strategy. Instead of posing the problem in a binary way—is there "real disagreement" between Yum and Yuk, and if so, can the relativist account capture it?—the idea was to ask which of the varieties of disagreement we have distinguished are present in the dispute between Yum and Yuk, and which semantic theories allow for these. So, let's go to it.

We certainly have practical noncotenability. Yuk has an attitude towards licorice that Yum cannot coherently take on board herself without changing her own attitudes towards licorice. Even if Yum does not disagree with anything Yuk *believes*, then, there may be reason for them to argue. Yum may want to change Yuk's attitude about licorice, making it congruent with her own, and to do this she may try to call Yuk's attention to various salient facts about the licorice. These facts will play a role much like that of premises in an argument, except that their intended effect is not a change of belief but a change in taste.

Explaining how there can be disputes about matters of taste, then, does not seem to require that there are disagreements of taste in any sense stronger than practical noncotenability. And every theory of meaning for taste predicates predicts that we will have at least this. On expressivist accounts, Yum's and Yuk's speech acts are nothing more than expressions of their noncotenable attitudes towards licorice. But contextualists, too, can make use of practical noncotenability to explain disagreements of taste. For although according to the contextualist, Yum and Yuk have *asserted* compatible contents, in doing so they have expressed their noncotenable attitudes of liking and hating licorice, respectively. Indeed, even if Yum had said "I like this" and Yuk had said "Well, I hate it," they could be said to disagree.

However, some of the ways in which Yuk might naturally express his disagreement with Yum seem to require something beyond practical non-cotenability. First, there's the word "No" in "No, it's not tasty at all." "No" would be quite infelicitous, I think, with explicit self-avowals of attitude:

(6) Yum: I like this.
    Yuk: No, I don't like it.

Second, Yuk could naturally express his disagreement using devices of propositional anaphora:

(7) I don't believe that!
    What you're saying is false!
    I can't accept that.

This is hard to explain unless Yuk takes himself to disagree with what Yum has asserted, or with a belief Yum thereby expresses. It seems to require not just practical but doxastic noncotenability. And it is hard to see how standard contextualist or expressivist accounts are going to get that.

One interesting avenue for the contextualist, explored by de Sa (2008), is to suppose that in cases like that of Yum and Yuk, one or both speakers is presupposing that they do not have relevantly different tastes. If Yuk is presupposing that Yum's tastes are like his, then the belief expressed by Yum's claim, on the contextualist account—Yum's belief that licorice tastes good to her—*is not* doxastically co-tenable with Yuk's attitudes: Yuk could take it on board only by rejecting his belief that Yum's tastes are like his.

The problem with this approach is that it just isn't plausible to suppose that the presupposition of shared taste is in place in all cases of disagreement about matters of taste. Let it be mutually known by Yum and Yuk that their tastes in foods tend to be very different. The dialogue with which we began still sounds natural, and it still looks like a disagreement.

Perhaps a better approach for the contextualist is to retreat to a nonindexical version of contextualism. On such a view, there is a single proposition, the proposition *that licorice is tasty*, which Yum believes and Yuk disbelieves, but whether this proposition is true at a context of use depends on the tastes of the agent of the context.[15] This approach would retain the key contextualist idea that the accuracy of Yuk's belief about the tastiness of licorice depends on Yuk's tastes, while the accuracy of Yum's belief depends on Yum's tastes. But it would secure doxastic noncotenability, since it would take Yum's and Yuk's beliefs to have incompatible intensions. Even though Yuk could acknowledge that Yum's belief is accurate, he could not regard its content as true,[16] and he could not come to believe what Yum believes without giving up a belief of his own. This would be enough to vindicate responses like those in (7).

Can we stop here? Although nonindexical contextualism does predict doxastic noncotenability, it does not secure preclusion of joint accuracy, since it allows that Yum's and Yuk's beliefs, despite their incompatible contents, can both be accurate. Relativism, by contrast, secures preclusion of joint accuracy, since from any given context of assessment, a single taste (the taste of the assessor) is relevant to the accuracy of all beliefs about what is tasty. As assessed from Yum's context, her belief is accurate and Yuk's is inaccurate, while as assessed from Yuk's context, his belief is accurate and Yum's is inaccurate. Do we have any reason to suppose that disputes of taste, like the one between Yum and Yuk, involve preclusion of joint accuracy?

The matter is delicate. But things tip in favor of relativism if the parties to such disagreements think of themselves not just as trying to change the other party's attitudes, but as trying to *refute* them—where the sign of successful refutation is not just that the other party now holds the content of her original claim to be false, but that she retracts her original assertion as inaccurate.

Disputes of taste do seem to have this flavor. If Yuk eventually gets Yum to dislike the taste of licorice, Yum will feel pressure to withdraw her earlier assertion that it is tasty. In this respect, disputes of taste are like disputes about any objective matter—for example, the age of the earth.

---

[15]Compare the account of "beautiful" discussed in §4.6.

[16]Cf. MacFarlane (2009: §7).

In another respect, though, they are not much like disputes about paradigm objective matters. For Yuk can only compel Yum to retract her assertion by, so to speak, changing Yum's perspective—bringing it about that Yum occupies a context of assessment that differs in semantically relevant ways from the one she occupied before. For, as long as Yum persists in her liking for licorice, the relativist account predicts, she is warranted in standing by her original assertion (even if it is inaccurate from Yuk's perspective). As long as what she asserted remains true as assessed from her current context, she need not retract. In cases of maximally robust disagreement, by contrast, retraction can be compelled (when it can be compelled at all) without any change of perspective. The very same facts that show a claim to be false as assessed from one perspective will suffice to show it false as assessed from any other.

By distinguishing between preclusion of joint accuracy and preclusion of joint reflexive accuracy, we can mark this difference. I think that in disputes of taste we can find the former but not the latter.

6.7 On "faultless disagreement"

Some recent advocates of truth relativism—most prominently Kölbel (2004a, 2002, 2008a)—have argued that disputes of taste are characterized by "faultless disagreement," and that only the relativist can explain how faultless disagreement is possible. I have avoided using this phrase here, because it is dangerously ambiguous. Both "faultless" and "disagreement" can be understood in several ways, and how we understand them matters greatly for the plausibility of "faultless disagreement" and its significance for the debate about relative truth.

We have already discussed some possible senses of "disagreement." The ones that will matter most for us here will be

disagreement$_n$ doxastic noncotenability

disagreement$_p$ preclusion of joint accuracy

What about "faultless"? What is it for a belief or assertion to be faultless? Here are four possibilities:

faultless$_w$ epistemically warranted

faultless$_t$ true

faultless$_a$ accurate

faultless$_n$ not in violation of constitutive norms governing belief/assertion

Now, what of the claim that faultless disagreement is possible? Clearly faultless$_w$ disagreement is possible, no matter what we mean by "disagreement." Two people can hold contradictory but equally warranted beliefs about a perfectly objective subject matter—say, the age of the earth—if one of them has misleading evidence.

Faultless$_t$ disagreement is not possible on either construal of "disagreement." If you can coherently characterize another's belief as "true" (using the monadic propositional truth predicate), then you could come to have a belief with the same content without giving up any of your current beliefs, so the other's attitude is doxastically cotenable with your own. It is not coherent to say, "I disagree with you about that, but what you believe is true." (I suspect that many opponents of truth relativism take its goal to be vindicating faultless disagreement in this sense. Clearly *that* is not a viable goal.)

Faultless$_a$ disagreement$_p$ is not possible. To say that joint accuracy is precluded is to say that at least one of the disagreeing attitudes must be at fault in the sense of being inaccurate.

However, faultless$_a$ disagreement$_n$ *is* possible. As we have seen, on a nonindexical contextualist treatment of "tasty," Yum's and Yuk's beliefs can both be accurate, even though they are not doxastically cotenable.

Assuming, as we have been, that the norms governing assertion and belief are keyed to accuracy relative to the asserter's or believer's context of assessment, faultless$_n$ disagreement$_p$ is possible. Preclusion of joint accuracy means that there is no single context of assessment relative to which both beliefs or assertions are accurate. But it may be that the beliefs or assertions are both reflexively accurate—that is, both accurate as assessed by those who hold them. So it may be that both satisfy the relevant norms.

There are, then, at least three coherent, but very different, ways to construe relativists' claim that there is "faultless disagreement" in disputes of taste. (For a summary, see Table 6.1.) First, the claim might be that both parties in such a dispute can be *warranted* in holding the views they do. Of course, this general phenomenon—disagreeing views, both of which are justified or warranted—is hardly distinctive of relativism. But it could be that truth relativism is needed to explain how the considerations the disagreeing parties take to warrant their claims could possibly do so. Why, in particular, should people regard their own subjective reactions as sufficient warrant for claims about what is tasty (cf. §1.1)?

Second, the claim might be that two parties who hold contradictory beliefs might both be "getting it right," in the sense that their beliefs are accurate. If this is the point, then the view supported is nonindexical contextualism, and the kind of disagreement at stake is doxastic noncotenability.

Third, the claim might be that two parties whose beliefs or assertions preclude each others' accuracy are both succeeding in living up to the norms governing the formation and retention of beliefs and the making and retracting of assertions. This is predicted by the kind of truth relativism we have been articulating in these pages—a truth relativism that countenances genuine assessment sensitivity and makes sense of it by relating truth at a context of assessment to norms governing belief and assertion. From Yuk's point of view, Yum's assertion that the licorice is tasty is inaccurate. But Yuk can agree that Yum has succeeded in conforming her assertions to the Reflexive Truth Rule (§5.3), which only forbids Yum from asserting things that are inaccurate as assessed from her own perspective, and the Retraction Rule (§5.4), which only requires her to retract assertions that are inaccurate as assessed from her current perspective.

TABLE 6.1. Can there be "faultless disagreement" about matters of taste?

Sense of "faultless"	w	w	t	t	a	a	n	n
Sense of "disagreement"	n	p	n	p	n	p	n	p
Standard contextualism	✓	✓						
Nonindexical contextualism	✓	✓			✓	✓		
Relativism	✓	✓			✓		✓	✓
Objectivism	✓	✓						

Kölbel's official definition of "faultless disagreement" does not by itself discriminate between these three construals:

A faultless disagreement is a situation where there is a thinker *A*, a thinker *B*, and a proposition (content of judgement) *p*, such that:

(a) *A* believes (judges) that *p* and *B* believes (judges) that not-*p*
(b) Neither *A* nor *B* has made a mistake (is at fault). (Kölbel 2004a: 53–4)

As we have seen, condition (a) is too weak to capture preclusion of joint accuracy, so the notion of disagreement at stake here seems to be doxastic noncotenability. And the talk of "mistake" in condition (b) is too generic to select between the various interpretations of "faultlessness" considered above. However, Kölbel's subsequent commentary points strongly towards construing "faultless" as *faultless$_n$*, and hence towards the third construal above. He endorses the principle

TR. *It is a mistake to believe a proposition that is not true in one's own perspective*

(Kölbel 2004a: 70), which closely resembles our Reflexive Truth Norm (§5.3). (He does not state the additional norm governing retraction that would be required to distinguish relativism from nonindexical contextualism.) So it seems that the "mistakes" he has in mind are violations of constitutive norms, and not (say) violations of epistemic norms.

If by "faultless disagreement" Kölbel means faultless$_n$ disagreement$_n$, then we can agree that the notion is coherent, even if it is not distinctive of truth relativism in the sense used here. But it is all too easy to give "faultless disagreement" other construals—including construals on which it is incoherent. For example, when Richard (2008: ch. 5) argues that a truth-relativist view makes faultless disagreement about matters of taste impossible, he assumes that regarding another's view as false rules out regarding it as "faultless." But this is not so if "faultless" means *faultless$_n$* (see MacFarlane 2012). If one does not want to be misunderstood, it is best to avoid the phrase "faultless disagreement" entirely. It is not needed for motivating or explaining truth relativism.

6.8 Conclusion

Disagreement is the crux of debates between relativists, objectivists, and contextualists. Objectivism accounts for the disagreement we feel in disputes of taste, at the cost of imputing implausible kinds of error and chauvinism to speakers; contextualism avoids chauvinism at the cost of losing the disagreement. Relativism, it is alleged, does better than objectivism because it avoids imputing error and chauvinism, and better than contextualism because it vindicates our intuitions of disagreement.

But if the question is posed in a binary, all-or-nothing way—does relativism allow that disputes of tastes are genuine disagreements, or does it not?—it tends to generate conflicting answers. It is common for objectivists to balk at accepting the relativist's claim to vindicate genuine disagreement about matters of taste. After all, on the relativist views, aren't both parties right from their own perspectives? And doesn't that show that it isn't *really* disagreement at all? On the other hand, it is common for contextualists to balk at the relativist's claim that there *is* genuine disagreement about matters of taste.

By distinguishing varieties of disagreement, we can sharpen up the question and explain why the original question provokes such disparate answers. The question is not whether there is "genuine" disagreement about matters of taste, but rather which of the varieties of disagreement we have distinguished characterizes disagreements of taste. And the main kinds of account we have considered can be defined by the answers they give to this question. In the case we were evaluating, standard contextualism and expressivism secure only practical noncotenability; nonindexical contextualism secures doxastic noncotenability; relativism secures preclusion of joint accuracy; and objectivism secures preclusion of joint reflexive accuracy.

Evaluating the case for relativism about predicates of taste, then, does not require settling what kinds of disagreement are "genuine," an issue that seems merely terminological. It just requires determining whether disputes of taste are characterized by preclusion of joint accuracy, for example, or just by doxastic noncotenability. And we can do this by considering the diagnostics outlined above for these varieties of disagreement.

These considerations show that the relativist can use disagreement as the crux of an argument against the contextualist, while still conceding to the objectivist that there are ways in which the kind of disagreement vindicated by the relativist account falls short of the kind of disagreement one finds about paradigm matters of objective fact. Indeed, the relativist can claim to have found a comfortable middle ground between the objectivist position, which attributes to disputes of taste more robust disagreement than there actually is, and the contextualist position, which does not find enough disagreement.

PART II

APPLICATIONS

7

TASTY

At the end of Chapter 1, we were left with the following desiderata for an account of the meaning of "tasty":

1. *Generality.* Our account should explain the contribution "tasty" makes, not just to simple sentences, but to all of the sentences in which it can occur.

2. *Assertion conditions.* Our account should explain why speakers who know first-hand how something tastes are warranted in calling something tasty just in case its flavor is pleasing to them (*TP*).

3. *Retraction conditions.* Our account should explain why speakers will retract (rather than stand by) an earlier assertion that something was tasty, if the flavor the thing had at the time of the assertion is not pleasing to their *present* tastes—even if it was pleasing to the tastes they had then.

4. *Disagreement.* Our account should explain how there can be genuine disagreements about whether something is tasty, even when both parties have first-hand knowledge of its flavor and know that its flavor is pleasing to one of them but not the other.

5. *Expression of attitude.* Our account should explain why, in calling something tasty, one expresses one's liking for its flavor.

I argued that none of the standard options for a theory of the meaning of "tasty"—objectivism, contextualism, and classical expressivism—secures all of these desiderata, although each secures some of them. I suggested that a relativist account could meet all of the desiderata, but at the time we did not have the conceptual machinery in place to vindicate this claim, or even state the view precisely. Now we are in a position to do better.

In §7.1 I will describe what a relativist account would say about simple, standalone sentences like "That licorice is tasty," abstracting from compositional details. We will see how the relativist account forges a kind of middle ground between objectivist and contextualist accounts, preserving what is correct in each. Next (§7.2) we will consider how to construct a compositional semantics that generates truth conditions for these simple sentences, as well as complex sentences in which "tasty" occurs embedded under truth-functional operators, attitude verbs, quantifiers, temporal modifiers, and modals. Finally (§7.3) we will see how Allan Gibbard's sophisticated modern version of expressivism might be extended to an account of "tasty" that includes a compositional semantics much like that in §7.2. The aim here will be to see why the Gibbard-inspired view, despite its many points of similarity with the relativist account, still counts as a form of expressivism, and to identify the substantive differences between it and the relativist view.

7.1   A relativist account

Since our main purpose here is to illustrate what is distinctive about a relativist account of "tasty," we will abstract from certain complexities that would have to be faced in a full treatment. A more complete account would have to explain the fact that "tasty" is synonymous with "tastes good," which is itself semantically complex. Assuming that "tastes good" is assessment-sensitive, is its assessment sensitivity due to "tastes," to "good," or to both in combination? In answering this question, one would have to look very generally at evaluative adjectives ("good," "bad," "strange") and at sensory appearance verbs ("tastes," "looks," "feels"). One might conclude that all evaluative adjectives are assessment-sensitive, or that all sensory appearance verbs are assessment-sensitive. But it could also turn out that the assessment sensitivity of "tastes good" arises from the *interaction* of appearance verbs with evaluative predicates. I do not currently know how to resolve these interesting questions, but their import is considerable. If assessment sensitivity is a feature of all evaluative terms, for example, then we would be committed to a relativist semantics for moral terms.

Second, we will not try to resolve thorny questions about the proper bearers of the property of being tasty. I will write as if the extension of this property at a circumstance of evaluation is a set of edible things—licorice, for example, or Joe's chili, or this apple in front of me. But that seems too simplistic. Suppose that Ali and Ben are both drinking from a particular bottle of Muscatel, but Ali is drinking it with dessert, while Ben is drinking it with a steak. Ali might judge the wine tasty, while Ben might find it horrible, its sweetness clashing badly with the taste of the steak.[1] This difference in judgment need

---

[1] I am grateful to Dirk Kindermann for getting me to think about this case.

not indicate any difference in their tastes, or in the flavor of the wine they are drinking. Nor does it seem that they are really in disagreement. Reflecting on this case, it is tempting to say that what is really tasty (or not) is not the wine, but something like a wine-in-context: the wine as accompaniment to steak, or as accompaniment to dessert. Alternatively, one might say that what is really tasty (or not) is not the wine, but its *flavor*, which can vary depending on what one is eating and smelling while drinking it. This would motivate a certain degree of contextualism about "tasty," since context would help fix which of the possible flavors a food can have is being called "tasty" on a particular occasion. But it would be consistent with a relativist account of "tasty" as applied to flavors. In any case, we will not explore these issues here; in this chapter, we will proceed as if the foods we discuss each have a single flavor at a given world and time.

Third, as we observed in Chapter 1, it seems inappropriate to call something "tasty" unless one has first-hand knowledge of its taste. A full account of the meaning of "tasty" ought to explain this feature of "tasty," which is arguably shared by other terms of aesthetic evaluation. The account given here does not do that.

Think of what follows as a simple, first-pass model of the meaning of "tasty," detailed enough to show how it differs from more familiar objectivist, contextualist, and expressivist models, and detailed enough to illustrate a number of interesting semantic issues.

7.1.1 *Tastes*

We will need the notion of a *taste*. The notion is the familiar one we use when we say that different people have "different tastes," or accuse someone of having "crude taste," or praise someone for having "good taste"—though we will focus only on the gustatory aspects of taste. I take it that a taste is a kind of *standard*—a gustatory standard—and I will sometimes use that label instead of "taste." Talk of a standard can suggest something intellectual: a set of principles the agent uses in assessing whether something is tasty. Nothing like that is intended here. Think of a standard, rather, as something that determines a scale. The International Prototype Kilogram in Sèvres, France is, in this sense, a standard for weight—the "standard kilogram." One's tastes, too, serve as a gustatory standard, quite independently of whether one can articulate this standard. It is possible that our gustatory standards depend to a significant degree on brute physiological differences, though they are also shaped greatly by our experiences with food.

Our tastes do not remain constant. They change as we experience new things, and even without experience, they can depend on our transient emotional states. I will assume that it makes sense to talk of an agent's taste *in a context*. More generally, one might want to talk of the taste that is *relevant* in a context. This is usually the taste of the agent of the context (the person who would be denoted by an occurrence of "I" in the context), but it might, in certain contexts, be some other taste—say, the taste shared by a contextually relevant group.

For the purposes of our semantics, we need not say much more about the metaphysics of tastes: for example, about what makes it the case that someone has a particular taste, or how tastes differ from each other. But I do want to insist on an analytic connection between one's tastes and what flavors one *likes*. Roughly: if one knows a flavor and likes it, then that flavor is evaluated positively by one's tastes; if one dislikes it, then that flavor is evaluated negatively by one's tastes; and if one neither likes nor dislikes it, then the flavor is evaluated neutrally by one's tastes. I don't think we can make much sense of the idea that a person might have a taste for overripe peaches but not like them, or love the flavor of licorice but not have a taste for it.

7.1.2   *A relativist account*

On a simple contextualist view,

(1)   This is tasty

is true, as used at a context c and assessed from any context, just in case the flavor of the referent of "this" at the time and world of c is evaluated positively by the taste of the agent of c (the speaker). On a simple relativist view, by contrast, (1) is true, as used at a context c and assessed from a context c', just in case the flavor of the referent of "this" at the time and world of c is evaluated positively by the taste of the agent of c' (the assessor).[2]

Note that both the context of use and the context of assessment play a role in the relativist account. The context of assessment tells us which taste to use

---

[2]Both the contextualist and the relativist view might be made more flexible by talking of the "taste relevant at a context" rather than the "taste of the agent of the context"—leaving room for special cases in which the relevant taste is not the taste of the agent of the context. To keep things simple, we will ignore this refinement here.

as a standard for evaluating flavors, but the context of use determines which flavor is to be evaluated: the flavor the referent of "this" has at the time and world of the context of use. Suppose I asserted (1) of a plate of fresh pasta at noon. Three hours later, the pasta has hardened in the sun and is beginning to attract flies. Clearly, the changes in the flavor of the dish over the last three hours are not relevant to the accuracy of my original assertion. What matters is the flavor the dish had at the time I made the assertion; that's what the assertion was about, after all. Assuming my tastes have not changed, then, I should continue to regard my original assertion as accurate.

However, if my tastes have changed, so that they no longer positively evaluate the original flavor of the dish, then according to the relativist account I should no longer consider my original assertion accurate. It is here that the relativist account differs from a contextualist one. According to a contextualist account, I should continue to consider my original assertion accurate, since the dish was good according to the tastes I had when I made the assertion. The relativist account denies that my original tastes are relevant. My claim was about the flavor of the dish; it was not about the tastes I happened to have at the time, and did not concern them.[3]

We have said how the contextualist and relativist views differ in their assignments of truth conditions to (1). But what difference does this make in practice? How do the two accounts differ in their predictions about how speakers use sentences like (1)? Here we can appeal to Chapter 5's bridge principles linking assessment-relative truth to proprieties for assertion and retraction.

When we look at proprieties for *making* assertions, the two views do not seem to differ at all. According to the Reflexive Truth Rule (§5.3), an assertion is licensed if its content is true as used at and assessed from the context one occupies in making the assertion. Since the context of use coincides with the context of assessment in this case, the relativist and contextualist accounts will settle this issue in the same way. Both will say that (1) may be asserted if the demonstrated food has a flavor that is evaluated positively by the asserter's tastes at the time of the assertion.

To see the practical difference between the views, we need to look at proprieties for retraction. According to the Retraction Rule (§5.4), an assertion of (1) made at c must be retracted at c' if its content is untrue as used at c and

---

[3]For the distinction between *being about* and *concerning*, see §4.5.2.

assessed from c'. This condition will be met, according to the contextualist view, if the flavor the food had in c is not pleasing to the speaker's tastes at c. It will be met, according to the relativist view, if the flavor the food had in c is not pleasing to the assessor's tastes at c'. So, if the speaker's tastes have changed since she made the assertion, and the original flavor of the food is no longer pleasing to them, then the relativist view, but not the contextualist view, says that an earlier assertion of (1) must be retracted.

Looking back at our desiderata, then, the relativist view seems to satisfy *Assertion conditions* just as well as the contextualist view did. But it also satisfies *Retraction conditions*, as the contextualist view did not.

What about the fourth desideratum, *Disagreement*? Suppose Yum likes the flavor of the salient food, while Yuk dislikes it. Then the truth norm, together with the relativist semantics, implies that Yum may assert (1) and Yuk may assert its negation,

(2)   No, it is not tasty.

As assessed from any context, the accuracy of Yum's assertion precludes the accuracy of Yuk's, and vice versa. Thus we have the kind of disagreement we characterized in Chapter 6 as *preclusion of joint accuracy*. This is a disagreement that Yum and Yuk are unlikely to resolve, since that would require at least one of them to change their tastes. But suppose that after extended discussion and further experience, Yuk's tastes do change, and he comes to like the food. Then not only would Yuk change his mind, proclaiming that the food "is tasty," he would also feel compelled to retract his earlier assertion of (2), and Yum could take herself to have refuted him. All of these things are marks of disagreement of a more robust kind than contextualists can account for.[4]

The relativist account also satisfies the fifth desideratum, *Expression of attitude*. In asserting (1), a speaker performs an action that is mutually known to be correct only if her tastes approve of the flavor of the demonstrated food. Performing such an action thus gives others *pro tanto* reasons to think that the speaker likes the food in question and intends others to recognize this. In that sense it expresses the attitude of liking the food.[5] Indeed, like the classical expressivist view, and unlike the contextualist view, the relativist view allows

---

[4] As noted in §1.2.1, collective contextualism can explain *Disagreement*, but only at the cost of losing *Assertion conditions*.

[5] For this sense of expression, see Bach and Harnish (1979: 15, 58, 291).

us to say that the speaker expresses a liking for the food without *asserting* anything about her own tastes or attitudes.

Only one desideratum remains: *Generality*. Here the relativist view does not face any special problems; it fits into the framework of truth-conditional semantics, and can expect to use the same methods contextualist and objectivist views use to explain the contributions of embedded occurrences. But there are a number of interesting issues of detail that might be thought to make things harder for the relativist. So, in §7.2, we will look in detail at how a relativist might handle a number of constructions that can embed "tasty."

7.1.3 *Can an epicure be a relativist about taste?*

It is sometimes thought that a relativist about taste must hold that all possible tastes are "on a par," or that there is "no disputing tastes." I suspect that this belief is an important source of resistance to the relativist view. Those who care deeply about food and drink, seeking out fine examples of both and priding themselves on their discriminating tastes, cannot easily accept a view that implies that their tastes are no better than anyone else's.

However, the relativist view does not imply that. Indeed, in a certain way, the relativist view vindicates the epicure's attitude. If "better" means "more likely to favor flavors that are actually tasty," then a relativist cannot coherently regard anyone else's tastes as better than her own. For, to the extent that their tastes are different from hers, they will inevitably approve of flavors that are not tasty (as assessed from her own context).

The epicure will reply that this is a hollow vindication. Having good tastes is supposed to be an *achievement*, something one aspires to, not something that (from one's own perspective) is guaranteed trivially by the semantics of "tasty." It ought to be possible, the epicure will say, to see one's tastes as better than many, but still subject to improvement, and the relativist view may seem to rule this out.

But in fact, it is perfectly coherent for a relativist to acknowledge that others' tastes are "better" than her own, in many sense of "better." As we have seen, "better" here cannot mean "more accurate," or "more likely to favor flavors that are actually tasty," on pain of incoherence. But there are many other things one might mean in saying that one taste is "better" than another. It may be that people with more refined tastes derive more pleasure from food, care more about food, are more intellectually stimulated by food, and have better lives as a result. It may even be part of living a virtuous life, as Aristotle thought, to take pleasure in the right kinds of food and drink. It is not incoherent for a relativist to aspire to have tastes that are better along any of these dimensions, while recognizing her own tastes as the ones that determine whether she may correctly call something "tasty."[6]

An epicure, then, need not be an objectivist about "tasty." That is fortunate, because being an objectivist would require refraining from calling things tasty at all until one has reached the pinnacle of refinement, and deferring to others about which foods are tasty. That is not how we (even the epicures among us) use the word "tasty," and it is not a way that a word with the social role of "tasty" *could* be used.

7.2   Compositional semantics

It is one thing to give truth conditions for a few simple sentences "tasty," and quite another to show how these truth conditions fall out of a compositional semantics that also gives plausible truth conditions to indefinitely many sentences in which "tasty" occurs embedded under other constructions. To that task we now turn. "Tasty" is unlike some adjectives in allowing explicit relativization to a taster. We can say not just that the cookies are tasty, but that they are "tasty for kids" or "tasty to John." A compositional semantics for "tasty" ought to explain how these constructions work. It should also yield sensible predictions about embeddings of "tasty" under propositional attitude verbs ("Jill believes it is tasty"), quantifiers ("everyone got a tasty cookie"), tense modifiers ("it was tasty"), and modals ("it would be tasty"). All of these constructions raise interesting questions, and some have been used as the basis of arguments for contextualist treatments of "tasty," so it is important to explore what a relativist can say about them.

7.2.1   *Atomic formulas*

We'll build up our semantics bit by bit, starting with atomic formulas and adding constructions that form more complex sentences one by one.

---

[6]In the same way, it is not incoherent for a relativist to aspire to have more information, while recognizing her current information as the information state that determines whether she may correctly say that something is "possible" (Chapter 10). Note that information states have a natural and objective ranking as better and worse: one body of information is better than another if it contains all the information the other does, plus some information the other does not. Despite this, there is no temptation to objectivism: nobody would say that, because information states can be better or worse, all epistemic modals should be interpreted relative to the best possible information state—full omniscience.

Grammar.

Singular terms: *"Joe," "Sally," "licorice," "Two Buck Chuck,"*[7] *"I," "you"*

Variables: *"x," "y," "z"*

One-place predicates: *"is tasty," "is poisonous," "is a person," "is a cookie"*

Two-place predicates: *"likes the taste of," "gets"*

Atomic formulas: *If α and β are singular terms or variables, Φ is a one-place predicate, and Ψ is a two-place predicate, $\ulcorner \alpha\ \Phi \urcorner$ and $\ulcorner \alpha\ \Psi\ \beta \urcorner$ are atomic formulas.*

Anticipating needs that will arise when we add quantifiers, tense and modal operators, and other constructions to our language, we define an index as follows:

Index. *An index is a quadruple $\langle w, t, g, a \rangle$, where w is a possible world, t a time, g a taste or gustatory standard, and a an assignment of values to the variables.*

We use a time parameter here because we will be treating tense and temporal modifiers as sentential operators. There are strong considerations in favor of treating tense using quantifiers instead (see King 2003). However, the operator approach allows a simpler account of predicates and predication, so we prefer it here. Our discussion below of interactions with tense can be transposed, with small modifications, to either framework.

The *taste* coordinate also deserves notice. Lasersohn (2005) uses a *judge* coordinate, rather than a taste, in his indices. This has a couple of drawbacks. First, a single judge may have different tastes at different times. So, strictly speaking, what we need is not just a judge, but a judge and a time. We already have a time coordinate in our indices, in order to deal with tense and temporal modifiers. But, as I will argue in §7.2.10, if we let *that* be the relevant time, we get incorrect results. We could add a *second* time coordinate, whose role is just to answer the question, "the judge's tastes *when?*" But it seems simpler just to let the taste serve itself as the coordinate.

Second, if we use a judge rather than a taste, we close off the possibility that some judge-dependent expressions are assessment-sensitive while others are use-sensitive. For if, in the definition of truth at a context of use and context of assessment, the judge is initialized by the context of assessment, *every* expression whose extension is sensitive to the judge will be assessment-sensitive. This excludes, for example, combining a relativist treatment of "tasty" with a

---

[7]Nickname of a notoriously cheap California wine.

nonindexical contextualist treatment of "beautiful." The point here is not that we should want such a combination, but that our basic framework should not rule it out from the start. If we have separate coordinates for gustatory and aesthetic standards, we have the possibility of letting one be initialized by the context of assessment and the other by the context of use.[8]

We can now define truth at a context and index for atomic formulas. We do this by defining the extension of arbitrary expressions at a context and index. The extension of a term at a context and index is an object, the extension of a one-place predicate is a set, the extension of a two-place predicate is a set of pairs, and the extension of a formula is a truth value.

Semantics. *We use* $[\![\alpha]\!]^c_{\langle w,t,g,a\rangle}$ *to denote the extension of α at c, $\langle w, t, g, a\rangle$.*[9]

Singular terms:

$$[\![\text{"Joe"}]\!]^c_{\langle w,t,g,a\rangle} = Joe$$

$$[\![\text{"Sally"}]\!]^c_{\langle w,t,g,a\rangle} = Sally$$

$$[\![\text{"licorice"}]\!]^c_{\langle w,t,g,a\rangle} = licorice$$

$$[\![\text{"Two Buck Chuck"}]\!]^c_{\langle w,t,g,a\rangle} = Two\ Buck\ Chuck$$

$$[\![\text{"I"}]\!]^c_{\langle w,t,g,a\rangle} = the\ agent\ of\ c$$

$$[\![\text{"you"}]\!]^c_{\langle w,t,g,a\rangle} = the\ addressee\ at\ c$$

Variables:

$$[\![\alpha]\!]^c_{\langle w,t,g,a\rangle} = a(\alpha),\ where\ \alpha\ is\ a\ variable$$

One-place predicates:

$$[\![\text{"is tasty"}]\!]^c_{\langle w,t,g,a\rangle} = \{x \mid x\ is\ tasty\text{-}according\text{-}to\text{-}g\ at\ w\ and\ t\}$$

$$[\![\text{"is poisonous"}]\!]^c_{\langle w,t,g,a\rangle} = \{x \mid x\ is\ poisonous\ at\ w\ and\ t\}$$

$$[\![\text{"is a person"}]\!]^c_{\langle w,t,g,a\rangle} = \{x \mid x\ is\ a\ person\ at\ w\ and\ t\}$$

$$[\![\text{"is a cookie"}]\!]^c_{\langle w,t,g,a\rangle} = \{x \mid x\ is\ a\ cookie\ at\ w\ and\ t\}$$

---

[8]Of course, it would also be possible to have two separate judge coordinates.

[9]Here I avoid issues about the semantics of mass terms by treating "licorice" and "Two Buck Chuck" as proper names.

Two-place predicates:

$$[\![\text{"likes the taste of"}]\!]^c_{\langle w,t,g,a \rangle} = \{\langle x,y \rangle \mid x \text{ likes the taste of } y \text{ at } w \text{ and } t\}$$

$$[\![\text{"gets"}]\!]^c_{\langle w,t,g,a \rangle} = \{\langle x,y \rangle \mid x \text{ gets } y \text{ at } w \text{ and } t\}$$

Atomic formulas:

$$[\![\alpha\ \Phi]\!]^c_{\langle w,t,g,a \rangle} = \begin{cases} True & \text{if } [\![\alpha]\!]^c_{\langle w,t,g,a \rangle} \in [\![\Phi]\!]^c_{\langle w,t,g,a \rangle} \\ False & \text{otherwise} \end{cases}$$

$$[\![\alpha\ \Psi\ \beta]\!]^c_{\langle w,t,g,a \rangle} = \begin{cases} True & \text{if } \langle [\![\alpha]\!]^c_{\langle w,t,g,a \rangle}, [\![\beta]\!]^c_{\langle w,t,g,a \rangle} \rangle \in [\![\Psi]\!]^c_{\langle w,t,g,a \rangle} \\ False & \text{otherwise} \end{cases}$$

7.2.2 *Postsemantics*

Note that up to this point, we have not needed to mention contexts of assessment. That is because, in this semantics, contexts of assessment are not *locally relevant* in the sense of §3.2.3. Contexts of assessment are needed only in the next phase, the definition of truth relative to a context of use and context of assessment in terms of truth at a context of use and index. To distinguish this phase from the definition of truth at a context of use and index, we call it the *postsemantics*:

Postsemantics. *A sentence S is true as used at context c_1 and assessed from a context c_2 iff for all assignments a,*

$$[\![S]\!]^{c_1}_{\langle w_{c_1}, t_{c_1}, g_{c_2}, a \rangle} = True$$

where w_{c_1} is the world of c_1, t_{c_1} is the time of c_1, and g_{c_2} is the taste of the agent of c_2 (the assessor) at the time of c_2.[10]

7.2.3 *Contents and circumstances*

Following Kaplan (1989: 546), we can superimpose a theory of contents (properties and propositions) onto this semantics.

---

[10] As noted earlier, a more flexible postsemantics might appeal instead to the taste *relevant* at c_2, leaving it a possibility that this might be a taste other than the assessor's.

Circumstance of evaluation.   *Let a circumstance of evaluation be a triple* $\langle w, t, g \rangle$*, where w is a world, t a time, and g a taste.*

Content.   *Where α is a formula, predicate, or singular term, let $|\alpha|_c^a$ denote its content at context of use c under the assignment a.*

Intensions of contents.   *The intension of $|\alpha|_c^a$ is the function f from circumstances of evaluation to extensions such that $f(\langle w, t, g \rangle) = [\![\alpha]\!]_{\langle w,t,g,a \rangle}^c$.*

Contents are relativized to contexts of use, but not to contexts of assessment, because we are developing a form of truth-value relativism, not content relativism (§4.2). Since the semantics we have given implies that the extension of "tasty" at a context and index is independent of the context and assignment, and depends only on the world, time, and taste parameters of the index, we can consistently stipulate that "tasty" invariantly expresses a single property, the property of being tasty.

7.2.4 *Boolean connectives*

It is easy to add truth-functional sentential connectives to our language:

Grammar.   *Where ϕ and ψ are formulas,* $\ulcorner \neg \phi \urcorner$*,* $\ulcorner \phi \wedge \psi \urcorner$*, and* $\ulcorner \phi \vee \psi \urcorner$ *are formulas.*

Semantics.

$$[\![\neg \phi]\!]_{\langle w,t,g,a \rangle}^c = \begin{cases} \textit{False} & \textit{if } [\![\phi]\!]_{\langle w,t,g,a \rangle}^c = \textit{True} \\ \textit{True} & \textit{otherwise} \end{cases}$$

$$[\![\phi \wedge \psi]\!]_{\langle w,t,g,a \rangle}^c = \begin{cases} \textit{True} & \textit{if } [\![\phi]\!]_{\langle w,t,g,a \rangle}^c = [\![\psi]\!]_{\langle w,t,g,a \rangle}^c = \textit{True} \\ \textit{False} & \textit{otherwise} \end{cases}$$

$$[\![\phi \vee \psi]\!]_{\langle w,t,g,a \rangle}^c = \begin{cases} \textit{False} & \textit{if } [\![\phi]\!]_{\langle w,t,g,a \rangle}^c = [\![\psi]\!]_{\langle w,t,g,a \rangle}^c = \textit{False} \\ \textit{True} & \textit{otherwise} \end{cases}$$

These clauses are simple and straightforward, and they allow us to extend our account of truth at a context of use and context of assessment from atomic sentences to arbitrary truth-functional compounds of such sentences. Operating in a truth-conditional framework gives us a simple solution to the embedding problem that proves so difficult for classical expressivism (§1.3.2).

7.2.5   *Explicit relativizations*

As noted in §1.2, "tasty" can be explicitly relativized to a judge:

(3)   That brand of peanut butter is very tasty to young kids.

(4)   Yuk, that isn't tasty at all to me.

(5)   Have you got anything that will be tasty to everybody?

There is reason to think this capacity for relativization is a semantic feature of "tasty," because similar relativizations seem out of place for other kinds of adjectives—even adjectives whose application requires a judgment call:

(6)   #Sam is strong to/for young kids.[11]

(7)   #Sam may be bald to/for you, but he isn't bald to/for me at all.

(8)   #Can you send someone who will be intelligent to/for everybody?

It is difficult to see how an objectivist about "tasty" would account for these data. And it is easy to see how a certain kind of contextualist can account for them. If "tasty" expresses the relational property of being *tasty to* a judge, then we should expect to find sentences in which the judge is explicitly specified, as well as sentences in which it is not (in which case the judge argument place is to be filled by context). But what account of (3)–(5) can a relativist give?

The approach favored here, due to Lasersohn (2005), is to treat "tasty to Sal" as a complex predicate, as follows:

Grammar.   *Where α is a one-place predicate and β a singular term or variable, $\ulcorner \alpha$ to $\beta \urcorner$ is a one-place predicate.*[12]

Semantics. $[\![\alpha \text{ to } \beta]\!]^c_{\langle w,t,g,a \rangle} = [\![\alpha]\!]^c_{\langle w,t,g',a \rangle}$, *where g' = the taste of $[\![\beta]\!]^c_{\langle w,t,g,a \rangle}$ at t.*[13]

We can now see how, on a relativist account, the intension of "tasty" (as used at some context) differs from the intension of "tasty to me" (as used at the

---

[11]"Sam is strong for a kid" is okay, but here "for a kid" gives a comparison class, not a judge. To say that Sam is strong for a kid is not to say that he is strong as judged by the standards of kids, but that he is stronger than the norm for kids.

[12]Perhaps α should be required to be a predicate whose extension varies with the taste of the index. For simplicity, we do not require that here, so "is a cookie to Joe" counts as grammatically well-formed, though semantically it will be equivalent to "is a cookie."

[13]This clause differs slightly from the one at Lasersohn (2005: 666), because his indices contain judges while mine contain tastes.

same context). As we look at different circumstances of evaluation that agree on the world and time but differ in the taste, the extension of "tasty" varies, while the extension of "tasty to me" stays the same. Logically speaking, "Two Buck Chuck is tasty" and "Two Buck Chuck is tasty to me" are neither strictly equivalent nor logically equivalent (§3.4). But they are *diagonally equivalent*; for any context c, "Two Buck Chuck is tasty" is true as used at and assessed from c just in case "Two Buck Chuck is tasty to me" is true as used at and assessed from c. This means that the Truth Rule for assertion will license asserting one just when it licenses asserting the other, which explains why it is so tempting to think that they are equivalent in some stronger sense.[14]

Stephenson (2007) takes an interesting alternative approach. Like Lasersohn, she includes a "judge" coordinate in her indices, but instead of taking "tasty" to be a one-place predicate whose extension is sensitive to this coordinate, she takes it to be a two-place predicate. The extra argument place can be filled either (i) by a regular pronoun (as in "tasty to Sal"), (ii) by a semantically equivalent null pronoun pro_{Sal}, or (iii) by a special silent nominal PRO_J, which denotes (at any context and index) the judge of the index. When "tasty" occurs without explicit qualification, Stephenson holds, its underlying syntax can be either (ii)—which is semantically equivalent to (i)—or (iii), whose extension is sensitive to the judge coordinate of the index.

Stephenson's view differs from ours both in its syntax and in its semantics. The syntactic difference is that "tasty" is taken to be a two-place predicate. The main semantic difference is that a judge is used instead of a taste; this has implications for temporal embeddings, which will be discussed below. Our view could be revised to resemble Stephenson's syntactically without matching it semantically. We could think of "tasty" as a two-place predicate with the meaning: "ψ tastes good by the taste ζ." The semantic value of "to" in "to Sal" could be understood as a function from judges to their tastes at the time of the index. Instead of PRO_J, which denotes the judge of the index, we could use PRO_G, which denotes the taste of the assessor at the time of assessment (or more flexibly, the taste that is relevant at the context of assessment). The resulting view would agree with ours in its predictions about the truth (at a context of use, context of assessment, and index) of every sentence. The syntactic issues, then, can be factored out from the semantic ones.

---

[14]Compare Lasersohn (2005: 688, Remarks 8 and 9).

7.2.6 *Implicit relativizations*

Lasersohn (2005) points out that there are some cases in which predicates like "tasty" that are clearly intended to be evaluated with respect to a particular judge or standard. He calls these uses "exocentric," distinguishing them from the more usual "autocentric" uses, which we evaluate relative to ourselves as judge (whether as speaker or as a third-party assessor). For example, in the dialogue

(9) Mary: How did Bill like the rides?
John: Well, the merry-go-round was fun, but the water slide was a little too scary.

"we intuitively regard John's utterance as true if the merry-go-round was fun for Bill, not if it was fun for ourselves (or for John)" (Lasersohn 2005: 672). Similarly, in buying dog food we might ask ourselves,

(10) I wonder which brand is most tasty?

In answering the question, we try to figure out which brand would be most tasty to the dog, not to ourselves.

Lasersohn takes John to be asserting in (9) the very same proposition he would be asserting if he used the same sentence autocentrically. A proper appreciation of the significance of John's speech act, then, requires not just a grasp of its force and content, but also an awareness of whether John was adopting an exocentric or an autocentric stance towards the asserted proposition. If we judge that he was adopting an autocentric stance, it is appropriate for us to take an autocentric stance in evaluating his claim. But if we judge that he was adopting an exocentric stance, then we should evaluate his claim relative to the judge he intended.

This approach is incompatible with the framework being developed here, on which it is an intrinsic property of a *content* that it is assessment-sensitive (or not). So I am committed to offering an alternative account of exocentric uses. It seems to me that in (9), John is not asserting the same proposition he would be asserting if he used "fun" autocentrically. He is, rather, asserting what would be literally expressed by the sentence

(11) The merry-go-round was fun *for Bill*, but the water slide was a little too scary *for him*.

Here "for Bill" works in much the same way as "to Bill" in "tasty to Bill"; it converts assessment-sensitive predicates ("fun," "scary") into non-assessment-sensitive ones. John doesn't use the words "for Bill," because he doesn't need to: it is obvious from context which proposition he is asserting, and he uses the minimum linguistic resources to get that across. This kind of laziness is to be expected. We tend not to make things explicit unless our audience is likely to misunderstand us.[15]

There are two additional considerations favoring the content-centered approach over Lasersohn's approach. First, as we will see in §7.2.9, we need to posit implicit relativizations anyway to account for binding phenomena, so there is no additional cost to using them here. Second, as we will see in §7.2.7, Lasersohn's account of attitude verbs is warped by his account of exocentric uses. By contrast, the implicit content approach advocated here is compatible with a simple and conservative semantics for attitude verbs.[16]

7.2.7   *Attitude verbs*

The simplest semantics for attitude verbs takes them to express relations between persons and contents. For example:

Grammar. *"believes" is a two-place predicate.*

If ϕ is a sentence (formula with no free variables), $\ulcorner that\ \phi \urcorner$ is a singular term.

Semantics.

$$\llbracket \text{"believes"} \rrbracket^c_{\langle w,t,g,a \rangle} = \{ \langle x,y \rangle \mid x \text{ has a belief with content } y \text{ at world } w \text{ and time } t \}$$

$$\llbracket \ulcorner that\ \phi \urcorner \rrbracket^c_{\langle w,t,g,a \rangle} = |\phi|^a_c$$

Another alternative, pioneered by Hintikka (1962) and favored by Stephenson (2007), construes attitude verbs as modal operators. Roughly, "Joe believes

---

[15]Stephenson's approach, discussed in §7.2.5, is similar to this one in taking the difference between exocentric and autocentric uses to be a difference in the *contents* of the asserted propositions. But on her view, there is also a syntactic difference: in the exocentric uses, the "judge" argument place of "tasty" is filled by a null pronoun, while in the autocentric uses, it is filled by PRO$_J$.

[16]Stephenson (2007) criticizes Lasersohn's account of exocentric uses on other grounds. She thinks that exocentric uses are available for "tasty," but not for epistemic modals, and that this must be explained by a semantic difference between them. (She takes "tasty," but not epistemic modals, to have an extra argument place for a judge.) But it seems to me that epistemic modals *are* sometimes used "exocentrically": for example, Bill might explain why Ann is hiding in the bushes by saying, "I might be on that bus" (Egan, Hawthorne, and Weatherson 2005: 140).

that p" is true at w just in case p is true at all the worlds w' that are doxastic live possibilities for Joe at w. (Stephenson argues, plausibly, that these operators shift the judge as well.) We prefer the relational analysis here, because it more smoothly handles complements that are not that-clauses ("Joe believes Goldbach's conjecture," "There is something that Joe and Mary both believe") and avoids the Hintikka approach's commitment to the closure of belief over necessary entailment.

Lasersohn too favors a relational semantics, but thinks that the belief relation has an extra, covert argument place. For on his view, a believer may believe a proposition exocentrically while not believing it autocentrically. It may be, for example, that Joan does not believe (autocentrically) that the dog food is tasty, but does believe (exocentrically, taking the dog as relevant judge) that the dog food is tasty. Thus, Lasersohn concludes, "we must now treat *believe* as a 3-place relation between an individual, a context, and a sentence content" (Lasersohn 2005: 676). The context argument allows us to distinguish between autocentric and various exocentric uses.[17]

The suggestion is implausible, because there is no independent evidence that "believe" has a third argument place for a context, judge, or standard. If "believe" did have such an argument place, it should be possible to specify a value for it, and to bind it with quantifiers. There should be a natural English way to say that Joan believes, taking the dog as judge, that the dog food is tasty. But this seems to be something we can express only in Lasersohn's own quasi-technical metalanguage. The most natural English equivalent—"Joan believes that the dog food is tasty to the dog"—builds the relativity to the dog into the content believed, rather than taking it to be an extra argument. This strikes heavily against the proposal that "believe" in English has the third argument place.

If, as suggested in §7.2.6, we understand the difference between exocentric and autocentric perspectives as a difference in the *contents* of the relevant beliefs, there is no longer any need to take "believe" to have an extra argument place. We simply say that the sentence

---

[17]In Lasersohn (2009), Lasersohn distinguishes "believe" from "consider," which he takes to be two-place, always requiring an autocentric perspective (for comment, see Cappelen and Hawthorne 2009: 106 n. 11). Lasersohn also raises the possibility that genuinely autocentric uses of "believe" express a two-place relation, like "consider." For the three-place relation cannot distinguish autocentric uses from exocentric uses that are targeted on the speaker, but not in a *de se* way (Lasersohn 2009: §4).

(12)   I believe that California Natural dog food is tasty.

can (depending on the context) be used to assert either that the speaker stands in the belief relation to the proposition that California Natural dog food is tasty, or that he stands in the belief relation to the proposition that California Natural dog food is tasty *to the dog*.

7.2.8   *Factive attitude verbs*

Factive attitude verbs like "knows" and "recognizes" are an interesting special case. Lasersohn (2009) observes that a speaker who asserted

(13)   John recognizes that licorice is tasty

would normally be thought to be committed both to

(a) Licorice's being tasty to John, and to

(b) Licorice's being tasty to himself.

This fact, he argues, is difficult for contextualists to explain. A contextualist account will take "tasty" in (13) to have an implicit argument—the relevant taster. If the implicit argument is John, then we can explain commitment (a) but not commitment (b). On the other hand, if the implicit argument is the speaker, then we can explain commitment (b) but not commitment (a). A relativist account, by contrast, nicely explains both commitments. Recognizing that licorice is tasty requires taking it to be true that licorice is tasty. Barring unexpected cognitive error, John will take it to be true that licorice is tasty only if he likes the taste of licorice—and hence only if licorice is tasty to him. That gives us commitment (a). Recognizing is also a factive attitude, so saying that John recognizes that licorice is tasty commits to the speaker to holding that licorice is tasty. But it will be true (as used at and assessed from the speaker's context) that licorice is tasty only if licorice is tasty to the speaker. That gives us commitment (b).

One might suppose that the contextualist can explain both commitments by taking the implicit argument to be a group containing both the speaker and John. But this won't work either, Lasersohn argues, as we can see from the following case:

John considers licorice to be tasty, and erroneously believes that he is the only person to do so. Unbeknownst to John, the speaker also considers licorice to be tasty, and knows that John does too. In this situation, surely the speaker could truthfully and felicitously say *John recognizes that licorice is tasty*, but it is not the case that both John and the speaker are committed to the claim that licorice is tasty for a group containing both John and the speaker. (Lasersohn 2009: 371)

As it stands, this is a bit too quick: even if John thinks that he is the only person who likes licorice, he might still be committed to the claim that licorice is tasty for a group that, in fact, contains both John and the speaker. He would just have to think of this group under a description that does not fully enumerate its members—say, as "those who are relevantly similar to me in their gustatory capacities."[18] I think, though, that in such a scenario the speaker could no longer "truly and felicitously" say that John *recognizes* that licorice is tasty. For "recognizes" is an epistemic verb; to recognize something is to come to know it, and that is a cognitive achievement that goes beyond mere correct belief.[19] In the case we have imagined, John has managed to acquire a true belief about whether licorice is tasty to the relevant group, but he cannot know this, since he formed his belief on the basis of the false assumption that he is the only member of the relevant group. It is not right, then, to say that he "recognizes" that licorice is tasty.

Seeing that "recognize" is not just factive but epistemic helps fend off the contextualist's rejoinder to Lasersohn's argument. But it also undermines one of the assumptions on which the argument is based: the assumption that, when our speaker takes John to believe that licorice is tasty, and finds licorice tasty himself, he can truly and felicitously say that John *recognizes* that licorice is tasty.

Let us say, rather vaguely, that one knows that p if one forms one's belief that p in a way that is appropriately sensitive to the truth of p. When we consider our own beliefs about which foods are tasty, then, they seem to be excellent candidates for knowledge. I believe that licorice is tasty because I like the flavor of licorice, and the proposition that licorice is tasty is true (as used at and assessed from my current context) just in case I like the flavor of licorice. So my grounds for believing the proposition are precisely the facts that are sufficient for its truth. It seems, then, that I can not only believe but *know* (recognize, realize) that licorice is tasty.

---

[18] As Lasersohn (2009: 371) notes, a specification of the group that leaves it an open question whether John himself is a member will not do, as it deprives us of an explanation of commitment (a). But the description I have given here allows John to know a priori that he is a member of the group, since he is maximally similar to himself.

[19] Williamson (2000: 34) argues that *all* stative factive attitude verbs imply knowledge.

But what about other people? I should say that someone else (say, John) knows (recognizes, realizes) that licorice is tasty only if I think that his belief that licorice is tasty is appropriately sensitive to the tastiness of licorice. But I know that John forms his belief on the basis of his tastes, which stand in no special relation to the truth of the proposition that licorice is tasty (as assessed from my context). If John suddenly acquired a liking for fried grasshoppers, that would change his beliefs about what is tasty, but (from my perspective) it would have no relevance whatever to the truth of these beliefs. It seems, then, that I cannot regard him as knowing, recognizing, or realizing that licorice is tasty, but at best as believing this truly.

What this means is that I will be in a position to assert (13) only in the special case where I can assume that John's tastes track my own. But in the presence of such an assumption, (a) entails (b), so an account that can explain a commitment to (a) can explain a commitment to (b). Thus Lasersohn's argument against contextualism has little force.

7.2.9 *Quantifiers and binding*

We can add binary quantifiers to the language in the usual way:

Grammar. *Where ϕ and ψ are formulas and α a variable, $\ulcorner All_\alpha(\phi, \psi)\urcorner$ and $\ulcorner Some_\alpha(\phi, \psi)\urcorner$ are formulas.*

Semantics.

 Notation: $a[x/\alpha](y) = x$ if $y = \alpha$ and $a(y)$ otherwise.

$$[\![All_\alpha(\phi, \psi)]\!]^c_{\langle w,t,g,a\rangle} = \begin{cases} True & \text{if for every object } x \text{ such that} \\ & [\![\phi]\!]^c_{\langle w,t,g,a[x/\alpha]\rangle} = True, \\ & [\![\psi]\!]^c_{\langle w,t,g,a[x/\alpha]\rangle} = True \\ False & \text{otherwise.} \end{cases}$$

$$[\![Some_\alpha(\phi, \psi)]\!]^c_{\langle w,t,g,a\rangle} = \begin{cases} True & \text{if for some object } x \text{ such that} \\ & [\![\phi]\!]^c_{\langle w,t,g,a[x/\alpha]\rangle} = True, \\ & [\![\psi]\!]^c_{\langle w,t,g,a[x/\alpha]\rangle} = True \\ False & \text{otherwise.} \end{cases}$$

The quantifiers shift the assignment function and leave the other coordinates of the index, including the taste, alone. This creates a prima facie problem with sentences like

(14)   Every person gets some tasty cookies
        $All_x(x$ is a person, $Some_y(y$ is a cookie $\land y$ is tasty, x gets $y))$[20]

Sentence (14) seems to have (at least) two different readings. On the first reading, it says that every person gets some cookies that are tasty (full stop). One should endorse the claim, thus construed, only if one finds every cookie given out to be tasty. On the second reading, it says that every person gets some cookies that are tasty *to that person*. One can endorse the claim, thus construed, even if one finds some of the cookies given out disgusting. Suppose that children and adults have different tastes in cookies. The green cookies are tasty to children, but not to adults, while the red cookies are tasty to adults, but not to children. All the children get two green cookies (and no red ones), and all the adults get two red cookies (and no green ones). On the first reading, (14) is not true as assessed by an adult; on the second reading, it is true.

The problem is that the relativist account seems to predict only the first reading. By contrast, a standard sort of contextualist account—one that takes "tasty" to work like "local"—easily predicts both readings. If "tasty" has an extra argument place for a judge or taste, then we should expect that it can be either filled by context (the first reading) or bound by a quantifier (the second reading).

There are two ways for a relativist to meet the objection. The first way is to join the contextualist in positing an extra argument place in "tasty," but argue, with Stephenson, that it can sometimes be filled by a special silent nominal whose denotation is determined by features of the context of assessment. A relativist who goes this way can give the same explanation of the ambiguity as the contextualist. Indeed, Stephenson's account predicts that there should be *three* interpretations of (14):

(15) $All_x(x$ is a person, $Some_y(y$ is a cookie $\land y$ is tasty to PRO_J, x gets $y))$

(16) $All_x(x$ is a person, $Some_y(y$ is a cookie $\land y$ is tasty to pro_{Sal}, x gets $y))$

(17) $All_x(x$ is a person, $Some_y(y$ is a cookie $\land y$ is tasty to x, x gets $y))$

Sentence (15) is assessment-sensitive; it is true (relative to a context of assessment) if every person gets a cookie whose taste is pleasing to the assessor.

[20]Cf. Lasersohn (2005: 681).

Sentence (16) involves an exocentric use of "tasty"; it is true if every person gets a cookie whose taste is pleasing to Sal. Sentence (17) is the bound reading; it is true if every person gets a cookie whose taste is pleasing to him or her.

Another approach—one that is consistent with the semantics given in §7.2.1, which does not take "tasty" to have an extra argument place—is to hold that the sentence (14) can be used to assert the proposition that would be literally expressed by

(18) $All_x(x$ is a person, $Some_y(y$ is a cookie $\wedge y$ is tasty *to x, x* gets $y))$,

using the predicate-modifying operator "ϕ *to* α" defined in §7.2.5. Here no syntactic mechanism is posited that gets us this interpretation. Instead, we simply suppose that the speaker expects the hearer to be able discern that the proposition expressed by (18) is the one she intends to assert. The second approach is in many ways more conservative, as it does not require positing a hitherto unknown syntactic element, PRO_J.[21]

7.2.10   *Tense*

For present purposes, we treat temporal modifiers as sentential operators, in the tradition of tense logic. As noted above, nothing essential hangs on this decision. We need a definite syntax and semantics in order to discuss interactions between temporal modifiers and "tasty," and the operator approach is simple. But the discussion below could be recast in a framework that treats temporal modifiers quantificationally.

Grammar.   *Where ϕ is a formula,* $\ulcorner Now\ \phi \urcorner$ $\ulcorner Will\ \phi \urcorner$, $\ulcorner Was\ \phi \urcorner$, *and* $\ulcorner One\ year\ ago\ \phi \urcorner$ *are formulas.*

---

[21]See also Lasersohn (2005: 681) for a syntactic argument against any proposal that explains the bound readings by positing an extra argument place in "tasty" that gets filled by a syntactically realized but unpronounced pronoun. (This would include Stephenson's proposal, discussed above, and more standard forms of contextualism.)

Semantics.

$$[\![Now\ \phi]\!]^c_{\langle w,t,g,a\rangle} = \begin{cases} True & if\ [\![\phi]\!]^c_{\langle w,t_c,g,a\rangle} = True, \\ False & otherwise \end{cases}$$

$$[\![Will\ \phi]\!]^c_{\langle w,t,g,a\rangle} = \begin{cases} True & if\ for\ some\ t' > t,\ [\![\phi]\!]^c_{\langle w,t',g,a\rangle} = True \\ False & otherwise \end{cases}$$

$$[\![Was\ \phi]\!]^c_{\langle w,t,g,a\rangle} = \begin{cases} True & if\ for\ some\ t' < t,\ [\![\phi]\!]^c_{\langle w,t',g,a\rangle} = True \\ False & otherwise \end{cases}$$

$$[\![One\ year\ ago\ \phi]\!]^c_{\langle w,t,g,a\rangle} = \begin{cases} True & if\ [\![\phi]\!]^c_{\langle w,t_c-1\ year,g,a\rangle} = True \\ False & otherwise \end{cases}$$

These temporal operators shift the time coordinate of the index, but they leave the taste coordinate untouched. This has a consequence that might seem surprising. Suppose that one's tastes change. At c_1, one likes the taste of licorice, while at c_2 (one year later), one dislikes the taste—not because the taste has changed, but because one's reactions to it have changed. Then at c_2 one can permissibly assert not only

(19)   Licorice is not tasty
       ¬(licorice is tasty)

but also

(20)   Licorice was not tasty a year ago
       ¬*One year ago* licorice is tasty.

Some readers may disagree with this prediction, and think that it should be correct in such a situation to assert

(21)   Licorice was tasty a year ago
       One year ago licorice is tasty.

Lasersohn (2005) and Stephenson (2007) both offer semantics for "tasty" that give this result. On their views, "is tasty" (or, for Stephenson, "is tasty PRO$_J$") is true of an object at an index if the judge of the index likes the taste of the object at the time of the index. So, even if the flavor of licorice has not changed through an interval,

(22)   Licorice was tasty before, but is not tasty any longer

can be true, because the judge's tastes have changed during that interval.

Here is one way of seeing the difference between the two approaches. On Lasersohn's and Stephenson's approaches, the time of the index plays a double role. It tells us not only what time-slice of the object to look at (which is important because objects can change their flavors over time), but also what time-slice of the judge to look at (which is important because judges can change their tastes over time). On the approach being recommended here, by contrast, the time of the index plays only the first role; there is no need to determine which time-slice of the judge is relevant, because the index already contains a complete taste.

Although it may at first seem a good feature of Lasersohn's and Stephenson's views that they endorse (21), there are several good reasons for rejecting the judge-in-the-index approach. First, it predicts that

(23)   Licorice will still be tasty in fifty years

should entail

(24)   Someone will be alive in fifty years.

(I assume here that it is not the case that any dead creature likes the taste of licorice, or any other food, while dead.) But this entailment seems dubious.[22]

Second, it would seem odd to say:

(25)   Last year licorice was tasty, but this year it isn't. It has exactly the same flavor this year that it did last year, but after eating too much of it, I now find this flavor crude and unappealing.

By contrast, it would not be at all odd to say:

(26)   Last year licorice was tasty to me, but this year it isn't. It has exactly the same flavor now this year that it did last year, but after eating too much of it, I now find this flavor crude and unappealing.

But the judge-in-index view would not predict a difference in acceptability here.[23]

[22]See Lasersohn (2005: 663 n. 13) for a similar point (attributed to an anonymous referee), using a modal operator rather than a temporal one.

[23]On the other hand, as Sophie Dandelet emphasized to me, the relativist needs to explain why "Licorice tasted good to me last year, but it wasn't tasty then" sounds marked, even in the context described. One possible explanation is that we are overgeneralizing from the diagonal equivalence of "Licorice is tasty" and "Licorice tastes good to me" (§7.2.5) to their strict equivalence (§3.4).

Third, endorsing (21) does not sit well with saying that an assertion in c_1 of

(27) Licorice is tasty

must be retracted in c_2. It would be odd (at the very least) to say:

(28) Last year I asserted that licorice was tasty. And last year licorice *was* tasty. Still, my assertion was not accurate and must be retracted.

This is a strong reason for an assessment-sensitive semantics for "tasty" to reject the judge-in-index approach.

7.2.11 *Alethic modals and counterfactuals*

Alethic necessity and possibility operators and counterfactual conditionals can be added in the standard way.

Grammar. *Where ϕ and ψ are formulas, $\ulcorner\Box\phi\urcorner$, $\ulcorner\Diamond\phi\urcorner$, and $\ulcorner\phi \rightarrow \psi\urcorner$ are formulas.*

Semantics.

$$[\![\Box\phi]\!]^c_{\langle w,t,g,a\rangle} = \begin{cases} \textit{True} & \textit{if for all worlds w' accessible from w,} \\ & [\![\phi]\!]^c_{\langle w',t,g,a\rangle} = \textit{True} \\ \textit{False} & \textit{otherwise} \end{cases}$$

$$[\![\Diamond\phi]\!]^c_{\langle w,t,g,a\rangle} = \begin{cases} \textit{True} & \textit{if for some world w' accessible from w,} \\ & [\![\phi]\!]^c_{\langle w',t,g,a\rangle} = \textit{True} \\ \textit{False} & \textit{otherwise} \end{cases}$$

$$[\![\phi \rightarrow \psi]\!]^c_{\langle w,t,g,a\rangle} = \begin{cases} \textit{True} & \textit{if $[\![\psi]\!]^c_{\langle w',t,g,a\rangle}$ = True, where w' is the closest} \\ & \textit{world to w (by the metric relevant at c)} \\ & \textit{such that $[\![\phi]\!]^c_{\langle w',t,g,a\rangle}$ = True} \\ \textit{False} & \textit{otherwise} \end{cases}$$

These connectives shift the world coordinate of indices, leaving the other coordinates—including the taste coordinate—alone. Thus,

(29) Licorice could have been tasty
     $\Diamond$licorice is tasty

is accurate (as assessed by someone with taste g) just in case licorice could have had a flavor that is tasty according to g. The fact that the assessor (or anyone else) could have had a different taste than g is irrelevant to the truth of (29). This is as it should be. To wonder what things would be like if horse manure were tasty is to wonder what things would be like if horse manure had a different flavor than it in fact has, not to wonder what things would be like if one had (say) the tastes of a dog.

For similar reasons, although the counterfactual conditional

(30) If I had not trained my palate on many better wines, Two Buck Chuck would be tasty to me

is true,

(31) If I had not trained my palate on many better wines, Two Buck Chuck would be tasty

is false (as used and assessed by me now). For, the closest possible world where I had not tried many better wines—call it w'—is presumably a world where Two Buck Chuck has the same flavor it has in the actual world. And it is false, in w', relative to my actual tastes, that Two Buck Chuck is tasty.[24]

One might have supposed that on the relativist view, the property of tastiness is mind-dependent; after all, our tastiness judgments seem to be projections of our own reactions onto the things that cause them. But in at least one sense of "mind-dependent," this charge is not valid. For the counterfactual

(32) If no sentient beings had ever existed, nothing would be tasty

comes out false on the proposed semantics. What matters for its truth is not whether, in the imagined humanless world, anything would be pleasing to a creature, but whether the flavors things would have had in such a world are pleasing by the taste of the assessor (here, us). This means that quick defenses of the objectivity of values that appeal to our intuitions about such conditionals cannot rule out relativist views.[25]

---

[24]More formally, $[\![$Two Buck Chuck is tasty *to I*$]\!]^c_{\langle w',t_c,g_c,a\rangle}$ = True (for any assignment a), whereas $[\![$Two Buck Chuck is tasty$]\!]^c_{\langle w',t_c,g_c,a\rangle}$ = False (for any a).

[25]Indeed, many contextualist views will also pass muster—those that take the proposition expressed to concern the speaker's tastes, rather than the speaker herself. And some relativist views, including those of Lasersohn and Stephenson, will have trouble with (32); see Lasersohn (2005: 663 n. 13). This is another reason to put a standard of taste, rather than a judge, in the index.

7.3 Relativism and expressivism

Now that we have seen how the relativist view copes with the desiderata we identified in Chapter 1 for an adequate account of the meaning of "tasty," it is time to consider a different sort of view that might claim to do so: a modern expressivist view modeled on Allan Gibbard's treatment of normative discourse. As we will see, this view has some similarities to the relativist view. Working out where the substantive differences lie will help to illuminate both approaches.

7.3.1 *Modern expressivism*

Whereas classical expressivism focused on the speech acts performed using words like "ought" and "tasty," modern expressivism tends to focus on the underlying mental states. The differences between the actions one performs by saying "That's tasty," on the one hand, and "That's green," on the other, are explained in terms of the differences between the underlying states these speech acts express.[26] In the latter case, what is expressed is a belief—a mental state with what Searle (1979: 3–4) calls *mind-to-world* direction of fit. In the former case, what is expressed is a liking, taste, or preference—a state with *world-to-mind* direction of fit.

Expressivists concede that we can use the language of belief and judgment to attribute states of the former kind. We can say, for example, that Yum believes that licorice is tasty, while Yuk thinks it is disgusting. But we can distinguish, expressivists argue, between a thin sense of "belief"—a sense in which any state that can be attributed using the word "believes" counts as a belief—and a thicker sense that is limited to states with mind-to-world direction of fit. In the thin or minimal sense, Gibbard claims, "I genuinely believe that pain is bad, and my expressivist theory, filled out, explains what believing this consists in" (Gibbard 2003: 183). It consists in being in a mental state with a world-to-mind direction of fit: in Gibbard's terms, a "plan-laden" state. The expressivist can also appeal to a minimal truth predicate, for which the Equivalence Schema holds (§2.4), and a minimal notion of a fact as a true claim. In this sense, "it's true that pain is bad and it's a fact that pain is bad—so long as, indeed, pain is bad" (Gibbard 2003: 183). In this way, the expressivist can deal with two of the objections we considered to classical

---

[26]See MacFarlane (2011b: §1) for some reservations about accounting for the force of speech acts like assertion entirely in terms of the expression of attitudes.

expressivism: the worries about attitude reports (§1.3.2) and propositional anaphora (§1.3.2).

But what of the more general worry about embeddings (§1.3.2)? The expressivist says what it is to believe that one ought to go to the party, or that a certain flavor is tasty, by identifying these thin beliefs with plan-like or desire-like mental states. But that does not give us an understanding of what it is to believe that everything Joe serves at his party will be tasty, or that Bill ought to go to the party only if Sally will be there, or that no bottle of wine is both cheap and tasty. These states are not pure beliefs (in the thick sense) or pure desiderative or planning states, but involve elements of both. Two people with opposite tastes could agree that everything Joe serves at his party will be tasty, because they have different ideas about what foods Joe will serve. Two people who endorse the same practical norms could disagree about whether Bill ought to go to the party only if Sally will be there, because they disagree about whether Sally likes Bill. Two people with the same taste in wine could disagree about whether no bottle is both cheap and tasty, because they disagree about the price of a particular bottle. The expressivist needs to give us some way to leverage her explanation of the "pure" desiderative and planning states to an explanation of these "mixed" states.

Blackburn (1984) attempts to solve this problem by giving a direct description of each of the mixed states. On Blackburn's account, simple sentences like

(33)   Gambling is wrong

express first-order attitudes of approval or disapproval (in this case, disapproval of gambling), while complex sentences express approval or disapproval of certain combinations of attitudes. For example,

(34)   If gambling is wrong, then helping others gamble is wrong.

expresses the mental state of approving of sensibilities that disapprove of helping other gamble when they disapprove of gambling. Using this analysis, Blackburn claims, we can explain why it is incoherent to accept (33) and (34), while refusing to accept

(35)   Helping others gamble is wrong.[27]

---

[27]In fact, the most Blackburn's analysis gives us is that a person who accepted (33) and (34) but refused to accept (35) would approve of other sensibilities than her own. It would not follow that

But this strategy threatens to make *all* conditionals, even those with purely descriptive antecedents and consequents, expressions of attitudes of approval. For consider the following argument:

(36) If gambling causes poverty, then gambling is wrong.
      If gambling is wrong, then Jim will avoid gambling.
      So, if gambling causes poverty, then Jim will avoid gambling.

Presumably Blackburn will understand the premises of (36) as expressions of approval for the sensibilities that combine certain attitudes, as before— only here one of the attitudes is a *belief*. But then he must understand the conclusion, too, as an expression of approval: approval for sensibilities that include the belief that Jim will avoid gambling when they include the belief that gambling causes poverty. Otherwise Blackburn has no account of the argument's validity. The upshot, then, is that *all* conditionals (and indeed, all other kinds of compound sentences) are to be understood as expressions of attitudes.

Schroeder (2008), who like Blackburn attempts to give a direct description of the attitude expressed by all complex sentences, explicitly embraces this consequence. On Schroeder's account, all sentences—even purely descriptive sentences—are taken to express states of "being for" some kind of act, described in non-normative terms. Schroeder admits that this

should seem like an unlikely conclusion for expressivists to draw. One of the principal motivations for expressivism in the first place was the idea that belief and desire are two very different kinds of psychological state, and belief is of the wrong kind in order to motivate. But now we are considering the view that believing is really a certain kind of being for. The proposal sounds both implausible on its face, and not at all like the kind of thing to which one would have antecedently expected expressivists to be friendly. Yet I don't see any way around it. (Schroeder 2008: 92)

Both Schroeder and Blackburn, then, have trouble hanging on to the basic expressivist idea that descriptive and normative beliefs differ in their "direction of fit."

In addition, their accounts require a complex and piecemeal rebuilding of semantic theory. Blackburn argues that we have no choice: "For what plays the

she disapproves of her own sensibility, or even that she does not approve of it. In what way, then, would she be incoherent? It would be better, given Blackburn's purposes, to take the conditional to express an attitude of *disapproval* of sensibilities that include disapproval of gambling but not disapproval of helping others gamble. Then the person who refused the modus ponens would have a sensibility that she herself disapproves of, which sounds more like proper incoherence.

role of Copernicus to the allegedly Ptolemaic complexities?" (Blackburn 1984: 196). But he only gets as far as conjunction and the conditional. Schroeder gets considerably farther, but his account founders on temporal and modal constructions (Schroeder 2008: ch. 12).

7.3.2 *Gibbard's two insights*

Gibbard's distinctive approach to these problems rests on two insights. The first insight is that the expressivist does not need to give a direct description of the mixed attitudes, as Blackburn and Schroeder attempt to. It is enough, Gibbard suggests, to provide an indirect grip on these attitudes, by specifying which other attitudes they are compatible with and which they conflict with.[28] If we identify judging that one ought to pack as being in a state of planning to pack, for example, then we can understand judging that one ought *not* to pack as being in a state that is incompatible with every state in which one plans to pack.

Schroeder (2008: 9) complains:

But this does not really tell us anything about what this state of mind is like! All it does is to tell us what properties it must have. It is like giving a list of the criteria that an expressivist account of this mental state must satisfy, in lieu of actually giving an account of that state and showing that it satisfies those criteria.

It is not clear, though, that this complaint is fair. Arguably, our grip on logically complex *descriptive* beliefs, such as the belief that the beer is either in the refrigerator or under the porch, consists in knowing what combinations of beliefs they are compatible with. If one knows this, one knows quite a lot about what this state of mind is like: indeed, it is not clear what more one would need in order to grasp it fully.

Gibbard's second insight is that the expressivist can coopt the methods of truth-conditional semantics to give a systematic account of these relations of compatibility and incompatibility between mental states. Let a *hyperstate* be a completely decided state of mind, which we can represent as an ordered pair consisting of a possible state of affairs and a maximally determinate *hyperplan* that settles what to do in all contingencies. Then we can associate each state of judging—whether normative, descriptive, or mixed—with a set of hyperstates, which we might think of as its content (Gibbard 2003: 53–8). The state of judging that one ought to pack, for example, is associated with

---

[28]Gibbard's first statement of this view is in Gibbard (1990: ch. 5). Blackburn (1988) develops a similar view, abandoning his earlier approach.

the set of all hyperstates whose plan components include a plan to pack (in the relevant circumstances). The state of judging that one ought to pack unless the train has already come is associated with the set of all hyperstates whose plan components include a plan to pack just in case their belief components do not represent the train as having already come. Judgments, generically, can be understood as *ruling out* all hyperstates not contained in the associated set—and thus as disagreeing with all judgments whose contents are disjoint from theirs, and being compatible with all others.[29]

The problem of compositionality is now easy to solve. The content of a disjunctive judgment, for example, is the union of the contents of the disjuncts, the content of a negated judgment is the complement, and the content of a conjunctive judgment is the intersection—just as in truth-conditional semantics.

It is not difficult to apply Gibbard's strategy to an expressivist view of "tasty." Instead of fact-plan worlds, we can talk of fact-taste worlds, which are ordered pairs of a factual possible world w and a taste t. We can take each sentence to "obtain" or not at a fact-taste world (Gibbard 2003: 57–8), and we can take the content of the sentence to be the set of fact-taste worlds at which it obtains. Then all we need for a compositional semantics is a recursive definition of "S obtains at the fact-taste world $\langle w, t \rangle$" for arbitrary sentences. The compositional semantics developed above in §7.2 will do nicely, with some relabeling ("obtains" for "true"). In this way the expressivist can get a systematic account of the compatibility and incompatibility relations between all the pure and mixed states, which, by the first Gibbardian insight above, suffices for an understanding of the mixed states.

The resulting version of expressivism satisfies our desiderata much better than classical expressivism. It captures the assertion conditions of taste claims, and the idea that taste claims express an attitude, in the same way as classical expressivism. But unlike classical expressivism, it has a compositional semantics. It also more directly vindicates the idea that there can be real disagreements about what is tasty, since it explains judging that licorice is *not* tasty as the mental state that disagrees with all states that judge licorice to be tasty.

---

[29]Ordinary states of mind are not hyperstates, but hyperstates represent ways in which these ordinary states could be developed without "change of mind." Gibbard assumes, reasonably, that if one rules out every possible way a less determinate state could be developed as one gains knowledge and firms up plans, one disagrees with the state.

7.3.3   *How do the views differ?*

One might now ask whether there is any real difference between this puri-
fied, Gibbardian expressivist view and the relativist view. Though they use
different rhetoric, they seem to agree on most of the issues at stake:

1. They use essentially the same compositional semantics.
2. They both countenance contents that can be represented as sets of
   world/taste pairs.
3. They both countenance a generic mental state type which is attributed
   in ordinary language using "believes" and which can have contents of
   this kind.
4. They both hold that these contents cannot, in general, be assigned truth
   values given just a state of the world (though both can distinguish a
   "purely descriptive" subclass of contents that are insensitive to the taste
   component and can be assigned truth values given just a state of the
   world).
5. They both explain compatibility relations between states in terms of
   relations between these states' contents.
6. They both hold that there is a monadic truth predicate that can be
   predicated of these contents.

Where, if anywhere, do the views differ? Surely it cannot matter greatly
whether in the recursive clauses of the compositional semantics we use the
terminology of being "true at" a world/taste pair as opposed to "obtaining at"
one.[30]

   The central difference, I think, is this. While both the relativist and the
expressivist hold that one can believe a content whose intension is a set of
world/taste pairs, they give very different explanations of what it is to do this.
As we have seen, the expressivist distinguishes between pure states, which
are explained directly, and mixed states, which are explained only indirectly,
in terms of their compatibility relations to other states. Call a content *world-
insensitive* if whenever its intension contains $\langle t, w \rangle$, it contains $\langle t, w' \rangle$ for all w',
and *taste-insensitive* if whenever its intension contains $\langle t, w \rangle$, it contains $\langle t', w \rangle$
for all t'. Then the expressivist says that to believe a taste-insensitive content
just is to have a thick belief, and to believe a world-insensitive content *just*

---

[30]Recognizing this, Kölbel (2002: 113–14) argues that Gibbard's view is, in fact, a form of
relativism. But if this were right, it would be equally fair to say that relativism is just relabeled
Gibbardian expressivism.

is to have certain gustatory preferences. Beliefs whose contents are neither taste-insensitive nor world-insensitive are explained indirectly, in terms of their relations of agreement and disagreement with other states, both pure and mixed. For the expressivist, then, the surface language of "believing" masks a deep difference in psychological kind. In saying "he believes that it is tasty," we attribute the *very same* kind of state we could also attribute using the language of preference: "he doesn't like its flavor."

For the relativist, by contrast, there is a real difference between the state we attribute using "he believes that it is tasty" and any state we could attribute using the language of preference. Where the expressivist sees only one state, which can be attributed in either way, the relativist sees two states. Where the expressivist appeals to the identification with a preference to explain what it is to believe that a particular flavor is tasty, the relativist appeals to generic features of beliefs.[31] To be sure, a belief that something is tasty will have a different functional role than a belief that it is red, but that (the relativist holds) can be explained in terms of differences between the contents believed, given an appropriate generic understanding of what it is to believe something.

Why might it matter whether there is one state or two? The expressivist view makes it *conceptually impossible* to think that something whose taste one knows first-hand is tasty while not liking its taste, while the relativist view allows that one could be in such a state. The expressivist might claim an advantage here. Part of Gibbard's motivation for an expressivist account of *ought* judgments is the conviction that there should not be a gap between judging that you ought to do something and deciding to do it.[32] Judging that you ought to pack while deciding not to pack is not irrational, on his view, but *impossible*: someone who evidently does not plan to pack shows in her actions that she does not really think she ought to pack, even if her words suggest otherwise (Gibbard 2003: 12). If there were a gap, Gibbard thinks, then we would not have any rational means to bridge it. Once we have settled what we ought to do, we have made a decision; there is no residual question that still

---

[31]For example, beliefs "aim at truth," in the sense that they must be given up when their contents are seen to be untrue (as used at and assessed from the believer's context); beliefs combine with preferences to motivate actions ("He doesn't think it is tasty; he only wants to eat tasty things; so he won't eat it"); beliefs can be formed perceptually; and so on.

[32]Note that the "ought" here is not a specifically moral ought, but an all-things-considered practical "ought," the sort of "ought" an amoralist could employ in saying that we ought to disregard the dictates of law and morality.

needs to be answered. "I the chooser don't face two clear, distinct questions, the question what to do and the question what I ought to do" (Gibbard 2003: 11). Similarly, one might think, I don't face two distinct questions, whether licorice is tasty and whether I like its taste. These are different ways of posing the same question.

I think that there is something right in Gibbard's motivation, but he goes too far. In one sense, it is surely right that there are not two separate questions, whether licorice is tasty and whether I like its taste. For, if I am asked whether licorice is tasty, I resolve the question by asking whether I like the taste of licorice. This is a strike against objectivist accounts of "tasty," which take very different sorts of considerations to bear on the two questions. But it carries no weight against the relativist view, which implies that one should believe that licorice is tasty just in case one likes the taste of licorice. The relativist, then, can agree that the questions are "not separate" in the following sense: first-person deliberation about each gets resolved by the same considerations. It does not follow from this, however, that the questions concern the same psychological state.[33]

Once the "separate questions" point has been defanged, Gibbard's denial of a gap looks more like a liability than an advantage. Intuitively, there *can* be a gap between believing that one ought to do something and deciding to do it. As Scanlon (2006: 726) notes, "judging that what I have most reason to do right now is to defy the bully, and getting myself, right now, to defy him, seem to be two different things." Getting into one state but not the other may be irrational, but it does not seem impossible. The same goes for believing that licorice is tasty while not liking its taste. Alex might find herself unable to believe that licorice is tasty because she aspires to greatness and thinks (on the basis of reading) that only uneducated people think that licorice is tasty. Though she likes the taste of licorice, and hence has sufficient reason to conclude that it tasty, she just can't bring herself to draw that conclusion. This is a form of irrationality, but perfectly intelligible.

---

[33] As Evans (1982: 225) notes, if you are asked whether you believe there will be a third world war, you will appeal to the same sorts of considerations you would appeal to if you were asked whether there will be a third world war. Nonetheless, the two questions are distinct and can have different true answers.

7.3.4 *Retraction and disagreement*

Some other important differences between relativism and Gibbardian expressivism emerge when we move from belief to assertion. The relativist view can explain why speakers tend to retract earlier taste assertions when their tastes change—a fact that might seem to point towards objectivism. Can the expressivist do the same? As noted in §1.3.1, it is not clear what it would be to "take back" or "retract" the expression of an attitude, where this goes beyond simply not still having the attitude.

Perhaps it is enough if the expressivist can make sense of the idea that one's present attitude (say, thinking that licorice is tasty) *disagrees with* one's earlier attitude (thinking that licorice is disgusting). And that is the sort of thing one might think the expressivist can do. After all, the expressivist account of embedding presupposes that we can make sense of relations of agreement and disagreement holding between these states.[34] However, there is room to doubt whether the expressivist has sufficient resources to articulate a concept of disagreement that would work for this purpose. What we need is something like what in Chapter 6 we called *preclusion of joint accuracy* and spelled out in terms of contexts-relative truth. Gibbard, though, cannot appeal to an antecedent notion of truth or accuracy in explicating what he means by disagreement. Instead of talking about one mental state precluding the accuracy of another, he talks of a state precluding *being in* another without change of mind (Gibbard 2003: 56). This is close to our notion of *noncotenability*, which we argued suffices only for a flimsy sort of disagreement.[35] A temporalist will take believing that Socrates is sitting and believing that Socrates is standing to noncotenable, in the sense that having one precludes being in the other, but there is no disagreement between two people who have these beliefs at different times. It is not clear, then, that Gibbard has a robust enough notion of disagreement to do the work he needs it to do, particularly when one considers states of mind held in different contexts.

---

[34] "The orthodox explain disagreeing with a claim as accepting its negation, whereas I go the other way around: I explain accepting the negation as disagreeing with the claim. Agreement and disagreement are what must ground an expressivistic account of logic" (Gibbard 2003: 73).

[35] Gibbard's notion is not quite the same as our notion of noncotenability, because he holds that the agnostic and the atheist do not disagree (Gibbard 2003: 73). We said that a state S is noncotenable with one's cognitive set if one could not come to have S without change of mind; Gibbard limits this to "decided states" and does not count moves from indecision to decision, or uncertainty to certainty, as changes of mind. But I do not think this difference matters much for the issue at hand.

8

KNOWS

Our ordinary practices of attributing knowledge lead us quickly to a conundrum. If you ask me whether I know that I have two dollars in my pocket, I will say that I do. I remember getting two dollar bills this morning as change for my breakfast; I would have stuffed them into my pocket, and I haven't bought anything else since. On the other hand, if you ask me whether I know that my pockets have not been picked in the last few hours, I will say that I do not. Pickpockets are stealthy; one doesn't always notice them. But how *can* I know that I have two dollars in my pocket if I don't know that my pockets haven't been picked? After all, if my pockets were picked, then I *don't* have two dollars in my pocket.

It is tempting to concede that I don't know that I have two dollars in my pocket. And this capitulation seems harmless enough. All I have to do to gain the knowledge I thought I had is check my pockets. But we can play the same game again. I see the bills I received this morning. They are right there in my pocket. But can I rule out the possibility that they are counterfeits? Surely not. I don't have the special skills that are needed to tell counterfeit from genuine bills. How, then, can I know that I have two dollars in my pocket? After all, if the bills are counterfeit, then I don't have two dollars in my pocket.

How should we respond to the conundrum? We might take the side of the skeptic, and concede that we know very little. Or we might take the side of the dogmatist, arguing that I *do* know that my pockets haven't been picked, and that the bills in them aren't counterfeit. Neither option has seemed very appealing to most philosophers; both seem to involve taking our ordinary practices in attributing and evaluating knowledge claims to be deeply mistaken.[1]

An attractive alternative is to reject the forced choice between skepticism and dogmatism, by rejecting the reasoning being used in the conundrum. Let us look again at the form of the argument:

---

[1] For a sophisticated defense of this kind of error theory, see Nagel (2011).

1. p obviously entails q. [premise]

2. If α knows that p, then α could come to know that q without further empirical investigation. [1, Closure]

3. α does not know that q and could not come to know that q without further empirical investigation. [premise]

4. Hence α does not know that p. [2, 3, modus tollens]

The second step relies crucially on a principle we may call

Closure. *If α knows that p, and p obviously entails q, then α could come to know q without further empirical investigation.*

So one way to reject the forced choice is to reject *Closure*, and allow that I can know that I have two dollars in my pockets without being in a position to know that my pockets haven't been picked. One might motivate such a position, following Nozick (1981), by noting that if I didn't have two dollars in my pocket, I would not believe that I did; whereas if my pockets had been picked, I would still believe that they hadn't been picked. However, abandoning *Closure* seems to deprive deductive inference of its ability to extend knowledge. Most philosophers have found this intolerable and sought a fourth option.

The fourth option is to suppose that what is meant by "knows" shifts with the context. On the most natural form of this view, "knowing" that p requires being able to rule out contextually relevant alternatives to p.[2] Which alternatives are relevant depends on the context.

When I am first asked whether I know that I have two dollars in my pocket, I am in context A. In order to count as "knowing" in this context, I have to be able to rule out the possibility that I spent all my money on breakfast, that I spent all but one dollar, and that I had no money in the morning. I can rule those out based on my memories of the day's events, so I count as "knowing." Though I can't rule out the possibility that my pockets were picked, that is not a relevant possibility in this context, and I needn't rule it out to count as "knowing."

However, when I am asked whether I know that my pockets have been picked, the possibility that my pockets have been picked becomes a relevant

---

[2]What is it to "rule out" an alternative? Various possible answers could be given here, some more internalist, others more externalist. We can abstract from this issue for our purposes here.

alternative. In this context (*B*), I don't "know" that I have two dollars in my pocket unless I can rule out this alternative.

Once I have ruled out this alternative by checking my pockets, I count once again as "knowing" that I have two dollars in my pocket. I can't rule out the possibility that the bills I see are counterfeit, but I needn't do that to count as "knowing," since that possibility isn't relevant in context *B*. When this possibility is explicitly raised, however, it becomes relevant. Now, in context *C*, I no longer count as "knowing" that I have two dollars in my pocket unless I can rule out the possibility that the bills are counterfeit.

On this sort of a view, which we will call *contextualism*, *Closure* holds within any one context.[3] However, there can be *apparent* violations of *Closure* when there are contextual shifts in the relevant alternatives. For example, the following knowledge attributions can both express truths if (1) is used in context *A* and (2) in context *B*:

(1)   John knows that he has two dollars in his pocket.

(2)   John does not know that his pockets haven't been emptied by a pick-pocket.

In this way we can respect the ordinary judgments that generate the conundrum without rejecting *Closure*.

Contextualism looks like an appealing response to the conundrum—more appealing, anyway, than skepticism, dogmatism, or the denial of *Closure*. In what follows, we will consider some of the problems faced by contextualist views, and we will look at an alternative way of forging a middle path between skepticism and dogmatism, called "subject-sensitive invariantism." The upshot of our discussion will be that both contextualism and invariantism are getting *something* right, but neither is getting everything right. What is needed is a synthesis that captures what is right about both one-sided views—a *relativist* semantics for knowledge attributions.

8.1   Contextualism

Contextualism offers us a way of saving ordinary knowledge claims from the challenge posed by the conundrum. It explains the contextual variation in our willingness to make knowledge attributions by positing that "knows" is semantically context-sensitive, like "today," "local," and "tall."

---

[3]Of the many versions of contextualism in the literature, Lewis (1996) is perhaps closest to the version described here.

There are other ways one might try to explain contextual variation in our willingness to attribute knowledge. A skeptic might try saying that, although most of the knowledge claims we make are strictly speaking false, it is reasonable to make them nonetheless—just as it is often reasonable to engage in hyperbole, harmless simplification, irony, and metaphor (Schaffer 2004; Davis 2007). When I say that it is 400 miles from San Francisco to Los Angeles, what I say is strictly false (it is 327 miles as the crow flies, 382 by road), but close enough to the truth for practical purposes. Could the same be said of my claim to know that I have two dollars in my pocket?

No. When we exaggerate or simplify, saying what is strictly false to convey something true (or true enough), we are typically aware of this. If I say that San Francisco is 400 miles from Los Angeles, and someone objects, "That is isn't strictly speaking true; it's really 382 miles," I'll concede that and say that I was only speaking loosely. But we don't regard ourselves as exaggerating or "only speaking loosely" when we make ordinary knowledge claims, like "I know that I have two dollars in my pocket." If we did, we'd be happy to accept the skeptic's arguments, admitting that *strictly speaking* we don't know much of anything, but declaring this irrelevant to our ordinary talk.

On the other hand, a dogmatist might try saying that, although many of the knowledge claims we resist making are actually true, we resist making them for fear of engendering misleading expectations. Even if I don't need to rule out the possibility of counterfeits in order to know, making the knowledge claim when this possibility is salient may suggest to others that I can rule it out (Rysiew 2001).

But although worries about misleading implicatures may be good reasons to refrain from asserting something, they aren't good reasons to assert its *negation*. So they don't explain why, beyond just refraining from asserting that I know I have two dollars, I will assert that I *don't* know this.

It is plausible, then, that some kind of semantic context sensitivity explains the contextual variability in our willingness to say that people "know" or "don't know." However, other aspects of our use of "knows" seem to speak against this hypothesis.[4]

In general, speakers know what they are saying. When they employ

[4]The points I will make in the remainder of this section are independent of how exactly a contextualist view is formulated. They will apply to the view that "knows" is an indexical verb, views that take "knows" to have a hidden argument place that is filled in implicitly by the context, and even views that appeal to "free enrichment."

context-sensitive words like "I," "today," or "this," they are aware that the thoughts they are expressing depend on features of the context, and they are able to offer paraphrases to those who have not been able to understand them based on the contextual cues. For example:

> A: That horse is going to win!
>
> B: Which do you mean, the bay or the roan?
>
> A: The bay.

When speakers rely on implicit arguments or completions, as with "tall," "ready," or "local," they are able to make these explicit when asked:

> A: Manuel is tall.
>
> B: What? He's not even six feet!
>
> A: I meant that he's tall for a Peruvian.

So, if the propositions expressed by sentences involving "knows" generally varied with contextually determined standards or relevant alternatives, we would expect speakers to be aware of this dependence, and to be prepared to make it explicit when needed. But, as Schiffer (1996: 326–7) observes, "no ordinary person who utters 'I know that p,' however articulate, would dream of telling you that what he meant and was implicitly stating was that he knew that p relative to such-and-such standard" (see also Feldman 2001: 74, 78–9; Hawthorne 2004: §2.7). Parallels to the dialogues above do not seem natural:

> A: I know I signed the contract.
>
> B: Do you mean you know this by the standards of ordinary life,
>   or by the standards of the courtroom?
>
> A: ?? Just the former.

> A: I know I've got two dollars in my pocket.
>
> B: How do you know they're not counterfeit?
>
> A: ?? I only meant that I could rule out the alternatives that were
>   relevant before you brought up the possibility of counterfeits.

One might maintain that speakers are subject to a certain kind of "semantic blindness," and don't realize the extent to which the contents of their own knowledge claims depend on context (DeRose 2006). But this is a difficult line to take. One would have to give a convincing explanation of why speakers are semantically blind in this case, but not in others. Moreover, once one allows the hypothesis that speakers' usage may reflect semantic errors, the contextual variability in speakers' readiness to ascribe "knowledge" becomes far weaker evidence for contextualism. For one might attribute *this* to semantic blindness.

Relatedly, contextualist views make faulty predictions about when speakers will take "knowledge"-attributing claims to be true, when they will take themselves to be in agreement and disagreement on such claims, and when such claims ought to be retracted (Feldman 2001: 77; Rosenberg 2002: 164; Hawthorne 2004: 163; MacFarlane 2005a: §2.3; Stanley 2005b: 52–6). Here there seems to be a real contrast between "know" and context-sensitive words like "tall." If Joe says "Chiara is tall" (meaning tall *for a fifth-grader*) and Sarah says "Chiara is not tall" (meaning tall *for an American female*), they have not disagreed, and (barring misunderstanding) Joe will not take Sarah's claim to be any kind of challenge to his own. He will take both Sarah's claim and his own to be true, despite their contradictory surface forms. It would be positively bizarre for Joe to say to Sarah, "Yes, you're right, she *isn't* tall after all; what I said was false, and I take it back."

Things are otherwise with "know." If I say "I know that I have two dollars in my pocket," and you later say, "You didn't know that you had two dollars in your pocket, because you couldn't rule out the possibility that the bills were counterfeit," I will naturally take your claim to be a challenge to my own, which I will consider myself obliged either to defend or to withdraw. It does not seem an option for me to say, as the contextualist account would suggest I should: "Yes, you're right, I didn't know. Still, what I said was true, and I stick by it. I only meant that I could rule out the alternatives that were relevant then." Similarly, the skeptic regards herself as *disagreeing* with ordinary knowledge claims—otherwise skepticism would not be very interesting. But if the contextualist is right, this is just a confusion.

Thus the contextualist seems forced to say that ordinary speakers are *mistakenly* taking themselves to disagree (or to agree). But attributing this kind of error tends to undermine the positive case for contextualism, which rests largely on observations about speakers' propensities to use "know" in various contexts. The more error we attribute to speakers, the less their usage can tell us about the meanings of their words.[5]

---

[5]DeRose (2004) is able to make sense of *some* cases of epistemic disagreement, for example between the skeptic and her opponent, by supposing that all parties in a conversation are governed by the same epistemic standard. The various parties to the conversation can then legitimately regard their claims as incompatible, and their conversational moves can be seen as attempts to shift the standard governing the conversation through accommodation (Lewis 1979b).

8.2   Subject-sensitive invariantism

The foregoing considerations seem to favor *invariantism*, the view that "knows" is not context-sensitive. As we have seen, standard (skeptical and dogmatic) forms of invariantism have difficulty accounting for the variability in our willingness to attribute knowledge. But as a number of philosophers have pointed out, it is possible to account for quite a bit of variability while still being an invariantist (Fantl and McGrath 2002; Hawthorne 2004; Stanley 2005b). Even if "knows" is not itself context-sensitive, the truth of sentences like "I know that I have two dollars" and "She knows that she has two dollars" might vary with context in more or less the way contextualists say they do.

Whether a subject has the property of *weighing more than 200 pounds* depends only on how much he weighs. Whether he has the property of *being too big for one's pants*, by contrast, depends not just on how much he weighs, but on how big his pants are. Suppose, then, that *knowing that p* is a matter of *being in an epistemic position that is good enough for one's situation*, and not of being in an epistemic position that surpasses some fixed standard. Then we would expect to see a lot of variability of the sort discussed at the beginning of this chapter. As one's situation changes, and new possibilities become practically relevant, so does the strength of the epistemic position one must be in to have the property of *knowing that p*.

This kind of view is called *subject-sensitive invariantism* (SSI), because it holds that "knows" invariantly expresses a property whose extension at a circumstance of evaluation depends on features of the subject's practical situation.[6] Proponents of SSI generally argue that the concept of knowledge is conceptually linked with the concept of rationality, so that someone knows that *p* just in case it would be rational for her to act as if *p*. Since what it is

On DeRose's favored version of this view, when the there is no agreement on what the shared standard is, then "*S* knows that *p*" is true just in case it is true on both of the two disputed settings of the epistemic standard, false if it is true on neither, and neither true nor false if there is a split decision (DeRose 2004: 15–16). However, this strategy is limited. It applies only to cases where the two disagreeing parties take themselves to be participating in a single conversation, so it does not predict that they disagree if they merely *think* to themselves "*S* knows that *p*" and "*S* does not know that *p*," respectively, or if one considers the other's written or taped comments months later. Moreover, it does not explain why the parties should continue to make their claims even after it has become clear that neither is going to acquiesce in her attempt to shift the epistemic standard, and hence (on DeRose's assumptions) that neither is speaking truly.

[6]Stanley (2005b: 122) prefers the term "interest-relative invariantism," noting that on *every* view of knowledge, whether a subject knows that *p* is sensitive to features of the subject—such as whether the subject believes that *p*.

rational for a subject to do depends on the practical circumstances the subject is in, so does what is required for the subject to know that p.

To better see the difference between contextualism and SSI, compare the semantic clauses for "knows" one might find in a version of each:

Contextualist semantics for "knows." $[\![\textit{"knows"}]\!]^c_{\langle w,t,a \rangle} =$
$\{\langle x,y \rangle \mid y$ *is true at the circumstance* $\langle w,t \rangle$ & x *believes* y *at* $\langle w,t \rangle$ &
x *can rule out all the alternatives to* y *that are relevant at* $c \}.$

SSI semantics for "knows." $[\![\textit{"knows"}]\!]^c_{\langle w,t,a \rangle} =$
$\{\langle x,y \rangle \mid y$ *is true at the circumstance* $\langle w,t \rangle$ & x *believes* y *at* $\langle w,t \rangle$ &
x *can rule out all the alternatives to* y *that are relevant in* x*'s situation at* $\langle w,t \rangle \}.$

Note that the context c plays a significant role in the contextualist semantics, but not the SSI semantics.

These two views yield the same predictions for first-person, present-tensed knowledge attributions, where the context of use and the subject's circumstances coincide. To distinguish the two views, then, we must consider cases where the subject of the knowledge attribution is not in the same situation as the knowledge attributor. Suppose we are in a situation where the possibility of counterfeit bills is relevant, and we are discussing Fred, who is not in such a situation. Suppose that Fred can rule out the possibility that he has been pickpocketed, but not the possibility that the bills in his pocket are fake. Suppose, further, that *we* know that the bills in Fred's pocket are genuine. Should we say that Fred knows that he has two dollars in his pocket? According to the contextualist, we should not. "Fred knows that he has two dollars" is true at our context only if Fred can rule out the counterpossibilities that are relevant at our context—and he can't. According to SSI, however, it is Fred's situation, not ours, that matters. SSI says that Fred knows that he has two dollars just in case he can rule out the counterpossibilities that are relevant in *his* circumstances—and he can.

To adjudicate between contextualism and SSI, then, we need to think about the *shape* of the variability data. Does the variation in our willingness to ascribe knowledge track variations in our own context, or variation in the subject's circumstances? We can't see the difference if we confine ourselves to present-tensed self-attributions of knowledge, but we can see it if we look at attributions of knowledge to others who are in different situations than we are, or to ourselves in the past.

Proponents of SSI have urged that they do better than contextualists in cases where the knowledge attributor is in a "low-stakes" situation and the subject is in a "high-stakes" situation. Suppose Fred has to make a very important payment to the IRS, and they will be inspecting his bills carefully. Does he know he has enough money, in the case where he cannot be sure whether his bills are counterfeit? It seems wrong to answer "yes" even if we are in a "low-stakes" situation, where counterfeiting is not a significant practical concern. It seems, rather, that we should use the evidential standards appropriate to Fred's situation, whatever situation we are in. And that is what SSI prescribes.

However, as Keith DeRose points out, contextualists can handle such cases, too. For the mere fact that we are considering Fred's plight can make counterfeiting a relevant possibility for us:

On contextualism, the speaker's context does always call the shot. . . . But sometimes speakers' own conversational purposes call for employing standards that are appropriate to the practical situation of the far-away subjects they are discussing, and so the shot that the speakers' context calls can be, and often quite naturally will be, to invoke the standards appropriate to the practical situation faced by the subject being discussed. (DeRose 2005: 189)

Both views, then, can handle these cases. But contextualism seems to do much better on the converse kind of case, where the attributor is in a high-stakes situation and the subject is in a low-stakes situation. When I'm concerned about the possibility of counterfeits, I don't think to myself:

(3)   I don't know whether I have two dollars in my pocket, but all of those people walking in and out of the coffee shop know whether they have two dollars.

If I take my inability to discriminate between counterfeits and real bills to rule out *my* knowing that I have two dollars, then I also take your inability to discriminate to rule out *your* knowing this, even if you are not in a practical situation where the possibility of counterfeits is particularly relevant. Contextualism gets this right, and SSI owes, at the least, a special story.

Similarly, when I'm not concerned about the possibility of counterfeits, I don't think to myself:

(4)   I know that I had two dollars in my pocket after breakfast, but I didn't know it this morning, when the possibility of counterfeits was relevant

to my practical deliberations—even though I believed it then on the same grounds that I do now.

Nor do I think:

(5) I know that I have two dollars in my pocket, but if the possibility of counterfeiting were relevant to my practical situation, I would not know this—even if I believed it on the same grounds as now.

However the evidential standards for "knowing" are fixed, they seem to be fixed rigidly across times and counterfactual situations. But this contradicts the central thesis of SSI, which is that they vary with the subject's situation in the circumstances of evaluation. Compare the property of being too big for one's pants. It is perfectly coherent to say

(6) I am too big for my pants, but last year I wasn't, even though last year I weighed the same as I do now, since I had bigger pants then, or

(7) I am too big for my pants, but I wouldn't have been if I had bigger pants.

Proponents of SSI acknowledge these problems as genuine difficulties for their view. What they say in response is not persuasive. John Hawthorne suggests that we tend to "project" the standards currently in play to other putative knowers, times, and circumstances, supposing that, "as more and more possibilities of error become salient to us, we are reaching an ever more enlightened perspective" (Hawthorne 2004: 164–5). Seeing the relevance of counterfeiting to our own practical situation, we assume that it is relevant to everyone else's practical situation as well. However, even if this kind of psychological tendency can explain occasional or even frequent mistakes, it cannot account for our universal resistance to sentences like (4) or (5).

Moreover, even if the projection strategy works, it is a double-edged sword. If it succeeds in explaining why we evaluate *embedded* occurrences of "know" in light of present standards, it should also explain why we evaluate occurrences of "know" at other *contexts of use* in light of present standards. That is, it should provide an explanation of the data about truth ascriptions, disagreement and retraction that is available even to the contextualist.[7] The problem is that one of the best arguments for an invariantist semantics for

---

[7]Hawthorne suggests as much himself: "And, if pressed, we are willing, moreover, to say that 'I was mistaken in thinking that I did know that'" (Hawthorne 2004: 163).

"know" is that it explains the data about truth ascriptions, disagreement, and retraction. If that data is explained instead by the story about projection, then the argument for preferring SSI to contextualism is significantly weakened.

Stanley (2005b: 101–3) takes a different approach. He explains why (3) seems strange by noting that, to the extent that I am interested in others as potential knowers, what I really care about is whether their evidence would suffice to give *me* knowledge. Thus, he argues, when we are asked about the truth of (3), our responses actually track our views about the truth of

(8)   I don't know whether I have two dollars in my pocket, but all of those people walking in and out of the coffee shop would know whether they have two dollars, were they in my practical situation.

However, as Schaffer (2006: 93–4) points out, this sort of explanation threatens to overgeneralize. Suppose we are in a practical situation where the threat of counterfeits is not relevant, and we are discussing Fred, who is in a situation where the threat of counterfeits *is* relevant. Applying Stanley's strategy, we ought to expect our intuitions about whether Fred knows to track whether we think Fred would count as knowing were he in *our* practical situation. But that does not seem to be the case. Indeed, as noted above, proponents of SSI take the fact that we judge Fred not to know in this sort of case to be strong evidence in favor of SSI, as against contextualism. So Stanley's strategy for dealing with (3) would undermine the positive case for SSI.

Stanley acknowledges that modal embeddings, like (5), are problem cases for SSI. He argues that they are not reasons to prefer contextualism to SSI, because contextualism faces the same problems (Stanley 2005b: 110–112). All he really shows, though, is that it is possible to formulate a version of contextualism that would face the same problems. As Blome-Tillmann (2009) demonstrates, it is also possible (and desirable) to formulate a contextualist view in such a way that it avoids the problem. Moreover, Stanley says nothing that would explain the oddity of temporal embeddings like (4). He does consider the sentence

(9)   I didn't know *O* on Thursday, but on Friday I did,

pointing out that if in fact the speaker was going to be in a high-stakes situation on Friday, that may be enough to put her in a high-stakes situation on Thursday, even if she doesn't realize this (Stanley 2005b: 107). But that does not help with (4), where the high-stakes situation was in the past. It seems, then, that some of SSI's predictions about the truth conditions of sentences do not accord well with our considered judgments.[8]

8.3 Relativism

Let us review the dialectical situation. There are three main kinds of views on the table: standard invariantism, contextualism, and SSI. Each has its strengths and weaknesses:

Standard invariantism does not have the resources to explain the variability in our wilingness to ascribe knowledge, and seems to saddle us with an unattractive choice between rejecting *Closure*, embracing skepticism, or embracing dogmatism.

Contextualism explains the variability data and lets us keep *Closure*, but it has trouble explaining our judgments about when others' "knowledge" attributions (or our earlier ones) are true, when such attributions are in disagreement, and when they must be retracted.

SSI handles these things much better than contextualism, but it seems to get the variability data wrong, and makes incorrect predictions about how knowledge attributions behave under modal and temporal constructions.

In the literature, the choice between these views is often presented as a choice of the least of three evils: given that they all have shortcomings, which short-comings are easiest to stomach? This view of the dialectical situation is explicit in Hawthorne (2004) and Stanley (2005b), who respond to some objections to SSI not by showing how they can be met, but by arguing that contextualism faces equivalent or worse objections. But this way of arguing for a view only makes sense if we are certain that we have all of the options on the table.[9] For the most straightforward conclusion to draw from the problems facing all three kinds of views is that we need a different kind of view, one that avoids all of the objections.

Let us reflect on the features such a view would need to have. It would need to explain the way in which the alternatives a subject must rule out in

---

[8]For further criticisms, see Blome-Tillmann (2009: §4).

[9]It also presupposes that there *is* a coherent semantics for "knows." Some have suggested that our use of "knows" is simply incoherent (Schiffer 1996; Weiner 2009). The rational course of action would then be to reform our thought and talk by introducing new, unconfused terms of epistemic assessment. An unattractive prospect, granted—but its disadvantages would have to be weighed against the disadvantages of the three views scouted above.

order to count as "knowing" vary with context. However, it would not join standard contextualism in taking this variation to be keyed to the context of use, since that is what makes it difficult for contextualists to explain truth ascriptions, disagreement, and retraction. Nor would it join SSI in taking this variation to be keyed to the circumstances of the subject to whom knowledge is ascribed, since that is what makes it difficult for SSI to explain our judgments about (3) and embedded cases like (4) and (5). Since we have now exhausted the possibilities for variation that are countenanced in traditional semantic frameworks—variation with context of use or with circumstance of evaluation—we can be sure that the view we are seeking cannot be found in such frameworks.

However, once we make room for assessment sensitivity, a new option opens up. We can take the relevant alternatives to be determined by the context of assessment, rather than the context of use. The resulting view would agree with contextualism in its predictions about when speakers can attribute knowledge, since when one is considering whether to make a claim, one is assessing it from one's current context of use. So it would explain the variability data as ably as contextualism does, and offer the same way of rescuing *Closure* from the challenge posed by the conundrum. But it would differ from contextualism in its predictions about truth assessments of knowledge claims made by other speakers, and about when knowledge claims made earlier must be retracted. Moreover, if the considerations in Chapter 6 are sound, it would vindicate our judgments about disagreement between knowledge claims across contexts.

Semantically, the view can be implemented as follows. We add to our indices a parameter s for a set of contextually relevant possibilities. It is convenient to model this as a set of maximally specific possibilities—in our framework, world/time pairs.[10] In general, s will not contain all of the world/time pairs; pairs outside of s are assumed to be non-actual and "properly ignored" (Lewis 1996: 554). To "know" that p, relative to a set s of relevant possibilities, one must be able to rule out all members of s in which p is false:

Semantics for "knows." $[\![\textit{"knows"}]\!]^c_{\langle w,t,s,a\rangle} =$
$\{\langle x,y\rangle \mid y$ *is true at the circumstance* $\langle w,t,s\rangle$ & x *believes* y *at* $\langle w,t,s\rangle$ & *at* $\langle w,t\rangle$,

---

[10]Including the temporal element will allow us to represent knowledge and ignorance of one's location in time. To know that it is 2 p.m., one must rule out the possibility that it is 1 p.m., but one needn't rule out any complete world-history.

x can rule out every possibility $(w', t') \in s$ *such that y is false at* $\langle w', t', s \rangle$ }

Because the relevant alternatives, world, and time are distinct parameters of indices, shifting the world or time of evaluation leaves the relevant alternatives unchanged. Hence, like standard contextualist views, the relativist view gets the right predictions for sentences like (4) and (5), which we have seen are problematic for SSI.

To get a definition of truth at a context of use and context of assessment, we initialize the relevant possibilities parameter with the possibilities relevant at the context of assessment:

Relativist postsemantics.   *A sentence S is true as used at context* c_1 *and assessed from a context* c_2 *iff for all assignments a,*

$$[\![S]\!]^{c_1}_{\langle w_{c_1}, t_{c_1}, s_{c_2}, a \rangle} = True$$

where w_{c_1} *is the world of* c_1, t_{c_1} *is the time of* c_1, *and* s_{c_2} *is the set of possibilities relevant at* c_2.

We can take the contents of attitudes to be "relevant-alternatives-neutral"—that is, to have truth values that vary not just with the state of the world but with the relevant alternatives:

Circumstance of evaluation.   *Let a* circumstance of evaluation *be a triple* $\langle w, t, s \rangle$, *where w is a world, t a time, and s a set of relevant possibilities.*

Content.   *Where* α *is a formula, predicate, or singular term, let* $|\alpha|^a_c$ *denote its content at context of use c under the assignment a.*

Intensions of contents.   *The intension of* $|\alpha|^a_c$ *is the function f from circumstances of evaluation to extensions such that* $f(\langle w, t, s \rangle) = [\![\alpha]\!]^c_{\langle w, t, s, a \rangle}$.

On this view, the relation "knows" expresses does not vary with the context—there is just a single knowing relation—but the extension of that relation varies across relevant alternatives. As a result, it makes sense to ask about the extension of "knows" only relative to both a context of use (which fixes the world and time) and a context of assessment (which fixes the relevant alternatives).

From the relativist's point of view, invariantism and contextualism each capture part of the truth about knowledge attributions. Invariantism is right that there is a single knowledge relation, but contextualism is right that our willingness to ascribe knowledge depends on a contextually variable set of relevant alternatives, rather than a fixed set of alternatives or one determined by the subject's practical situation. Relativism synthesizes these insights, while avoiding the weaknesses of the two one-sided views. There is a single knowledge relation, but its extension (as assessed from a particular context) depends on which possibilities are relevant at the context of assessment.

8.4   Other alternatives

It is worth mentioning two other alternatives that share some of the virtues of the relativist account.

8.4.1   *Nonindexical contextualism*

If one accepts the account of the contents of knowledge attributions suggested above, but balks at the assessment sensitivity, one can be a nonindexical contextualist (in the sense of §4.6), replacing the *Relativist postsemantics* with a

Nonindexical contextualist postsemantics.   *A sentence S is true as used at context c (and assessed from any context) iff for all assignments a,*

$$[\![S]\!]^c_{\langle w_c, t_c, s_c, a \rangle} = \textit{True}$$

where w_c is the world of c, t_c is the time of c, and s_c is the set of possibilities relevant at c.

On this view, the truth values of sentences containing "know" depend on which possibilities are relevant at the context of use, not because this affects which proposition is expressed, but because it helps determine which circumstance of evaluation to look at in deciding whether these sentences are true or false at the context.[11]

Nonindexical contextualism shares some, but not all, of relativism's features. Like relativism, and unlike standard contextualism, it takes "knows" to express a single property across all contexts of use, irrespective of which possibilities are relevant. Like relativism, and unlike standard contextualism, it takes this property to have an extension that varies with the relevant alternatives. But unlike relativism, it takes the accuracy of assertions and beliefs

---

[11]The view is stated, though not endorsed, in MacFarlane (2005a, 2007b, 2009), and defended by Brogaard (2008). As noted in MacFarlane (2009), Kompa (2002) and Ludlow (2005: 27) seem to have had something similar in mind. Richard (2004, 2008) defends a view that might be either nonindexical contextualism or relativism, without making the distinctions that would be needed to decide between these interpretations.

to depend on the alternatives that are relevant at the context of *use*. In this respect it resembles traditional forms of contextualism (hence the name).

Because nonindexical contextualism does not require assessment sensitivity, it is a more conservative departure from mainstream views than relativism, and that is a point in its favor. It has substantial advantages over standard ("indexical") forms of contextualism, which take the *contents* of knowledge claims to be affected by epistemic factors relevant at the context of use. Unlike standard contextualism, for example, it yields the right predictions about ascriptions of monadic truth to knowledge claims made in other contexts. Suppose that yesterday Sam said,

(10)   I know that I have two dollars in my pocket.

And suppose that although Sam's epistemic position yesterday was sufficient to rule out the alternatives to his having two dollars that were relevant in his context yesterday, it is not sufficient to rule out the alternatives that are relevant in our context today. Standard forms of contextualism then predict, wrongly, that it should be correct to say today,

(11)   What Sam said yesterday was true (even though he didn't know that he had two dollars in his pocket).

Nonindexical contextualism predicts, by contrast, that it is correct to say,

(12)   What Sam said yesterday was not true (since he didn't know that he had two dollars in his pocket).[12]

Because it vindicates (12), nonindexical contextualism goes farther than standard contextualism at vindicating our sense that, in thinking that Sam didn't know he had two dollars, we are *disagreeing* with him. However, the kind of disagreement it vindicates is just *doxastic noncotenability* (§6.2), and one might question whether this is disagreement enough. According to nonindexical contextualism, the accuracy of an assertion of (12) does not preclude the accuracy of Sam's earlier assertion; so Sam can come to accept (12) without feeling any normative pressure to retract. (Recall that the Retraction Norm does not require him to retract his assertion if its content is true as used at the context

---

[12]Recall from §4.8 that the extension of "true" at a circumstance of evaluation e is the set of propositions that are true at e. An assertion of (12) is therefore accurate just in case the proposition that Sam asserted the previous day is not true at the circumstance of the context, that is, at $\langle w_c, t_c, s_c \rangle$, where w_c is the actual world, t_c is the present time, and s_c is the (bigger) set of possibilities now relevant.

where he made it and assessed from his current context; and on the nonindexical contextualist view, it is.) This mismatch between ascriptions of monadic truth and falsity and evaluations of assertions as accurate or inaccurate is counterintuitive, and the relativist view avoids it.

Although nonindexical contextualism makes the same predictions as relativism about the accuracy of ascriptions of monadic truth to earlier knowledge claims, then, it does not make the same predictions about the accuracy of the claims themselves, or about when such claims must be retracted. If we were correct to suggest in Chapter 6 that an important sort of disagreement requires that, were the opponent to be convinced, she would have to retract her claim, then nonindexical contextualism does not do much better than standard contextualism in making sense of the disagreement we perceive between knowledge claims made in relevantly different contexts.

8.4.2 *Expressivism*

A different way of responding to the problems facing contextualism and invariantism is to be an *expressivist* about knowledge attributions (cf. §1.3, §7.3). On an expressivist approach, the meanings of knowledge-attributing sentences would be explained not by assigning them truth conditions, but by saying what mental states they characteristically express. For example, Chrisman (2007: 241) argues that in saying

(13) S knows that p

in context c, a speaker is expressing two states of mind:

1. a belief that S's true belief that p meets the epistemic standards relevant at c, and

2. acceptance of these epistemic standards.

This account can explain the contextual variability in our willingness to attribute "knowledge" in much the same way as contextualism. But it claims to do better than contextualism in accounting for intercontextual disagreement and agreement, since it holds that in such cases "the speakers are expressing pragmatically opposed or concurring states of norm acceptance, rather than logically contradictory or identical descriptive beliefs" (Chrisman 2007: 244).

Dialectically, the strategy is an odd one, if the aim is to do better than contextualism. For the contextualist can agree that in attributing knowledge, one normally expresses one's endorsement of the contextually relevant standards. In saying, "my moral code forbids lying unless a life is in danger," I express my endorsment of this norm. And, in general, whenever I claim that a norm is *my* norm, I express endorsement of the norm, even though the content of the claim is entirely descriptive—as witnessed by the fact that someone else can make the same claim, that this norm is my norm, without endorsing it. According to the epistemic contextualist, in saying "S knows that p," one is saying what one could have said with "S's true belief that p satisfies the epistemic standard relevant at my context."[13] One would expect such a claim to express endorsement of the contextually relevant standard—after all, in *claiming* that a standard is the relevant one, one is expressing commitment to its relevance, which is a way of endorsing it. So a contextualist can agree with Chrisman that knowledge attributions normally express both a belief that the subject's belief satisfies a certain epistemic standard, and endorsement of this standard.[14] And that means that the explanation for intercontextual disagreement that the expressivist offers is available to the contextualist as well. So much for the claimed advantage of expressivism over contextualism!

This is little comfort for the contextualist, though, because the expressivist's explanation of intercontextual disagreement and agreement in terms of " pragmatically opposed or concurring states of norm acceptance" does not work. Suppose Alex, in a high-stakes context, denies that Sam knows that he has two dollars, while Beth, in a low-stakes context, says that Sam knows that he has two dollars. On the expressivist account, Alex has expressed

A1 a belief that Sam's true belief that he has two dollars does not satisfy the standards s_A that are relevant at Alex's context, and

A2 endorsement of the standards s_A,

while Beth has expressed

B1 a belief that Sam's true belief that he has two dollars does satisfy the standards s_B that are relevant at Beth's context, and

B2 endorsement of the standards s_B.

The disagreement, on this account, is due entirely to A2 and B2, since A1 and B1 are compatible, and may even be common ground between Alex and Beth. It is what Stevenson called a "disagreement in attitude" (see §6.3). Now

---

[13] I talk of standards here rather than relevant alternatives, to more closely match Chrisman's presentation. A relevant alternatives contextualist can think of the epistemic standard governing a context as a standard one meets by being able to rule out all of the relevant alternatives.

[14] The views will still be distinct, in that the expressivist holds that mentioning this endorsement is required for explaining the meaning of "knows," while the contextualist thinks it is not.

consider Candace, whose context is in all relevant respects the same as Beth's, but who thinks that Sam's belief does not meet s_B. When Candace says that Sam does not know that he has two dollars, she expresses

C1 a belief that Sam's true belief that he has two dollars does not satisfy the standards s_B that are relevant at her (and Beth's) context, and

C2 endorsement of the standards s_B,

If the disagreement between Alex and Beth is entirely due to the clash between attitudes A2 and B2, then there should be a disagreement *in just the same sense* between Alex and Candace, even though both deny that Sam "knows" that he has two dollars. Inuitively, though, Candace *agrees* with Alex, while Beth disagrees with him. So, although the expressivist *has* identified a respect in which Alex and Beth disagree—they endorse incompatible standards—that does not seem to exhaust the disagreement we perceive there to be between Alex and Beth, as shown by the fact that we think Alex and Beth disagree in a way that Alex and Candace do not.

8.5   Factivity

Stanley (2005b: 147) objects that

It is extremely unclear what the factivity of knowledge comes to, on a relativist semantic theory. But any account of the data, no matter what the predictions about particular cases, is more charitable than one that renders mysterious an inference as basic as the factivity of knowledge.

However, the account presented above clearly validates factivity, in just the sense Stanley intends: "the inference from Kp to p" (147). For any contexts c_1 and c_2, if

(14) $\ulcorner S$ knows *that* $\phi\urcorner$

is true as used at c_1 and assessed from c_2, then ϕ is true as used at c_1 and assessed from c_2. That is, ϕ is an *absolute logical consequence* of (14) (in the sense of §3.4). For suppose that (14) is true as used at c_1 and assessed from c_2. Then, by the *Relativist postsemantics*,

$$[\![(14)]\!]^{c_1}_{\langle w_{c_1}, t_{c_1}, s_{c_2}, a\rangle} = \text{True}.$$

By the semantics for atomic propositions, it follows that

$$\langle [\![S]\!]^{c_1}_{w_{c_1}, t_{c_1}, s_{c_2}, a}, [\![that\ \phi]\!]^{c_1}_{w_{c_1}, t_{c_1}, s_{c_2}, a}\rangle \in [\![\text{"knows"}]\!]^{c_1}_{w_{c_1}, t_{c_1}, s_{c_2}, a}.$$

By the semantics for *"that,"*

$$[\![that \; \phi]\!]^{c_1}_{w_{c_1},t_{c_1},s_{c_2},a} = |\phi|^{a}_{c_1},$$

and by the *Semantics for "knows,"* this content is true at the circumstance $\langle w_{c_1}, t_{c_1}, s_{c_2} \rangle$. By *Intensions of contents*, it follows that

$$[\![\phi]\!]^{c_1}_{\langle w_{c_1},t_{c_1},s_{c_2},a \rangle} = \text{True}.$$

But then it follows from the *Relativist postsemantics* that ϕ is true as used at c_1 and assessed from c_2.

There must be something wrong, then, with Stanley's argument against factivity. It proceeds as follows. Suppose that "John knows that p" is true as used and assessed from John's (low-stakes) context, while it is false as used at John's context but assessed from Hannah's (high-stakes) context. Then John may say, "I know that p," and Hannah may say, "John does not know that p." Stanley says:

On the relativist resolution of the intuitions, John and Hannah are each supposed to be vindicated in their respective judgments, despite their genuine disagreement. It is therefore deeply implausible that John and Hannah each is merely lucky to be right. That is, it is not enough that, for John, he is right, and for Hannah, she is right. This is not genuine vindication. It must be that, if they are both correct, then John *knows* that he is right, and Hannah *knows* that she is right. That is, in the evisaged case, John knows that John knows that p, and Hannah knows that John does not know that p. A neutral observer can then point out that John knows that John knows that p, and Hannah knows that John does not know that p (as I have just done). (Stanley 2005b: 146)

But this "neutral observer" would then be committed to a contradiction, by factivity.

Stanley concludes that the relativist must abandon factivity. But before taking such drastic measures, we should reexamine the premise of Stanley's argument: that both John and Hannah *know* that they are right. The relativist takes them both to be "right" in the following sense: what John believes is true as assessed from John's context, and what Hannah believes is true as assessed from Hannah's context. This is an important kind of "rightness" because it shows that both John and Hannah are conforming to the truth norm for belief (§5.7), which enjoins believing only propositions that are true as used at and assessed from one's current context. There is no difficulty in claiming that both

John and Hannah know that they are right in this sense (faultless$_n$, §6.7). But it does not follow, from the claim that they both know that they are right in this sense, that John knows that John knows that p and Hannah knows that John does not know that p. Relative to some contexts of assessment, it will be true that John knows that p and that John knows that he knows that p; relative to others, it will be true that John does not know that p and that Hannah knows that he does not know that p; but there will be no single context relative to which John knows that he knows that p and Hannah knows that he does not know that p. So Stanley's argument can be rejected (for similiar responses, see Montminy 2009: 345–6; Richard 2008: 169).

8.6 Speaker error

Unlike contextualism, relativism vindicates speakers' ordinary judgments about when two knowledge attributions disagree, when an earlier knowledge attribution must be retracted, and so on. This seems a major point in its favor. However, Montminy (2009) argues that relativism too must impute error to speakers, and so is not to be preferred on these grounds. For ordinary speakers would reject the relativist's predictions about how knowledge claims should be assessed for truth or falsity in other contexts. The relativist, then, needs an error theory, just like the contextualist.

Montminy illustrates his point with the following dialogue between John and Bob, who are in a low-stakes context, *Low*, in which odd conspiracy theories are properly ignored:

> JOHN: We both know that Neil Armstrong was the first man to set
>   foot on the moon.
> BOB: That's true.

Now suppose Hannah is in a high-stakes context *High*, where the possibility that the government faked the moon landing is relevant, and so takes John to have spoken incorrectly. As Montminy notes, Hannah will also take Bob to have spoken incorrectly. And this, he says, "is a problem for relativism: according to this view, since Bob's assessment of John's knowledge claim is made in Low, it is correct" (Montminy 2009: 345).

But this example cannot be used to make the point—at least not against the relativist view of this chapter (or MacFarlane 2005a). Bob has not said:

(15)   That's true as used at your context and assessed from mine.

but rather:

(16)   That's true.

According to our account of the monadic truth predicate, then, he has expressed a proposition that is true at a circumstance of evaluation just in case the proposition John asserted is true at that circumstance (§4.8). So, if Hannah takes John to have spoken falsely, she should take Bob to have spoken falsely too. Here, the relativist predictions are in accord with what Montminy takes to be ordinary speakers' judgments.

Could Montminy simply use a different dialogue? If Bob had said

(17)   That's true as used at your context and assessed from mine,

then the relativist view *would* predict that Hannah should agree with Bob. But here there is no conflict with ordinary judgments. Bob's claim is couched in technical vocabulary, and ordinary speakers will not have judgments about its truth until they are informed how this vocabulary works. Montminy sees this worry and tries replacing the technical claim with a counterfactual:

(18)   If the stakes were low and no error possibilities had been mentioned, then John's assertion would be true.

He argues that relativism predicts that (18) is true, but that Hannah (in High) would judge it to be false (353). Recall, though, that on the relativist view, the world and relevant alternatives parameters shift independently (see §8.3). In (18), the counterfactual antecedent shifts the world, but leaves the relevant alternatives the same, so the consequent is evaluated with respect to the same relevant alternatives as an unembedded claim would be. So the relativist account predicts that (18) is false as assessed from Hannah's context, and again there is no conflict with ordinary judgments.

How, one might wonder, *can* we probe ordinary judgments relating to truth at a context of assessment? Recall the conceptual connections we forged in Chapter 5 between truth relative to a context of assessment and retraction. We can get at ordinary speakers' judgments by asking them to consider proprieties for retraction, and that is what Montminy does at the very end of his paper. Hannah thinks that John's evidence about the moon landing rules out the alternatives relevant in *Low*, but not those relevant in her current context, *High*. She says:

(19)   John does not know that Neil Armstrong was the first man to set foot on the moon.

Later, she finds herself in a low-stakes context, *Lower*. In this context, she says:

(20)   John did know that Neil Armstrong was the first man to set foot on
the moon.

The relativist account predicts that, having said this, Hannah will be prepared
to retract the assertion she made with (19). And Montminy does not dispute
this. What he disputes is that, when in High, Hannah will accept that if she
later comes to be in Lower, she will be obliged to retract (19):

the fact that a speaker in Low would withdraw her previous denial of knowledge
made in High does not entail that *when she is in High,* the speaker takes herself to be
committed to withdrawing her current knowledge denial, if this denial is challenged
in some future Low. As a matter of fact, a speaker in High would reject this commitment, that is, such a speaker would hold that it would be *incorrect* to withdraw her
current knowledge denial in some future low-standards context. . . . This means that
if relativism is correct, ordinary speakers are systematically mistaken about whether
their current knowledge claims should be withdrawn in future contexts. (Montminy
2009: 354)

Suppose that Montminy is right about what ordinary speakers would think
about the correctness of withdrawing their knowledge attributions in the
envisioned future context. Would the fact that the relativist view attributes
this kind error to ordinary speakers be a reason to reject relativism?

No—because the error the relativist has to attribute is less extreme, and
more easily explicable, than that which contextualists have to attribute. The
contextualist must attribute mistakes about when two claims are in disagreement, of a sort which it would be very surprising to find elsewhere. If a
speaker says that a particular ant is "large"—meaning large for an ant—she
will feel absolutely no tension between that claim and an earlier assertion
that "ants are not large." So why, if the contextualist account of knowledge
attributions is correct, do speakers feel tension between knowledge attributions and denials made in different contexts? The contextualist owes us an
explanation of why speakers make the error in one case but not in another
that is semantically similar. The argument against contextualism is not *just*
that it attributes error to speakers—speakers do make errors!—but that we
cannot understand why speakers would make the error it attributes.

The relativist is in a much better position here. If Montminy is right about
the data, then speakers do not have a clear view of just what they are commit-
ting themselves to when they attribute knowledge. That isn't so surprising,
really. As any Socratic dialogue will reveal, speakers aren't typically explicitly

aware of everything they're committed to. How many people regard themselves as committed to staying with both their jobs and their families, without
envisioning circumstances in which these commitments conflict? If one wants
to probe what a speaker is really committed to, one needs not a first, gut
reaction to a question, but a judgment informed by due reflection. In this case,
the speaker would have to consider questions like the following:

1. If I'm later in Lower, should I stand by this denial of knowledge or
   retract it?
2. If I should stand by it, does that mean I shouldn't then attribute the
   knowledge I'm now denying?
3. If I shouldn't then attribute the knowledge I'm now denying, how will I
   then justify refraining from attributing knowledge, when I'm willing to
   attribute knowledge in other evidentially similar cases?
4. If, on the other hand, I *should* then attribute the knowledge I'm now
   denying, how will I square that with standing by my current denial?
   Will I take there to be no disagreement between these two attitudes?

Coming to a reflective judgment about what one is committed to will require recapitulating the considerations that originally motivated relativism as
against contextualism and invariantism. And my view is that, having done
that, speakers will plump for the relativist choices as the ones that best reflect
their practices in attributing and denying knowledge.

Having said that, I do want to acknowledge that there *is* something odd
about judging that, in a future context Lower, you ought to retract an assertion
that you now regard as accurate—not because you've gotten new evidence,
but simply because the contextually relevant alternatives are different. After
all, from your present point of view, there is something wrong with the
standard governing Lower: it counts people who do not know as knowers![15]
It can seem, then, that thinking that you ought to retract your current assertion
if you later come to be in Lower is a bit like thinking that you ought to retract
your current assertion if you later come to accept misleading evidence against
it.

I think that the confusion one feels in answering questions about what
one ought to do in future contexts with different relevant alternatives can
be explained. From the inside, relativism feels a lot like invariantism. In
any given context, you treat all knowledge attributions as governed by the

---

[15] I am grateful to Paul Boghossian for pressing this worry.

same standard (or the same set of relevant possibilities), regardless of the context in which they were produced. When you encounter others who ascribe knowledge where you deny it, or deny it where you ascribe it, you take them to have spoken inaccurately, and to have false beliefs. You don't say "Well, they're right too." There *is* a judgment in that vicinity that you can make: you can say that the others are asserting propositions that are true as used and assessed from *their* contexts, and hence that they are conforming correctly to the norms governing assertion and retraction. But this judgment requires deployment of more sophisticated concepts, and it is not one that you often need to make. For the most part, a practicing relativist can pretend that invariantism is true, as long as she doesn't think too hard about how the judgments she makes in different contexts fit together.

The kind of question Montminy is asking forces us to snap out of this comfortable, natural, invariantist illusion. The continued pull of the invariantist ways of thinking that work so well for the most part make us confused in our answers. But if we reflect, we can see that the somewhat counterintuitive answers the relativist gives to these questions are what is required to make good sense of our knowledge-attributing practices. The alternative is to regard ourselves as confused and very forgetful invariantists.[16]

[16]See Weiner (2009), who argues that our concept of knowing is incoherent, but that this is "mostly harmless."

9

TOMORROW

It is natural to think of time as a *line* running from past to future. Talk about the past concerns the part of the line that lies behind us, while talk of the future concerns the part that lies ahead. But reflection on the contingency of the future suggests an alternative picture of time as *forking* or *branching*. The branches represent possible future continuations of history. At a given moment in time there may be many possible continuations—many branches—none of them marked out as "the" future.

The branching picture has been taken seriously, both in literature and in science.[1] But can we really make sense of branching? On the branching picture, it seems, there is no such thing as *the* future—yet we make claims about the future all the time. For example, I said ten days ago that it would be sunny today. It is sunny, so it seems my assertion was accurate. But how *could* it have been accurate if, as the branching picture has it, there were both rainy and cloudy branches ahead of me when I made it? What facts about its content and context make it the case that it was accurate rather than inaccurate? Not the fact that *the* future of that context held a sunny day, because on the hypothesis of branching, none of the branches through a point can be picked out as *the* future.

This is the puzzle I want to discuss. Faced with the same puzzle, David Lewis concludes that we must either reject branching or accept that our future-directed talk and attitudes are fundamentally confused (Lewis 1986: 199–209). This is a troubling dilemma, because whether there is branching seems, in part, an empirical issue, and some kind of branching temporal structure is called for by prominent interpretations of our best current physical theories (Barrett 2001). If Lewis is right, then endorsing these theories means making talk about what will happen tomorrow incoherent.

---

[1]See Borges' story "Truth in the Garden of Forking Paths" (Borges 1964) for a literary exploration, Barrett (2001) for a scientific one.

I think Lewis's dilemma is a false one. A proper account of the semantics of future contingents can vindicate ordinary thought and talk about the future in a way that is compatible with branching. However, such an account requires assessment sensitivity. We must accept that the truth of a sentence like "There will be a sea battle tomorrow" (or the proposition it expresses) depends not just on the context in which it is used but on the context from which it is assessed. From today's point of view, we (on the sunny branch) can rightly assess yesterday's prediction of sunny weather as accurate. But equally, the "branched" versions of ourselves (on the rainy branch) can rightly assess it as inaccurate, as can our past selves, moments after the claim was made.

9.1   Metaphysical background

To state the problem more rigorously, we will need to be more explicit about concepts like determinism, branching, and possible futures. Our approach here will be to define concepts that should be acceptable to those with many different kinds of modal metaphysics. The problem is a semantic one at root, not a metaphysical one.

9.1.1   *Times*

We will assume, first, a totally ordered set of *times*. It will not matter, for our purposes, whether this set is finite or infinite, dense or discrete, continuous or noncontinuous. All that matters is that for any two times t_1 and t_2, $t_1 \leq t_2$ or $t_2 \leq t_1$.

In assuming that it makes sense to talk of "times" independent of a frame of reference, we are ignoring special relativity. It would be possible to make our framework compatible with special relativity, but the added complexity would make the central semantic points harder to see.[2] Pretend, for now, that the worlds we consider are all Newtonian.

9.1.2   *Worlds*

We will assume a set of *worlds*, together with a domain function D, which maps a world and time to a set of objects, and a valuation function V, which maps an atomic predicate, a world, and a time to an extension—intuitively, the set of objects (or tuples of objects) that satisfy that predicate, given its actual meaning, in that world at that time.

---

[2]For a discussion of indeterminism in a relativistic framework, see Belnap (1992).

We do not assume that our worlds are real, concrete wholes, as in Lewis (1986). Nor do we assume that they are ersatz representations. We abstract from the "implementation details" that distinguish ersatz from realist conceptions. All we will assume about worlds, metaphysically speaking, is that they determine the extension of every atomic predicate in the language under study at every time. Both realists and ersatzists should thus be able to follow the argument.

We will impose one further restriction on our worlds: their temporal evolutions must be consistent with physical law. Although we can certainly conceive of worlds governed by alien physical laws—"where animals speak and stars stand still, where men are turned to stone and trees turn into men, where the drowning haul themselves up out of swamps by their own top-knots" (Frege 1953: §14)—we will restrict our attention here to worlds that are physically possible.

9.1.3 *Accessibility and branching structure*

In the sense of possibility we will be concerned with here, what is possible at one time may no longer be possible at a later time. Imagine that you are planning a road trip. If you leave by daybreak, you can get to Death Valley by nightfall, but if you leave by noon, you can only get as far as Bakersfield. So, as of daybreak, it is possible for you to be in Death Valley at nightfall, but as of noon, it is no longer possible for you to be in Death Valley at nightfall. As time passes, the set of accessible possibilities contracts.

Branching requires that which worlds are possible, from a given world's point of view, can vary with time. We model this by making the *accessibility* (or relative possibility) relation time-relative. Accessibility can be defined in terms of our D and V functions as follows:

Accessibility. w_2 *is accessible from w_1 at t just in case for every time $t' \leq t$ and every atomic predicate Φ, $D(w_1, t') = D(w_2, t')$ and $V(\Phi, w_1, t') = V(\Phi, w_2, t')$.*

Intuitively: w_2 is accessible from w_1 at t if w_1 and w_2 have a common past and present and differ only in the future.[3] It follows immediately from the definition that

(i) Accessibility-at-t is reflexive, symmetric, and transitive—an equivalence relation.

---

[3]This definition implies that if objects are world-bound, as David Lewis holds, then each world is accessible only to itself, and hence there is no branching.

(ii) There is *no backwards branching*, in the sense of Belnap, Perloff, and Xu (2001): if w_2 is accessible from w_1 at t, then w_2 is accessible from w_1 at every $t' \leq t$.

At any given time, then, the accessibility relation *partitions* the worlds into clumps of mutually accessible worlds, which may split into smaller branches at later times, or combine into trunks at earlier times. The structure is that of a branching tree.

9.1.4 *Determinism and indeterminism*

A world is *deterministic* at a time t if every world accessible to it at t is accessible to it at all times $t' > t$. (Intuitively: there is no future branching.) A world is *indeterministic* if it is not deterministic.

Physical law is deterministic if every world is deterministic at every time.[4] But it is possible for a world to be deterministic at a time even if physical law is not deterministic.

In what follows, we assume neither that physical law is deterministic nor that it is not. That is a question for physics. Semantics, conceived as a theory of linguistic meaning, should not presuppose any particular answer to this question. The project is not to give a semantics for future-directed talk that assumes indeterminism, but rather to give one that does not assume determinism.

9.2 Ockhamist semantics

For our purposes in setting up the semantic problem, we can work with a very simple language, with just a few terms and predicates, and without quantifiers:

Grammar.

Singular terms: *"Albuquerque," "Berkeley," "Here"*

One-place predicates: *"is sunny," "is rainy"*

Atomic formulas: *If α is a singular term and Φ a one-place predicate, $\ulcorner \alpha\Phi \urcorner$ is an atomic formula.*

Boolean connectives: *If ϕ and ψ are formulas, then $\ulcorner \phi \wedge \psi \urcorner$, $\ulcorner \phi \vee \psi \urcorner$, and $\ulcorner \neg \phi \urcorner$ are formulas.*

---

[4]Compare Montague's definition of a deterministic theory: a theory is deterministic iff, for any histories S_1 and S_2 compatible with the theory, if S_1 and S_2 agree at a time t_0, they agree at every time $t > t_0$ (Montague 1974: 320, Def. 1).

Temporal operators: *If ϕ is a formula, then $\ulcorner$Tomorrow $\phi\urcorner$, $\ulcorner$Yesterday $\phi\urcorner$, and $\ulcorner$Now $\phi\urcorner$ are formulas.*[5]

Modal operators: *If ϕ is a formula, then $\ulcorner\Diamond\phi\urcorner$ and $\ulcorner\Box\phi\urcorner$ are formulas.*

The compositional semantics, as usual, will take the form of a recursive definition of truth relative to a context and an index—in this case, a world/time pair. (It is called "Ockhamist" in the temporal logic literature because it validates some theses of William of Ockham.)

Ockhamist Semantics. *We use $[\![\alpha]\!]^c_{\langle w,t\rangle}$ to denote the extension of α at c, $\langle w,t\rangle$.*

Singular terms:

$$[\![\text{"Albuquerque"}]\!]^c_{\langle w,t\rangle} = \textit{Albuquerque}$$
$$[\![\text{"Berkeley"}]\!]^c_{\langle w,t\rangle} = \textit{Berkeley}$$
$$[\![\text{"Here"}]\!]^c_{\langle w,t\rangle} = \textit{the location of } c$$

One-place predicates:

$$[\![\text{"is sunny"}]\!]^c_{\langle w,t\rangle} = \{x \mid x \text{ is sunny at world } w \text{ and time } t\}$$
$$[\![\text{"is rainy"}]\!]^c_{\langle w,t\rangle} = \{x \mid x \text{ is rainy at world } w \text{ and time } t\}$$

Atomic formulas:

$$[\![\alpha\ \Phi]\!]^c_{\langle w,t\rangle} = \begin{cases} \textit{True} & \textit{if } [\![\alpha]\!]^c_{\langle w,t\rangle} \in [\![\Phi]\!]^c_{\langle w,t\rangle} \\ \textit{False} & \textit{otherwise} \end{cases}$$

Boolean connectives:

---

[5]A few temporal operators will suffice for demonstration purposes. In a real language, we'd need many more, including non-context-sensitive ones.

$$[\![\neg\phi]\!]^c_{\langle w,t\rangle} = \begin{cases} \textit{True} & \text{if } [\![\phi]\!]^c_{\langle w,t\rangle} = \textit{False} \\ \textit{False} & \textit{otherwise} \end{cases}$$

$$[\![\phi \wedge \psi]\!]^c_{\langle w,t\rangle} = \begin{cases} \textit{True} & \text{if } [\![\phi]\!]^c_{\langle w,t\rangle} = [\![\psi]\!]^c_{\langle w,t\rangle} = \textit{True} \\ \textit{False} & \textit{otherwise} \end{cases}$$

$$[\![\phi \vee \psi]\!]^c_{\langle w,t\rangle} = \begin{cases} \textit{False} & \text{if } [\![\phi]\!]^c_{\langle w,t\rangle} = [\![\psi]\!]^c_{\langle w,t\rangle} = \textit{False} \\ \textit{True} & \textit{otherwise} \end{cases}$$

Temporal operators:[6]

$$[\![\textit{Tomorrow } \phi]\!]^c_{\langle w,t\rangle} = [\![\phi]\!]^c_{\langle w,t_c+24\,hours\rangle}$$

$$[\![\textit{Yesterday } \phi]\!]^c_{\langle w,t\rangle} = [\![\phi]\!]^c_{\langle w,t_c-24\,hours\rangle}$$

$$[\![\textit{Now } \phi]\!]^c_{\langle w,t\rangle} = [\![\phi]\!]^c_{\langle w,t_c\rangle}$$

Modal operators:

$$[\![\Diamond\phi]\!]^c_{\langle w,t\rangle} = \begin{cases} \textit{True} & \text{if } [\![\phi]\!]^c_{\langle w',t\rangle} = \textit{True for some } w' \textit{ accessible from } w \textit{ at } t \\ \textit{False} & \textit{otherwise} \end{cases}$$

$$[\![\Box\phi]\!]^c_{\langle w,t\rangle} = \begin{cases} \textit{True} & \text{if } [\![\phi]\!]^c_{\langle w',t\rangle} = \textit{True for all } w' \textit{ accessible from } w \textit{ at } t \\ \textit{False} & \textit{otherwise} \end{cases}$$

The modal operators defined here are "historical modals," since what is possible or necessary in this sense depends on the time. As time passes, things that were contingent become necessary (settled) or impossible. What has already happened counts as "necessary" in this sense. True, it could have failed to happen—but that just means that it *was* possible that it would not happen (1), not that it is now possible for it not to happen (2):

(1)   *Yesterday* $\Diamond\neg$*Now P*
       Yesterday it was possible that it would not now be the case that *P*

---

[6]Here t_c denotes the time of *c*. Note that "tomorrow" and "yesterday" have the meanings "tomorrow at this time" and "yesterday at this time." The meanings of the words in English are looser.

(2) $\Diamond \neg Now\ P$

    It is possible for it not now to be the case that P.

9.3   Propositions

It is not difficult to add a theory of propositions that fits the semantics. In fact, there are two reasonable ways of doing this, one corresponding to the "temporalist" view of propositions, the other to the "eternalist" view.

    Temporalist propositions are "time-neutral"; they have truth values relative to a world and a time. A *circumstance of evaluation*, then, will be a world/time pair, and the intension of a proposition will be a function from world/time pairs to truth values:

Temporalist propositions.   *Where ϕ is a sentence, let $|\phi|_c^T$ denote the temporalist proposition it expresses at context of use c.*

    The intension of $|\phi|_c^T$ is the function f from world/time pairs to truth values such that $f(\langle w, t \rangle) = [\![\phi]\!]_{\langle w,t \rangle}^c$.

The definition is straightforward, since both the indices relative to which we define sentence truth and the circumstances of evaluation relative to which we define propositional truth are world/time pairs. However, as we have already seen in §4.5.1, there is no reason in principle for these two roles to be played by the same thing. So we are free to join our semantic theory with an *eternalist* theory of propositions, on which circumstances of evaluation are just worlds:

Eternalist propositions.   *Where ϕ is a sentence, let $|\phi|_c^E$ denote the eternalist proposition it expresses at context of use c.*

    The intension of $|\phi|_c^E$ is the function f from worlds to truth values such that $f(w) = [\![\phi]\!]_{\langle w,t_c \rangle}^c$ (where, as usual, t_c is the time of c).

The issues that concern us in what follows will be independent of the choice between temporalist and eternalist propositions. For simplicity, we will work with eternalist propositions. This will help illustrate our earlier claim (§3.1.3) that assessment sensitivity does not require propositional truth to be relativized to anything besides possible worlds.

9.4   The postsemantic problem

Our Ockhamist semantics (§9.2) gives us a definition of truth at a context and index (world/time pair) for arbitrary sentences in our language. But how can we move from this to the pragmatically relevant notion of truth at a context?

A parallel problem arises for propositions. We have an account of truth relative to a world for the propositions expressed by arbitrary sentences in context. But what is it for such a proposition to be true at a context? What does it take for an assertion of such a proposition to be accurate or inaccurate?

In frameworks without branching, these questions have a standard answer. A sentence S is true at a context c just in case $[\![S]\!]^c_{\langle w_c, t_c \rangle} = \text{True}$, where w_c and t_c are the world and time of c. Similarly, a proposition p is true at a context c just in case it is true at w_c, and an assertion is accurate just in case its content is true at w_c.

However, these simple answers aren't available on the branching picture. For they all assume that it makes sense to talk of "the world of the context of use."[7] And

Nondetermination Thesis. *In frameworks with branching worlds, a context of use does not, in general, determine a unique "world of the context of use," but at most a class of worlds that overlap at the context.*

Consider a concrete case in which a sentence is used—say, by being uttered in an assertion. There will be many worlds, in general, that represent the very same past and present happenings, up to and including the production of the very utterance we are interested in, and that diverge only on the future history. None of them, it seems, has any better claim to be *the* world of the context of use than any of the others. The concrete episode of use takes place in all of them. A way to see this is to note that, if we include in the language a name for this episode, say, "Ep," then the sentence "Ep occurs" will be true in all of the overlapping worlds.

It will be convenient for further discussion to introduce some notation for the "worlds of a context":

$W(c)$. *Where c is a context, let $W(c)$ be the class of worlds that overlap at the context.*

Since our branching structure is determined by the time-relative accessibility relation, we can assume that the worlds overlapping at a context, which *qua* overlapping must belong to the same branch, are mutually accessible:

Mutual accessibility. *For all $w_1, w_2 \in W(c)$, w_1 is accessible from w_2 at t_c.*

---

[7] See Lewis (1980: §7), Kaplan (1989: 522, 547). For the observation that talk of the "history of the context" does not make sense in a branching-time framework, see Belnap, Perloff, and Xu (2001: 231–3).

9.4.1   *The Thin Red Line*

The argument we have given so far for the Nondetermination Thesis can be resisted. Granted, if there are branching worlds, then none of the *present* and *past* facts about a concrete speech episode singles out one of them from the others. But why should we limit ourselves to present and past facts? Why not also consider facts about the episode's *future*?

Consider a concrete speech episode Ep that occurs at time t_0, and suppose that the state of the universe at t_0 is compatible with both sunny and cloudy weather at t_1 (one day later). If Ep will be followed in one day by sunny weather, this is a fact about Ep. If Ep won't be followed in one day by sunny weather, this is a fact about Ep. Either way, then, there is a fact about Ep that can discriminate between two worlds that coincide in their present and past states up through the time of Ep, but diverge thereafter.

Of course, someone might deny that there *is* any fact about what kind of weather will follow Ep in one day. But some additional reason should be given for this denial; it does not follow merely from the claim that the next day's weather is not determined by the present state of the universe.

Why should we not say, then, that of the many worlds that coincide up through the production of Ep—all of which accurately represent the present state of the universe and its past evolution—only one also accurately represents what is actually going to happen? And *that* world is the "world of the context."

Following Belnap and Green (1994), let us call this view the *Thin Red Line* view. According to the Thin Red Line view, there is a function *TRL* that maps each context of use c onto a unique world, $TRL(c)$.[8] We can then identify "the world of c" (w_c) with $TRL(c)$, and define truth at a context c as truth at the point of evaluation $c, \langle w_c, t_c \rangle$.

9.4.2   *Against a Thin Red Line*

There is good reason to reject this picture. The reason is not metaphysical, but semantic—or, rather, postsemantic. The Thin Red Line view yields bizarre predictions about merely counterfactual retrospective assessments of future contingent claims.

---

[8] Belnap and Green (1994) and Belnap, Perloff, and Xu (2001: ch. 6) consider theories that give a Thin Red Line a role to play in the semantics proper rather than the postsemantics. They give persuasive objections to these theories, so here I only consider views that give the Thin Red Line a role in the postsemantics.

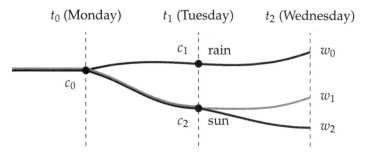

FIG. 9.1. The Thin Red Line. $TRL(c_0) = w_1$.

Let's look at a concrete example (Fig. 9.1). Suppose that at c_0 (on Monday), Jake asserts,

(3)   Tomorrow Berkeley will be sunny.
       Tomorrow Berkeley is sunny

Suppose $TRL(c_0) = w_1$ (as indicated by the gray line in the diagram). Then the Thin Red Line view says that (3) is true at c_0 just in case $[\![(3)]\!]^{c_0}_{\langle w_1, t_0 \rangle} = \text{True}$. By the semantic clause for *Tomorrow* and the fact that $t_0 + 24$ hours $= t_1$,

$$[\![(3)]\!]^{c_0}_{\langle w_1, t_0 \rangle} = [\![\text{"Berkeley is sunny"}]\!]^{c_0}_{\langle w_1, t_1 \rangle} = \text{True.}$$

So (3) is true at c_0.

Now imagine someone at c_2 looking back at Jake's assertion and wondering about its accuracy. This assessor will take the accuracy of Jake's assertion to depend on whether the sentence he asserted, (3), is true at the context in which he asserted it, c_0. Since, according to the Thin Red Line view, (3) is true at c_0, the assessor should take Jake to have made an accurate assertion, not one he needs to retract. And this seems right; after all, the assessor has only to feel the sun on her skin to know that Jake's assertion was accurate.

Things don't work so well, though, if we imagine someone at c_1 looking back and assessing Jake's assertion at c_0. As before, the assessor should take Jake to have spoken accurately just in case (3) is true at c_0. Since, according to the Thin Red Line view, (3) *is* true at c_0, the assessor should take Jake to have spoken accurately. But that seems wrong; the assessor has only to feel the rain on her skin to know that Jake's assertion was inaccurate.

Intuitively, the assessor at c_1 should take Jake to have spoken accurately just in case Berkeley is sunny at t_1 and w_0, not w_1. But since the *TRL* function maps c_0 to w_1, the Thin Red Line view does not deliver this result.

A proponent of the Thin Red Line could perhaps meet the objection by saying that the Thin Red Line is different for each of the two observers. But this would amount to taking the *TRL* function to be a function from a context of use *and* a context of assessment to a world. Because the view would give a semantic role to contexts of assessment, it would be a version of a relativist view, not an alternative to one.

9.4.3   *Undermining Thin Red Line intuitions*

The intuition behind the Thin Red Line view is strong. It can seem very counterintuitive to deny that, of the many worlds overlapping at a context, one of them is singled out as the "actual future history," the one that is really going to be actualized. Yet, as we have seen, a postsemantics based on the Thin Red Line view will give the wrong verdicts about counterfactual retrospective assessments of future-tensed assertions. Can we do anything to weaken the intuitive grip of the Thin Red Line picture?

Yes. We can undermine the picture by looking closely at several considerations that may seem to support it, and seeing that in fact they do not.

It won't be both ways.   Perhaps it will be sunny here at this time tomorrow, perhaps it won't. But we know it won't be *both* ways—it will be one or the other. Doesn't that mean that there is no branching? Or, if there is branching, that only one of the worlds overlapping at the present context (c_0) is the actual world, the one that is going to be realized, the "Thin Red Line"?

No. All we conclude from the datum that it won't be both ways is that our semantic theory must avoid making

(4)   Tomorrow it will be sunny here and won't be sunny here.
      Tomorrow (Here is sunny $\land \neg$Here is sunny)

true at any context.[9] The no-branching and Thin Red Line views can secure this result, but so can many semantic theories that accept branching and reject a Thin Red Line. Given the Ockhamist semantics of §9.2, (4) is false at every context and index $c, \langle w, t \rangle$. So presumably no postsemantics that works with this semantic theory will make (4) true at a context. Indeed, this consideration does not support the Thin Red Line postsemantics as against any of the alternative views described in §§9.5–9.8, below.

---

[9]Recall that our operator *Tomorrow* means "at this time tomorrow," not "at some time tomorrow."

The fallacy of the moving dot. When we look at a diagram representing a branching tree of possible histories, like Fig. 9.1, it is tempting to think of our present location on the tree as a dot that moves slowly from the past into the future. To think of the diagram this way is to think of it like a branching network of roads that we are traveling down (in the back of a pickup truck, perhaps—not in the driver's seat). So we naturally reason as follows:

Even though I'm now on *both* Route 66 and Interstate 40—they overlap here—there's a fact of the matter as to which one I'll be going down when they diverge ahead. I may not know at this point which one it will be, but I'll find out when we get there. I know I won't be going *both* ways!

Similarly, even if I'm now located in many worlds that overlap in the present but diverge in the future, there's a fact of the matter as to which one is the actual future. To find out, I just have to wait and see what happens as I travel forward in time.

But this "moving dot" picture embodies a fundamental confusion. We've already represented time as one of the spatial dimensions of our tree (in Fig. 9.1, the horizontal dimension). So what could possibly be represented by the *motion* of a point along this dimension? Certainly not a process that takes place in time, since all such processes are already represented spatially on the tree. There is nothing in the branching model that corresponds to a car moving along the branching road, and nothing that corresponds to the decision the car will have to make to go down one branch or the other. If worlds branch, then *we branch too*.

Perhaps it is the counterintuitiveness of that idea—that we branch too—that supports the Thin Red Line. But the idea is not counterintuitive when properly understood. It comes down to no more than the fact, already registered, that all of the branching worlds through our present context are worlds that contain us. As we have just seen, it does not imply, for example, that we will come to have contradictory properties.

Tomorrow we'll find out. It seems clear that tomorrow we will know more about which of the various possible future contingencies facing us at present were realized. For example, if it is sunny, we'll look back and say,

(5) Yesterday it was the case that Berkeley would be sunny now. *Yesterday Now* Berkeley is sunny

and hence (given a monadic truth predicate like the one described in §4.8)

(6) If we had said yesterday that it would be sunny now, what we said would have been true.

Wouldn't this show that

(7) w_0 is not the world of the context c_0?

And doesn't that mean that which world is the world of the context—the Thin Red Line—is a discoverable fact of the matter?

No. The Thin Red Line postsemantics is not needed to make sense of our judgments about (5) and (6). Given the Ockhamist semantics (§9.2), (5) is true at $c, \langle w, t \rangle$ if and only if

(8) Berkeley is sunny

is true at $c, \langle w, t_c \rangle$. So any account that uses this semantics will have to allow (5) and (6) to be true as used at c_1. And as we will see in §§9.5–9.8, the Ockhamist semantics does not require a Thin Red Line postsemantics. Both supervaluationist and relativist postsemantics can vindicate (5) and (6), without any need for a Thin Red Line.

The postsemantic problem, then, is this. Given the Nondetermination Thesis, how do we move from the notion we have defined in our recursive semantic clauses—truth relative to a context, a world, and a time—to the directly pragmatically relevant notion of truth at a context? The problem is pressing, because if all we have is truth at a context and index, it is unclear how to move from our semantic theory to predictions about the use of sentences.[10]

What are our options in dealing with the postsemantic problem? One can find three approaches in the literature. The first two avoid the problem by altering the compositional semantics so that a a future-tense sentence does not vary in truth value across the worlds that overlap at the context of use. The third leaves the semantics as it is and tries to get by in the postsemantics without a "world of the context of use."

9.5 Peircean semantics

The postsemantic problem arises because, given the Ockhamist semantics for "tomorrow," future-tensed sentences can have different truth values at the

---

[10]It might be charged that the problem comes from thinking of contexts as concrete speech situations rather than abstract sequences of parameters. If we think of contexts abstractly, then nothing stops us from taking a context to determine a world. But this just moves the bump in the rug, since now we have a problem determining which abstract context is relevant for evaluating a particular concrete speech episode. If we appeal to facts about the context of assessment to make this choice, then we will have, I think, a notational variant of an assessment-sensitive view.

various worlds compatible with a context. So we can avoid it by adopting a semantics that makes our future-directed sentences *moment-determinate*:

Moment-determinate. *A formula ϕ is moment-determinate iff for all c, t, w, w', if w' is accessible from w at t, then $\llbracket \phi \rrbracket^c_{\langle w,t \rangle} = \llbracket \phi \rrbracket^c_{\langle w',t \rangle}$. (Cf. Belnap and Green 1994: 374)*

If every sentence is moment-determinate, we can safely define truth at a context by quantifying over the worlds that are compatible with the context:

Universal Postsemantics. *A sentence S is true at c iff for every $w \in W(c)$, $\llbracket S \rrbracket^c_{\langle w,t_c \rangle} = True$.*
   An eternalist proposition p is true at c iff for every $w \in W(c)$, p is true at w.
   A temporalist proposition p is true at c iff for every $w \in W(c)$, p is true at w, t_c.

The fact that all the sentences of the language are moment-determinate, together with *Mutual accessibility*, guarantees that this postsemantics will not produce gaps: for every sentence S and context c, either S or the negation of S will be true at c. It may be helpful to compare the Tarskian definition of truth for quantified sentences. Because truth for sentences doesn't vary with the assignment, we can define truth simpliciter as truth on every assignment. (We could have just as well said "some assignment," or picked an arbitrary assignment.) Similarly, if sentences don't vary in truth across the worlds that overlap at a context, we can define truth at a context as truth at that context, the time of the context, and *all* of the overlapping worlds. (And, just like Tarski, we could have used the quantifier "some" instead of "all.") We don't *need* a "world of the context," any more than we need an assignment of the context.

   In our Ockhamist semantics, the only operator that can introduce moment-indeterminacy is "*Tomorrow*."[11] So it suffices to replace this. The semantics Prior calls "Peircean" (Prior 1967: 132) would do the trick:

---

[11] Of course, in a real language there would be many more.

Peircean Semantics.

$$[\![Tomorrow_\square \; \phi]\!]^c_{\langle w,t \rangle} = \begin{cases} True & \text{if } [\![\phi]\!]^c_{\langle w',t_c+24 \; hours \rangle} = True \\ & \text{for all } w' \text{ accessible from } w \text{ at } t \\ False & \text{otherwise} \end{cases}$$

$$[\![Tomorrow_\lozenge \; \phi]\!]^c_{\langle w,t \rangle} = \begin{cases} True & \text{if } [\![\phi]\!]^c_{\langle w',t_c+24 \; hours \rangle} = True \\ & \text{for some } w' \text{ accessible from } w \text{ at } t \\ False & \text{otherwise} \end{cases}$$

The Peircean "*Tomorrow_□*" operator is, in effect, a "fusion" of the Ockhamist "*Tomorrow*" and the Ockhamist historical necessity operator, and can be defined in terms of them (Prior 1967: 130):

(9) $Tomorrow_\square \; \phi \equiv_{def} \square Tomorrow \; \phi$

Hence the Peircean language, which contains "*Tomorrow_□*" but not "*Tomorrow*," has less expressive power than our original one: it cannot express the non-moment-determinate contents that led to the postsemantic problem. As Prior notes:

To the Ockhamist, Peircean tense-logic is incomplete; it is simply a fragment of his own system—a fragment in which contingently true predictions are, perversely, inexpressible. The Peircean can only say 'it will be that p' when p's futurition is necessary; when it is not necessary but will occur all the same, he has to say that 'It will be that p' is false; the sense in which it is true eludes him. (Prior 1967: 130–1)

We will take the Peircean view, then, to be the view that

1. ordinary statements about tomorrow are to be rendered using the fused operator "*Tomorrow_□*," and
2. we simply can't say or think anything expressible using the Ockhamist "*Tomorrow*" but not with the Peircean operators.[12]

Belnap, Perloff, and Xu (2001: 159) object that the Peircean view "makes no sense of someone who purports to assert that the coin will land heads even though it might not, that is, who sincerely asserts both that *Will:A* and that *Poss:* ∼ *Will:A*." For, on the Peircean semantics,

(10) $Tomorrow_\square \; \phi \wedge Tomorrow_\lozenge \; \neg\phi$

---

[12]McArthur (1974), who endorses this view, describes it as the view that "all future-tense statements should be viewed as being either overtly or covertly (when in a factual guise) modal."

is a logical falsehood. It is not clear, though, how forceful this objection is, since arguably there *would* be something odd about asserting

(11)   It will be sunny tomorrow, but it is possible that it will not be sunny tomorrow / but it is not inevitable that it will be sunny tomorrow.[13]

However, there are several additional reasons to reject the Peircean view.

Missing scope ambiguities.   Our syntactic decision to regiment "tomorrow" as a sentential operator implies that there are two syntactic disambiguations of

(12)   It will not be sunny tomorrow,

depending on the relative scopes of "not" and "tomorrow":

(13)   It is not the case that it will be sunny tomorrow
       ¬Tomorrow S

(14)   It will be the case tomorrow that it is not sunny
       Tomorrow ¬S

It is striking, though, that although we can mark the syntactic distinction by resorting to cumbersome circumlocutions, as in (13)–(14), these variants seem like different ways of saying the same thing. If you ask somebody who utters (12) whether they meant (13) or (14), you are likely to be met with a blank stare. That is consistent with the Ockhamist semantics of §9.2, according to which (13) and (14) have the same truth value at every context and index. But it is quite difficult to explain on the Peircean semantics, since

(15)   ¬Tomorrow$_\square$ S

can be true while

(16)   Tomorrow$_\square$ ¬S

is false.

---

[13]Many views besides the Peircean view—including the three-valued semantics to be considered in §9.6, the supervaluationist view to be considered in §9.7, and the relativist view to be considered in §9.8—imply that (11) is not properly assertible. (Of the views considered here, only the Thin Red Line view predicts that (11) has a non-defective use.) DeRose (1999: 17) takes the oddity of sentences like (11) to be evidence for an epistemic reading of "possible" in them. But it would not be evidence against the alethic readings of "possible" provided by any of the theories listed above, since they all predict that (11) is bad.

One or the other will happen. On the Peircean view, it is always false to say

(17) It is possible that it will be sunny tomorrow, and it is possible that it won't be, but either it will be or it won't be.
$Tomorrow_\Diamond\ S \land Tomorrow_\Diamond\ \neg S \land (Tomorrow_\Box\ S \lor Tomorrow_\Box\ \neg S)$

But this seems like something we can say truly: Thomason (1970: 267) even says that it "has the force of a tautology." It expresses the natural thought that, even if the future is open, one or the other of the alternatives will take place. Perhaps we could give up thinking this, but it would be a great cost of the Peircean semantics. Ordinary thinking about the future allows that

(18) Either it will be rainy tomorrow or it will be sunny tomorrow.

can be true even when

(19) Either it is inevitable that it will be rainy tomorrow or it is inevitable that it will be sunny tomorrow.

is false, but this distinction cannot be made on the Peircean view.

Retrospective truth judgments. The Peircean view is also at odds with our retrospective judgments of the truth of future-directed propositions. Consider again Fig. 9.1. At c_0 Jake utters (3), and thereby asserts the eternalist proposition

P $|Tomorrow$ Berkeley is sunny$|_{c_0}^E$

Now imagine that at c_2, Jake says

(20) What I said yesterday—namely, P—was[14] true.

Intuitively, (20) expresses a truth. On Monday Jake said that it would be sunny the next day. So if on Tuesday he discovers that it is sunny, he should take the claim he made on Monday to be true. Yet, on the Peircean account, P, the proposition Jake asserted on Monday, is false at every possible world overlapping at c_0.

A related point, pressed by Belnap, Perloff, and Xu (2001: 160), is that one might win a bet that it will be sunny the next day without winning a bet that it is necessary that it will be sunny the next day. But for the Peircean these

---

[14]Because the proposition is eternalist, the tense of the copula is irrelevant here. In English one would naturally say "was" rather than "is," but that isn't important for the argument.

should come to the same bet. (Whether one wins, of course, is determined by a retrospective assessment of the truth of the content of the bet.)

We can shed more light on the problem by looking at a simple argument for (20) that Jake could give at c_2:

(21)   The proposition that it is sunny today (call it "Q") is true.

(22)   The proposition that I asserted yesterday when I said "tomorrow it will be sunny" is the proposition that it is sunny today. That is, $P = Q$.

(23)   So the proposition that I asserted yesterday (P) is true. (And, since it is an eternalist proposition, it was true yesterday.)

How does the Peircean avoid this conclusion? Clearly, she must reject (22). For on her account, the proposition Jake asserted yesterday has the same intension as the proposition he would have asserted had he said,

(24)   It is inevitable that tomorrow Berkeley will be sunny.

and *this* proposition, the proposition that it was inevitable yesterday that it would be sunny today, does not have the same intension as the proposition that it is sunny today. This seems a hard bullet to bite (though Heck 2006 does bite it). Surely what Jake asserted yesterday, when he said that it would be sunny today, is the same as what he asserts today when he says that it is sunny today.[15]

9.6   Three-valued semantics

The Thin Red Line view will always give a future contingent sentence and its negation opposite truth values at a context. That is problematic, though, if we suppose that nothing about the context favors one possible continuation over another. And it gives bad results when we consider retrospective assessments of a prediction from contexts that are not on the Thin Red Line. Ideally, what we would like is

Symmetry. *Where* $\ulcorner Tomorrow\ \phi \urcorner$ *is a future contingent, it has the same truth status (at every context) as* $\ulcorner Tomorrow\ \neg\phi \urcorner$.

The Peircean approach secures Symmetry by adopting a semantics on which future contingents are all false. One of our objections to this approach was that it predicted a scope ambiguity we don't seem to hear, between

---

[15]Remember that we are working with eternalist propositions here. Note also that nothing in this argument depends on its use of indexicals like "today" and "tomorrow": if we replaced these with spelled-out dates, the argument would still go through.

(13)   It is not the case that it will be sunny tomorrow

and

(14)   It will be the case tomorrow that it is not sunny.

If the Peircean approach is correct, this scope difference is semantically significant: (14) is a future contingent, hence false, while (13) is the negation of a
future contingent, hence true. And this seems wrong; the sentences ought to
have the same truth value. Ideally, then, we would like

Transparency. *Where* $\ulcorner$*Tomorrow* $\neg\phi\urcorner$ *is a future contingent, it has the same truth
status (at every context) as* $\ulcorner\neg$*Tomorrow* $\phi\urcorner$.

The Thin Red Line view secures Transparency but not Symmetry; the Peircean
view secures Symmetry but not Transparency. Is there a way to have both?
One way, due to Łukasiewicz (1920, 1967), is to introduce a third truth value
for future contingents (i for "indeterminate"). Łukasiewicz proposed using a
three-valued logic to compute truth values for compound sentences, according
to the tables in Table 9.1.

TABLE 9.1. Łukasiewicz's three-valued truth tables.

$\neg$		$\wedge$	t	i	f		$\vee$	t	i	f		$\supset$	t	i	f
t	f		t	t	i	f		t	t	t	t		t	t	i	f
i	i		i	i	i	f		i	t	i	i		i	t	t	i
f	t		f	f	f	f		f	t	i	f		f	t	t	t

Integrating Łukasiewicz's semantics into our framework for combining tense
and modality, we get the following changes:

Three-valued Semantics.

Temporal operators:

$$[\![Tomorrow\ \phi]\!]^c_{\langle w,t \rangle} = \begin{cases} True & if\ [\![\phi]\!]^c_{\langle w',t_c+24\ hours \rangle} = True \\ & for\ all\ w'\ accessible\ from\ w\ at\ t \\ False & if\ [\![\phi]\!]^c_{\langle w',t_c+24\ hours \rangle} = False \\ & for\ all\ w'\ accessible\ from\ w\ at\ t \\ Indeterminate & otherwise \end{cases}$$

$$[\![Yesterday\ \phi]\!]^c_{\langle w,t \rangle} = [\![\phi]\!]^c_{\langle w,t_c-24\ hours \rangle}$$

$$[\![Now\ \phi]\!]^c_{\langle w,t \rangle} = [\![\phi]\!]^c_{\langle w,t_c \rangle}$$

Modal operators:

$$[\![\lozenge \phi]\!]^c_{\langle w,t\rangle} = \begin{cases} \textit{True} & \textit{if } [\![\phi]\!]^c_{\langle w,t\rangle} \neq \textit{False} \\ \textit{False} & \textit{otherwise} \end{cases}$$

$$[\![\square \phi]\!]^c_{\langle w,t\rangle} = \begin{cases} \textit{True} & \textit{if } [\![\phi]\!]^c_{\langle w,t\rangle} = \textit{True} \\ \textit{False} & \textit{otherwise} \end{cases}$$

Basic connectives:

$$[\![\neg \phi]\!]^c_{\langle w,t\rangle} = \begin{cases} \textit{True} & \textit{if } [\![\phi]\!]^c_{\langle w,t\rangle} = \textit{False} \\ \textit{False} & \textit{if } [\![\phi]\!]^c_{\langle w,t\rangle} = \textit{True} \\ \textit{Indeterminate} & \textit{otherwise} \end{cases}$$

$$[\![\phi \vee \psi]\!]^c_{\langle w,t\rangle} = \begin{cases} \textit{True} & \textit{if } [\![\phi]\!]^c_{\langle w,t\rangle} = \textit{True or } [\![\psi]\!]^c_{\langle w,t\rangle} = \textit{True} \\ \textit{False} & \textit{if } [\![\phi]\!]^c_{\langle w,t\rangle} = \textit{False and } [\![\psi]\!]^c_{\langle w,t\rangle} = \textit{False} \\ \textit{Indeterminate} & \textit{otherwise} \end{cases}$$

$$[\![\phi \wedge \psi]\!]^c_{\langle w,t\rangle} = \begin{cases} \textit{True} & \textit{if } [\![\phi]\!]^c_{\langle w,t\rangle} = \textit{True and } [\![\psi]\!]^c_{\langle w,t\rangle} = \textit{True} \\ \textit{False} & \textit{if } [\![\phi]\!]^c_{\langle w,t\rangle} = \textit{False or } [\![\psi]\!]^c_{\langle w,t\rangle} = \textit{False} \\ \textit{Indeterminate} & \textit{otherwise} \end{cases}$$

This semantics secures Symmetry, since when ⌜*Tomorrow* ϕ⌝ is a future contingent, both it and ⌜*Tomorrow* ¬ϕ⌝ will get the value *i*. And it secures Transparency, since ⌜¬*Tomorrow* ϕ⌝ will always get the same value as ⌜*Tomorrow* ¬ϕ⌝. In this way, Łukasiewicz's approach nicely avoids one of the three problems we found with the Peircian approach (*Missing scope ambiguities*). However, it does nothing to solve the other two.

One or the other will happen.   Like the Peircean view, Łukasiewicz's view does not allow (17) to be true. Perhaps it is some improvement that it comes out indeterminate rather than false. And, unlike the Peircean view, Łukasiewicz's view at least allows a distinction between (18), which comes out indeterminate when tomorrow's weather is undetermined, and (19), which comes out plain false. But, when "It will be sunny tomorrow" (*S*) and "It will be windy tomorrow" (*W*) are independent future contingents, the three-valued view does not allow a distinction between

(25) Either it will be windy tomorrow or it won't be sunny tomorrow
      Tomorrow W ∨ *Tomorrow* ¬*S*,

and

(26) Either it will be sunny tomorrow or it won't be sunny tomorrow
      Tomorrow S ∨ *Tomorrow* ¬*S*.

Both will get the value *i*, since both are disjunctions whose disjuncts have the value *i*. But intuitively, only the former is a future contingent. It will not help to fine-tune the truth tables; the fundamental problem (noted by Prior 1953: 326; Prior 1967: 135) is that there is no way for a truth-functional semantics to give all future contingents the value *i* without also assigning *i* to sentences like (26).

Retrospective truth judgments.   We faulted the Peircean view for predicting that on a sunny Tuesday Jake should take what he said Monday, in uttering "It will be sunny tomorrow," to have been false. Surely, we said, Jake should take what he said to have been true, since he said that it would be sunny, and it is. The three-valued view does only marginally better: it holds that Jake should take his earlier assertion to be neither true nor false. This means that the three-valued view, like the Peircean view, must reject the extremely plausible premise (22).

　　Can we do better?

9.7 Supervaluationism

We have looked at two ways to solve the postsemantic problem by *avoiding* it—adopting a compositional semantics that makes all sentences moment-determinate. An alternative approach is to retain our original, Ockhamist semantics, and address the postsemantic problem directly. This is the approach taken by Thomason (1970), who adopts the "supervaluationist" technique first used by van Fraassen (1966) for the semantics of nonreferring singular terms.

9.7.1 *Supervaluational postsemantics*

Let's review the postsemantic problem. Our Ockhamist semantics gives us a definition of truth at a context and index (world/time pair) for every sentence of the language. The postsemantics needs to define truth at a context in terms of truth at a context and index. A context determines a unique time—the time of the context—but not, according to the Nondetermination Thesis, a unique world.

The supervaluationist response to the problem is simple: if there is no unique world of the context, then we must look at *all* of the worlds of the context. A sentence that is true at all of these worlds is true at the context; one that is false at all of these worlds is false at the context; and one that is true at some and false at others is neither true nor false at the context. If we define the falsity of ϕ as the truth of $\ulcorner \neg \phi \urcorner$, this idea is captured by the

Universal Postsemantics. *A sentence S is true at c iff for all $w \in W(c)$,*
$[\![S]\!]^c_{\langle w, t_c \rangle} = \textit{True}.$
  An eternalist proposition p is true at c iff for every $w \in W(c)$, p is true at w.
  A temporalist proposition p is true at c iff for every $w \in W(c)$, p is true at w, t_c.

This is the same postsemantics we used with the Peircean semantics (§9.5). The difference is that we now use the Ockhamist semantics and tolerate the resulting truth value gaps, rather than trying to prevent them with a semantics that makes every sentence moment-determinate.

This account satisfies all of the conditions of adequacy we have considered so far. We have Symmetry, because a future contingent sentence and its negation will both have the same truth status (neither true nor false). We have Transparency, because the Ockhamist semantics implies that

(27)   For every c, $\langle w, t \rangle$, $[\![Tomorrow \; \neg\phi]\!]^c_{\langle w, t \rangle} = [\![\neg Tomorrow \; \phi]\!]^c_{\langle w, t \rangle}$,

and hence (given the Universal Postsemantics) that

(28)   For every c, $\ulcorner Tomorrow \; \neg\phi \urcorner$ is true at c iff $\ulcorner \neg Tomorrow \; \phi \urcorner$ is true at c.

So no problem of *Missing scope ambiguities* arises.

We also secure *One or the other will happen*, since on the Ockhamist semantics,

(29)   For every c, $\langle w, t \rangle$, $[\![Tomorrow \; \phi \vee Tomorrow \; \neg\phi]\!]^c_{\langle w, t \rangle} = \textit{True}$,

and hence

(30)   For every c, $\ulcorner Tomorrow \; \phi \vee Tomorrow \; \neg\phi \urcorner$ is true at c.

Finally, we get correct predictions about *Retrospective truth judgments*. To see this, we'll need to add the monadic predicate "true" to our object language, as described in §4.8:

(31) $[\![\text{is true}]\!]^c_{\langle w,t\rangle} = \{x \mid (x \text{ is an eternalist proposition} \wedge x \text{ is true at } w) \vee$
       $(x \text{ is a temporalist proposition} \wedge x \text{ is true at } \langle w, t\rangle)\}$

We can now ask whether (20), which we can regiment as

(32)   *Yesterday* (P is true),

is true at c_2, on the supervaluationist's account. The Universal Postsemantics
says that (32) is true at c_2 just in case

$$\forall w \in W(c_2), [\![(32)]\!]^{c_2}_{\langle w,t_{c_2}\rangle} = \text{True},$$

or equivalently (plugging in the semantics for "*Yesterday*"),

$$\forall w \in W(c_2), [\![P \text{ is true}]\!]^{c_2}_{\langle w,t_{c_2}-24\text{ hours}\rangle} = \text{True},$$

or (plugging in the semantics for "true"),

$$\forall w \in W(c_2), P \text{ is true at } w.$$

Recalling that
$$P = |Tomorrow \text{ Berkeley is sunny}|^E_{c_0},$$

and recalling our definition of the intension of an eternalist proposition, this
is equivalent to

$$\forall w \in W(c_2), [\![Tomorrow \text{ Berkeley is sunny}]\!]^{c_0}_{\langle w,t_{c_0}\rangle} = \text{True},$$

and thus (by the semantics for "*Tomorrow*" and the fact that $t_{c_2} = t_{c_0} +$
24 hours) to

$$\forall w \in W(c_2), [\![Berkeley \text{ is sunny}]\!]^{c_0}_{\langle w,t_{c_2}\rangle} = \text{True}.$$

The upshot is that (20) is true at c_2, on the supervaluational account, just
in case Berkeley is sunny at t_1 ($= t_{c_2}$) on all of the worlds in $W(c_2)$. Since
$W(c_2) = \{w_1, w_2\}$, and Berkeley is sunny at t_1 in both w_1 and w_2, (20) is true
at c_2.

We have gone through this example at some length, because one might
naturally assume that a nonrelativist account cannot get the retrospective
truth judgments right. Heck (2006) takes MacFarlane (2003) to be arguing
along these lines. As Heck sees it, the case for a relativist treatment of future

contingents hangs on intuitions about the correctness of claims like "What Jake said was true (when he said it)." Heck suggests that the argument can be blocked by taking "what Jake said" to pick out a different proposition at c_2 than it does at c_0. That seems a desperate expedient. Even if "what Jake said" has some degree of flexibility and contextual sensitivity, one ought to be able to use it to pick out the same proposition twice, and that is the most natural reading in this case. But the foregoing considerations show that Heck's maneuver is not even necessary. The supervaluationist can *already* explain how "what Jake said was true" can express a truth at c_2 and not at c_0, even if both occurrences of "what Jake said" denote the same proposition, P. So the case against a supervaluationist treatment of future contingents cannot rest on intuitions about the correctness of ordinary truth ascriptions, expressed using a monadic truth predicate.

On what, then, does it rest?

9.7.2   *The retraction problem*

The supervaluationist view, as elaborated in §9.7.1, is a form of nonindexical contextualism (§4.6). It takes a sentence like

(33)   There will be a sea battle in the year 2100

to express the same proposition whenever it is uttered. But whether an assertion of this proposition is accurate depends on the time at which the assertion occurs. (Equivalently: whether (33) is true at a context c depends on the time of c.) Even though the proposition (33) expresses is an eternalist proposition, and does not vary in truth with the time of evaluation, its truth at a context depends on the time of the context, because the time of the context affects which worlds matter for its truth at the context.

As we have seen (§8.4.1), it is characteristic of nonindexical contextualist views that monadic truth ascriptions can come apart from accuracy judgments and retraction obligations. For a monadic truth ascription of the form

(34)   What was asserted is/was true

is correct just in case the proposition denoted by "what was asserted" is true at all the circumstances compatible with the context of the *ascription* (here, all of the worlds that overlap at that context). But the assertion under discussion is accurate just in case the proposition denoted by "what was asserted" is true at all the circumstances compatible with the context of the *assertion*. When the context of the monadic truth ascription diverges from the context of the assertion in relevant ways, the truth ascription can be correct even though the assertion was not accurate, and the truth ascription can be incorrect even though the assertion was accurate. Thus, one may be obligated to retract an earlier assertion even when it is correct for one to say that its content is (or was) true.[16]

This is exactly what the supervaluationist account implies about Jake's assertion. As we have seen, the supervaluationist account implies that at c_2, it would be correct for Jake to assert

(20)   What I said yesterday—namely, *P*—was true.

But it *also* implies that Jake's assertion at c_0 was inaccurate, and hence that Jake ought to retract it.

And that seems wrong. For assessors at c_2, the fact that rain was still a possibility when Jake made his assertion isn't relevant to its accuracy. Thus, although the supervaluationist can explain retrospective *truth* judgments, she cannot explain retrospective *accuracy* judgments, or the consequent retraction obligations. In determining whether an earlier assertion was accurate (and can stand) or inaccurate (and must be retracted), one considers its truth relative to the worlds that are still open possibilities, not the worlds that were open possibilities when the assertion was made.

To see how strange the supervaluationist's verdict is, suppose that at c_2, the Director of the Bureau of Quantum Weather Prediction offers Jake an irrefutable proof that, at t_0, it was still an open possibility that it would not be sunny at t_2. Should such a proof compel Jake to withdraw his assertion? Clearly not. If he had asserted that it was *settled* that it would be sunny on Tuesday, he would have to stand corrected. But he did not assert that. He just said that it *would be* sunny on Tuesday—and it is.

On the other hand, if the Director had visited Jake at t_0, just after he made his assertion, and confronted him with exactly the same facts, then arguably he would have had to retract. His assertion did not concern any particular one of the many worlds he occupied; all of these worlds are equally relevant to its truth. (It is useless, recall, to appeal to the "actual world" in this context.) By showing that some of those overlapping worlds contained a sunny tomorrow, while others did not, the Director would have shown that Jake's assertion was not accurate.

[16] Again, for eternalist contents, the distinction between "is" and "was" is irrelevant.

When we consider Jake's assertion just after it was made, then, the Director's proof seems to show that it was not accurate. But when we consider it from a different vantage point—the vantage point of c_2—then the Director's proof seems altogether irrelevant to its accuracy. Of course, *justification* is well known to exhibit this kind of perspectival variation. The very same considerations that count as solid grounds for belief in one context may be utterly insufficient in another, because new evidence has become available. But that's not what we're dealing with here. It's not that Jake's new evidence that it's sunny at c_2 somehow undermines the Director's proof that it was not settled at c_0 that it would be sunny on Tuesday. No, the Director's proof still stands. Jake still accepts its conclusion. It's just that, from Jake's current point of view, this proof isn't at all relevant to the accuracy of his assertion.

This, then, is the puzzle:

- present assertions concerning the future can be shown to be inaccurate by a proof of present unsettledness, but
- past claims concerning the present cannot be shown to have been inaccurate by a proof of past unsettledness.

In order to solve this puzzle, we will need assessment sensitivity.

9.8 Relativism

The supervaluational semantics had many virtues: it secures Symmetry and Transparency, avoids the problem of *Missing scope ambiguities*, ensures that *One or the other will happen*, and explains *Retrospective truth judgments*. So we don't want to throw it out completely; we just want to tweak it minimally so that it can give correct predictions about *Retrospective accuracy judgments*.

9.8.1   *A relativist postsemantics*

The needed fix is not hard to see: instead of quantifying over all the worlds that overlap at the context of use, as the supervaluational theory does, we will need to quantify over all the worlds that overlap at the context of use and the context of assessment:

Relativist Postsemantics.   *A sentence S is true as used at c_0 and assessed from c_1 iff for all $w \in W(c_0, c_1)$, $[\![S]\!]^{c_0}_{\langle w, t_{c_0} \rangle} = True$,*

  where

$$W(c_0, c_1) = \begin{cases} W(c_1) & \text{if } W(c_1) \subset W(c_0) \\ W(c_0) & \text{otherwise} \end{cases}$$

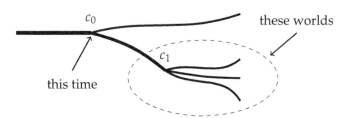

FIG. 9.2. The context of use (c_0) fixes the time, the context of assessment (c_1) the worlds.

An eternalist proposition p is true as used at c_0 and assessed from c_1 iff for every $w \in W(c_0, c_1)$, p is true at w.

A temporalist proposition p is true as used at c_0 and assessed from c_1 iff for every $w \in W(c_0, c_1)$, p is true at w, t_{c_0}.

On the relativist account, the context of use tells us which time to look at, while the context of assessment tells us which worlds to look at (see Fig. 9.2).[17]

This postsemantics explains the retrospective accuracy judgments. When c_0 is in the past of c_1, $W(c_0, c_1) = W(c_1)$, so an assessor at c_1 should take an assertion made at c_0 to be accurate just in case its content is true at all the worlds overlapping at c_1. That is why a proof of past unsettledness is not sufficient to compell retraction. But when $c_0 = c_1$, the assessor should take the assertion to be accurate just in case its content is true at all the worlds overlapping at c_0. That is why a proof of present unsettledness is sufficient to compel retraction.

9.8.2 *Explaining the pull of the Thin Red Line*

The Thin Red Line picture derives much of its intuitive plausibility, I think, from the following thought:

---

[17] The essential structural feature of this account is what Nuel Belnap calls "double time references" (Belnap, Perloff, and Xu 2001: 14; Belnap 2001: 1–22; the idea can also be found in Dummett 1981: 395). Belnap, however, does not use a notion of truth at a context of use and context of assessment. Instead, he gives an account of when an assertion is "vindicated" or "impugned" in terms of truth at a point of evaluation (context and index). My approach imposes another layer, the definition of truth at a context of use and context of assessment, between the definition of truth at a point of evaluation and the account of assertion. This allows the account of assertion to abstract from peculiarities of particular linguistic constructions. Everything specific to the index, and hence to the particular expressive resources of a language, is handled in the postsemantics, and "screened off" from the theory of speech acts, which can remain through changes in the index that might be motivated by the addition of additional linguistic resources. This is an attractive kind of modularity.

When tomorrow comes.   Right now it may not be settled whether it will be
sunny tomorrow. But when tomorrow comes, we will be able to look back at a
present utterance of "It will be sunny tomorrow" and say that it was accurate
(if it is sunny) or that it was not accurate (if it is not).

As we have seen, none of the classical alternatives to the Thin Red Line picture
can vindicate *When tomorrow comes*. They all predict that, even if it is sunny
tomorrow, we should judge our prediction today "it will be sunny tomorrow"
as inaccurate. And that just seems wrong.

However, the relativist account does vindicate *When tomorrow comes*, without positing a Thin Red Line. And, unlike the Thin Red Line account, the
relativist account gives correct predictions about counterfactual retrospective
assessments. When it rains tomorrow, the relativist can say not only that
yesterday's prediction of sunshine was accurate, but also that it wouldn't
have been accurate if it had rained today. (That is, it isn't accurate as assessed
from a context on the other branch.)

The relativist, then, can diagnose the flaw in the case for the Thin Red
Line. The case starts innocently, with a correct intuition about retrospective
assessments (*When tomorrow comes*). But it then makes a fallacious inference
(referring to Fig. 9.1):

(35)   An assessor at c_2 will be correct in assessing today's assertion that it
       will be sunny tomorrow as accurate.

(36)   It's (epistemically) possible that it will be sunny tomorrow.

(37)   Thus, it's (epistemically) possible that we'll be at c_2.

(38)   So, it's (epistemically) possible that tomorrow we'll be correct in as-
       sessing today's assertion that it will be sunny tomorrow as accurate.

(39)   So, it's (epistemically) possible that today we'd be correct in assessing
       today's assertion that it will be sunny tomorrow as accurate.

The fishy move is the last step, from (38) to (39). It assumes, in effect, that
accuracy does not vary with the context of assessment. If we make that
assumption—the denial of assessment sensitivity—then the argument from
When tomorrow comes to the Thin Red Line looks irresistible. But if we countenance assessment sensitivity, the argument stops at step (38).

9.8.3 *Some logical subtleties*

According to the supervaluational semantics, $\ulcorner\Box\phi\urcorner$ is an (absolute) logical consequence of ϕ, and vice versa, even though the two formulas cannot be intersubstituted in embedded contexts. ($\ulcorner$*Yesterday* $\phi\urcorner$ can be true at a context even when $\ulcorner$*Yesterday* $\Box\phi\urcorner$ is not.) The absolute logical equivalence of ϕ and $\ulcorner\Box\phi\urcorner$ is reflected in the plausible normative claim that one should assert ϕ only if one is in a position to assert $\ulcorner\Box\phi\urcorner$. Unfortunately, it also implies, less plausibly, that one is obliged to retract an earlier assertion of ϕ if one would have been obliged to retract an earlier assertion of $\ulcorner\Box\phi\urcorner$.

The relativist semantics allows us to split the difference. It implies that $\ulcorner\Box\phi\urcorner$ is a *diagonal* consequence, but not an absolute consequence, of ϕ (see §3.4). The diagonal equivalence of $\ulcorner\Box\phi\urcorner$ and ϕ is reflected in the norm that one should assert only what is settled true. But it implies nothing about retraction, because the context in which one considers retracting an assertion is not the same as the context in which one made the assertion. So the relativist can allow that an assertion of ϕ can stand even in cases where an assertion of $\ulcorner\Box\phi\urcorner$ would have to have been retracted.

The reader might worry that both supervaluationism and relativism afford an easy argument for determinism, along the following lines:

(40) $\ulcorner\phi \vee \neg\phi\urcorner$ is logically true.

(41) $\ulcorner\Box\phi\urcorner$ is a logical consequence of ϕ.

(42) $\ulcorner\Box\neg\phi\urcorner$ is a logical consequence of $\neg\phi$.

(43) So, $\ulcorner\Box\phi \vee \Box\neg\phi\urcorner$ is logically true—there are no future contingents.

The supervaluationist will endorse all the premises. And, while the relativist can reject premises (41) and (42) when "logical consequence" is construed as "absolute logical consequence," she will accept all the premises when "logical consequence" and "logically true" are interpreted as "diagonal logical consequence" and "diagonally logically true." How, then, can these theorists avoid accepting the conclusion, (43)? They can do it by rejecting the inference pattern that seems to license the move from (40)–(42) to (43). And indeed, the meta-rule

Semantic case argument. *If $\phi \models \xi$ and $\psi \models \xi$ then $\phi \vee \psi \models \xi$.*

fails on both the supervaluational and the relativist semantics.

This may seem strange, and indeed, some have thought it a compelling reason to reject the supervaluational account. For example, Timothy Williamson charges that "supervaluations invalidate our natural mode of deductive think-ing" (cf. Williamson 1994: 152). Granted, *Semantic case argument* holds in classical semantics, and has counterexamples with supervaluations. But un-less we dogmatically hold every principle that holds in classical logic and semantics sacrosanct, that by itself cannot be a strike against supervaluations.

Williamson's talk of "deductive thinking" suggests that his real concern is not with *Semantic case argument*, but with a corresponding natural deduction rule:

Case argument rule.

$$
\cfrac{\phi \vee \psi \quad \overset{\displaystyle\overset{\phi}{\vdots}}{\zeta} \quad \overset{\displaystyle\overset{\psi}{\vdots}}{\zeta}}{\zeta}
$$

It is plausible that some form of the *Case argument rule* is fundamental to the meaning of disjunction; and certainly the rule is a useful one. But the super-valuationist (and by extension the relativist) can have a natural deduction rule that looks like this, by distinguishing between rules that can be used in subproof contexts (replacing the vertical dots in the proof schema above) and rules that can only be used at the top level. Rules that can be used in subproofs are required to generate logical implications (§3.4), not just logical consequences. The rule allowing one to infer $\Box\phi$ from ϕ would, then, not be usable in a subproof. In this way we can keep the *Case argument rule* while still blocking the fatalist inference (40)–(43).[18]

9.9 Asserting future contingents

Together with our norms for assertion and retraction, the relativist semantics implies that one should never assert a future contingent, and that one should retract an assertion when its content is shown to be still unsettled. This may seem unreasonably stringent. We assert future contingents all the time. It does not seem that I have to be able to rule out the possibility of a strike or derailment in order to assert that I will be arriving at Paddington Station on the 9:30 train.

This is not an objection to the relativist view alone: it strikes equally against any view that takes future contingents to be untrue, including the supervaluational, three-valued, and Peircean views. Avoiding it would seem

---

[18]For a similar response to Williamson, see McGee and McLaughlin (2004: §3).

to require either adopting a TRL view or rejecting the Truth Norm for assertion in favor of something weaker (such as the norm that one should assert p only if one reasonably believes that p).

It is better simply to bite the bullet here. If I assert, "I'll arrive on the 9:30 train," and you challenge me—"Even if there is a strike or accident on the rails?"—then I must do one of the following:

1. *Retract* my assertion.

2. *Back up* my assertion by asserting that there will not be a strike or an accident.

3. *Clarify* that what I meant—what I asserted—was not the proposition that I would arrive on the 9:30 train, but something weaker: that I would arrive on the 9:30 train, barring strikes, accidents, or other rare and unpredictable mishaps; or that I would *very likely* arrive on the 9:30 train.

I cannot concede that there might be a strike or accident while standing by the unqualified assertion that I will arrive on the 9:30 train.

In practice, the third option—*Clarify*—is probably the most common. We seek efficiency in our use of tools general, including linguistic tools. When it is obvious that I mean to be talking about the afternoon, I can say "4:30" instead of "4:30 p.m." When it is obvious that I am not talking about an exact time, I can say "The meeting will start at noon" instead of "The meeting will start at noon or a few minutes after." When it is obvious that we are dealing with ordinary situations, I can say "The salt will dissolve in water" instead of "The salt will dissolve in water, provided that the water is not already supersaturated with salt." I mean to be asserting the same proposition with the pithy formulation that I could have asserted, at the cost of pedantry, with the longer one. If my audience mistakenly takes me to be asserting the proposition that the shorter sentence literally expresses, I will explain that this was not what I meant.

So, although the relativist view predicts that we should not assert future contingent propositions, it does not predict that we should not make assertions using sentences whose literal contents are future contingents. For we can quite reasonably use such sentences to assert propositions that are not future contingents—propositions about what is likely, or about what will happen barring unforeseen circumstances. It is not surprising that we should leave out pedantic qualifications when it is obvious what is intended.

For readers who are not happy with biting the bullet in this way, there is a simple way the relativist view might be modified so that it does not forbid the assertion of future contingents. *Relativist Postsemantics*, as stated in §9.8.1, gives a determinate verdict in every case. For every sentence S and contexts c_0, c_1, either S is determinately true as used at c_0 and assessed from c_1 or S is determinately not true as used at c_0 and assessed from c_1. Sentences expressing future contingents are determinately not true, and that is why the Truth Norm forbids asserting them. But we could tweak the postsemantics so that instead of a necessary and sufficient condition for truth, it provides only a sufficient condition for truth and a sufficient condition for non-truth, leaving some cases indeterminate:

Indeterminate Relativist Postsemantics. *A sentence S is true as used at c_0 and assessed from c_1 if for all $w \in W(c_0, c_1)$, $[\![S]\!]^{c_0}_{\langle w, t_{c_0} \rangle} = True$, and not true as used at c_0 and assessed from c_1 if if for all $w \in W(c_0, c_1)$, $[\![S]\!]^{c_0}_{\langle w, t_{c_0} \rangle} \neq True$.*

If neither of these conditions is met, S is neither determinately true or determinately not true as used at c_0 and assessed from c_1. (There is no "fact of the matter," we might say.)

Consider a future contingent proposition p—say, the proposition that I will arrive on the 9:30 train—and let c be a context at which p is not yet settled. Where the *Relativist Postsemantics* classes p as determinately not true (as used at and assessed from c), the *Indeterminate Relativist Postsemantics* classes p as not determinately true but also not determinately not true (as used at and assessed from c). Where the original postsemantics (in conjunction with the Truth Norm for assertion) determines that p should not be asserted at c, the modified postsemantics leaves it indeterminate whether p should be asserted at c, and indeterminate whether an assertion of p made prior to c should be retracted at c. It will still be determinate, though, that an assertion of p should be retracted at a context c' containing only worlds at which p is false.

The modified view will not satisfy those who think that asserting a future contingent can be determinately permissible. But it may assuage those who simply rebel at the idea that asserting a future contingent is always impermissible. The price is that the modified theory has gaps in its normative implications; it says nothing in cases where the original theory provides a verdict.[19]

---

[19] I am grateful to Michael Caie for getting me to think about this sort of view.

9.10   Future-directed attitudes

Perhaps the biggest difficulty facing the relativist—and any other approach that takes future contingents to be neither true nor false at a context—is making sense of future-directed attitudes. David Lewis argues:

The trouble with branching exactly is that it conflicts with our ordinary presupposition that we have a single future. If two futures are equally mine, one with a sea fight tomorrow and one without, it is nonsense to wonder which way it will be—it will be both ways—and yet I do wonder. (Lewis 1986: 207–8)

As we have seen, neither the supervaluational nor the relativist account predicts that "it will be both ways." According to both theories,

(44)   There will be a sea battle tomorrow and there will not be a sea battle tomorrow
       Tomorrow F ∧ *Tomorrow* ¬*F*

comes out false when both a sea battle and peace are objectively possible. Still, even if Lewis's reason for thinking that "it is nonsense to wonder which way it will be" is not quite right, one might remain puzzled. On the relativist account, an agent who takes it to be objectively contingent whether there will be a sea battle tomorrow should regard neither "there will be a sea battle" nor "there will not be a sea battle" as true (as used at and assessed from her present context). She should also hold that neither the proposition that there will be a sea battle the next day nor the proposition that there will not be a sea battle the next day is true at all of the possible worlds she occupies. With these things settled, what scope is left for wondering? Call this the *Wondering problem*.

There is a closely related problem about partial belief, which we might call the *Credence problem*. The relativist account predicts, plausibly, that an agent who thinks both a sea battle and peace are possible should not believe either that there will be a sea battle or that there will not be a sea battle. (Both propositions are untrue as used and assessed from the agent's context; see §5.7.) But in addition to asking about full belief, we can ask about partial belief. What credence (subjective probability) should the agent have in the proposition that there will be a sea battle?

Here competing considerations seem to point in different directions. On the one hand, the agent knows that the proposition that there will be a sea battle is not true, as used at and assessed from her context. Normally we give a very low credence to things we are certain are untrue. That suggests that the agent should have a very low (perhaps 0) credence in both the proposition that there will be a sea battle and its negation.[20]

On the other hand, when an agent has a credence of 0 that p, we generally take it to be irrational for her to accept a bet on p *at any odds*. (The expected utility of the bet is the value of the bet times the credence in p minus the cost of the bet; so if the credence in p is 0, then the expected utility of the bet cannot be greater than 0.) So, if the considerations in the preceding paragraph are correct, an agent who thinks that both Heads and Tails are objectively possible outcomes of a coin flip should not accept a bet at any odds on the outcome. And that is surely wrong. Surely it would be rational for the agent to pay one dollar for a chance to win a hundred dollars if a fair coin lands Heads, and irrational to decline such a bet.

So we have a dilemma. Either we preserve the connections between degree of belief and truth—the idea that, when one is certain a proposition is not true (as used at and assessed from one's context), one believes it to degree 0—or we preserve the connections between degree of belief and rational action (for example, in accepting bets). We cannot have both, but both seem essential.

Williams (2010), who is pessimistic about the prospects for resolving this dilemma, suggests that the best way out is to think of degrees of belief in future contingents as degrees of belief "under the fiction" that there is a single, determinate future. But this proposal seems unpromising, quite apart from the technical worries Williams raises. It is not generally rational to engage in make-believe while making bets. I may believe "under the fiction that I am a great basketball player" that I can sink ten balls in a row from ten yards distance, but I would be ill advised to bet on this. Why should things be any different for future contingents?

One might think that the dilemma can be resolved by observing that the rationality of betting depends on the chance one will get the payoff. This, in turn, depends not on whether the proposition that the coin will land Heads is true as assessed from the present moment, but whether it will be assessed as true after the coin lands, when the payoff will be determined. So, the fact that the proposition is neither true nor false as assessed from the present moment

---

[20]The agent will simultaneously have a high credence in the disjunctive proposition that either there will be a sea battle or there won't be one. Of course, this combination of credences violates standard probability axioms. However, there are nonstandard theories of subjective credence that reject finite additivity. Field (2000) argues that taking a proposition to be indeterminate in truth value just *is* having a low credence in both it and its negation.

is irrelevant to the rationality of the bet. But this doesn't really help, since the proposition that *is* relevant to the bet—namely, that the proposition that the coin will land Heads will be assessed as true after it lands—is itself a future contingent.

   Instead, we need to revisit the assumption behind the first horn of the dilemma:

Context-relative Truth and Credence. *If an agent takes a proposition to be untrue as used at and assessed from the context she currently occupies, she ought to have a very low degree of belief in that proposition.*

This assumption seems plausible, I suggest, because it is easily confused with the following *true* assumption:

Monadic Truth and Credence. *If an agent takes a proposition to be untrue, she ought to have a very low degree of belief in that proposition.*

Given our semantics for monadic "true" (§4.8), a proposition p is not true just in case it is not the case that p. So, assuming this is transparent to the agent, *Monadic Truth and Credence* is equivalent to

Negative Belief and Credence. *If an agent believes not-p, she ought to have a very low degree of belief in p.*

This is a minimal constraint on the relation between binary belief and credence—one that presumably everyone will accept. So we ought to accept *Monadic Truth and Credence*. But that is not to say that we should accept *Context-relative Truth and Credence*, which is a stronger principle. When one takes neither a proposition nor its negation to be true as used at and assessed from one's current context, one should believe neither the proposition nor its negation. Hence, one should believe neither that the proposition is true (in the monadic sense) nor that it is not true—since believing that it is not true would require believing its negation. Since one should not believe that a future contingent is untrue (in the monadic sense), *Monadic Truth and Credence* yields no constraint on one's credences in future contingents.

   It is important to recall here that the context(s)-relative truth predicate we use in semantics is a theoretical term, whose sense is given in part by the norms for truth and binary belief. These norms specify that, when a proposition is untrue as used at and assessed from one's current context, one should not assert it or believe it outright.[21] But they say nothing about what degree of partial belief one may have, so long as it does not suffice for full belief. That leaves it open that one may have, say, 0.5 credence in a proposition one regards as a future contingent. The first horn of the dilemma gets its force from the reflection that, if one believed that a future contingent were *not true* (in the monadic sense), it would follow that one ought not to have an 0.5 credence; after all, given the disquotational behavior of monadic truth, believing that it is not true is tantamount to believing its negation, which requires giving it a very low credence. But one can believe that a proposition is not true as used at and assessed from one's context without believing that it is not true (in the monadic sense). Indeed, when one believes that neither the proposition nor its negation is true as used at and assessed from one's context, one must believe *neither* that the proposition is true (in the monadic sense) *nor* that it is not true. So the first horn of the dilemma is based on a kind of confusion.

So much for the *Credence problem*. Similar considerations can be brought to bear on the *Wondering problem*. It would be crazy to wonder whether p while believing that p is not true (in the monadic sense), for believing that p is not true is tantamount to believing that not-p. But believing that p is not true as used and assessed from one's context does not require believing that p is not true (in the monadic sense). Indeed, when one believes that neither p nor its negation is true as used and assessed from one's context, one cannot coherently believe that p is not true (in the monadic sense). As we have seen, it can be rational in such a case to have intermediate credences in p and not-p, and that is just the state in which it makes sense to wonder whether p.

9.11 Conclusion

David Lewis thought that the idea that worlds overlap and branch "conflicts with our ordinary presupposition that we have a single future," and that we must either reject it or accept that much of our talk about the future is incoherent (Lewis 1986: 206–209). Faced with this choice, Lewis rejects branching:

---

[21] In practice, we may use fuzzy versions of these norms. We think that the things we assert or believe should be *close enough* to being true at our current contexts. How close is close enough depends on what we're doing and what our interests are. Even if quantum mechanics tells me there's a possible future on which the particles in the bus that is approaching spontaneously form into a lion, that doesn't make me hesitate to assert or believe that I won't be eaten by a lion in the next minute. I ignore this complication here.

he thinks that we can dismiss on "common sense" grounds the suggestion that "we ourselves are involved in branching" (209). This is an odd argument for Lewis to make, given his generally deferential attitude towards science (cf. Lewis 1991: 58–59), since some prominent interpretations of our best physical theories seem to require a branching structure of historical possibilities. Belnap, Perloff, and Xu (2001: 205) point out that a similar argument from common sense could be used against the claim that there are no reference-frame-independent facts about simultaneity. If we have to choose between what science tells us about the world and the coherence of our ordinary talk, it seems we should plump for science and reform our talk to fit.

Still, the thought that science could reveal that all of our future-directed thought and talk is incoherent is deeply unsettling. When we discover that our ordinary talk of simultaneity presupposes falsely that simultaneity is absolute, reform is not so difficult. We can learn to relativize our simultaneity claims to a reference frame, and we can explain why most of our ordinary simultaneity talk is successful despite its false presupposition. What would we do, though, if we found that all of our future-directed talk falsely presupposes that there is an "actual future"? What replacement could we find that served the same purpose? *Could* we stop wondering about what will happen, content that all the alternatives are realized in different futures that are equally ours? Could we learn to confine ourselves to talk about what is possible and inevitable?

I have argued in this chapter that we can avoid both horns of Lewis's terrible dilemma. If we countenance assessment sensitivity, we can make good sense of ordinary thought and talk about the future, whether or not branching obtains.

10

MIGHT

If I say, "Goldbach's conjecture might be true, and it might be false," I am not making a claim about what could have been the case, had things gone differently. Nor am I expressing a belief in the metaphysical contingency of mathematics. Rather, I am expressing my uncertainty—or perhaps our collective uncertainty—about the truth or falsity of Goldbach's conjecture. Similarly, if I say "Joe can't be running," I am not saying that Joe's constitution prohibits him from running, or that Joe is essentially a non-runner, or that Joe isn't allowed to run. My basis for making the claim may be nothing more than that I see Joe's running shoes hanging on a hook. Here I am expressing certainty.

Modal adjectives and adverbs whose primary use is to express states of certainty or uncertainty are called *epistemic* modals. To add a few more examples:

(1) P is probably equal to NP.

(2) There's a ten percent chance of rain tonight.

(3) It must be Tuesday.

(4) He could be coming in on Wednesday.

(5) It is possible that she didn't pass the exam.

It is uncontroversial that such sentences are commonly used to express a state of certainty or uncertainty, and to indicate to the audience what possibilities the speaker takes to be open. But there is little agreement about their truth conditions, or even whether they have truth conditions.

One natural thought is that epistemic modals are used to make claims whose truth or falsity depends on what the speaker knows. According to *Solipsistic Contextualism*, "Joe might be running" expresses a truth just in case what the speaker knows does not rule out that Joe is running, and "Joe must be running" expresses a truth just in case what the speaker knows rules out that Joe is not running.[1]

Solipsistic Contextualism promises to explain two facts about epistemic modals that would otherwise seem quite puzzling. First, it explains why we are normally prepared to make epistemic possibility claims on the basis of our own ignorance. If someone asks me whether Joe is in China, it is generally okay for me to reply, "He might be," unless I know that he is not. This is just what we should expect if the truth of "He might be" depends on what the speaker knows. It is not what we should expect if the truth of "He might be" depends in part on what others know, or on what one could come to know. As we will see in what follows, the more "objective" we make claims about epistemic possibility, the larger the gap between the circumstances in which we are warranted in making them and the circumstances in which we actually do make them. Solipsistic Contextualism explains why we are willing to assert "It might be that *p*" in roughly the same cases as "For all I know, *p*."

Second, Solipsistic Contextualism explains why the following sentences sound paradoxical:

(6) Joe might be in China, but I know he isn't.

(7) Joe might be in China, but he isn't.

According to Solipsistic Contextualism, (6) is a contradiction: when the second conjunct expresses a truth, the first must express a falsehood. And, while (7) isn't a contradiction—possibility had better not imply actuality!—it is pragmatically infelicitous, since in asserting that Joe isn't in China, one represents oneself as knowing that he isn't, contrary to what is conveyed by the first conjunct.[2]

However, there are serious problems with Solipsistic Contextualism. I will not be alone in pointing them out: most of them have been noticed already by nonsolipsistic contextualists and expressivists. But I think that the former have failed to appreciate how deep these problems are, while the

[1]For present purposes, we can leave the notion of "ruling out" schematic: we need not decide, for instance, whether knowledge that *p* rules out everything logically inconsistent with *p*. Our discussion of Solipsistic Contextualism and its variants will turn only on *whose* knowledge is at stake, not on what "ruling out" consists in. Hence we will regard theories that understand epistemic modals as quantifiers over "epistemically possible worlds" as versions of Solipsistic Contextualism, provided they take the relevant set of worlds (together with an ordering, perhaps) as determined by the *speaker's* knowledge or evidence.

[2]Cf. DeRose (1991: 600), Stanley (2005a).

latter have appreciated them but overreacted. There is, as I will argue, a viable truth-conditional semantics for epistemic modals, provided we are willing to embrace assessment sensitivity.

10.1   Against Solipsistic Contextualism

Suppose you are standing in a coffee line, and you overhear Sally and George discussing a mutual acquaintance, Joe:

> *Coffee Shop*
> SALLY: Joe might be in China. I didn't see him today.
> GEORGE: No, he can't be in China. He doesn't have his visa yet.
> SALLY: Oh, really? Then I guess I was wrong.

It seems that George is contradicting Sally and rejecting her claim. It also seems that, having learned something from George, Sally concedes that she was wrong. Finally, it seems appropriate for her to retract her original claim, rather than continuing to stand by it.[3] Think how odd it would be were she to respond:

> SALLY: Oh, really? #Still, I was right when I said "Joe might be in
>   China," and I stand by my claim.

Some have suggested that George's "No" might be read as targeting not Sally's claim that Joe might be in China, but its prejacent, the proposition that Joe is in China (von Fintel and Gillies 2008: 83–4; Portner 2009: 175). Compare:

> A: It's rumored that you are leaving California.
> B: No, that's false.

Here what is being rejected is just the suggestion that B is leaving California, not the claim that this is rumored. But this maneuver is not plausible in *Coffee Shop*. First, George can make explicit what he is rejecting: "It's not the case that he might be in China." Second, Sally's concession and retraction would not make sense if George were just rejecting the prejacent; she didn't assert that Joe *was* in China, but only that he might be. By contrast, retraction would be completely bizarre in the dialogue between A and B, above.

---

[3]Note that Sally's retraction is not tantamount to an admission that she should not have made the assertion in the first place; cf. §5.4. To say that one was wrong *in claiming* that *p* is not to say that one was wrong *to claim* that *p*. Sometimes it is right to make a claim that turns out to have been wrong (false)—say, because one had an abundance of misleading evidence. So, if you find it implausible that Sally would say "I was wrong" in the dialogue above, make sure you're not interpreting her as saying "I was wrong to say that."

If all of this is right, then any view about epistemic modals must have answers to the following questions:

Warrant Question. On what basis did Sally take herself to be warranted in making her first claim?

Rejection Question. On what basis did George take himself to be warranted in rejecting Sally's claim as incorrect?

Retraction Question. On what basis did Sally concede that she was wrong, after George's intervention? What did she learn from George's remark that made her retract her original claim?

Solipsistic Contextualism has an easy answer to the Warrant Question: Sally knows that she can't rule out Joe's being in China, and that is precisely the condition for "Joe might be in China" to be true in her context. But it seems to have no good answer to the Rejection Question and the Retraction Question. If Solipsistic Contextualism is correct, it is just a confusion to think that George is in a position to reject Sally's claim—for that, he'd need to know something about what *she* knew, not about Joe's location. And it is just a confusion to think that Sally should retract her claim after learning that Joe still lacks a visa. After all, she still knows that nothing she knew at the time of her utterance ruled out Joe's being in China.

It might still be possible to tell a story about how George could *mistakenly* think that he is in a position to contradict Sally, and how Sally could *mistakenly* think that she ought to retract her assertion. Perhaps George mistakenly takes Sally to have asserted what *he* would have asserted by saying "Joe might be in China." Perhaps Sally, assessing her own past assertion, mistakenly takes it to have the content she would *now* express if she used the same sentence. And perhaps the two are mistakenly taking themselves to contradict each other, when in reality they are simply talking past each other.

But that is a lot of error to impute to speakers. One wants some explanation of why speakers are systematically confused in this way, and why this confusion doesn't generalize to other cases that should be similar if Solipsistic Contextualism is correct. For example, if speakers are systematically blind to unobvious context sensitivity, why doesn't the following dialogue seem natural?

> A: Joe is tall. In fact, he's the tallest graduate student in our department.

B: No, he isn't tall. He's shorter than nearly every NBA player.

A: Okay, then, scratch that. I was wrong.

One would also need to explain why the data that seems to support Solipsistic Contextualism (primarily data about when speakers take themselves to be warranted in making epistemic modal claims) should be taken so seriously, when the data about third-party assessments, retraction, and disputes are just thrown away. There is no clear reason to favor the "positive" data in this way. On the contrary, semantics is typically driven more by data about perceived incompatibilities and entailments than by data about when people are willing to accept sentences. I propose, then, to put this approach to defending Solipsistic Contextualism on the back burner, as a last resort should no alternative view prove viable.

10.2   Flexible Contextualism

These problems with Solipsistic Contextualism are relatively well known. Indeed, although Solipsistic Contextualism is sometimes assumed in discussions of other matters (e.g. in Stanley 2005a: 128), no one who has staked out a serious position on the semantics of epistemic modals defends the view.[4]

The usual assumption, however, is that the problems with Solipsistic Contextualism lie with its solipsism, and that the solution is to move towards a form of contextualism that is less solipsistic. If "Joe might be in China" doesn't mean "For all I know, Joe is in China," perhaps it means "For all *we* know, Joe is in China," or "For all we know or could easily come to know, Joe is in China." All of these can be thought of as variants on "What is known does not rule out Joe's being in China," with different glosses on "what is known." According to *Flexible Contextualism*, occurrences of "might" are to be evaluated with respect to the body of information that is relevant at the context of use, but the relevant body of information can extend beyond what

---

[4]Solipsistic Contextualism is sometimes attributed to G. E. Moore (perhaps the first philosopher to clearly distinguish epistemic uses of modals from others) on the basis of passages like this one: "People *in philosophy* say: The *props.* that I'm not sitting down now, that I'm not male, that I'm dead, that I died before the murder of Julius Caesar, that I shall die before 12 to-night, are 'logically possible'. But it's not English to say, with this meaning: It's possible that I'm not sitting down now etc.—*this* only means 'It's not certain that I am' or 'I don't know that I am'" (Moore 1962: 184). However, Moore did not accept the Solipsistic Contextualist analysis of "must." He denied that "It *must* be that *p*" means the same as "It's impossible that not-*p*" (188), on the grounds that it is appropriate to say the former only when one does not know *directly* (e.g. by seeing) that *p*. It seems that he also rejected the solipsistic view for "probably" (402).

is known by the speaker. This is the orthodox view in both philosophy and linguistics.

In what follows, we will look at how Flexible Contextualism has been motivated as a response to the problems facing Solipsistic Contextualism. I will argue that the proposed cure fails, because it is based on a misdiagnosis of the disease. The fundamental problem with Solipsistic Contextualism lies with its contextualism, not its solipsism.

10.2.1   *Widening the relevant community*

A natural thought is that the solipsist's inability to answer the Rejection and Retraction Questions shows that the truth conditions she assigns are too weak. By strengthening the claim we take Sally to be making, we can make George's rejection and Sally's retraction intelligible. The obvious move is to suppose that the knowledge relevant to the truth of Sally's epistemic modal claim is not just *her* knowledge, but her knowledge together with George's. This proposal would allow the contextualist to answer the Rejection and Retraction Questions as follows:

Rejection Question.   George takes himself to be warranted in rejecting Sally's claim, because at the time of her claim he already knew enough to rule out Joe's being in China. Since, on the hypothesis being considered, the truth of her claim depends not just on what Sally knew when she made it, but also on what George knew, this is sufficient basis for rejecting it.

Retraction Question.   Sally retracts her claim because she has learned from George that he knew something, at the time she made the claim, that ruled out Joe's being in China.

Generalizing, we arrive at the idea that "It might be that p" is true at a context if what is known by the contextually relevant group does not rule out that p.[5] Such a view could still explain the paradoxical ring of (6) and (7), provided it is assumed that the agent of the context (speaker) always belongs to the contextually relevant group, and that the group counts as knowing if any member does. On these assumptions, if the speaker knows that Joe isn't in China, then "Joe might be in China" cannot express a truth. It follows that (6) is a contradiction and that (7) is pragmatically infelicitous.

---

[5]What is it for the knowledge of a group G to rule out that p? A variety of answers are possible. Teller (1972) argues that a group's knowledge can rule out that p even if no group member's knowledge rules out that p, provided that p is inconsistent with the totality of facts known by various members of the group.

So far, the move away from solipsism seems well-motivated and plausible. But there is a problem. We made it easier for the contextualist to answer the Rejection and Retraction Questions by strengthening the truth conditions of epistemic possibility sentences: stronger claims are easier to reject and retract. But the more we do that, the harder it becomes to answer the Warrant Question: stronger claims are harder to assert. At the very least, then, the contextualist faces a delicate balancing act.

In the case of *Coffee Shop*, balance seems possible. In order to answer the Warrant Question, we must assume that Sally had grounds for thinking that nothing she *or* George knew ruled out Joe's being in China. If George is a close acquaintance, it's not implausible that she should have such grounds.

But we can tweak the case in ways that make the Warrant Question much more difficult. Suppose that George does not know about Joe's visa, but you do:

Eavesdropping

SALLY: Joe might be in China. I didn't see him today.

GEORGE: Neither did I.

YOU: Forgive me for eavesdropping, but Joe can't be in China. He doesn't have his visa yet.

SALLY: Oh, really? Then I guess I was wrong.

You reject Sally's claim as false, not because you think Sally or George knows about Joe's visa situation, but because *you* know. And Sally is prepared to retract her claim after your correction. To answer the Rejection and Retraction Questions, then, the contextualist must include you (along with Sally and George) in the contextually relevant group. Sally didn't know that you were there when she made her claim; indeed, we may suppose that she did not notice you were there until you spoke, and even that she does not know who you are. If you were part of the contextually relevant group, then, it is just by virtue of being a random eavesdropper. But if the contextually relevant group contains all random eavesdroppers, Sally's claim becomes a very strong one, since it can only be true if nobody within earshot has information that rules out Joe's being in China. How could Sally have thought herself warranted in asserting *that*? She would certainly not have asserted that nobody in earshot has any information that would exclude Joe's being in China. The Warrant Question now seems impossible to answer.

And why limit ourselves to earshot? It doesn't matter much to our story that you are in the same room as Sally. You'd assess her claim the same way if you were thousands of miles away, listening through a wiretap. Indeed, it seems to me that it does not even matter whether you are listening to the wiretap live or reviewing a recording the next day—or the next year. (In that case it will be your knowledge concerning Joe's whereabouts on the day the recording was made that is relevant—but still *your* knowledge, not Sally's, and your knowledge *now*.) To answer the Rejection Question, the Flexible Contextualist would have to extend the relevant group of knowers not just to those within earshot, but to all those who will one day hear of, read of, or perhaps even conjecture about, Sally's claim. There's no natural stopping point short of that.[6]

The worry, then, is that the arguments that motivate a move from the "for all I know" reading of epistemic modals to the "for all we know" reading also motivate extending the scope of "we" to include not just the participants in the conversation but eavesdroppers, no matter how well hidden or how distantly separated in time and space. "It is possible that p" thus becomes "p is not ruled out by what is known by anyone who will ever consider this claim." But if this is what epistemic modals mean, then most ordinary uses of them are completely irresponsible. Surely Sally would not be warranted in asserting "Nothing known by me *or by anyone who will ever consider this claim* excludes Joe's being in China." Indeed, she may have good reason to deny this. But intuitively Sally *is* warranted in asserting that Joe might be in China; her assertion is a paradigm use of an epistemic modal.

---

[6]Von Fintel and Gillies (2008: 86) claim that Rejection becomes much less natural with time lag. They say that it would be very odd if Detective Parker, reading an old transcript of a court case where Al Capone says "The loot might be in the safe," were to say,

(a) Al was wrong/What Al said is false. The safe was cracked by Geraldo in the 80s and there was nothing inside.

While I agree that it would be odd for Parker to say this, I think that is because it is unclear what purpose he would have in doing so. As Fabrizio Cariani pointed out to me, this diagnosis is supported by the fact that it would be at least as odd for him to say:

(b) Al was right/What Al said is true. He had no idea where the loot was.

If we suppose that the reason Parker is reviewing these transcripts is that he wants to find the stash of loot Capone was searching for—so that it is a live question for him where the loot is—then I think (a) sounds entirely natural.

10.2.2 *Objective factors*

Hacking (1967) has a somewhat different argument for the same conclusion—
that widening the relevant group of knowers to include the speaker's conversational partners is the wrong response to the problems facing Solipsistic
Contextualism.

> Imagine a salvage crew searching for a ship that sank a long time ago. The mate of the
> salvage ship works from an old log, makes a mistake in his calculations, and concludes
> that the wreck may be in a certain bay. It is possible, he says, that the hulk is in these
> waters. No one knows anything to the contrary. But in fact, as it turns out later, it
> simply was not possible for the vessel to be in that bay; more careful examination of
> the log shows that the boat must have gone down at least thirty miles further south.
> The mate said something false when he said, "It is possible that we shall find the
> treasure here," but the falsehood did not arise from what anyone actually knew at the
> time. (Hacking 1967: 148)

Hacking concludes that the truth of epistemic modal claims must depend not
just on what is known, but on objective features of the situation—here, the
presence of relevant information in the log.

   This is another way in which contextualism might be made nonsolipsistic:
instead of (or in addition to) widening the community of relevant epistemic
agents, we can relax the strength of the relation these agents must stand in
to the relevant facts. In addition to looking at what they *do* know, we look
at what they could *come* to know through a "practicable investigation" (as
Hacking puts it), or what is within their "epistemic reach" (as Egan 2007 puts
it). We might say that "it is possible that *p*" expresses a truth if what is within
the speaker's epistemic reach (or perhaps the epistemic reach of a contextually
relevant group) does not rule out *p*. In a similar vein, DeRose (1991) appeals
to "relevant way[s] by which members of the relevant community can come
to know," and Moore (1962: 402) to a distinction between what the speaker
and hearers "easily might know" and what they "couldn't easily know or
have known."

   On this view, the answers to the Rejection and Retraction Questions in
Coffee Shop are as follows:

Rejection Question. George takes himself to be warranted in rejecting Sally's
   claim, because at the time of her claim, information that ruled out Joe's
   being in China was within her epistemic reach. (She had only to ask him.)

Retraction Question. Sally retracts her claim because she has learned that, at
   the time she made the claim, information that ruled out Joe's being in

China was within her epistemic reach.

The main problem with this strategy is much the same as the problem with widening the relevant community. In order to answer the Rejection and Retraction Questions, not just for *Coffee Shop*, but in general, we will have to make "epistemic reach" very broad indeed. To handle *Eavesdropping*, for example, we will have to construe everything an eavesdropper might potentially say as within one's epistemic reach. And Sally will retract her assertion just as surely if she finds an itinerary on the floor as she will in response to George's intervention—even if her finding this scrap of paper is completely fortuitous. Thus the notion of epistemic reach that is needed extends far beyond intuitive ideas of a "practicable investigation" or "contextually relevant way of coming to know." This extension of epistemic reach makes epistemic possibility claims much stronger, to the point where it is difficult to see how we can answer the Warrant Question.

Even leaving aside worries about the Warrant Question, it is hard to see how extending epistemic reach can be a fully adequate answer to the Rejection Question. People used to think that it was possible that there were even numbers greater than 2 and less than 10^{17} that were not the sum of two primes. It seems correct to say that they were wrong in this belief—since we have now verified computationally that there cannot be any such numbers. But surely this computation was not within *their* epistemic reach. Similarly, we will judge Sally's claim false (on the basis of what we know) even if we are listening in remotely, so that Sally is unable to take advantage of our information about Joe's wherabouts.

Hacking is right that extending the contextually relevant group of knowers cannot explain our rejection of the mate's claim in the salvage ship case. But his alternative strategy of looking instead at what could be ruled out by "practicable investigations" fails too. It would be perfectly natural for the mate to say:

(8) It's possible that the ship sank in this bay, but it's also possible that it went down on the reef to the south. Let's examine the log more closely before we dive: maybe we can find something that rules out one of these locations.

In his second sentence, the mate is acknowledging the possibility that a "practicable investigation" will rule out one of the two possibilities. If Hacking is right, that is tantamount to acknowledging that one of the two conjuncts of the mate's first sentence might be false. So if Hacking's proposal is right, then the mate's speech should sound as infelicitous as

(9)   Jane is in China and Al is in New York. Maybe Jane is in Japan.

But it doesn't; it is perfectly felicitous. We need another approach.

10.2.3   *The puzzle*

All of the proposals we've considered in this section are attempts to preserve the core contextualism of Solipsistic Contextualism—the idea that epistemic modals are contextually sensitive to what is known at the context of use—while dropping the implausible solipsism. And all of them face the same basic problem. We can answer the Rejection and Retraction Questions within the framework of a contextualist theory only by making the truth conditions of epistemic possibility claims stronger. But the stronger we make them, the harder it is to answer the Warrant Question. The less solipsistic the theory becomes, the harder it is to explain why speakers feel entitled to make the epistemic modal claims they do.

Although we have focused so far on expressions of epistemic possibility, the same arguments can be applied, *mutatis mutandis*, to "it is likely that," "it is probable that," "it is more likely than not that," "there is a 30 percent chance that," and other expressions of epistemic probability. Solipsistic contextualist accounts of these locutions give bad predictions about retraction and disagreement, but if we drop the solipsism while retaining the contextualism, we get bad predictions about when one is warranted in making assertions using these locutions.

We are left, then, with a puzzle: although the truth of a claim made using epistemic modals must depend somehow on what is known—that is what makes it "epistemic"—it does not seem to depend on any *particular* body of knowledge. There is no way to account for this in the framework of contextualism, which requires that the relevant body of knowledge be determined by features of the context of use. The fundamental problem with Solipsistic Contextualism lies with its contextualism, not its solipsism.

10.3   Expressivism

If these arguments seem familiar, perhaps it's because they've been made before. Consider how Price (1983) argues against truth-conditional treatments of "probably." First, he points out that we do not treat claims about what is "probable" as claims about what is likely given the *speaker's* evidence:

If I disagree with your claim that it is probably going to snow, I am not disagreeing that given *your* evidence it is likely that this is so; but indicating what follows from *my* evidence. Indeed, I might *agree* that it is probably going to snow and yet think it false that this follows from your evidence. (403)

He then notes that if we fix this problem by expanding the relevant body of evidence to include evidence that is available in principle, we can no longer understand how speakers take themselves to be justified in making the probability judgments they do:

Consider the surgeon who says, 'Your operation has probably been successful. We could find out for sure, but since the tests are painful and expensive, it is best to avoid them.' The accessibility, in principle, of evidence which would override that on which the SP judgement is based, is here explicitly acknowledged. (405)

If we look at when speakers make "probably" claims, we are pushed toward a solipsistic semantics, while if we look at third-party assessments of such claims, we are pushed toward something more objective. The upshot is that there is no way of filling in the X in "Given evidence X, it is probable that q" that would yield plausible truth conditions for the unqualified "It is probable that q."

Price takes these arguments to show that "probably" does not contribute to the propositional content of a speech act at all. His view is that "probably" contributes to the *force* of a speech act, not its content. Other philosophers and linguists have proposed similar accounts of "possibly" and other epistemic modals. So it is worth considering whether such approaches might provide a satisfactory resolution to the problems scouted in the preceding two sections.

10.3.1 *Force modifiers*

It would be misguided to ask how "speaking frankly" contributes to the truth conditions of

(10)   Speaking frankly, she's too good for him.

When (10) is used to make an assertion, what is asserted is simply *that she's too good for him*. "Speaking frankly" does not contribute anything to the content of the assertion; its role is rather to comment on the kind of speech act being made. We should not puzzle ourselves about when the proposition *that speaking frankly she's too good for him* is true, because there is no such proposition.

Perhaps asking how epistemic modals affect truth conditions is equally misguided. We have assumed so far that Sally is making an assertion, and this assumption leads directly to questions about the truth conditions of her claim. But we need not understand her speech act as an assertion. Perhaps she is simply signaling her unwillingness to assert that Joe *isn't* in China. As Hare argues, "We have a use for a way of volubly and loquaciously *not* making a certain statement; and perhaps there is one sense of 'may' in which it fulfils this function" (1967: 321). Or perhaps she is *perhapserting* the proposition *that Joe is in China*—where a "perhapsertion" is a distinct kind of speech act, which we might understand as the expression of some minimal degree of credence, or advice not to ignore a possibility. If the linguistic role of epistemic modals is to signal that the speaker is making a perhapsertion, then we need not trouble ourselves about the contribution it makes to truth conditions.[7]

Such views account well for our uses of (standalone) sentences involving epistemic modals, while allowing us to dodge the questions about truth conditions that we saw above to be so problematic. However, they make it difficult to explain embedded uses of epistemic modals.

10.3.2 *Embeddings*

Epistemic modals can occur embedded under quantifiers, truth-functional connectives, conditionals, attitude verbs, adjectives, and other constructions.[8] In this they differ greatly from "speaking frankly," which does not embed in these ways:

(11) (a) If it might be raining, we should bring umbrellas.

      (b) #If speaking frankly she's too good for him, she'll realize this.

(12) (a) It's not possible that Joe is in China.

      (b) #It's not the case that speaking frankly, Joe is in China.

(13) (a) Sally believes that it's possible that Joe is in China.

      (b) #Sally believes that speaking frankly, she's too good for him.

The force modifier approach tells us nothing about the contribution made by "might" in (11a) or "possible" in (12a). It is clear that "might" in (11a) is *not* indicating that anything is being perhapserted. In typical uses of (11a), the whole conditional is being asserted full stop, and the antecedent is neither

[7]Compare also Frege (1879) on "must"; and van Heijenoort (1967: 5), Boyd and Thorne (1969: 71), and Stalnaker (1999: 45) on "may."

[8]However, there are some interesting restrictions. For example, von Fintel and Iatridou (2003) argue that in many contexts epistemic modals must take wide scope over quantifiers.

asserted nor perhapserted. (It's perfectly coherent to say, "If p, then q. But not p.") There is clearly a difference between (11a) and

(14)   If it is raining, we should bring umbrellas,

but the force-modifier account of "might" does not help us understand what it is, since "might" is not serving as a force modifier in (11a).

Similarly, the force-modifier account of

(15)   It's possible that Joe is in China

gives us no guidance whatsoever about the meaning of (12a). Clearly "possible" occurs here within the scope of the negation—(12a) does not mean the same thing as

(16)   It's possible that Joe is not in China

—but little sense can be made of the negation of a *speech act*.

Finally, in (13a), "possible" occurs in the description of the content of a cognitive state, not a speech act. Although it is fairly clear how we could leverage our understanding of the kind of speech act conventionally made by (15) into an understanding of (13a), this requires that we treat "believe" differently when its complement is modified by an epistemic modal than when it is not. (Roughly: when "believes" takes a complement clause in which an epistemic modal takes wide scope, it will attribute credence above some minimal threshold, while in other cases it will attribute full belief.) Similar modifications will be needed for other attitude verbs. This complicates the (already difficult) project of giving a compositional semantics for attitude verbs by undermining the neat division of labor between force (supplied by the attitude verb) and content (supplied by the complement clause).

10.3.3   *Hare's gambit*

Defending a force-modifier view of evaluative terms from a similar objection, Hare (1970) suggested that an understanding of conditionals like

(17)   If that is a good movie, then Sam liked it

(18)   If Sam liked it, it is a good movie

can be derived from a generic understanding of the conditional as a modus ponens license, together with an understanding of the significance of *unembedded* occurrences of "that is a good movie" and "Sam liked it."

To know the meaning of the whole sentence "If the cat is on the mat, it is purring," we have to know (1) the meaning of the hypothetical sentence form, which we know if we know how to do *modus ponens*; (2) the meanings of the categoricals which have got encaged in this sentence form; and we know the latter if we know (a) that they are (when not encaged) used to make assertions and (b) what assertions they are used to make. (17)

Is there, in fact, anything to prevent us treating "That is a good movie," when it goes into a conditional clause, in exactly the same way as we have treated "The cat is on the mat"? As before, we know the meaning of the hypothetical sentence form. And we know the meanings of the categoricals that are encaged in it. So we can easily perform the standard maneuver for letting the consequent of the hypothetical out of its cage. (19)

If Hare is right, then no compositional semantics is required to explain our competence with sentences in which epistemic modals occur embedded. No surprise, then, that many expressivists (and more broadly "use theorists of meaning") have clung to what we might call "Hare's gambit" (see, for example, Price 1994; Horwich 2005).

But Hare is not right. There are subtleties about the way epistemic modals interact with conditionals that cannot be predicted just on the basis of an understanding of how standalone epistemic modal sentences are used and an understanding of conditionals as modus ponens licenses. Consider three case studies.

Modus tollens   The following inference seems fine:

(19)   If it is raining, then the streets are not dry.
       The streets are dry.
       So, it isn't raining.

But if we insert an epistemic modal, we get a bad inference:

(20)   If it is raining, then it is not possible that the streets are dry.
       It is possible that the streets are dry.
       So, it isn't raining.

If this inference were good, then Niko, who has been sitting in his office all day with the blinds closed and thinks that the streets might be wet and might be dry, could conclude that it isn't raining, without even looking outside! That would be a case of "evidence-free weather forecasting" (Kolodny and

MacFarlane 2010: 26). Apparently (19) is a good inference and (20) is not: how can that difference be predicted on the basis Hare offers?[9]

Yalcin's observation   Conditionals with the following pattern are easily intelligible:

(21)   If it is raining and none of us know this, then —.

But these, as Yalcin (2007) notes, are not:

(22)   # If it is raining and it is possible that it isn't raining, then —.

How can this difference be predicted on the basis Hare offers? Both antecedents are infelicitous when "let out of their cages." So why the difference when they are "encaged" in conditionals?

Counterfactuals   Suppose that we have just opened a desk drawer and found conclusive evidence that Joe is in China. We might say:

(23)   It is not possible that Joe is in Boston.

But it would not be correct to say:

(24)   If we hadn't looked in that drawer, it would still be possible that Joe is in Boston.

Here, we do not evaluate the epistemic possibility operator relative to what we would have known in counterfactual possibilities where we didn't look in the drawer. Could we have predicted this, knowing just what Hare tells us about epistemic modals and conditionals?

Any satisfactory account of the meanings of indicative conditionals and epistemic modals must be able to capture these subtle facts, known by ordinary speakers. A speaker who just knew the unembedded behavior of epistemic modals, and that the conditional was a modus ponens license, would not know enough. So appeals to Hare's gambit should not satisfy us: we need a real compositional semantics to explain how epistemic modals interact with other expressions. I know of only one expressivist account of epistemic modals that provides one—that of Yalcin (2011). We will return to Yalcin's view in §10.6, after describing the relativist alternative.

___

[9]Your first reaction may be to find a syntactic difference, taking the conditional in (20) to scope under the modal. There are reasons not to do that, to be discussed further in §10.5.5.

10.4   Relativism

It is notable that expressivist views are motivated almost entirely by arguments *against* truth-conditional approaches. Typically, these arguments assume that any truth-conditional view must have a contextualist shape.[10] In the case of epistemic modals, this means that the body of information relative to which the modal is assessed must be determined by features of the context of use. We have seen above how one might argue quite generally that no view with this shape accurately captures the way we use epistemic modals.

But must a truth-conditional semantics for epistemic modals have this shape? Not if we countenance assessment sensitivity. In this section, we will explore the possibility that the truth of epistemic modal claims depends on a body of information determined not by the context of use, but by the *context of assessment*. This semantics offers prospects for meeting the objections to contextualist views in a broadly truth-conditional framework, thereby undermining the motivation for the expressivist approach.

We started with the intuitively compelling idea that the truth of epistemic modal claims depends on *what is known*. That is why they are called "epistemic." But we ran into trouble when we tried to answer the question, "known to whom?" For it seemed that people tend to assess epistemic modal claims for truth in light of what *they* (the assessors) know, even if they realize that they know more than the speaker (or relevant group) did at the time of utterance.[11] A straightforward way to account for this puzzling fact is to suppose that epistemic modals are assessment-sensitive: the truth of an epistemic modal claim depends on what is known by the assessor, and thus varies with the context of assessment. On this view, epistemic modal claims have no "absolute" truth values, only assessment-relative truth values. This is why they resist being captured in standard frameworks for truth-conditional semantics.

For the sake of concreteness, we will work at first with the most austere kind of relativist view—what one might call *Solipsistic Relativism*. (Later we will consider some complications that motivate a more flexible form of the view.) On this view, "Joe might be running" expresses a truth, as assessed by

---

[10]This is as true of Yalcin (2011) as it is of Price (1983). Much of Yalcin's argument is directed against "descriptivism," a view that is also rejected by the relativist. Such arguments can motivate expressivism as an alternative to contextualism, but not as an alternative to truth-conditional approaches generally, if we include relativist approaches in their number.

[11]This phenomenon was first called to my attention by Hawthorne (2004: 27 n. 68).

Sam, just in case what *Sam* knows (at the time of assessment) does not rule out that Joe is running. This is not yet a compositional semantics for "might," since we have not yet explained how to handle embedded occurrences. More on that later (§10.5). But we can already see from this sketch of a theory how Solipsistic Relativism will handle the data that seemed most problematic for the various forms of contextualism.

10.4.1 *Explaining Warrant, Rejection, and Retraction*

The Warrant Question. Why is Sally warranted in making her original claim, that Joe might be in China? Assume that assertion is governed by the Reflexive Truth Rule (§5.3). The proposition *that Joe might be in China* is true, as used at and assessed from Sally's context, just in case Sally's information does not preclude Joe's being in China. Since Sally has good reason to think that this condition is met, she is warranted in making the assertion.

The Rejection Question. Why is George warranted in rejecting Sally's claim? The proposition she asserted is true as used at her context and assessed from his only if *his* information does not preclude Joe's being in China at the time of Sally's assertion. But his knowledge that Joe does not have a visa yet *does* preclude Joe's being in China. So, relative to the context he occupies, Sally's claim is false.

Recall that the contextualist could only answer the Rejection and Retraction Questions by strengthening truth conditions for claims of epistemic possibility to the point where it became impossible to answer the Warrant Question. The relativist does not have this problem. In general, Solipsistic Relativism counts a sentence as true as used at c and assessed at c just when Solipsistic Contextualism counts it as true as used at c. The relativist semantics will diverge from the contextualist semantics only when the context of assessment is distinct from the context of use. So the Solipsistic Relativist will be able to explain *production* of epistemic modals in much the same way as the Solipsistic Contextualist, while explaining *assessments* in a way that is not available to the contextualist.[12]

---

[12]This needs some qualification, since it's not clear that deliberation about whether to assert an assessment-sensitive proposition shouldn't take into account its truth value relative to contexts of assessment other than the one occupied by the speaker. For example, one might refrain from asserting something one knows one will have to retract almost immediately, when one's context changes, even if it is true relative to one's current context.

Note, also, that for the Solipsistic Relativist, Hacking's "salvage ship" case (§10.2.2) presents no new difficulties. It is really just another third-party assessment case, in which *we* (Hacking's readers) are the third party. According to Solipsistic Relativism, the truth of the mate's claim (as assessed by us) depends on what *we* know. Since we know (from Hacking's narrative) that the treasure lies elsewhere, the mate's claim is false, relative to the context of assessment we occupy. The fact that there was a "practicable investigation" the mate could have carried out is simply irrelevant. What is crucial is something Hacking did not explicitly point out: that we, the readers, come to know, through Hacking's testimony, that the treasure lies elsewhere.

The Retraction Question.   Why should Sally retract her claim after hearing what George has to say? Our framework assumes that retraction is governed by the Retraction Rule (§5.4). So Sally ought to retract her original assertion if its content is false, as used at the context in which she made the assertion (c_1) and assessed from the context she is in now (c_2). These contexts are different in at least one key respect. In c_1, Sally did not know anything that would preclude Joe's being in China. But in c_2, she has learned from George that Joe does not yet have his visa. This means that the proposition she asserted is false as assessed from c_2, and she ought to retract her claim.

Note the change of perspective. The contextualist assumes that, if George's claim gives Sally reason to retract her claim as false, then George must be part of the group whose knowledge matters to the (non-relative) truth of Sally's claim. The relativist, by contrast, holds that what is important is not that *George* knew that Joe was in Berkeley, but that *Sally* comes to know this. It is irrelevant, for the relativist, that Sally comes to know this through the testimony of someone else who already knew it at the time she made the claim. What is known by others is relevant only insofar as they are potential informants of the speaker (in this case, Sally). If they don't speak up, or if they do speak up but Sally doesn't believe them (and so doesn't acquire knowledge), then our retraction norm does not demand that Sally retract her assertion. Conversely, if Sally comes to know that Joe does not yet have his visa through her own new observations, or through serendipitous discovery of evidence, she has just as much reason to retract her original claim as she would if she had learned this through others' testimony. That the contextualist isn't getting the right generalization here comes out clearly in the need for epicycles: for example, the appeal to "contextually relevant ways of coming to know" and "distributed knowledge" in addition to a "contextually relevant group of knowers."

10.4.2 *Hacking's lottery*

Immediately after presenting his "salvage ship" case, Hacking writes:

When one starts collecting examples like this, it begins to look as if, whenever it turns out to be false that *p*, we say, of an earlier era, that in those times it may have seemed possible that *p*, but it was not really possible at all. (Hacking 1967: 148)

If Hacking had endorsed this description of the data, he would have been well on the road to relativism. For only a relativist semantics can explain why earlier epistemic modal claims are *always* evaluated in light of what we know now (at the time of assessment), even when we know much more than was known at the time the claim was made.

However, Hacking thinks that this description of the data "would be too strong":

Consider a person who buys a lottery ticket. At the time he buys his ticket we shall say it is possible he will win, though probably he will not. As expected, he loses. But retrospectively it would be absurd to report that it only *seemed* possible that the man would win. It was perfectly possible that he would win. To see this clearly, consider a slightly different case, in which the lottery is not above board; it is rigged so that only the proprietors can win. Thus, however it may have seemed to the gullible customer, it really was not possible that he would win. It only seemed so. "Seemed possible" and "was possible" both have work cut out for them. (148)

If Hacking is interpreting his example correctly, it spells trouble for the relativist. For it suggests that the retrospective assessment data used to motivate relativism do not extend as far as the relativist needs them to. In the case of the non-rigged lottery, it seems, we *do not* assess our earlier claim that it was possible that the man would win as false, despite the fact that what we know now (after the lottery) excludes his having won. This seems to favor some version of contextualism over relativism.

However, it is far from clear that Hacking's interpretation of the example is correct. Hacking says,

(25) It was perfectly possible that he would win,

and this seems right. But assent to (25) is only problematic for the relativist if the occurrence of "possible" in it is given an epistemic reading, and that is precluded by the subjunctive mood of the complement. If we force an epistemic reading by putting the clause in the indicative[13] (rephrasing it a bit to avoid grammatical difficulties),

(26)   It was perfectly possible that he had the winning ticket,

then my willingness to accept the sentence vanishes. We know he did not, in fact, have the winning ticket, so we can't assert that it was possible that he did (though of course it *seemed* possible).

10.4.3   *Resisting retraction*

Von Fintel and Gillies (2008) note that

not all *might*s are retracted or rejected in the face of new evidence. Speakers can quite often *resist* the invitation to retract even if they have become better informed. Billy is looking for her keys. Alex is trying to help.

(27)   a.   Alex: The keys might be in the drawer.

b.   Billy: (*Looks in the drawer, agitated.*) They're not. Why did you say that?

c.   Alex: Look, I didn't say they *were* in the drawer. I said they *might* be there—and they might have been. Sheesh.

They take such cases to cast doubt on the relativist's prediction that retraction is called for in cases where the speaker gains new information that rules out the prejacent of her modal claim.

The phrasing of their example is misleading. It encourages the reader to confuse two very different questions:

(i)   Was the assertion made responsibly?

(ii)   Must the speaker retract the assertion?

Billy's question "Why did you say that?" is most naturally read as a request for Alex to address (i). And, even on the relativist account, Alex ought to push back here: after all, she had excellent grounds for making her assertion. But an affirmative answer to (i) does not imply an affirmative answer to (ii). Everyone should concede that one can be obliged to retract an assertion that was responsibly made: evidence sometimes turns out to be misleading. So, even though we have a strong intuition that Alex is being unfairly criticized

---

[13] In ordinary English (excluding the technical talk of some philosophers), "it is possible that" plus the present or past indicative can only express epistemic modality (Hacking 1967; DeRose 1991). "It is possible that the ship sank, but we all know it didn't" just isn't felicitous on any available reading.

here, it is entirely irrelevant to the question whether she should retract her assertion.

Once we have separated retraction from responsibility, the intuition that Alex is resisting retraction is cloudier. One might interpret her as meaning this:

(28) I didn't assert that the keys *were* in the drawer (which is something I wouldn't have been warranted in asserting), but only that the keys *might be* in the drawer. And I was warranted in asserting that because *for all I knew then,* they might have been in the drawer.[14]

On this interpretation, Alex's claim "they might have been there" is intended to explain the reasonableness of her assertion. It shows that, in making the assertion, Alex was confirming to the Reflexive Truth Rule. But it does not support a refusal to retract. For that, Alex would need to be in a position to assert not just that *for all she knew,* the keys might have been in the drawer, but that the keys might have been in the drawer. And if the relativist is right, she can't assert that, because she knows now that the keys weren't in the drawer when she made her claim.[15]

We might rewrite the dialogue so that Alex makes it clear that she is standing by her claim, and refusing to retract. The relativist account does not rule that out. It says that Alex ought to retract if the proposition she asserted was the assessment-sensitive proposition that the keys might be in the drawer. But Alex might have used the words "The keys might be in the drawer" to assert the assessment-invariant proposition that, for all she knew at the time, the keys might be in the drawer (compare §7.2.6 and §9.9). If that is all Alex intended to assert in the first place, then she is in her rights to stand by her claim, explaining to her challenger that she only meant to assert something about what her information at the time left open.[16]

---

[14]See §10.5.4 for the "for all I know" operator.

[15]See §10.5.6 for an argument that shifting the time of evaluation to the past does not shift the information relevant to an epistemic modal.

[16]This move may seem unprincipled, but I think it is just realistic. We are lazy and flexible in our use of tools quite generally, and sentences are tools for making assertions and other speech acts. Here, as elsewhere, we use the tool that will get the job done with the minimum of work. Suppose I want to assert that it's around 3:10 p.m. I could say, "It's around 3:10 p.m." But I'm lazy, and I know that given the context it will be obvious to you both that I'm talking about the afternoon and that I'm not claiming that it's *exactly* 3:10. So I just say, "It's 3:10." There's nothing mysterious about what's happening here, and no reason to suppose that there must be hidden syntactic hooks corresponding to the unpronounced "about" and "p.m."

What is interesting is not that we can imagine a natural dialogue where Alex refuses retraction, but that we can imagine a natural dialogue where Alex *does* retract. The former case is not particularly problematic for relativists, but the latter case, as we have seen, poses great difficulties for contextualists. The situation is not symmetrical: the relativist can recognize the assessment-invariant contents that the contextualist takes to be expressed by epistemic modal claims as possible contents of assertion, but the relativist's assessment-sensitive contents are not available to the contextualist.

10.4.4 *Ignorant assessors*

Dietz (2008) has observed that although our intuitions about retrospective assessments seem to support relativist semantics when the assessor knows *more* than the original asserter, they do not do so when the assessor knows *less*. Here is a variation on one of Dietz's examples. Suppose that yesterday I proved Theorem X and asserted "Theorem X must be true." Today, however, my memory has gone fuzzy. I recall that I was working on Theorem X, but I don't remember whether I proved it, refuted it, or did neither. If Solipsistic Relativism is correct, I should be able to say:

(29)   If I said "Theorem X must be true" yesterday, then what I said was false.

For what I know now (at the context of assessment) leaves open the possibility that Theorem X is false. And this seems bizarre. Intuitively, I don't have warrant to pronounce on the falsity of claims made by my better-informed past self, even when these claims contain epistemic modals.

If epistemic possibility is perspectival, this data suggests, it is *asymmetrically* perspectival. The truth of epistemic modal claims can depend on what is known by the assessor, but only if the assessor knows more than the original asserter.

The source of this difficulty is not the relativism in Solipsistic Relativism, but the solipsism. What is essential to a relativist account of epistemic modals is that the relevant body of information be determined by features of the context of assessment. Solipsistic Relativism embodies a simple and inflexible view about how this information is determined: it is just the information possessed by the assessor. But we need not build this into the theory. According to *Flexible Relativism*, the relevant body of information is the one that is *relevant* at the context of assessment. In many cases, this will be the assessor's information, but it need not be.

This response is analogous to Keith DeRose's contextualist treatment of cases where epistemic standards seem to depend on the situation of the *subject* of the knowledge attribution, not the attributor (discussed in §8.2). DeRose notes that the contextualist account, properly understood, can handle such cases without modification:

On contextualism, the speaker's context does always call the shot. . . . But sometimes speakers' own conversational purposes call for employing standards that are appropriate to the practical situation of the far-away subjects they are discussing, and so the shot that the speakers' context calls can be, and often quite naturally will be, to invoke the standards appropriate to the practical situation faced by the subject being discussed. (DeRose 2005: 189)

The essential point here is that it is the *speaker's* context that determines whether it is appropriate to take into account the situation of the subject. So the view is genuinely contextualist, not a hybrid of a contextualist and a subject-centered view.

Flexible Relativism affords a similar kind of response to worries about ignorant assessors. The idea is that, although in some cases the speaker's information *is* relevant to the evaluation of epistemic modal claims, it is the *assessor's* context that determines when this is so. In contexts where the primary point of the assessment is critical evaluation of a speaker's assertion, the relevant information state will generally be the information the speaker had at the time of the assertion, while in contexts where the assessor is simply trying to guide her own inquiry, the relevant information state will generally be the assessor's current information. But in each case, it is features of the context of assessment that determine which information is relevant. So the view is genuinely relativist, and not a hybrid of relativism and contextualism.

10.5 Compositional Semantics

So far we have contented ourselves with describing what the various contending views say about simple standalone sentences in which epistemic modals take wide scope, like "Joe might be in China." But a full account of epistemic modals must also explain how they behave in other contexts: how they interact with truth-functional connectives, quantifiers, conditionals, and other expressions. To this task we now turn.

10.5.1   *The framework*

As usual, our semantics will take the form of a recursive definition of truth at a context and index. It is customary in semantics for modals to include a *world*, and sometimes a *time*, in the indices. We will include both (though nothing hangs on the inclusion of a time parameter). But we will depart from tradition in also including an *information state*, which will determine which worlds the modal operators quantify over. (Traditionally, the modals are taken to quantify over the worlds that are *accessible* from the world of evaluation, so that the relevant information state is determined by the world and a contextually fixed accessibility relation, and no separate representation of the information state is needed.) This departure from tradition can be motivated on purely compositional grounds: as we will see in §10.5.5, a proper account of the interaction of epistemic modals with indicative conditionals requires that the information state be a shiftable parameter.

We will represent an information state as a set of worlds—intuitively, the worlds that are open possibilites given the information. This simple representation will suffice for dealing with simple modals like "might" and "must." If we wanted to deal with quantitative probability operators like "it is more likely than not than" or "there is a 67 percent chance that," we would probably want a more complex representation of information states that defines a probability distribution on an algebra of subsets of worlds (see Yalcin 2007). But the extra complexity this would involve is not needed for our purposes here.

Our compositional semantics, then, will recursively define truth relative to a context and an index consisting of a world, time, information state, and assignment. This does not yet commit us to assessment sensitivity, since a compositional semantics with this shape is compatible with a variety of different *postsemantics*:

Solipsistic Contextualist Postsemantics. *A sentence S is true as used at context c_1 and assessed from a context c_2 iff for all assignments a,*

$$[\![S]\!]^{c_1}_{\langle w_{c_1}, t_{c_1}, i_{c_1}, a \rangle} = \textit{True}$$

where w_{c_1} is the world of c_1, t_{c_1} is the time of c_1, and i_{c_1} is the information state determined by what is known by the agent of c_1 at t_{c_1}.

Flexible Contextualist Postsemantics. *A sentence S is true as used at context c_1 and assessed from a context c_2 iff for all assignments a,*

$$[\![S]\!]^{c_1}_{\langle w_{c_1}, t_{c_1}, i_{c_1}, a\rangle} = True$$

where w_{c_1} is the world of c_1, t_{c_1} is the time of c_1, and i_{c_1} is the information state relevant at c_1.

Solipsistic Relativist Postsemantics. *A sentence S is true as used at context c_1 and assessed from a context c_2 iff for all assignments a,*

$$[\![S]\!]^{c_1}_{\langle w_{c_1}, t_{c_1}, i_{c_2}, a\rangle} = True$$

where w_{c_1} is the world of c_1, t_{c_1} is the time of c_1, and i_{c_2} is the information state determined by the what is known by the agent of c_2 at t_{c_2}.

Flexible Relativist Postsemantics. *A sentence S is true as used at context c_1 and assessed from a context c_2 iff for all assignments a,*

$$[\![S]\!]^{c_1}_{\langle w_{c_1}, t_{c_1}, i_{c_2}, a\rangle} = True$$

where w_{c_1} is the world of c_1, t_{c_1} is the time of c_1, and i_{c_2} is the information state relevant at c_2.

(It is also possible to deny that there *is* a meaningful postsemantics, as Yalcin 2011 does.)

Our compositional semantics is also compatible with a variety of views about what propositions are expressed by epistemic modal sentences, including:

Eternalist propositions. *The intension of $|S|^E_c$ (the eternalist proposition expressed by S at c) is the function f from circumstances of evaluation to truth values such that $f(\langle w\rangle) = [\![S]\!]^c_{\langle w, t_c, i_c, a\rangle}$ for an arbitrary assignment a. (Note that the choice of a should not matter, since S is a sentence.)*

Temporalist propositions. *The intension of $|S|^T_c$ is the function f from circumstances of evaluation to truth values such that $f(\langle w, t\rangle) = [\![S]\!]^c_{\langle w, t, i_c, a\rangle}$ for an arbitrary assignment a.*

Information-neutral eternalist propositions. *The intension of* $|S|_c^{IE}$ *is the function* f *from circumstances of evaluation to truth values such that* $f(\langle w, i\rangle) = [\![S]\!]^c_{\langle w, t_c, i, a\rangle}$ *for an arbitrary assignment a.*

Information-neutral temporalist propositions. *The intension of* $|S|_c^{IT}$ *is the function* f *from circumstances of evaluation to truth values such that* $f(\langle w, t, i\rangle) = [\![S]\!]^c_{\langle w, t, i, a\rangle}$ *for an arbitrary assignment a.*

There may be substantive issues about whether the contents of beliefs and assertions vary with the information state, but these questions are not settled by compositional considerations alone.

10.5.2 *Epistemic modals*

The semantics for the epistemic possibility and necessity modals are straightforward: they behave like existential and universal quantifiers over the worlds in the information state.

$\Diamond_e$ **and** $\Box_e$**.**

$$[\![\Diamond_e \phi]\!]^c_{\langle w, t, i, a\rangle} = \begin{cases} \textit{True} & \textit{if } [\![\phi]\!]^c_{\langle w', t, i, a\rangle} = \textit{True for some } w' \textit{ in } i \\ \textit{False} & \textit{otherwise} \end{cases}$$

$$[\![\Box_e \phi]\!]^c_{\langle w, t, i, a\rangle} = \begin{cases} \textit{True} & \textit{if } [\![\phi]\!]^c_{\langle w', t, i, a\rangle} = \textit{True for all } w' \textit{ in } i \\ \textit{False} & \textit{otherwise} \end{cases}$$

These compositional clauses are not inherently relativist or contextualist. When combined with the *Relativist Postsemantics*, they yield a relativist account of epistemic modals, while when combined with the *Contextualist Postsemantics*, they yield a contextualist account.[17]

10.5.3 *Boolean connectives*

Explaining interactions of epistemic modals and Boolean connectives is straightforward in this framework. The Boolean connectives work just as one

---

[17] According to a Contextualist Postsemantics, $\ulcorner \Diamond_e \phi \urcorner$ is true at c just in case $[\![\Diamond_e\phi]\!]^c_{\langle w_c, t_c, i_c, a\rangle} =$ True for any a. By the compositional clause, this is so just in case $[\![\phi]\!]^c_{\langle w, t_c, i_c, a\rangle} =$ True for some $w' \in i_c$, that is, just in case ϕ is true at some world in the information state of the context of use. A similar derivation shows that, on a Relativist Postsemantics, $\ulcorner \Diamond_e\phi \urcorner$ is true as used at c and assessed from c' just in case $[\![\phi]\!]^c_{\langle w, t_c, i_{c'}, a\rangle} =$ True for some $w' \in i_{c'}$.

would expect:[18]

¬, ∧, and ∨.

$$[\![\neg\phi]\!]^c_{\langle w,t,i,a\rangle} = \begin{cases} \textit{True} & \textit{if } [\![\phi]\!]^c_{\langle w,t,i,a\rangle} = \textit{False} \\ \textit{False} & \textit{otherwise} \end{cases}$$

$$[\![\phi \wedge \psi]\!]^c_{\langle w,t,i,a\rangle} = \begin{cases} \textit{True} & \textit{if } [\![\phi]\!]^c_{\langle w,t,i,a\rangle} = [\![\psi]\!]^c_{\langle w,t,i,a\rangle} = \textit{True} \\ \textit{False} & \textit{otherwise} \end{cases}$$

$$[\![\phi \vee \psi]\!]^c_{\langle w,t,i,a\rangle} = \begin{cases} \textit{False} & \textit{if } [\![\phi]\!]^c_{\langle w,t,i,a\rangle} = [\![\psi]\!]^c_{\langle w,t,i,a\rangle} = \textit{False} \\ \textit{True} & \textit{otherwise} \end{cases}$$

It is easy to verify that this account of negation vindicates the equivalences

(30) $\neg\Diamond_e\phi \equiv \Box_e\neg\phi$

(31) $\neg\Box_e\phi \equiv \Diamond_e\neg\phi$

10.5.4 *For all I know*

We can also introduce an operator corresponding to the English phrase "for all α knows":

$FAK^\alpha\ \phi$.

$$[\![FAK^\alpha\ \phi]\!]^c_{\langle w,t,i,a\rangle} = \begin{cases} \textit{True} & [\![\phi]\!]^c_{\langle w',t,i',a\rangle} = \textit{True for some } w' \in i', \textit{where} \\ & i' \textit{ is the information state of } [\![\alpha]\!]^c_{\langle w,t,i,a\rangle} \textit{ at } w \textit{ and } t. \\ \textit{False} & \textit{otherwise} \end{cases}$$

The effect of the operator is to shift the information state to what was known by the person or group denoted by α at the time of evaluation, and to quantify over the worlds in the shifted information state. Thus, for example, "For all I know, it is raining" is true (as uttered by me now) just in case it is raining in every possible world not excluded by what I know now.

---

[18]Some semanticists have suggested that an alternative treatment of disjunction is needed in order to explain why $\ulcorner\Diamond_e(\phi \vee \psi)\urcorner$ seems to imply both $\ulcorner\Diamond_e\phi\urcorner$ and $\ulcorner\Diamond_e\psi\urcorner$. I am tempted to think that the data can be explained pragmatically, but the issues are complex, and beyond the scope of this book (see Zimmermann 2000; Geurts 2005).

Note that even when ϕ is information-sensitive (that is, its extension varies with the information state parameter), $\ulcorner FAK^\alpha \ \phi \urcorner$ is not.[19] Its extension depends only on the information α possesses at the time of the index, and not on the information state of the index. Despite this difference, $\ulcorner \Diamond_e \phi \urcorner$ and $\ulcorner FAK^I \ \Diamond_e \phi \urcorner$ stand in a close logical relationship on both the Solipsistic Contextualist and Solipsistic Relativist views.

For the Solipsistic Contextualist, each is an absolute logical consequence of the other (in the sense of §3.4).[20] This is a nice result, because Solipsistic Contextualism was motivated in large part by the intuition that "It might be that p" and "For all I know, p" are in some strong sense equivalent. However, even for the Solipsistic Contextualist, they are not equivalent in the stronger sense of logically *implying* each other (§3.4), since one can find a context and index where they diverge in truth value.[21] This makes a difference in embedded contexts: for example,

(32)   For all Sam knows, for all I know it is raining

can diverge in truth value from

(33)   For all Sam knows, it might be raining.

$\ulcorner FAK^I \ \phi \urcorner$ is, however, *strongly* equivalent to $\ulcorner FAK^I \ \Diamond_e \phi \urcorner$: they are true at just the same points of evaluation. This, too, is satisfying, insofar as we seem to use these two forms interchangeably in English:

(34)   For all I know, it is raining.

(35)   For all I know, it might be raining.

On a Solipsistic Relativist Postsemantics, we no longer get the result that $\ulcorner FAK^I \ \phi \urcorner$ and $\ulcorner \Diamond_e \phi \urcorner$ are absolutely logically equivalent. To see that they could

[19] Unless α is.

[20] Proof: Let c be any context. Let w_c be the world of c, t_c the time of c, s_c the agent of c, and i_c the set of worlds not excluded by what s_c knows at c. Let a be an arbitrary assignment: since we won't be dealing with open formulas, any formula that is satisfied by a can be assumed to be satisfied by any assignment. By the definition of truth at a context, $\ulcorner FAK^I \ \phi \urcorner$ is true at c iff $[\![FAK^I \ \phi]\!]^c_{\langle w_c, t_c, i_c, a\rangle}$ = True. By the recursive clause for "FAK," $[\![FAK^I \ \phi]\!]^c_{\langle w_c, t_c, i_c, a\rangle}$ = True iff $[\![\phi]\!]^c_{\langle w', t_c, i', a\rangle}$ = True for some $w' \in i'$, where i' is the set of worlds not excluded by what is known by $[\![I]\!]^c_{\langle w_c, t_c, i_c, a\rangle}$ at w_c and t_c. But $[\![I]\!]^c_{\langle w_c, t_c, i_c, a\rangle}$ = s_c, so $i' = i_c$. Thus $\ulcorner FAK^I \ \phi \urcorner$ is true at c iff $[\![\phi]\!]^c_{\langle w', t_c, i_c, a\rangle}$ = True for some world $w' \in i_c$. But as we have seen, this is just the condition for $\ulcorner \Diamond_e \phi \urcorner$ to be true at c.

[21] To see this, note that $[\![FAK^I \ \phi]\!]^c_{\langle w, t, i, a\rangle}$ does not depend at all on the value of i, while $[\![\Diamond_e \phi]\!]^c_{\langle w, t, i, a\rangle}$ does depend on the value of i.

not be, it suffices to notice that the latter is assessment-sensitive while the former is not. However, a weaker kind of equivalence holds: they are *diagonally equivalent* (§3.4). That is, whenever one is true as used at and assessed from a context c, so is the other.[22] This vindicates the intuition that it is correct to say "It is possible that p" just when what one knows does not exclude p. (The Flexible Relativist Postsemantics will not vindicate even these weaker results, though they may still hold "in general" if, in general, it is the assessor's information that is relevant at the context of assessment.)

10.5.5 *Conditionals*

The semantics described above straightforwardly explains the interaction of epistemic modals with truth-functional connectives: negation, conjunction, and disjunction. Interactions with indicative conditionals, though, require special treatment.

Suppose we are inquiring about Joe's whereabouts. The contextually relevant information leaves open the possibilities depicted in Fig. 10.1. Because w_0 and w_1 are open possibilities, the following sentences both appear to be true:

(36) It is possible that Joe is in Boston.

(37) It is possible that Joe is in China.

In addition, the sentence

(38) If Joe is in China, then it is not possible that he is in Boston

appears to express a truth—one we are in a position to know simply by virtue of our knowledge of elementary geography. But standard theories of indicative conditionals and modals cannot vindicate these judgments.

If the indicative is the material conditional, then in the context described above, we cannot know that (38) is true. For, in this context, we know that (36) is true, so we know that the consequent of (38) is false. Construed as a material conditional, then, (38) can only be true if its antecedent is also false—that is, if Joe is not in China. But we do not know that Joe is not in China. So we cannot know that (38) is true.

If, on the other hand, we use the familiar "closest possible worlds" semantics of (Stalnaker 1975), then (38) is false at every world in the context set. For according to Stalnaker's semantics, the conditional is true at a world w if its

---

[22]The proof is straightforward.

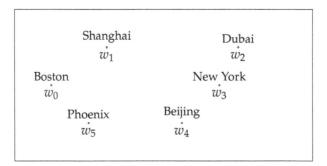

FIG. 10.1. The possibilites as to Joe's location.

consequent is true at the closest possible world to w in the context set at which its antecedent is true. But the consequent of (38) is false at *every* world in the context set, so *a fortiori* (38) will also be false at w. On neither, approach, then, do we get the desired result, which is that (38) is true, and its consequent false, at all of the worlds in the context set.

One way to avoid this undesirable conclusion is to suppose that the modal in (38) scopes over the conditional, so that the proper formalization of the sentence is not

(39) $[if\ C] \neg \Diamond_e B,$

or equivalently

(40) $[if\ C] \Box_e \neg B,$

but rather

(41) $\Box_e [if\ C] \neg B.$

But there are strong reasons not to solve the problem by appealing to this familiar distinction between *necessitas consequentiae* and *necessitas consequentis*. The first is that there are good syntactic and semantic reasons for thinking that "if"s modify modals, rather than the other way around (Kratzer 1981a; Kratzer 1986; Lycan 2001: ch. 1). If conditional antecedents are fundamentally modifiers of modals (which in some cases may be implicit), then the modals they modify cannot take wide scope over them.

Second, if there is really a scope distinction to be made, we should expect to hear an ambiguity in (38). That is, in addition to hearing it as (41), we should be able to hear it as (40) (and thus as false) in at least some discourse contexts. But I think the only available reading of (38) is one on which it is true.

Third, wide-scoping would not help with Yalcin's puzzle, already mentioned in §10.3.3, concerning epistemic modals in the *antecedents* of conditionals. Yalcin (2007) notes that conditionals of the form

(42)   If $(\phi \wedge \Diamond_e \neg \phi)$, then ψ

are odd to the point of unintelligibility. For example:

(43)   If Joe is in Boston but might not be in Boston, then he might be in China.

(44)   If Joe is in Boston but might not be in Boston, then he has his winter coat.

It is very difficult to see why these sentences should be odd, on standard views about modals and conditionals. Again, consider a Stalnaker-style semantics and the context represented by Fig. 10.1. It's presumably true at *every* world in the context set that Joe might not be in Boston.[23] So interpreting (43) or (44) should just be a matter of evaluating the consequent at the closest world at which Joe is in Boston. Sentence (43) should come out true at every world in the context set, while (44) will be true at some but not others. Whence the feeling of unintelligibility? Wide-scoping is no use here.

Let us return, then, to (38), and consider what we must say about the semantics of the conditional if it is to come out true, on the assumption that the modal governs the consequent, and not the entire conditional. Clearly, the antecedent cannot just shift the world of the index, because the truth of the consequent depends only on the information state of the index, and not at all on the world. The effect of the antecedent must therefore be to shift the information state. To evaluate (38), we throw out worlds at which Joe is not in China, until we have an information state at which it is *accepted* that Joe is in China (Fig. 10.2):

Accepted. ϕ is accepted *at an information state i (relative to a context c, time t, and assignment a) just in case for all $w \in i$, $\llbracket \phi \rrbracket^c_{\langle w,t,i,a \rangle} = True.$*[24] *We will use the*

---

[23] Technically, there is room to let the set of worlds the epistemic possibility operator quantifies over vary from world to world within a context; different worlds can be thought of as "accessible" from each world. But it is hard to see how this flexibility could be exploited to solve the puzzle, so I ignore it here.

[24] The term "accepted" derives from Stalnaker (1975) and is used in this sense by Yalcin (2007). Kolodny and MacFarlane (2010) use the clunkier term "true throughout."

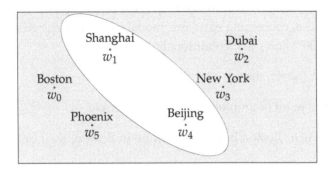

FIG. 10.2. The shifted information state.

notation "accepted$_{ta}^c$ at i" to mean "accepted at i (relative to context c, time t, and assignment a)."

We then see whether the consequent is also accepted at this information state. In this case, it is—there is no world in the shifted information state at which Joe is in Boston—so the conditional is true.

More precisely:[25]

$[if \; \phi]$.

$$[[if \; \phi]\psi]^c_{\langle w,t,i,a \rangle} = \begin{cases} True & \text{if } \psi \text{ is accepted}_{ta}^c \text{ at every } i' \subseteq i \text{ such that:} \\ & \quad \phi \text{ is accepted}_{ta}^c \text{ at } i', \text{ and} \\ & \quad \text{there is no } i'' \supset i' \text{ such that } \phi \text{ is accepted}_{ta}^c \text{ at } i''. \\ False & \text{otherwise} \end{cases}$$

Using this semantics, we can explain how (36), (37), and (38) can all be known to be true in a single informational context (such as that of Fig. 10.1). We can also explain why sentences like (43) and (44) sound unintelligible. To evaluate them, we need to evaluate their consequents relative to the largest subset of our information state at which their (common) antecedent

[25]For kindred proposals, see Kolodny and MacFarlane (2010), Yalcin (2007), and Gillies (2010). The definition given here differs from that in Kolodny and MacFarlane (2010) in requiring that ψ be accepted, rather than just true, at the shifted information state. (One upshot of this change is that we no longer need to require that ψ be modalized.) It differs from that in Yalcin (2007) in not assuming that there will be a *unique* maximal subset of i at which the antecedent is accepted (for motivation, see Kolodny and MacFarlane 2010: 136), and in allowing these subsets to be empty. It differs from that in Gillies (2010) in taking the conditional antecedent to shift a parameter of the index, rather than the context itself.

(45)   Joe is in Boston but might not be in Boston

is accepted. But the only information state at which (45) is accepted is the empty set of possibilities. Thus the sentences violate the presupposition, carried by the indicative mood, that the antecedent is not already ruled out. They are difficult to interpret for exactly the same reason that indicatives whose antecedents are known to be false are difficult to interpret.

Finally, we can explain why (19) is a good inference, while (20) is not. Suppose that the premises of (19) are accepted relative to a contextually relevant information state *i*. The second premise requires that every world in *i* be a world where the streets are dry, and the first premise requires that every world in *i* where it is raining be a world where the streets are not dry. These constraints can only be satisfied if no world in *i* is a world where it is raining—in which case the conclusion will be accepted at *i*. So (19) is a good inference in the sense of being acceptance-preserving.[26]

Suppose, now, that the premises of (20) are accepted at *i*. The second premise requires that *i* contain at least one world where the streets are dry, and the first premise requires that the subset of *i* containing just the worlds in *i* where it is raining not contain any worlds where the streets are dry. These constraints require that *i* contain some worlds where it is not raining, so the conclusion is not accepted at *i*. Inference (20) is not acceptance-preserving.

10.5.6   *Tense*

According to the semantics given above, epistemic modals are sensitive to an information-state that shifts independently of the time of the index. That means that epistemic modals are insensitive to the time of the index, and hence to temporal embeddings.[27] In evaluating whether it *was* possible yesterday that the letter would arrive today, for example, we do not ask whether *yesterday's* information left it open that the letter would arrive, but whether our present information leaves this open.

Von Fintel and Gillies (2008) think that this prediction is clearly false. They give the following example:

---

[26]It is not *valid* in any of the senses distinguished in §3.4. It is "quasi-valid" in the terminology of Kolodny and MacFarlane (2010), and its conclusion is an "informational consequence" of its premises in the terminology of Yalcin (2007: 1004).

[27]As noted in §10.3.3, they seem also to be insensitive to alethic modal embeddings of the sort we find in counterfactual conditionals. It seems natural to suppose that the situation would be similar with shifts in the time of the index; in general, modal and temporal rigidity go together.

Sophie is looking for some ice cream and checks the freezer. There is none in there. Asked why she opened the freezer, she replies:

(46)   a. There might have been ice cream in the freezer.

       b. PAST(MIGHT(ice cream in freezer))

It is possible for Sophie to have said something true, even though at the time of utterance she knows (and so do we) that there is no ice cream in the freezer. (87)

To explain Sophie's utterance, they think, we need to assume that the temporal modifier shifts the body of information relative to which the modal is evaluated. Sentence (46) is true, they think, if it was consistent with what Sophie knew before she checked the freezer that there was ice cream inside.

But there is another way to explain Sophie's utterance. The tensed epistemic modal in (46) occurs in a "becausal" context. Sophie is being asked to explain her action. She can do this by stating her reasons for acting as she did. In this case, she looked in the freezer because she believed that there might have been ice cream there. So she could have answered the question by saying: "I believed there might have been ice cream in the freezer." But because it is obvious that what is wanted is a rationalization of her action, not some other kind of explanation, she need not explicitly say "I believed"; instead, she can just give the *content* of her belief: "There might have been ice cream in the freezer."[28]

We can see the same kind of thing in cases that don't involve epistemic modals at all:

> TED: Why did you give up your career and follow Lisa to Europe?
>
> SAM: She loved me!

Sam's reply is felicitous even if it is common ground between Ted and Sam that Lisa did not love Sam. We understand Sam to be rationalizing his behavior by giving the content of the belief that led him to act as he did. (I assume nobody would suggest mucking with the semantics of "She loved me" to explain these facts.)

Similar considerations can help with a puzzle about embeddings of tensed epistemic modals under *because*. It seems that one can truly and felicitously assert

---

[28] Alternatively, we might take her to be asserting that *for all she knew then*, there might have been ice cream in the freezer. This claim, too, would help to rationalize her action, by describing her knowledge state at the time.

(47)   I studied that book because it was possible that Fermat's Last Theorem would be refuted using its techniques.

even if one knows that Fermat's Last Theorem is true, provided it was not known at the time one studied the book that the theorem was true. But "becausal" contexts are generally considered to be factive. So, if (47) is true and felicitous, then it seems we are committed to the truth of

(48)   It was possible that Fermat's Last Theorem would be refuted using its techniques,

even though we know now that the theorem would not be refuted. Honoring that commitment would seem to require interpreting the modal as quantifying over the possibilities that were in play at the time of the index.

Notice, however, that (47) gives the speaker's reasons for doing something, and in this kind of context, the presupposition of factivity is sometimes relaxed. Suppose Joe has just found out that the internet search company he invested in has gone bankrupt. He might felicitously say:

(49)   I bought that stock because it was going to be the next Google!

Similarly, the utterer of (47) might say:

(50)   I studied that book because it was going to show me how to refute Fermat's Last Theorem.

Was the book going to show her how to refute Fermat's Last Theorem? Presumably not, since the theorem can be proved. But the speech is still felicitous, in a context where the speaker is explaining her action by giving the content of the belief that motivated it. So the felicity of (47) in a similar context does not motivate taking epistemic modals to be temporally "shifty."

Let's try taking the modal in (46) out of its becausal context. Imagine Sophie saying:

(51)   A minute ago there might have been ice cream in the freezer, but now there can't be (I just checked).[29]

If von Fintel and Gillies are right, we should expect (51) to be ambiguous between a *present-uncertainty-about-the-past* reading

(52)   MIGHT(PAST(ice cream in freezer))

---

[29]Or: "A minute ago it was possible that there was ice cream in the freezer, but now it isn't."

and a truth-conditionally distinct *past-uncertainty-about-the-past* reading

(53)   PAST(MIGHT(ice cream in freezer)).

But it is not clear that it does have the *past-uncertainty-about-the-past* reading.
If such a reading is available at all, it should be salient in this context:

(54)   I just checked the freezer, and it is empty. And I know that before I
       checked it, the door had been closed for at least ten minutes. But a
       minute ago there might have been ice cream in there.

I find it hard not to hear Sophie as raising the bizarre possibility that there was
some ice cream in the freezer, but it vanished mysteriously despite the closed
door. We would not expect this reading to be salient if the *past-uncertainty-
about-the-past* reading were available.

One might argue that temporal shiftiness is needed to handle cases involving *binding*:

(55)   Whenever it was possible that Mary was drunk, the people she came
       with drove her home.[30]

On the most natural reading of this sentence, "possible" needs to be evaluated
with respect to the information people had on various occasions of partying.
This might be thought to require that the modals be evaluated relative to what
is known at the time of the index.

But (55) also has another reading. Suppose several groups of researchers
have been compiling data on Mary's drinking habits and transportation safety.
The groups might disagree about whether, on some particular occasion when
Mary drove herself home from a party, it was possible that she was drunk,
and because of this they might disagree about the truth of an occurrence of
(55). They would *not* be disagreeing about whether Mary's (or her friends')
knowledge left it open whether she was drunk on these occasions; they might
all agree that it did. What matters, rather, is whether their own knowledge
now leaves it open. It is hard to see how we could get this reading if the modals
are evaluated relative to what is known at the time of the index.

The relativist gets this second, "unbound" reading straightforwardly. But
she can also explain the bound readings of (55), by appealing to "free enrichment" with appropriately placed ⌜*FAK*^{α}⌝ operators. These operators provide
agent variables that can be bound by the enclosing quantifiers or given values

---

[30]I owe this example to Fabrizio Cariani.

contextually. The idea, then, is that one can use the *sentence* (55) to express a number of different propositions, including at least two assessment-invariant propositions with binding of the variables in $\ulcorner FAK^\alpha \urcorner$ operators, as well as one assessment-sensitive proposition with no binding:

(56)　that whenever it was possible (for all they knew) that Mary was drunk, the people she came with drove her home.

(57)　that whenever it was possible (for all I knew) that Mary was drunk, the people she came with drove her home.

(58)　that whenever it was possible that Mary was drunk, the people she came with drove her home.

The speaker relies on the audience's ability to figure out which proposition she intends to convey based on contextual clues. (When the ambiguity cannot be resolved contextually, the $\ulcorner FAK^\alpha \urcorner$ operators can be made explicit.) Those who favor a temporally shifty semantics can hardly complain about this strategy, because they too will have to appeal to unexpressed $\ulcorner FAK^\alpha \urcorner$ operators to ensure that "possible" in (55) is evaluated in relation to different groups' knowledge at different times, and to distinguish reading (56) from (57). (It is not clear they can get (58)—the proposition the researchers disagree about—at all.)

10.5.7　*Attitude verbs*

As in §7.2.7, we will take attitude verbs to have a relational semantics. So, for example, "believes" is a two-place predicate relating a person and a content. That-clauses denote contents. The semantics for "believes" can remain the same even if we take contents to be informationally sensitive. Of course, the informational relativity of contents may play a part in one's answer to the question: in virtue of what does a person stand in the believing relation to this content at this time? But this is a question about the metaphysics of beliefs, not the semantics of "believes."

An alternative approach is to construe "α believes" as an operator taking a sentential complement. Traditionally this operator is construed as a quantifier over the possible worlds left open by one's belief state; one believes p if p is true at every such world (Hintikka 1962). Things are more complicated, though, if the index contains not just a world but an information state. Since whether Sarah believes that Joe might be in Boston depends on *her* information, the operator must shift the information state, then quantify over the worlds in the shifted information state (Yalcin 2011: 324).

It is sometimes argued that *factive* attitude verbs, like "realize," pose a special problem for a relativist account of epistemic modals. Von Fintel and Gillies (2008: 93) ask us to consider the following case:

Blofeld and Number 2 are at SPECTRE headquarters plotting Bond's demise. Bond planted a bug and some misleading evidence pointing to his being in Zürich and slipped out. Now he and Leiter are listening in from London. As they listen, Leiter is getting a bit worried: Blofeld hasn't yet found the misleading evidence that points to Bond's being in Zürich. Leiter turns to Bond and says:

(59) If Blofeld realizes you might be in Zürich, you can breathe easy—he'll send his henchmen to Zürich to find you.

And he might continue:

(60) If he doesn't realize soon that you might be in Zürich, we better get you out of here.

They claim that (59) and (60) are perfectly felicitous, but should be cases of presupposition failure on the relativist account, since the relativist must take the complement of the factive verb "realize" to be false.

I agree that the factiveness of "realize" forces a reading of the complement "you might be in Zürich" on which the speaker takes it to be true. That means that the complement does not express the assessment-sensitive proposition *that Bond might be in Zürich*. But why is this a problem for the relativist account? The relativist can simply concede that the complement is not being used here to express that proposition. Instead, it is being used to express the assessment-invariant proposition *that for all Blofeld knows, Bond might be in Zürich*. Leiter could have expressed the same thing in wordier fashion:

(61) If Blofeld realizes you might (for all he knows) be in Zürich, you can breathe easy—he'll send his henchmen to Zürich to find you.

(62) If he doesn't realize soon that you might (for all he knows) be in Zürich, we better get you out of here.

He leaves out the "for all he knows," because it will be obvious enough from context. Like all of us, he tends to use the minimal linguistic means needed to get across his message. We can imagine, though, what he would say to make his meaning clear if confusion arose. If Bond were to reply, "What do you mean? It's not true that I might be in Zürich—we both know I'm here—so how can he *realize* that I might be in Zürich?", then Leiter would clarify by saying, "I meant, if he realizes that, for all *he* knows, you might be in Zürich."

10.6 Yalcin's nonfactualism

In §10.3, we noted that expressivist views face serious difficulties explaining the contributions of embedded occurrences of epistemic modals. The only plausible solution I have seen is that of Yalcin (2007, 2011). Yalcin mirrors Gibbard's strategy (§7.3), co-opting the machinery of truth-conditional semantics to give a systematic account of the mental states expressed by complex sentences. Indeed, Yalcin's semantics is essentially the same as the relativist semantics described in §10.5.

Yalcin's account and the relativist account agree in rejecting the contextualist's idea that epistemic modal sentences can be assigned truth values relative to (just) a context of use. The relativist response is to assign truth values relative to a context of use and context of assessment, and to use a generic account of assertion and retraction to account for the peculiar features of the use of the modal sentences. Yalcin, by contrast, does without contexts-relative truth values entirely. There is nothing corresponding to the "postsemantics" in his account; all that the semantics provides is a definition of truth at a context and index, where the indices include information states.[31]

This means that Yalcin's account cannot appeal to a generic story about assertion to explain the special features of epistemic modal assertions. Instead, Yalcin tells a special story tailored to the case: whereas assertions of straightfoward factual propositions express full beliefs, assertions of "It is possible that *p*" express a special cognitive state we might call *leaving-open*, and have the communicative function of achieving coordination on a set of open possibilities. (One *leaves-open* that *p* just in case one is sensitive to the question whether *p* and does not believe that not-*p*.) Yalcin does not say what states are expressed by mixed sentences, whose truth depends both on the world and on the information state (for example, "I packed every item I might need in Germany"). But his system allows him to give indirect specifications of these states, through their logical relations to "pure" states.

One apparent advantage of Yalcin's nonfactualism over relativism is that it does not seem to need distinctively modal belief contents. To believe that it might be raining, on Yalcin's account, is to have an attitude (*leaving-open*)

---

[31]In this respect the account resembles Belnap, Perloff, and Xu (2001)'s approach to future contingents; see MacFarlane (2003: 331–2) for discussion.

to the proposition *that it is raining*, and to describe this attitude one need not suppose that there is a distinct proposition *that it might be raining*. From this point of view, Yalcin's view looks more conservative.

However, this difference is less significant than it first appears. For consider this inference:

(63)   a. It might be raining.

     b. So, that it might be raining is true. [from (a)]

     c. Joe believes that it might be raining.

     d. So, Joe believes something true. [from (b), (c)]

Yalcin needs an account of the constructions occuring here that explains the validity of the two inferences. The task is easily solved if we take "that it might be raining" to denote a content, "believes" to denote a relation between a person and a content, and "true" to denote a property of a content.[32] But then we need to concede that there is a distinct, informationally neutral content *that it might be raining*, to which Joe stands in the *believing* relation (what other relation would be expressed by "believes")?

If Yalcin were forced by these considerations to embrace belief contents whose truth varies with the information state, would anything remain to distinguish his view from relativism? Yes. Yalcin's view would retain its core expressivist commitment: its *identification* of believing that $\Diamond_e P$ with not believing that $\neg P$, while being sensitive to the question whether P.[33] On this kind of view, it is *conceptually impossible* to believe that it might be raining while believing that it is not raining, or to fail to believe that it is not raining (while being sensitive to the question) without believing that it might be raining. For the relativist, by contrast, these are distinct states, and it is possible in principle to be in one without being in the other. Of course, on the relativist view one *ought not* be in one without being in the other. Given that one aims at believing what is true given one's evidence, and given the intension of *it might be raining*, it would be a mistake to believe this proposition while believing that it is not raining, and a mistake to fail to believe this proposition while considering whether it is raining and not

---

[32] Yalcin seems to favor a Hintikka-style semantics, on which "believes" is treated as a sentential operator, though he mentions a relational semantics as a possibility (Yalcin 2011: 324–5). But it is difficult to see how the Hintikka-style semantics can account for the validity of the inferences in (63).

[33] Compare the discussion of Gibbard's expressivism in §7.3.

believing that it is isn't. A mistake—but one it is possible to make, at least in principle.

Relatedly, on Yalcin's view, any creature with the conceptual resources to believe that it is raining can also believe that it might be raining. For believing that it might be raining *just is* being sensitive to the question whether it is raining and failing to believe that it is not. On the relativist view, by contrast, a creature could have the conceptual resources to consider the question whether it is raining, and to form a belief either way, without having the conceptual resources to believe that it might be raining.

These differences are substantive. While there is something attractive about identifying believing that $\Diamond_e\phi$ with leaving-open that ϕ, such a view rules out a kind of "epistemic *akrasia*" that seems genuinely possible—the state of believing that $\Diamond_e\phi$ while simultaneously believing $\neg\phi$, and hence not leaving-open that ϕ. The relativist view leaves such combinations possible, while explaining what is wrong with them, and why they are rare.

11

OUGHT

It is impossible to deliberate about what to do without thinking about likelihoods. Should I take the bet you offered me—even odds that the Giants will win? That depends on whether I think that it is likelier than not that the Giants will win. Should I go to graduate school in chemistry or work as a pharmacist? That depends on how likely it is that a graduate degree will lead to a more satisfying career. Should I switch from a variable rate mortgage to a fixed? That depends on how likely it is that mortgage rates will rise in the future. Should I have coffee or tea? That depends on which drink I think is likelier to be prepared well at this café.

In emphasizing this connection between oughts and likelihoods, I am not assuming a crude consequentialism, which reduces every decision to a calculation of expected utility. Different normative theories take probabilities into account in different ways, and, on most plausible moral views, there are considerations that can outweigh expected utility. But I do not know of any plausible normative view that considers likelihoods irrelevant to deliberation. Spending one's fortune on charitable ventures that have a very small likelihood of helping people is not magnanimous; it is wasteful. Rushing into a burning building at great risk to one's own life when it is extremely unlikely that anyone is inside is not courageous; it is foolhardy.

In Chapter 10, I argued that ordinary talk of what is possible, necessary, likely, and unlikely is assessment-sensitive. If that is right, then we should expect, given the connection between likelihood judgments and deontic judgments, that deontic talk is also assessment-sensitive. If the truth of an ought-judgment depends on the truth of a likely-judgment, and the truth of the likely-judgment depends on the context of assessment, then the truth of the ought-judgment must also depend on the context of assessment. And that

I developed the central ideas in this chapter jointly with Niko Kolodny. Some of them can be found in our joint paper Kolodny and MacFarlane (2010).

is what I will argue in what follows. First, though, we need to consider how orthodox frameworks handle the connection between likelihoods and oughts.

11.1 Objective and subjective oughts

11.1.1 *Subjectivism*

In the ethics literature, the connection between oughts and likelihoods is generally explained by taking "ought" to have a *subjective* sense:

Subjective Ought. *At time t, S ought (subjectively) to φ just in case φing is the appropriate thing for S to do in light of the credences that would be appropriate given S's information at t.*

If all of my evidence suggests that William is allergic to peanuts, then in the subjective sense, I ought not bring peanut butter cookies to the party— even if William is not in fact allergic, and everyone else knows this. And if my evidence suggests that Blue Blazer is a much faster horse than Exploder, I ought subjectively to bet on Blue Blazer, even if in fact my evidence is misleading and Exploder is the faster horse.

Subjectivism explains why there should be a connection between ought judgments and likelihood judgments when we consider things from the first-person present standpoint of the deliberator: it says that what I ought to do now depends on what is likely given my current evidence. However, the connection seems to hold even when we take an outside standpoint, and this subjectivism cannot explain. Suppose that I am about to bet on a race you know is fixed. I am doing what I ought to, in the subjective sense, since given my evidence Blue Blazer is more likely to win than Exploder. *You* know, though, that my evidence is incomplete and misleading: although Blue Blazer has done better in the past, tonight he will be suffering the effects of a drug. So if I ask your advice, you will say that I ought to bet on Exploder. You align your ought judgment with *your* likelihood judgment, not mine.[1] It would seem, then, that even if I am using "ought" in the subjective sense, *you* are not. For, if you are, you are saying something that both you and I know is false.

Granted, once you reveal what you know, I will no longer be in an evidential state relative to which Blue Blazer is more likely to win. So it will *become*

---

[1]Thomson (1986: 179) puts the point well: "On those rare occasions on which someone conceives the idea of asking for my advice on a moral matter, I do not take my field work to be limited to a study of what he believes is the case: I take it to be incumbent on me to find out what is the case."

true for me to say, in the subjective sense, "I ought to bet on Exploder." It is tempting to say, then, that although your advice is false when it is made, it is good advice because it will result in a belief that is both true and useful.[2]

But that hardly salvages subjectivism. What will lead to a true and useful belief is not your advice itself—your "ought" claim—but your revelation that the race is fixed. If subjectivism is correct, there is no real sense in which I come to *agree* with your advice when I later come to believe that I ought not bet on Blue Blazer. (The truth of my later belief depends on what I will know then, while the truth of your advice depends on what I know now.) It is mysterious, moreover, why I should expect your advice to be followed by evidence that Blue Blazer is not likely to win. After all, if subjectivism is correct, that evidence is just irrelevant to the truth of the advice.

More fundamentally, this sort of strategic consideration cannot explain why you would not only say, but *believe* that I ought to bet on Exploder.

11.1.2 *Objectivism*

It is natural to think that in advising me, you are using an "ought" that is relative not to my information, or even to your own, but to the facts. I would like to know what I ought to do in light of all the facts. I think that this is to bet on Blue Blazer. Knowing more of the facts than I do, you think I am wrong about this, and you advise me accordingly. We can make sense of our disagreement by supposing that we are both using "ought" in the "objective" sense:

Objective Ought. *At time t, S ought (objectively) to φ just in case φing is the appropriate thing for S to do in light of all the facts at t, known and unknown.*

But the objective "ought" cannot be the "ought" we use in deliberation. Suppose you buy three rubber duckies for your child, and later learn that one out of every hundred rubber duckies from this manufacturer leaches out toxic chemicals. What should you do? Clearly, you ought to throw away all three duckies. But that is almost certainly *not* what you ought to do in the objective sense. An omniscient being who knew all the facts would know which (if any) of your duckies were toxic, and would counsel you to discard only those, keeping the rest.

The problem is not just that, in our state of ignorance, we lack the knowledge to determine with certainty what we ought, objectively, to do. If that

---

[2]See Ross (1939: 152–3), paraphrasing Prichard (1949).

were the only problem, then we could try to figure out what it is most *prob-able* that we ought to do, and do that (Moore 1912: 100–1; Brandt 1959: 367; Thomson 1986: 178). In our case, though, we know that it is highly probable that all three of the duckies are safe, and hence highly probable that we ought, objectively, to keep them all. Despite that, we decide to throw them out, and rationally so—we would not risk a child's life for the price of three rubber duckies. Whatever "ought" we are using when we deliberate about what we ought to do in this case, it is not the objective one.[3]

11.1.3   *Ambiguity*

It seems, then, that the deliberator's "ought" cannot be the objective one, and the advisor's "ought" cannot be the subjective one. But this leaves open the possibility that the deliberator's "ought" is subjective and the advisor's objective. We might try saying that at the race track, I am deliberating about what I ought to do, given my information, while you are advising me about what I ought to do, given the facts.

But this resolution is not satisfactory. If I am saying, correctly, that giving my limited information I ought to bet on Blue Blazer, and you are saying, also correctly, that given the facts I ought not to bet on Blue Blazer, then our claims do not conflict. We are not in disagreement in *any* of the senses discussed in Chapter 6. Yet it does seem that when you say, "No, you ought not bet on Blue Blazer," you are contradicting what I said and disagreeing with me. Indeed, it seems important to the way we think about deliberation and advice that the advisor is speaking to the very same normative question the deliberator is asking. The ambiguity approach has to reject this natural view.

A further problem is that, if the motivation for disambiguating is sound, there is no stopping at two senses of "ought." Consider, again, the case of the rubber duckies. Suppose that you have no reason to doubt that the duckies are safe; you have not heard about the defects at the factory. You think that you ought to keep the duckies. *I*, on the other hand, know that there is a one percent chance that any given ducky is toxic. In this case I will tell you that you ought to get rid of all the duckies. Here my "ought" is not objective. Since it is very likely that all the duckies are safe, it is very likely that you ought objectively to keep them—as I am well aware. But my "ought" is not subjective, either. I can agree that what you ought subjectively to do, given

---

[3]For this general point, see Ewing (1947: 128), Prichard (1949), Parfit (1984: 25), Jackson (1991: 466–7), Broome (1991: 128), Wedgwood (2003: 204), Gibbard (2005: 345).

what you know, is keep all the duckies. So we need a third sense of "ought," and there will be no stopping here. By constructing more cases of this kind, we can motivate what Jackson (1991) calls an "annoying profusion of oughts."

11.2   Contextualism

These considerations suggest that, rather than being ambiguous, "ought" is univocal, but context-sensitive. On each occasion of use, it should be interpreted relative to a contextually relevant body of information.

Use-sensitive Ought.   *An occurrence of "S ought to φ" at a context c is true iff φ-ing is the appropriate thing for S to do in light of the information relevant at c (normally, the speaker's information).*

So, when I say that I "ought to bet on Blue Blazer," the truth of my claim depends on whether it makes sense for me to bet on Blue Blazer given what I know, and when you say that I "ought not bet on Blue Blazer," the truth of your claim depends on whether it makes sense for me to bet on Blue Blazer given what *you* know. In this way we can explain both the deliberator's and the advisor's uses of "ought" without positing a lexical ambiguity.

Contextualism solves Jackson's "annoying profusion" problem, and semantically it is more plausible than the ambiguity view (indeed, it is the orthodoxy in the linguistics literature; see, for example, Kratzer 1981b). However, it does not solve the fundamental problem with the ambiguity view. If deliberators and advisors are using "ought" in relation to different bodies of evidence, then they are talking past one another, not addressing a single normative question. To return, again, to our opening example: if you can accept that I have said something true in saying that I "ought to bet on Blue Blazer," and I can accept that you have said something true in saying that I "ought not bet on Blue Blazer," then we do not disagree except perhaps in a verbal sense.

This is not to say that the contextualist view makes it impossible to understand how a deliberator and advisor could *ever* disagree. In many cases, they will be using "ought" in relation to the same body of information, and in those cases the deliberator's "ought" is incompatible with the advisor's "ought not." However, disagreement does not seem to be limited to cases of this kind. Suppose that when I said "I ought to bet on Blue Blazer," I did not know of your presence. Suppose that you were a stranger, eavesdropping on my soliloquy from behind a bush. Even in such a case, it makes sense for you to think that I am wrong, and to say, "No, you ought to bet on Exploder." Surely it is not plausible that the force of my original assertion was that the appropriate thing to do in light of my information at the time, *and of any information possessed by anyone who might overhear or later consider my claim*, was to bet on Blue Blazer. I had no warrant for an assertion that strong.[4]

Alternatively, the contextualist could take the contextually relevant body of information to be the information the speaker now possesses plus any information she will acquire before having to act. This suggestion helps us see the advisor as disagreeing with the deliberator, but it has the odd result that whether the deliberator's judgment is true depends on whether the advisor will intervene. Suppose that you are trying to decide whether to offer your advice or just let me waste my money on Blue Blazer. According to this account, my claim "I ought to bet on Blue Blazer" will be true if you don't offer your advice, and false if you do offer your advice. This is, to say the least, a bizarre prediction. It means that your motive in offering me advice cannot be to bring me from an incorrect to a correct belief about what I ought to do.

Thus, although contextualism seems an improvement on the ambiguity view, it leaves us without adequate resources to explain how advisors and deliberators can be addressing a single question and disagreeing about the answer.

11.3 A relativist account

From the failures of subjectivism, objectivism, and contextualism, we can extract four desiderata for an adequate account of "ought":

1. The truth of "ought" claims depends on what is appropriate in light of some body of information, not on what is appropriate in light of all the facts.

2. However, this body of information is not fixed by features of the context of use. In particular, it is not the speaker's information at the time of use, or the information of some contextually relevant group, or the information the speaker will gather before having to act.

3. Nor is it the information possessed by the *subject* of the "ought" claim at the time of evaluation.

4. Advisors' "ought"s should be interpreted relative to the same body of information as deliberators'.

---

[4]Compare the parallel discussion of epistemic modals in §10.2.

All of these desiderata can be met with a relativist account. Instead of letting the context of use fix which information is relevant to the truth of "ought" claims, we let the context of assessment determine this. On this account, "ought" claims are not about any particular body of information (nor do they "concern" any particular body of information, in the sense introduced in §4.5.2). Their truth, relative to any context of assessment, depends on the information relevant at that context, and not the information relevant at the context of use, or the subject's information at the time of evaluation. So the first three desiderata are met. The fourth is also met, since from any given context of assessment, all "ought"s are interpreted relative to the same body of information—though which body of information this is will vary with the context of assessment.[5]

On this account, you are warranted in asserting "I ought to ϕ" if ϕing is the appropriate thing for you to do in light of your information. (On this, the relativist agrees with both the subjectivist and the contextualist.) You are warranted in asserting "S ought to ϕ" if ϕing is the appropriate thing for S to do in light of your information. (On this, the relativist agrees with the contextualist, but not the subjectivist.) And you are obliged to retract an earlier assertion of "S ought to ϕ" if ϕing is not the appropriate thing for S to have done in light of the information you have now. (Here the relativist diverges from both contextualism and subjectivism.) The relativist "ought" has a more subjective feel when the assessor knows no more than the subject, and a more objective feel when the assessor knows significantly more. These differences do not need to be explained by positing either an ambiguity or the usual kind of contextual sensitivity (use sensitivity) in "ought." Indeed, the relativist account deprives us of most of the usual reasons for thinking that "ought" has an objective sense at all. We will return to one remaining reason in §11.7. And we will address some lingering reasons for thinking that there is a subjective sense of "ought" in §11.6.

---

[5] The central idea here, that "ought" is perspectival rather than ambiguous or use-sensitive, is developed independently in Horty (2011) in the context of utilitarianism. Horty, however, is concerned with indeterminism rather than uncertainty, and objective states play the role in his theory that information states play in ours. Because of this, his theory is not directly applicable to cases in which there is uncertainty without objective indeterminism.

11.4 Compositional Semantics

Since on this account deontic modals are sensitive to the information relevant at the context of assessment, we can model them semantically in the same framework we used for epistemic modals (§10.5.1). We can then derive some interesting predictions about how deontic modals interact with epistemic modals, conditionals, and other constructions. After describing the compositional semantics, we will apply it to two puzzles from the literature.

As in §10.5.1, an index will consist of a world, time, assignment, and *information state*, which we may think of as a set of possible worlds.[6] Propositions will have truth values relative to worlds and information states, and the postsemantics will look to the context of assessment to initialize the information state parameter.

Traditionally, "ought" is treated semantically as a sentential operator: "Ought(ϕ)" is taken to be true if ϕ is true at all of the most ideal worlds in the contextually restricted "modal base." There are some uses of "ought" for which this treatment is appropriate. For example:

(1) There ought to be a law against loud car stereos.
  It ought to be the case that there is a law against loud car stereos.
  OUGHT(there is a law against loud car stereos).

Plausibly, (1) is true just in case all of the most ideal worlds are worlds where there is a law against loud car stereos.

However, as Schroeder (2011) argues, it is distorting to extend this treatment to the uses of "ought" with which we are concerned here—uses in the context of deliberation and advice. There are important syntactic and semantic differences between *evaluative* uses of ought, such as (1), and *deliberative* uses like

(2) Jim ought to choose Sarah.

Syntactically, the "ought" in (2) is a control verb, while the "ought" in (1) is a raising verb. This syntactic difference goes with a difference in meaning. (2) does not mean the same thing as

(3) It ought to be the case that Jim chooses Sarah.

---

[6] A more complex representation would include a probability distribution over an algebra of subsets of these worlds (see Yalcin 2007), but the simpler representation will suffice for purposes of this chapter.

If it did, it would also mean the same thing as

(4)   Sarah ought to be chosen by Jim,

and it does not. Sentences (3) and (4) give a positive evaluation of a certain state of affairs, but they do not say who is responsible for bringing about that state of affairs. Sentence (2), by contrast, implies that *Jim* is responsible for bringing it about that he chooses Sarah.[7] The "ought" in (2) expresses a relation between an agent (Jim) and an action (choosing Sarah), not a property of a state of affairs (Jim's choosing Sarah).

Accordingly, we will think of the deliberative "ought" as a two-place predicate whose argument places are filled by terms for an agent and an action. We will need a notation for actions:

Actions. $^x|\phi x|$ *is the action of making it the case that the open sentence ϕx applies to oneself.*

So, for example,

$$^x|x \text{ flies}|$$

is the action of flying, and

$$^x|\exists z(x \text{ is sitting next to } z \wedge z \text{ is sitting next to } y)|$$

is the action of sitting next to someone who is sitting next to y. It will not be necessary for our purposes to give a systematic theory of the metaphysics of actions, which could settle when the actions expressed by two open sentences are identical. We will assume, however, that actions are individuated in such a way that "is done intentionally" is an extensional predicate of actions. If you intentionally flipped the switch and in so doing unintentionally alerted the burglar, then your flipping the switch is not the same action as your alerting the burglar, even though given the circumstances you could not have performed the former without performing the latter.[8]

We will need three background notions to define the semantics for "ought." The first is the set of actions an agent can *choose* to perform:

---

[7] At least on its most natural reading. Schroeder allows that it has a less natural "evaluative" reading on which it is synonymous with (3), and on which "ought" functions as a raising verb.

[8] On Davidson's (1963) account, by contrast, these are the same action described differently, and "is done intentionally" applies to an action only under a description.

Choices. *Let Choice$_\alpha^{w,t}$ be the set of actions α can choose to perform at w, t.*

What actions an agent can choose to perform depends on what the agent knows and what abilities she has. For example, the action of buying a lottery ticket is one I can now choose to perform, but the action of buying a winning lottery ticket is not—unless I know ahead of time that the ticket I buy is going to win. If the ticket I buy wins the lottery, then buying a winning lottery ticket is something I did, but not something I chose to do. The intuitive distinction I am relying on here does not line up precisely with the distinction between things done intentionally and things done unintentionally: choice requires a degree of control that intentional action does not. If, in the last seconds of a basketball game, I make a desperate shot and it goes in, then scoring a basket is something I did intentionally, but not something I was in a position to *choose* to do. I chose to throw the ball and try for the basket, knowing that whether I succeeded was not entirely in my control. In general, let us say, one can choose to ϕ only if one expects that one will succeed in ϕing if one sets out to ϕ.

The second notion we will need is a *ranking* of actions in light of an information state:

Ranking. $\geq_\alpha^{w,t,i}$ *is a partial order defined on actions. To say that $x \geq_\alpha^{w,t,i} y$ is to say that in light of information i, action x is at least as good as action y for α to do at w, t.*[9]

Different substantive normative views will disagree about this underlying ranking. A consequentialist will define $\geq_\alpha^{w,t,i}$ in terms of the expected utility of the two actions for α in light of i, while a deontologist will use a different method. I will presuppose only some uncontroversial facts about the underlying relation: for example, that moving an injured patient to a more comfortable place is better than not moving her in light of information that she does not have a spinal injury, but worse than not moving her in light of information that leaves a spinal injury an open possibility.

Finally, we need the notion of one action's *requiring* another at a world and time:

---

[9]By only requiring the ranking to be a partial order, we leave it open that there could be *incomparable* actions: actions x and y such that it is not the case either that x is at least as good as y or that y is at least as good as x. This possibility is required by some substantive normative theories.

Requires. *An action x requires an action y by agent α at w, t (x $\xrightarrow[w,t]{\alpha}$ y) iff α cannot perform x at w, t without thereby performing y.*

For example, for a driver, the action of *accelerating up a hill* requires *pushing the gas pedal*. By contrast, the action of *picking up the apple* does not require *grabbing the apple with one's left hand*, since one could also pick up the apple with one's right hand. The modality here is situational and worldly, not epistemic. It doesn't matter whether anyone *knows* that one cannot accelerate up a hill without pressing the gas pedal: what matters is that, given the laws of nature, the design of the car, the slope of the hill, and the absence of strong electromagnets at the top, the car is not capable of accelerating up the hill unless the driver presses the gas pedal. Thus, in a situation where the winning number is 6, the action of *picking the winning number* requires *picking 6* (and vice versa), even if nobody knows this.

Which actions an agent can choose to perform depends on what the agent knows, but which actions are *required* by these actions depends on the objective facts of the situation, both known and unknown. The actions required by an action one can choose to perform will typically include many actions one would be performing unintentionally. For example, Oedipus's intentional action of striking the old man in the road requires the action of striking his father, since in fact the old man is his father. But, because Oedipus does not know this, striking his father is not something he *chooses* to do. This interplay between *Choice*$_\alpha^{w,t}$, which is sensitive to α's knowledge, and $\xrightarrow[w,t]{\alpha}$, which is not, will be important for understanding the semantics of the deliberative "ought."

The basic idea of the semantics is this. Take the set of actions that are under your control—the ones you can choose to do (or not do) right now. Of these, consider the subset of highest-ranking actions: those that are not ranked lower than any action in the set.

Optimal.

$$Optimal_\alpha^{\langle w,t,i \rangle} = \{x \in Choice_\alpha^{w,t} \mid \forall y \in Choice_\alpha^{w,t}(y \geq_\alpha^{w,t,i} x \supset x \geq_\alpha^{w,t,i} y)\}$$

Then you ought to do every action that is required by *all* of the actions in this highest ranking group:[10]

---

[10] At this point Niko Kolodny and I part company. He rejects the principle that if one ought to φ, and φing requires ψing, one ought to ψ.

Deliberative Ought.

$$\langle x, y \rangle \in [\![O]\!]^c_{\langle w,t,i,a \rangle} \text{ iff } \forall z \in Optimal_x^{\langle w,t,i \rangle} (z \xrightarrow[w,t]{x} y)$$

To take a simple example, suppose that two children, A and B, are drowning in a lake. You can rescue only one. They are equally far away, and equally precious to you. Simplifying somewhat, suppose that the set of highest-ranked actions that you can choose to perform is {*saving child A*, *saving child B*, *saving one of the children*}. Then it is not the case that you ought to save child A, or that you ought to save child B, but it is the case that you ought to save one of the children, since this action is required by all of the actions in the highest-ranking group. It is also the case that you ought to enter the water, that you ought to get wet, and countless other things, some of which you may not know you have done until later. For example, if in fact the children are twins, it will follow that you ought to save a twin—though you may never know that you have done this.

One immediate implication of the semantics is that "ought" is sensitive to the information state parameter of the index. So if we use the Relativist Postsemantics from §10.5.1, according to which this parameter is initialized by the context of assessment, it follows that "ought" is assessment-sensitive.

11.5   Ifs and oughts

There are many "ought" questions that this semantics will not settle, since they depend on the underlying ranking $\geq_\alpha^{w,t,i}$. These are properly normative questions, not semantic ones. As we will see, however, the semantics can help us with some thorny puzzles involving the relation of "ought" to conditionals and epistemic modals—puzzles that, left undiagnosed, might be taken to motivate one of the views we have rejected (subjectivism, objectivism, ambiguity, contextualism).

11.5.1   *The miner paradox*

You are standing in front of two mine shafts. Flood waters are approaching. You know that ten miners are in one of the shafts, but you don't know which. You have enough sand bags to block one of the shafts. If you block the shaft the miners are in, all the miners will live, but if you block the other shaft, all the miners will die. If you block neither shaft, or try ineffectually to block both, the water will be divided, and only the lowest miner in the shaft will die, leaving nine alive. What ought you to do?[11]

In the course of your deliberation, you might naturally endorse the following two conditionals:

(5) If the miners are in shaft A, I ought to block shaft A.
[*if miners-in-A*] $O\,(I,\,{}^{x}|x$ *blocks shaft A*$|)$

(6) If the miners are in shaft B, I ought to block shaft B.
[*if miners-in-B*] $O\,(I,\,{}^{x}|x$ *blocks shaft B*$|)$

Since you also accept

(7) Either the miners are in shaft A or the miners are in shaft B,
miners-in-A $\vee$ *miners-in-B*

it seems you should be able to conclude, by constructive dilemma:

(8) Either I ought to block shaft A or I ought to block shaft B.
$O\,(I,\,{}^{x}|x$ *blocks shaft A*$|)\vee O\,(I,\,{}^{x}|x$ *blocks shaft B*$|)$

But in fact, you ought not block either shaft, as that would be taking too big a risk with the lives of the miners (or so most substantive moral theories would conclude). The right conclusion to draw is the negation of (8):

(9) I ought not block shaft A and I ought not block shaft B.
$\neg\,O\,(I,\,{}^{x}|x$ *blocks shaft A*$|)\wedge\neg\,O\,(I,\,{}^{x}|x$ *blocks shaft B*$|)$

Our reasoning has gone wrong somewhere, but where?

Faced with this dilemma, one may feel the temptation to reject the eminently reasonable conditionals (5) and (6), as a hard-headed subjectivism would require; or to accept the implausible conclusion (8), as a hard-headed objectivism would require; or to argue that there is no conflict between (8) and (9), because the "ought"s in them are used in different senses, or relative to different contextual information states. We have already seen (in §11.1–11.2) why these responses are unsatisfactory.[12]

Another natural temptation is to suppose that the modals in (5) and (6) take wide scope over the conditionals, as follows:

(5') I ought to: [block shaft A if the miners are in shaft A].

---

[11] The example has been discussed by Parfit (1988), who credits Regan (1980: 265 n.1), and more recently by Kolodny and MacFarlane (2010) and Parfit (2011: 159–160).

[12] For further argument, tailored to this case, see Kolodny and MacFarlane (2010).

(6′)   I ought to: [block shaft B if the miners are in shaft B].

Since the argument from (5′), (6′), and (7) is not an instance of constructive dilemma, we no longer have anything resembling a formally valid argument for (8). But this does not really solve the problem, since (5′) and (6′) still seem to be incompatible with (9). If the miners are in shaft A and (5′) is true, then presumably I cannot do what I ought to do by blocking neither shaft. Similarly, if the miners are in shaft B and (6′) is true, I cannot do what I ought to do by blocking neither shaft. Since we know that the miners are in one of the shafts, we can again argue by constructive dilemma that (9) is false.[13]

The key to a more satisfactory solution to the puzzle is to recognize that "ought" is information-sensitive, in the way our semantics describes. As we have seen in §10.5.5, indicative conditionals shift the information state of the index. So, suppose that our current contextually relevant information state S is ignorant about which shaft the miners are in, but certain that they are either in shaft A or in shaft B. Let A be the set of worlds in which the miners are in A, and B the set of worlds in which the miners are in B. Then (5) is true relative to S just in case

(10) $O(I, {}^x|x \text{ blocks shaft } A|)$

is true relative to the contracted state $S \cap A$, and (6) is true relative to S just in case

(11) $O(I, {}^x|x \text{ blocks shaft } B|)$

is true relative to the contracted state $S \cap B$. What the premises of the argument require, then, is that

$(S \cap A) \cup (S \cap B) = S$

Blocking shaft A is what I ought to do in light of $S \cap A$.

Blocking shaft B is what I ought to do in light of $S \cap B$.

And these constraints are perfectly consistent with the truth of (9), which requires only that

Blocking neither shaft is what I ought to do in light of S.

On our semantics, then, (5), (6), and (7) are perfectly compatible with (9), and do not entail (8). So none of the desperate measures mentioned above are needed to respond to the puzzle.

---

[13]For further considerations against the idea that the modals scope over the conditionals, see §10.5.5 and Kolodny and MacFarlane (2010: §III.1).

It might be thought that any semantics that invalidates an instance of constructive dilemma is unacceptable. But we have already seen reasons to reject the unrestricted validity of this inference form (§10.5.5), and it is possible to delineate a precise range of applicability within which it is reliable (Kolodny and MacFarlane 2010: §IV.5). The sky will not fall.

11.5.2   *Gibbard on truth and correct belief*

Gibbard (2005: 338) poses the following puzzle:

For belief, correctness is truth. Correct belief is true belief. My belief that snow is white is correct just in case the belief is true, just in case snow is white. Correctness, now, seems normative. More precisely, as we should put it, the concept of correctness seems to be a normative concept—and that raises a puzzle: Hume worried about the transition from is to ought, and the lesson that many have drawn is that from purely non-normative premises alone, no normative conclusion can follow. . . . Yet from the truth of "Snow is white" follows the correctness of a belief that snow is white.

Gibbard's worry is that if

(12)   It is raining

entails

(13)   You ought to believe that it is raining

—and Gibbard thinks that it does—then it seems we have a straightforward case of a purely descriptive claim that entails a purely normative claim.

Gibbard defends Hume by distinguishing between objective and subjective sense of "ought":

You flip a coin and hide the result from both of us. If in fact the coin landed heads, then in the objective sense, I ought to believe that it landed heads. Believing the coin landed heads would be, we might say, epistemically fortunate. In the subjective sense, though, I ought neither to believe that it landed heads nor believe that it landed tails. I ought to give equal credence to its having landed heads and to its having landed tails. (340)

He argues that the subjective sense is fundamental, and that the objective sense can be defined in terms of it. On his account, "I ought (objectively) to ϕ" can be analyzed as

If a duplicate of mine I^+ were transformed so that he oughted [subjectively] to accept all the facts of my circumstance, and I^+ were to decide, for my circumstance, what to do, then I^+ would ought [subjectively] to decide, for my circumstance, to do A. (347)

Letting A be "accept that S," this implies (349):

(14) I ought [objectively] to accept that S iff I^+ ought [subjectively] to accept that S for my circumstance.

(15) I^+ ought [subjectively] to accept that S for my circumstance iff S obtains in my circumstance.

From which it follows trivially that

(16) I ought [objectively] to accept S iff S obtains in my circumstance.

So, Gibbard concludes, (12) really does entail (13). But that is because the objective ought claim in (13) just expresses a complex counterfactual relation between two subjective oughts, and not a genuine normative proposition. It is, as he says, "a normative claim only degeneratively," since when we expand it, it turns into a trivial relation between two subjective oughts (341).

Gibbard's solution relies on a distinction between objective and subjective senses of "ought" that we have already seen reason to reject. What is more, the counterfactual Gibbard uses to explain the objective sense of "ought" is at the very least "wild" (as Gibbard himself calls it), and at worst unintelligible. We are supposing that I^+ ought to accept all the facts of my circumstance. Let's suppose that these include the following: someone is approaching, but I have no evidence that anyone is approaching. Then we must suppose that I^+ ought to accept both that someone is approaching and that he has no evidence that anyone is approaching. But how can it be that he ought to accept both these things, if, as seems plausible, he ought not believe things contrary to his evidence? In imagining the counterfactual circumstance, then, we must imagine that different epistemic norms obtain, not just different facts (348). And it is not clear that we can do this. So it is not clear that we can even coherently entertain the counterfactual in terms of which Gibbard analyzes the objective "ought." It seems dubious, then, that this analysis captures what we mean when we say that we ought to believe what is true.

The semantics we have suggested provides a more straightforward resolution to Gibbard's puzzle. Let us ask first whether (12) entails (13), as Gibbard supposes. In §3.4, we distinguished three notions of entailment that might be used in a framework allowing assessment sensitivity:

logical implication: preservation of truth at every point of evaluation (context, index pair).

absolute logical consequence: preservation of truth at every context of use and context of assessment.

diagonal logical consequence: preservation of truth as assessed from the context
   of use, at every context of use.

Sentence (12) does not entail (13) in any of these senses. To see why, note that
the truth of (12) at a point of evaluation depends only on the world and time
of the index, while the truth of (13) depends on the information state. So it is
possible to find a point of evaluation c, $\langle w, t, i, a \rangle$ at which (12) is true but (13)
is false. This is enough to show that (13) is not logically implied by (12). To
see that it is not an absolute logical consequence, either, it suffices to note that
(13) is assessment-sensitive, while (12) is not. To see that it is not a diagonal
logical consequence, select a context c such that it is raining at t_c in w_c, but i_c
is ignorant about whether it is raining.

   Since (12) does not entail (13), it is not a counterexample to Hume's principle that a normative proposition cannot be derived from a purely descriptive
one. But, one might ask, why does (12) *seem to* entail (13)? Our semantics
offers two reasons. First, whenever (12) is *accepted* at a context (in the sense of
§10.5.5), (13) is also accepted at that context.[14] If I know that it is raining, then
the information state of my context contains only worlds where it is raining,
and relative to that information state, one ought to believe that it is raining.
This means that, whenever a speaker is in a position to assert (12), she is in a
position to assert (13) as well—a relation that might easily be confused with
entailment.[15]

   Second, given our semantics for conditionals, the conditional

(17)   If it is raining, then you ought to believe that it is raining

is logically true, in all three senses distinguished in §3.4: it is logically necessary, absolutely logically true, and diagonally logically true. One might
naturally think this means that its consequent (13) is a logical consequence of
its antecedent (12). But that does not follow, since on our semantics modus
ponens is not valid for the indicative conditional.[16] So our semantics allows
us to see why one might think that (12) entails (13), even though it does not.

---

[14]Yalcin (2007: 1004) calls this relation *informational consequence.*

[15]For kindred observations, see Stalnaker (1975)'s diagnosis of the plausibility of the "or-to-if"
inference.

[16]More precisely, its instances are not guaranteed to be logical implications, absolute logical consequences, or diagonal logical consequences. It is, however, acceptance-preserving. See
Kolodny and MacFarlane (2010).

11.6   Evaluative uses of "ought"

The relativist "ought" we have been describing lies between the subjective "ought" and the objective "ought." We have been arguing that it does the work of both, explaining both the first-personal deliberative uses that tempt us to appeal to a subjective "ought" and the third-personal advice uses that tempt us to appeal to an objective "ought." We might conjecture, then, that "ought" is never really used in the senses traditionally distinguished as "subjective" and "objective," and that the ambiguity theory was an unsuccessful first attempt to capture phenomena better explained in terms of assessment sensitivity. In this section and the next, we defend this conjecture against arguments that there are still essential roles for the subjective and objective senses of "ought" to play—roles that cannot be discharged by the assessment-sensitive "ought."

Suppose that Fatma is investigating a murder case. She has gathered a considerable amount of evidence pointing to the butler: the butler's gloves had the host's blood on them, the butler's knife was found buried outside, and the gardener, the only other person present on the property at the time of the murder, has a credible alibi. We, however, have some evidence that Fatma does not, and this evidence establishes conclusively that the gardener committed the murder and tried to frame the butler. Question: ought Fatma to believe that the gardener committed the murder?

If the "ought" here is the assessment-sensitive one we have been describing, then the answer, as assessed from our context, would appear to be yes. But that seems paradoxical. Given that all of her evidence points to the butler, Fatma would not be justified in believing that the gardener committed the murder. Surely, then, in at least one important sense of "ought," she ought not believe this. It is tempting to conclude, then, that even if the assessment-sensitive "ought" has a role in deliberation and advice, it is not the "ought" we are using when we consider Fatma's situation as detached critics rather than potential advisors.

But this argument is too quick. First, it ties "ought" too closely to criticism. If you ought to administer the medicine, and you do administer the medicine, thinking it is poison and aiming to kill the patient, then you are criticizable, though you have done what you ought. And if you don't administer the medicine, because you have been told that it is poison and want to help the patient, then you have an excuse for not doing what you ought to have done. We should be wary, then, of moving too quickly between claims about what people ought to do and claims about whether criticism is warranted.[17]

Second, the assessment-sensitive account does not predict that

(18)   Fatma ought not believe that the gardener committed the murder

is false as assessed by someone who knows that the gardener did it. What
it says is that (18) is false as assessed from a context where the *relevant* information state includes information that the gardener did it (see §10.4.4
and the Flexible Relativist Postsemantics in §10.5.1.) In normal contexts of
deliberation and advice, the relevant information state will be the information
possessed by the assessor. Deliberators want their normative conclusions to
be correctable by assessors who have more information than they do, because
they want to do what is really best, not just what others will judge to be
reasonable. But when the primary question at hand is not "what should be
done?" but rather "was the agent reasonable in doing what she did?", the
relevant information state may shift to the agent's information. That is what
happens when we say things like,

(19)   Don't beat yourself up over it. You believed then just what you ought
       to have believed, even though it turned out to be false.

This does not amount to a concession that there is a subjective sense of "ought."
On this view, "ought" is assessment-sensitive; it is just that sometimes features
of the context of assessment tell us to look at the agent's information rather
than the assessor's.[18]

Third, if one wants to make an assessment-invariant claim with the truth-
conditions of a subjective "ought," it is always possible to use the "for all α
knows" construction introduced in §10.5.4:

(20)   For all Fatma knows (or: given her evidence), she ought not believe
       that the gardener committed the murder.

The "ought" in this sentence is the "ought" whose semantics is given above,
but the explicit binding of the information state makes the sentence equivalent
to a subjective "ought" statement. So accommodating the data does not require
positing a separate, subjective sense of "ought."

---

[17]The point is often made by defenders of objectivism (Moore 1912; Thomson 1986). But (*pace*
Parfit 1984: 25) it holds even for the subjective "ought." Whether one does what one subjectively
ought to depends on one's information, but whether one is blameworthy depends on much else
besides, including one's beliefs and intentions.

[18]Cf. DeRose (2005: 189) and §§8.2 and 10.4.4, this volume.

11.7   Modal ignorance

When we are deliberating, we very often express ignorance about what we ought to do. For example, in the miners case discussed above, it would be natural to say:

(21)   I don't know whether I ought to close shaft *A* or shaft *B*. If the miners are in *A*, I should close *A*, and if they're in *B*, I should close *B*. But which shaft are they in? I don't know, so I'm not in a position to know what I ought to do.[19]

But the semantics offered above seems to predict that such professions of ignorance are unwarranted. For the deliberator's information leaves it open whether the miners are in shaft *A* or shaft *B*, and the deliberator knows that. By reflecting on these facts, the deliberator can easily come to know that

(22)   I ought to close neither shaft

is true as used at and assessed from her current context. So she should confidently say

(23)   I am in a position to know that I ought to close neither shaft,

not

(24)   I am not in a position to know what I ought to do.

To explain why she finds it natural to say (24), one might suppose, we need the objective sense of "ought."

A similar objection can be made against our semantics for epistemic modals (§10.5), and indeed against a whole range of contextualist proposals that take the assertability of "it is possible that ϕ" to depend on whether the speaker's information rules out ϕ. One version of the objection can be found in DeRose (1991). In the scenario DeRose describes, John's doctor sees some symptoms that might indicate cancer, and orders a test. If the test is negative, it means that cancer is completely ruled out. If the test is positive, then more tests must be conducted to determine whether John has cancer.

In this case, the test has been run, but not even the doctor knows the results of the test. A computer has calculated the results and printed them. A hospital employee has taken the printout and, without reading it, placed it in a sealed envelope. The policy

---

[19]Being in a position to know *p* is having grounds such that, were one to believe *p* on these grounds, one would know *p*.

of the hospital is that the patient should be the first to learn the results. Jane has made an appointment to pick up the results tomorrow. She knows that the envelope with the results has been generated and that nobody knows what the results are. Still, if Bill were to call her to find out the latest news, she might very well say, "I don't yet know whether it's possible that John has cancer. I'm going to find that out tomorrow when the results of the test are revealed." (DeRose 1991: 587)

What is it, DeRose asks, that Jane is uncertain of now, and will find out when she learns the test results? It can't be whether Jane's current information, or the information of a relevant group, rules out John's having cancer. For, as Jane is well aware, she does not yet have knowledge that would rule out John's having cancer—indeed, *nobody* does. (I assume, with DeRose, that we do not count the computer that printed the test results as a knower.) The moral, DeRose thinks, is that the truth of epistemic modal statements depends not just on what is known, but on what could come to be known through a relevant channel (here, the test).

Both of these arguments from "modal ignorance" assume that, in order to explain the naturalness of the professions of modal ignorance with which they start, we must find a way to construe these professions on which they are *true*. It is this that I want to question. We can explain why it seems natural for the speakers in our examples to utter (24) or

(25)   I am not in a position to know whether it is possible that John has cancer

without construing these sentences in a way that makes them true (as assessed from the speakers' contexts). I will argue that the speakers are taken in by a persuasive but fallacious line of reasoning—one whose invalidity is not obvious but can be seen using our semantics.

Before arguing this, though, let us remind ourselves why the alternatives that these arguments seem to recommend are unsatisfactory. Suppose we allow (24) to be true by construing the "ought" in it as the objective "ought." What about the "ought"s in the conditionals in (21)? Since they seem to be offered in support of (24), it seems we must construe them in the objective sense as well. But then what of the conclusion our deliberator ultimately reaches, namely (23)? Here we cannot construe the "ought" objectively, so it looks as if the deliberator has simply changed the subject. And that makes it very hard to see the considerations in (21) as even relevant to the deliberation. The deliberation is, after all, geared towards arriving at a (non-objective) ought claim that can form the basis of action; what, exactly, is the rational bearing of the objective "ought"s on this conclusion? Moreover, there does not *seem* to be an ambiguity here, and there is no explicit signaling of a change in sense.

Similarly, if we follow DeRose and take "possible" in (25) to mean *possible given the information the speaker has or could come to have through relevant channels*, then we can explain the naturalness of Jane's assertion of (25) by taking it to be true. But it would also be perfectly natural for Jane to say:

(26)   I know it's possible that the printout says Negative, and I know it's possible that it says Positive.

If "possible" means what DeRose says it does, then we can construe (26) as true only by taking the test *not* to be a relevant information channel. Of course, nothing precludes a contextualist from taking the test to be a relevant channel in one context, Jane's utterance of (25), but not in another, her utterance of (26). The problem is that (25) and (26) seem *jointly* assertible, without any context shift. Indeed, it seems plausible that (26) gives Jane's *reason* for believing (25). She thinks she is not in a position to know whether it is possible that John has cancer precisely *because* she knows that the printout might read Negative (in which case it is not possible that John has cancer) and might read Positive (in which case it is possible that John has cancer). If we construe the "possible" in (26) relative to a different body of information than the "possible" in (25), then we have to take her reasoning to be equivocal in a way that should be patent to Jane.

As I see things, there *is* something wrong with Jane's reasoning, but the flaw is subtle—one she might very well not notice. Let us break it down. Jane reckons she knows the following:

(27)   It is possible that the printout says Negative.

(28)   If the printout says Negative, then it is not possible that John has cancer.

She then reasons as follows:

(J1)   Suppose I were in a position to know that

   (29)   It is possible that John has cancer.

(J2)   Then it would follow logically from things I am in a position to know—namely, (29) and (28)—that

(30) The printout does not say Negative.

(J3) If it follows logically from things I am in a position to know that (30), then (27) is not true.

(J4) But (27) is true, since I know it.

(J5) So, by reductio, (J1) is false: I am not in a position to know that (29).

The basic thought is simple: since (29) and (28) logically imply (30), Jane cannot rationally be uncertain about (30) without being uncertain about (29) as well.

The problem with this reasoning is that it assumes that modus tollens is logically valid—and it is not, for our indicative conditional. As we have already seen (§10.5.5), it fails when the consequent of the conditional is informationally sensitive, as it is in this case. However, the failure is not obvious. Modus tollens is reliable in such a wide range of cases that the argument "sounds right," and we can understand how Jane is misled into believing its conclusion. Explaining the naturalness of her profession of ignorance, then, does not require construing it in a way that makes it true. It just requires a proper understanding of the semantics of modals and conditionals.

The same holds for our original puzzle (21). Here the deliberator is reasoning as follows:

(E1) If the miners are in shaft *A*, I ought to close shaft *A*.

(E2) If the miners are in shaft *B*, I ought to close shaft *B*.

(E3) It is possible that the miners are in shaft *A* and it is possible that the miners are in shaft *B*.

(E4) So, it is possible that I ought to close shaft *A* and it is possible that I ought to close shaft *B*.

This certainly *seems* like compelling reasoning, but, if our semantics is correct, the argument is invalid, for reasons that should be evident from our consideration of the miners paradox in §11.5.1. The truth of (E1) requires that I ought to close shaft *A* in light of information that locates the miners in shaft *A*. The truth of (E2) requires that I ought to close shaft *B* in light of information that locates the miners in shaft *B*. The truth of (E3) requires that the contextually relevant information state leave it open which shaft the miners are in. These requirements can all be met even if, in light of the contextually relevant information, I ought to close neither shaft.

Why, then, does the argument *seem* valid? Because it exemplifies a form of argument that is reliable as long as the consequents of the conditionals are not informationally sensitive.[20] The following argument, for example, is guaranteed to preserve truth:

(F1) If the miners are in shaft *A*, they have a jackhammer.

(F2) If the miners are in shaft *B*, they have a blowtorch.

(F3) It is possible that the miners are in shaft *A* and it is possible that the miners are in shaft *B*.

(F4) So, it is possible that the miners have a jackhammer and it is possible that they have a blowtorch.

It is natural to assume that there is no relevant difference in form between argument (E) and argument (F), and to extend our justified confidence in the reliability of the latter to the former. Our deliberator is overgeneralizing in an understandable way. Charity, then, does not demand that we construe her claim as true.

The upshot of these considerations is that we are prone to overestimate the extent of our modal ignorance, because we are drawn down well-worn paths of reasoning into fallacies. It might still be thought, though, that we *need* modal ignorance to rationalize investigation. After all, if I can come to a correct determination about what I ought to do just by considering my information, why should I even seek out new information—for example, by trying to listen for noises coming from one the shafts? Don't I investigate precisely because I want to come to know something I'm currently ignorant about—namely, what I ought to do?

Note, first, that the relativist account in no way precludes saying that, when action is not required immediately, one is obligated to seek more information. Suppose that I know I have an hour before the flood waters arrive at the mine. What ought I to do? I ought not now block either of the shafts, but that does not imply I may just sit there. Presumably, I ought to do everything possible to find out where the miners are. That is a moral obligation, and it can ultimately be explained, in part, in terms of the value of saving all ten miners and the likelihood that investigating further will show us how to do that (Parfit 2011: 160–1). We need not suppose that there is an unanswered "ought" question to justify the investigation.

[20]See Kolodny and MacFarlane (2010: Theorem 3) for a more precise condition.

This response does not directly help, however, with future-directed oughts. Ought I to close shaft A in an hour? It is tempting to say, "I don't know." After all, a lot can happen in an hour: by then I may know where the miners are. But according to the relativist account, one might think, I should be prepared to give a negative answer now, based on the information I now possess. That seems odd, indeed.

But in fact, the relativist account *does* predict, in this case, that I should be agnostic about whether I ought to close shaft A in an hour. According to the semantics given above, "I ought to close shaft A" is true at a context c and index $\langle w, t, i, a \rangle$ if closing shaft A is required for me at w, t by all of the best actions I could choose to perform at w, t. Here the ranking of actions as "best" depends on the information state i, but which actions I can choose to perform at w, t depends on what things are like at w and t. If in one hour I will have come to know that the miners are in A, for example, then one of the actions I will *then* be able to choose to perform will be the action of *saving all the miners*. That action outranks all others, even by the ordering set up by my *current* information state i. (The only reason it is not the case *now* that I ought to save all the miners is that this is not an action I can now choose to perform.) And that action (in that situation) requires closing shaft A. So, for such a w and t, "I ought to close shaft A" comes out true at c, $\langle w, t, i, a \rangle$.

Thus, although I know that closing shaft A is not what I ought to do now, I do not know whether it will be what I ought to do in an hour. Not because I do not know what information I will have in an hour, but because I do not know which actions I will be able to choose to perform in an hour—and hence which of the actions I will be able to choose to perform is optimal, in light of my *present* information.

Despite the prevalence of the distinction between objective and subjective senses of "ought" in the literature on moral theory, then, it is not clear that we need it. A univocal assessment-sensitive "ought" lies between the objective and subjective poles in just the right way to make sense of the way we use "ought" in contexts of deliberation and advice.

12

THE RATIONALITY OF RELATIVISM

In the first part of this book, we saw what it would *be* for some of our thought and talk to be assessment-sensitive. In the second part, we considered reasons for thinking that our thought and talk about what is tasty, what people know, what will happen in the future, what might be the case, and what we ought to do *is* in fact assessment-sensitive.

But even if one accepts that some of our thought and talk *is* assessment-sensitive, one might ask *whether it makes sense* for it to be assessment-sensitive, and if so why. After describing what assessment sensitivity comes to, I have often been met with replies like this one:

If that's what assessment sensitivity is, then I agree that it is intelligible. I might even agree that some of our linguistic practices exhibit the patterns characteristic of assessment sensitivity. But surely once we realize this, we have reason to reform these practices, finding assessment-invariant ways of talking to do the work now done by assessment-sensitive ones. For how could it be rational to make an assertion one will be obliged to retract when one comes to occupy a relevantly different context? Maybe we can be relativists, in the way you describe, but we can't do so with our eyes open.

The burden of this chapter is to argue that there is no irrationality in speaking an assessment-sensitive language with full awareness. I will argue this in two steps. First, I will argue that there is no good *general* argument against the pattern of norms that constitutes assessment sensitivity—and in particular, no general argument against the rationality of making an assertion one expects one will have to retract later (in a different context). We must therefore look at particular bits of discourse, and ask whether it is rational that they be assessment-sensitive, given the roles they play in our lives. Taking an engineering perspective, I will show why it might make sense for our knowledge-attributing locutions to be assessment-sensitive rather than use-sensitive. (The considerations are easily generalizable to other cases.) Once we see what purposes assessment-sensitive expressions serve, we can see that they are optimally suited to serve these purposes.

It is tempting to think that this explanation provides the ingredients for a teleological explanation of assessment sensitivity. That would be overreaching, but in a speculative vein, we will sketch a couple of just-so stories about how knowledge attributions might have come to be assessment-sensitive.

12.1   Rationality and reflection

It is characteristic of assessment sensitivity that one can be obliged to retract an assertion that was perfectly correct to make. This may seem puzzling. How can it be rational to assert something one might have to retract later, not because one has learned that one was mistaken in asserting it, but just because one occupies a relevantly different context?

If there is a worry here, it cannot be *just* that one might later be compelled to retract an assertion made blamelessly. For that threat is already present, I take it, in nearly all of our assertions. It is always possible that one's present evidence for a claim is misleading, and that future evidence will reveal this.

It would be very odd, however, if one thought it *likely* that such evidence would present itself, but made the assertion regardless. And relativist accounts allow this to happen quite frequently. For example, suppose one says, at the beginning of a pregnancy, "It might be a boy and it might be a girl." One knows that in approximately nine months, one will be in an information state relative to which the proposition one asserted is false, and one will be compelled to retract it. How, in such a case, can it be rational to make the assertion in the first place?

The objection here seems to depend on something like the following reflection principle:

Reflection-Assertion I.   *One cannot rationally assert that p now if one expects that one will later acquire good grounds for retracting this assertion.*

However, this principle is not very plausible. It implies, for example, that it can never be rational to tell a lie when one expects that the truth will eventually be revealed. The rationality of a speech act, like that of any other act, depends on many contingencies of the situation. In particular cases, the badness of future retraction may be outweighed by the beneficial effects the lie will have before it is detected.

Granted, assessment-sensitive assertions are not like lies, because they need not involve any concealment. So we might try the following variant of our reflection principle:

Reflection-Assertion II. *One cannot rationally assert that p now if it is generally expected that one will later acquire good grounds for retracting this assertion.*

But surely there are cases in which it can be rational to assert something that is generally expected to be proven false. One might do so to attract attention, for example, or to keep one's job, or because the rewards of having correctly made a surprising prophecy, if it turns out to be true, vastly outweigh the damage to one's reputation for having gotten it wrong.

It seems unlikely that we will find a true, general connection between the rationality of assertion and expectations about future retraction. But we might appeal to a similar reflection principle governing belief to question the rationality of *believing* assessment-sensitive propositions:

Reflection-Belief I. *One cannot rationally believe p now if one expects that one will later acquire good grounds for giving up the belief that p.*

This principle is much more plausible than the parallel principle governing assertion. Suppose that you expect that the medical test you have scheduled for tomorrow will be positive (as it is for 70 percent of the patients with your symptoms and history), and that a positive result would mean that you have a 60 percent chance of having the disease. Surely it would be irrational for you to believe today that you do not have the disease. It would be irrational to think, "Sure, after the test I'll probably acquire grounds that will compel me to give up this belief, but right now I'm going to keep believing that I don't have the disease."

This looks bad for relativism. Relativist accounts typically allow that there are cases in which one should believe that *p* even though one knows that one will later be obliged to disbelieve *p*. We have already given an example involving epistemic modals. According to the relativist, one should believe at the beginning of a pregnancy that it is possible that the child is a boy and possible that the child is a girl. But when the baby girl is delivered, one should think: *it was not possible even then that it would be a boy* (after all, we know that even then the embryo was female). For an example involving deontic modals, consider the miners case described in §11.5.1. When the flood waters are approaching, one should believe that one ought to close off neither mine shaft. But after the flood comes and the miners are found to have been in shaft *A*, one should think: *I ought to have closed shaft A*. For an example involving knowledge attributions, suppose that one is in a low-stakes context, but expects later to be in a high-stakes context, where various bizarre possibilities involving government tampering with videos are relevant. One might properly believe that John knows that Neil Armstrong was the first man on the moon, even though one expects later to properly disbelieve this, on the grounds that John cannot rule out the possibility of tampering. All of these cases, if the relativist account is right, involve violations of *Reflection-Belief I*.

The first thing to notice about this argument is that, if it is cogent, it rules out not just relativist theories, but all forms of nonindexical contextualism as well. Consider the archetypical nonindexical contextualist view, temporalism. Suppose that at noon John believes the tensed proposition *that Sally is sitting*. He may know that at midnight, he will have excellent grounds for disbelieving this very proposition (since Sally will be sleeping then). So *Reflection-Belief I* says that he cannot rationally believe the proposition now. That would be an intolerable result for the temporalist. So, either we have a compelling argument against temporalism (and allied views that take the contents of beliefs to be centered propositions), or there is something wrong with our reflection principle.

I suggest that *Reflection-Belief I* derives what intuitive plausibility it has from another principle,

Reflection-Belief II. *One cannot rationally believe p in a context c if one expects that one will later acquire good grounds for thinking that p was not true at c.*

Reflection-Belief I and *II* yield the same verdicts in a wide range of cases, but diverge in cases where judging a proposition to be untrue is compatible with taking past beliefs with this proposition as their content to have been true at the contexts in which they were held. In such cases, only *Reflection-Belief II* remains compelling. John's knowledge that at midnight he will disbelieve the proposition *that Sally is sitting* does not undermine the rationality of believing that same proposition at noon, because when he rejects the proposition at midnight, he will not regard that as showing that his earlier belief was inaccurate. We can conclude, then, that whatever intuitive plausibility *Reflection-Belief I* has derives from *Reflection-Belief II*.

Although *Reflection-Belief II* offers no ground for objection against temporalism and other forms of nonindexical contextualism, it may seem problematic for relativist views. For relativists, unlike nonindexical contextualists, hold that the accuracy of past beliefs can depend on features of the current context. As it stands, though, *Reflection-Belief II* is not directly applicable to relativist views, since it uses a truth predicate that is relativized to just one context, a context of use. There are two ways it could be generalized to the relativist case:

Reflection-Belief II(a).   *One cannot rationally believe p in a context c if one expects that one will later acquire good grounds for thinking that p was not true* as used at and assessed from *c*.

Reflection-Belief II(b).   *One cannot rationally believe p in a context c if one expects that one will later* (in some context *c'*) *acquire good grounds for thinking that p was not true* as used at *c* and assessed from *c'*.

Reflection-Belief II(b) provides the basis for an argument against the rationality of relativist views, along the lines suggested in the preceding paragraph, but *Reflection-Belief II(a)* does not. So we need to ask which of these is the natural generalization of *Reflection-Belief II*—which one captures and extends what was compelling about that principle.

   Why does *Reflection-Belief II* seem intuitively plausible? Why do we think it is irrational to form a belief when one expects later to have good grounds for thinking this belief was untrue in its context? Presumably because "belief aims at truth"—a thought we might cash out by saying that belief is constitutively governed by a "truth norm" forbidding formation of false beliefs. So we can see *Reflection-Belief II* as deriving its plausibility from a more general reflection principle,

Reflection-Belief III.   *One cannot rationally believe p in a context c if one expects that one will later acquire good grounds for thinking that one did this contrary to the norm against forming untrue beliefs,*

together with a truth norm for belief, as the nonrelativist would state it:

Truth Norm for Belief NR.   *One ought not believe that p at a context c unless p is true at c.*

When we put *Reflection-Belief III* together with the truth norm for belief, as the *relativist* would state it (§5.7),

Truth Norm for Belief R.   *One ought not believe that p at a context c unless p is true as used at and assessed from c,*

we get *Reflection-Belief II(a)*. Given *Truth Norm for Belief R*, the relativist can coherently accept *Reflection-Belief III* while rejecting *Reflection-Belief II(b)*—the principle that would be needed for a general criticism of relativism.

In §5.7, I pointed out that for creatures who *only* had beliefs and did not make assertions, there would be no practical difference between relativism and nonindexical contextualism. For the difference shows up in norms for *retraction*, an act that occurs at one context and targets another speech act occurring at another. Once this is appreciated, it should not be surprising that one cannot make a general case against the rationality of *believing* assessment-sensitive propositions that would not generalize also to forms of nonindexical contextualism. In order to drive a wedge between relativism and nonindexical contextualism, the criticism would have to target the rationality of *asserting* assessment-sensitive propositions. But, as we saw at the outset, the reflection principles one would need are just not plausible in the case of assertion.

It seems, then, that no general case against the rationality of assessment-sensitive practices can be made along these lines. There is nothing *structurally* incoherent in the pattern of norms that define a practice as assessment-sensitive. But one might still wonder whether practices like this could be sensible ones. Perhaps there is a coherent set of desires and beliefs that makes it rational to prefer a single blade of grass to one's own life and health, but we would still puzzle about how such a worldview could make sense for a human being. Similarly, even if there are coherent linguistic practices that display the pattern of norms for assertion and retraction that characterize assessment sensitivity, we might think such practices bizarre and badly adapted to our linguistic needs. A proper defense of assessment sensitivity should say something to dispel this worry.

Here it is useful to take an engineering approach to the bits of language we have considered in Chapters 7–11. An engineer building a device needs to start from a description of what the device is supposed to do. So, we will start by asking what these putatively assessment-sensitive bits of language are *for*. What role do they play in our lives? What purposes do they serve? With this job description in hand, we can consider whether the assessment-sensitive semantics serves these purposes better than a contextualist or invariantist semantics could. An affirmative answer will count as a vindication of the rationality of assessment-sensitive practices. For concreteness, we will focus on one case—that of knowledge attributions—but the considerations are easily generalized.

12.2   Assessment sensitivity: an engineer's perspective

Why do we talk about what people know, and not just what is true and what people believe? Plausibly, our knowledge talk serves our need to keep track of who is authoritative about what: who can be properly relied on as an informant on a given topic (Craig 1990; Chrisman 2007). If we are considering buying a motorcycle and want advice, we will ask for someone who knows a lot about motorcycles. When we say that someone's beliefs do not amount to knowledge, we are saying not to trust or rely on them in this matter. When we criticize people who act on mere belief (not knowledge), it is for acting rashly, relying on sources that are not authoritative.

If this hypothesis about the purpose of attributing knowledge is correct, then one should *expect* to find contextual variation in the strength of the epistemic position we require someone to be in to count as "knowing." After all, authoritativeness comes in degrees, and how much authority is required will depend on our purposes. If we are building a multimillion dollar dam, we will rely only on expert civil engineers for opinions about the strengths of various materials and designs. If we are building a small retaining wall to hold a garden, we will be content with the opinions of an experienced general contractor. If "knows" were invariantly keyed to a single, very high epistemic standard, it would not be useful for the purpose we have assigned it.

From a language engineering point of view, then, we might want "knows" to be contextually sensitive in some way. But should it be sensitive to features of the context of use or the context of assessment? If we just think about the knowledge attributions we are presently prepared to make, these options will seem no different, since in these cases the context of use and the context of assessment coincide. To see the practical differences between the two options, we have to consider what each view says about our past knowledge attributions, especially those made in contexts with different governing standards. And here the difference is very clear. The contextualist view says that we can let past knowledge attributions stand if their subjects satisfied the epistemic standards in place when they were made; the relativist view says that they must be retracted unless their subjects satisfied the epistemic standards that are *currently* in place. The contextualist view, then, says to evaluate past knowledge attributions in relation to the various epistemic standards that were relevant when they were made, while the relativist view says to evaluate all knowledge attributions, present and past, by the currently relevant standards.

Are there engineering considerations that favor one of these implementations of contextual variability over the other? The contextualist strategy has one potential advantage: it does not throw out information. It allows knowledge attributions that were made in different practical environments to stand, whereas the relativist strategy requires that they be retracted. But this advantage brings with it a disadvantage: added cognitive load. Contextualism requires us to keep track of the epistemic standards that were in place when each of the past knowledge attributions was made. And this requires more memory and an explicit way of representing epistemic standards.

To make this more concrete, consider how each strategy might be implemented on a computer. Imagine that the computer makes knowledge attributions and attends to those of others. It needs a way to keep track of the knowledge attributions that have been made. A computer constructed along contextualist lines would have to store the subject, the time the subject was said to know, the proposition the subject was said to know, and the epistemic standard that governed the attribution. The computer would also keep track of the standard governing the current context, which would be used in deciding whether to attribute further knowledge:

```
CURRENT_STANDARD = low
PERSON{John} knows PROPOSITION{snow is white}
   by STANDARD{high} at TIME{2011-03-22 03:33:20 UTC}
PERSON{Stan} knows PROPOSITION{Stan has ten dollars}
   by STANDARD{low} at TIME{2011-03-22 04:35:00 UTC}
```

Because retraction would be relatively rare, these records would accumulate steadily in memory. A record would be deleted only if it were determined that the PERSON did not meet the STANDARD with respect to the PROPOSITION at the TIME.

A computer constructed along relativist lines would be able to use a simpler representation. There would be no need to store a standard with each knowledge attribution, because all of the knowledge attributions would be evaluated in relation to the current standard:[1]

```
CURRENT_STANDARD = low
PERSON{John} knows PROPOSITION{snow is white}
   at TIME{2011-03-22 03:33:20 UTC}
PERSON{Stan} knows PROPOSITION{Stan has ten dollars}
```

---

[1] Compare the story of the two lovers in §5.7.

at TIME{2011-03-22 04:35:00 UTC}

The computer would simply delete records where the PERSON did not meet CURRENT_STANDARD with respect to PROPOSITION at TIME. Since CURRENT_STANDARD would change, such deletions would be much more frequent than in the contextualist implementation. The computer would only store knowledge attributions that it regarded as correct by the lights of the standards governing its current context, throwing out the rest.

Which strategy is optimal, for the purpose of keeping track of who is authoritative about various subject matters, with a view to guiding action? For this purpose, all that matters is who knows by current standards. Although both the relativist and the contextualist strategy keep track of this, the relativist strategy keeps track *only* of this, and this is an advantage in efficiency. When standards are high, we don't really care who knows what by low standards, but the contextualist strategy stores a good deal of such information. A principle of efficient engineering says that we should store no more than is needed for our purposes, and this steers us towards relativism.[2]

To get a feel for the kind of argument I am making here, consider a simpler problem. Suppose we are writing a computer program that plays a card game. After each round of the card game, each player wins a certain number of points. The first player to gain 100 points total wins. In order to determine when the game has been won, then, the program needs to be able to keep track of each player's total score. There are two different strategies it might use to do this:

Score per round Store a list of each player's score on each round. After each round, check to see if anyone has won by totaling the scores in each player's list.

BILL: 0, 4, 17, 2, 0

---

[2]Sherlock Holmes in *A Study in Scarlet*: "I consider that a man's brain originally is like a little empty attic, and you have to stock it with such furniture as you choose. A fool takes in all the lumber of every sort that he comes across, so that the knowledge which might be useful to him gets crowded out, or at best is jumbled up with a lot of other things, so that he has a difficulty in laying his hands upon it. Now the skillful workman is very careful indeed as to what he takes into his brain-attic. He will have nothing but the tools which may help him in doing his work, but of these he has a large assortment, and all in the most perfect order. It is a mistake to think that that little room has elastic walls and can distend to any extent. Depend upon it there comes a time when for every addition of knowledge you forget something that you knew before. It is of the highest importance, therefore, not to have useless facts elbowing out the useful ones." (Doyle 1986: 11-12)

```
SARA: 15, 13, 3, 10, 12
```

Running total Store a single number, a running total, for each player. After
each round, check to see if anyone has won by examining the running
totals.

```
BILL: 23
SARA: 53
```

Clearly *Running total* is the more efficient strategy. It requires less memory—
storing one number per player instead of n, where n is the number of rounds
of play. And it requires less computation—performing one addition per player
each round, instead of $n - 1$, where n is the number of rounds played so far.
Since *Score per round* does nothing with its list of scores per round other than
total them, there is no point in storing this information.

One might resist the analogy. Perhaps there is a point to storing "old"
knowledge attributions, together with their governing standards, even if our
purpose is to determine who is authoritative now. For we can often conclude
from the fact that someone knew-relative-to-standard-S_1 that p that they knew-
relative-to-standard-S_2 that p. Thus, information about who can meet other
contexts' governing standards can serve as an inferential base for conclusions
about who can meet our current governing standards. Suppose, for example,
that there are just three possible epistemic standards, Low, Medium, and High.
If we remember that John did not know-by-Medium that his car was in his
driveway, then we can conclude that he did not know-by-High. Conversely, if
we remember that he knew-by-High that he was born in Texas, then we can
conclude that he knew-by-Medium. Whatever our current context is, then, we
can make use of stored knowledge attributions made in other contexts.

It is not clear, however, that realistic forms of contextualism can make
such a response. Realistically, there are not going to be just three epistemic
standards, arranged hierarchically so that if a subject satisfies one, she satisfies
all the lower ones. Suppose, for example, that an epistemic standard is a set of
relevant alternatives that must be ruled out. Then it will be fairly rare that two
standards S_1 and S_2 are so related that meeting S_1 entails meeting S_2 (this will
be so precisely when the set of alternatives corresponding to S_1 is a superset
of the set corresponding to S_2). It will also be fairly rare for two contexts
to be governed by precisely the same standard. So a large database of past
knowledge attributions is not likely to be inferentially very productive, and
the cost of maintaining it (and extracting information from it) may outweigh

the value of the information that can be extracted.

One might think that another reason to store a database of past knowledge attributions is to keep track of an agent's reliability: how often it is the case that she knows, relative to the standards governing the context she is in, whether p. But reliability can be tracked far more efficiently by keeping a running "batting average," which does not require storing either the attributions themselves or the governing standards.

In addition to requiring greater storage capacity, the contextualist strategy requires greater representational capacity, and this too is a a cognitive cost. Both the contextualist and the relativist computers will need to be sensitive to current epistemic standards in making and evaluating knowledge attributions. We assumed above that the relativist computer would *explicitly* represent the current standards—say, by storing them in a global variable. That is the natural assumption on the assumption that the relativist device is a digital computer, since all sensitivities in a digital computer are mediated by explicit, manipulable representations. But although our device needs to be able to judge when agents have met the standard, it doesn't need the kind of representation of a standard that can be compared with other standards and used in inferences. Consider van Gelder's (1995) nice example of a centrifugal governor (Fig. 12.1). The purpose of the device is to keep a motor running at a constant speed, by reducing power to the motor when it runs too fast and increasing power when it runs too slow. The speed of the motor is "represented" by the height of the balls. This low-grade "representation" is sufficient for regulating the steam input, since the balls are directly connected to the input through a mechanical linkage. But it is not the sort of representation that could be used in inferences. Sometimes such explicit representations are not necessary.

Although both the contextualist and the relativist strategies require some way of representing epistemic standards, the contextualist strategy puts inferential demands on these representations that the relativist strategy does not. On the relativist strategy, the knowledge attributor needs some implicit grasp of the epistemic standard governing her present context, but she never needs to compare two epistemic standards, or to consider whether someone would count as knowing by some standard other than the presently active one. So the attributor does not need an explicit representation of the standard; an implicit sensitivity to it may suffice. The upshot is that the contextualist strategy is more expensive, not just in its memory requirements, but in its

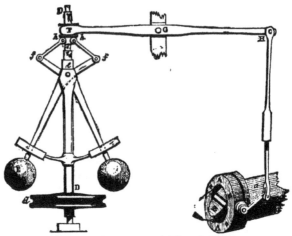

FIG. 4.---*Governor and Throttle-Valve.*

FIG. 12.1. Watt's centrifugal governor (Routledge 1881: 6). As the engine
    turns faster, the two balls rise due to centrifugal forces, causing the lever
    arm to restrict the flow of steam to the engine. As the engine turns slower,
    the balls fall, causing the lever arm to increase the flow of steam to the
    engine.

representational requirements.

This point is particularly compelling when we turn from knowledge attributions to claims of taste. Having an implicit sensitivity to a taste is easy:
one just needs to like some flavors when one tastes them, and dislike others.
Having an explicit representation of a taste—the sort of thing one would
need to get useful inferential knowledge from stored information about past
tastiness assertions—is much more difficult. In fact, we have such a paucity
of means for directly describing tastes that we tend to describe people's tastes
by listing things they like and dislike.

From an engineering point of view, any added cognitive burden needs to
be justified by the added value it gives us, given our purposes. The reflections
above suggest that the added burden of the contextualist implementation
is not worth it, if our interest in knowledge attributions lies in determining
who is authoritative in a way that matters for our decision-making. If that is
right, then in addition to seeing *that* our knowledge-attributing vocabulary is
assessment-sensitive (the conclusion of Chapter 8), we can see why it *makes
sense* that it should be so.

12.3 The evolution of assessment sensitivity

We have argued that it is *good*, given the purposes they serve, that knowledge attributions be assessment-sensitive. Does that mean we have a teleological explanation of *why* they are assessment-sensitive? Not necessarily. Good things can happen fortuitously, for reasons unrelated to their goodness. We would be closer to an explanation if we had reason to think that the relevant linguistic practices evolved through a process resembling natural selection, where variant conventions compete and the usefulness of a variant helps it spread in a population. It is plausible that such a mechanism is operative in the development of language (Croft 2000), but it is impossible to argue this in the particular case at hand without some knowledge of the history. Supposing that knowledge attributions are assessment-sensitive, were they always so? If not, what were they like before they became assessment-sensitive, and what triggered the change? We simply do not know, and I suspect we never will, as the relevant changes most likely predate the historical record.

All we can do here, then, is speculate. All the same, it seems useful to have at least one "just-so story" about how assessment-sensitive practices could have emerged, and been sustained, because of their usefulness for the purposes they serve. At the very least, that would answer a "how possible" question.

To aid imagination, then, let us end with a story. Or rather two stories—since I can think of two different ways in which assessment sensitivity might have evolved:

The upward path. The target expressions begin by being use-sensitive, and come to be assessment-sensitive.

The downward path. The target expressions begin by being invariantist, and come to be assessment-sensitive.

12.3.1 *The upward path*

ONCE upon a time, "knows" behaved just as contextualists say it does. Speakers took the truth of knowledge claims to depend on which alternatives were relevant at the context at which the claim was made. They kept track of the standards or alternatives that were relevant when various past knowledge claims were made, and they referred to these standards or alternatives when deciding whether to retract these claims.

For example, on Monday John asserted that Sue "did not know" that she would get home that night, because he was in a high-standards context involving actuarial calculations that took into account the possibility that Sue would be devoured by a saber-toothed tiger on the way home. But on Tuesday, in a context governed by lower standards, he asserted that Sue "knew" on Monday that she would get home that night. When pressed to defend his early assertion that she "did not know" this, he did so by noting that its truth depended on whether Sue could meet the higher standards governing his earlier context, not the lower standards governing his later context.

On Wednesday, though, John was feeling tired. Again he found himself in a low standards context, and again his earlier assertion that Sue had "not known" that she would get home Monday night was challenged. "I could defend my assertion," he thought to himself. "But why bother? I'm tired, and what point is there to keeping the thing on the books? After all, Monday's standards are of no importance to the projects I am engaged in now, which require me to identify people who are authoritative on questions I am now interested in." So, although he could have defended himself, he chose instead just to retract his earlier claim—not admitting fault, but just declining to defend it further. We might call this kind of retraction *lazy retraction*.

As time passed, and people got busier, more and more people found themselves thinking as John did. Sure, they *could* defend their past knowledge attributions. But why spend precious time and energy preserving something that is useless? If a thief comes and steals the old lawn furniture you'd been too busy to get rid of, do you call the police or give silent thanks?

As lazy retraction became more common, the norms began to change. Speakers began to *expect* others to retract earlier knowledge attributions if they were false by the lights of the standards governing the *present* context. Refusing to retract was considered, first, odd, then later, impolite, and finally, incorrect.

In this way, "knows" came to be assessment-sensitive.

12.3.2 *The downward path*

ONCE upon a time, "knows" had an invariantist semantics. The truth of knowledge claims did not depend on a contextually determined standard. Rather, there was a single set standard that agents had to meet in order to count as "knowing." This worked well enough, because life was simple. Inquiries mostly concerned basic necessities of life, and the matrix of risks and rewards stayed relatively constant.

As time passed, society became more complex. Instead of small houses, people began building large apartments housing many people. They built ambitious bridges over chasms. Failures of these large structures would be catastrophic, and many fewer people were regarded as authoritative about questions like "how thick a support do you need per unit weight?" when it came to these big projects.

People had been in the habit of settling questions about who is authoritative about a subject by asking who *knows* about it. Indeed, this was regarded as one of the main points of talking about knowledge. In order to preserve this link between attributions of knowledge and the project of identifying people who are authoritative on a subject, people began to demand that those who are said to "know" meet a higher standard in a context where much is at stake than in an ordinary context.

This was a step towards remaking "knows" along contextualist lines. Deciding whether to assert that somebody "knew" something now required deciding whether the person met the standards determined by the current context (the context of use). But this change was gradual, and it did not immediately bring with it a corresponding change in norms for *retracting* earlier assertions. People had been in the habit of evaluating past assertions in light of the very same standards that would apply to present ones, and even after these standards went from being fixed to being variable, this aspect of their practice persisted. A past assertion of "*S* knows that *p*," then, was deemed subject to retraction if *S* did not meet the epistemic standard relevant to the *current* context with regard to *p*—even if *S did* meet the standard relevant to the context in which the assertion was made.

Some more reflective people argued that there was something incoherent about the practice that emerged: that it was a Frankenstein's monster, an unholy combination of elements of contextualist and invariantist practices. They urged either a return to the old ways (invariantism), or a complete transition to a contextualist practice. But their pleas were largely ignored, because the practice *worked*. The increased complexities of life made a return to invariantism impractical, and the increased representational demands of the fully contextualist practice could not be justified by any compensating advantage. The practice solidified as it was, just as amphibians stabilized as an intermediate form between sea creatures and land creatures.

In this way, "knows" came to be assessment-sensitive.

REFERENCES

Ayer, A. J. (1959). *Language, Truth, and Logic*. New York: Dover.

Bach, Kent and Robert M. Harnish (1979). *Linguistic Communication and Speech Acts*. Cambridge, MA: MIT Press.

Baghramian, Maria (2004). *Relativism*. New York: Routledge.

Bar-Hillel, Y. (1973). Primary truth bearers. *Dialectica*, 27: 303–312.

Barrett, Jeffrey A. (2001). *The Quantum Mechanics of Minds and Worlds*. Oxford: Oxford University Press.

Belnap, Nuel (1992). Branching space-time. *Synthese*, 92: 385–434.

Belnap, Nuel (2001). Double time references: Speech-act reports as modalities in an indeterministic setting. In *Advances in Modal Logic*, iii, ed. F. Wolter, H. Wansing, M. D. Rijke, and M. Zakharyaschev. Stanford: CSLI, 1–22.

Belnap, Nuel and Mitchell Green (1994). Indeterminism and the thin red line. *Philosophical Perspectives*, 8: 365–388.

Belnap, Nuel, Michael Perloff, and Ming Xu (2001). *Facing the Future: Agents and Choices in Our Indeterministic World*. Oxford: Oxford University Press.

Bennigson, Thomas (1999). Is relativism really self-refuting? *Philosophical Studies*, 94: 211–236.

Blackburn, Simon (1984). *Spreading the Word*. Oxford: Oxford University Press.

Blackburn, Simon (1988). Attitudes and contents. *Ethics*, 98: 501–517.

Blome-Tillmann, Michael (2009). Contextualism, subject-sensitive invariantism, and the interaction of 'knowledge'-ascriptions with modal and temporal operators. *Philosophy and Phenomenological Research*, 79: 315–331.

Boghossian, Paul (2006). *Fear of Knowledge: Against Relativism and Constructivism*. Oxford: Oxford University Press.

Borges, Jorge Luis (1964). *Labyrinths: Selected Stories and Other Writings*. New York: New Directions.

Boyd, Julian and J. P. Thorne (1969). The semantics of modal verbs. *Journal of Linguistics*, 5: 57–74.

Brandom, Robert (1994). *Making It Explicit*. Cambridge, MA: Harvard University Press.

Brandt, R. B. (1959). *Ethical Theory*. Englewood Cliffs, NJ: Prentice Hall.

Brogaard, Berit (2008). In defence of a perspectival semantics for 'know'. *Australasian Journal of Philosophy*, 86: 439–459.

Broome, John (1991). *Weighing Goods*. Oxford: Blackwell.

Burke, T. E. (1979). The limits of relativism. *Philosophical Quarterly*, 29: 193–207.

Burnyeat, M. F. (1976a). Protagoras and self-refutation in later Greek philosophy. *Philosophical Review*, 85: 44–69.

Burnyeat, M. F. (1976b). Protagoras and self-refutation in Plato's *Theaetetus*. *Philosophical Review*, 85: 172–195.

Burnyeat, M. F. (1990). *The Theaetetus of Plato*. Indianapolis: Hackett.

Campbell, John (1997). The realism of memory. In *Language, Thought, and Logic*. Oxford: Oxford University Press, 157–181.

Cappelen, Herman (2008a). Content relativism and semantic blindness. In *Relative Truth*, ed. M. García-Carpintero and M. Kölbel. Oxford: Oxford University Press, 265–286.

Cappelen, Herman (2008b). The creative interpreter: Content relativism and assertion. *Philosophical Perspectives*, 22: 23–46.

Cappelen, Herman and John Hawthorne (2009). *Relativism and Monadic Truth*. Oxford: Oxford University Press.

Cappelen, Herman and Ernie Lepore (2005). *Insensitive Semantics: A Defense of Semantic Minimalism and Speech Act Pluralism*. Oxford: Blackwell.

Cartwright, Richard (1962). Propositions. In *Analytic Philosophy*, i, ed. R. Butler. Blackwell.

Chrisman, Matthew (2007). From epistemic contextualism to epistemic expressivism. *Philosophical Studies*, 135: 225–254.

Churchland, Paul (1979). *Scientific Realism and the Plasticity of Mind*. Cambridge: Cambridge University Press.

Craig, Edward (1990). *Knowledge and the State of Nature*. Oxford: Clarendon Press.

Croft, William (2000). *Explaining Language Change: An Evolutionary Approach*. Harlow, England: Longman.

Davidson, Donald (1963). Actions, reasons, and causes. *The Journal of Philosophy*, 60: 685–700.

Davidson, Donald (1990). The structure and content of truth. *Journal of Philosophy*, 87: 279–328.

Davidson, Donald (1997). The folly of trying to define truth. *Journal of Philosophy*, 94: 263–278.

Davis, Wayne A. (2007). Knowledge claims and context: Loose use. *Philosophical Studies*, 132: 395–438.

de Sa, Dan López (2008). Presuppositions of commonality: An indexical relativist account of disagreement. In *Relative Truth*, ed. M. García-Carpintero and M. Kölbel. Oxford: Oxford University Press, 297–310.

de Sa, Dan López (2009). Relativizing utterance-truth? *Synthese*, 170: 1–5.

DeRose, Keith (1991). Epistemic possibilities. *Philosophical Review*, 100(4): 581–605.

DeRose, Keith (1999). Can it be that it would have been even though it might not have been? *Philosophical Perspectives*, 13: 385–412.

DeRose, Keith (2004). Single scoreboard semantics. *Philosophical Studies*, 119: 1–21.

DeRose, Keith (2005). The ordinary language basis for contextualism and the new invariantism. *Philosophical Quarterly*, 55: 172–198.

DeRose, Keith (2006). 'Bamboozed by our own words': Semantic blindness and some arguments against contextualism. *Philosophy and Phenomenological Research*, 73: 316–338.

Dietz, Richard (2008). Epistemic modals and correct disagreement. In *Relative Truth*, ed. M. García-Carpintero and M. Kölbel. Oxford: Oxford University Press, 239–262.

Doyle, Sir Arthur Conan (1986). *Sherlock Holmes: The Complete Novels and Stories*, i. New York: Bantam.

Dreier, James (1999). Transforming expressivism. *Noûs*, 33: 558–572.

Dummett, Michael (1959). Truth. *Proceedings of the Aristotelian Society*, n.s. 59: 141–62.

Dummett, Michael (1978). *Truth and Other Enigmas*. Cambridge, MA: Harvard University Press.

Dummett, Michael (1981). *Frege: Philosophy of Language* (2nd edn). Cambridge, MA: Harvard University Press.

Egan, Andy (2007). Epistemic modals, relativism, and assertion. *Philosophical Studies*, 133: 1–22.

Egan, Andy (2009). Billboards, bombs, and shotgun weddings. *Synthese*, 166: 251–279.

Egan, Andy (2010). Disputing about taste. In *Disagreement*, ed. R. Feldman and T. A. Warfield. Oxford: Oxford University Press, 247–292.

Egan, Andy, John Hawthorne, and Brian Weatherson (2005). Epistemic modals in context. In *Contextualism in Philosophy*, ed. G. Preyer and G. Peter.

Oxford: Oxford University Press, 131–168.

Evans, Gareth (1982). *Varieties of Reference*. Oxford: Clarendon Press.

Evans, Gareth (1985). Does tense logic rest upon a mistake? In *Collected Papers*. Oxford: Oxford University Press, 343–363.

Ewing, A. C. (1947). *The Definition of Good*. New York: MacMillan.

Fantl, Jeremy and Matthew McGrath (2002). Evidence, pragmatics, and justification. *Philosophical Review*, 111: 67–95.

Feldman, Richard (2001). Skeptical problems, contextualist solutions. *Philosophical Studies*, 103: 61–85.

Fellman, Anita Clair (2008). *Little House, Long Shadow: Laura Ingalls Wilder's Impact on American Culture*. Columbia: University of Missouri Press.

Field, Hartry (1994). Deflationist views of meaning and content. *Mind*, 103: 249–85.

Field, Hartry (2000). Indeterminacy, degree of belief, and excluded middle. *Nous*, 34: 1–30.

Fine, Gail (1983). Plato's refutation of Protagoras in the *Theaetetus*. *Apeiron*, 31: 201–234.

Fitelson, Branden (2005). Inductive logic. In *Philosophy of Science: An Encyclopedia*, ed. J. Pfeifer and S. Sarkar. New York: Routledge.

Fox, John F. (1994). How must relativism be construed to be coherent? *Philosophy of the Social Sciences*, 24: 55–75.

Frege, Gottlob (1879). *Begriffsschrift, eine der arithmetischen nachgebildete Formelsprache des reinen Denkens*. Halle: Stefan Bauer-Meneglberg.

Frege, Gottlob (1953). *The Foundations of Arithmetic: A logico-mathematical enquiry into the concept of number*. Oxford: Blackwell.

Frege, Gottlob (1979). *Posthumous Writings*. Chicago: University of Chicago Press.

Geach, Peter (1960). Ascriptivism. *Philosophical Review*, 69: 221–225.

Geach, Peter (1965). Assertion. *Philosophical Review*, 74: 449–465.

Geurts, Bart (2005). Entertaining alternatives: Disjunctions as modals. *Natural Language Semantics*, 13: 383–410.

Gibbard, Allan (1990). *Wise Choices, Apt Feelings: A Theory of Normative Judgment*. Cambridge, MA: Harvard University Press.

Gibbard, Allan (2003). *Thinking How to Live*. Cambridge, MA: Harvard University Press.

Gibbard, Allan (2005). Truth and correct belief. *Philosophical Issues*, 15: 338–350.

Gillies, Anthony S. (2010). Iffiness. *Semantics and Pragmatics*, 3: 1–42.

Glanzberg, Michael (2007). Context, content, and relativism. *Philosophical Studies*, 136: 1–29.

Glanzberg, Michael (2009). Semantics and truth relative to a world. *Synthese*, 166: 281–307.

Goodman, Nelson (1979). *Fact, Fiction, and Forecast*. Cambridge, MA: Harvard University Press.

Grice, Paul (1989). *Studies in the Way of Words*. Cambridge, MA: Harvard University Press.

Groenendijk, Jeroen and Martin Stokhof (1997). Questions. In *Handbook of Logic and Language*, ed. J. van Benthem and A. T. Meulen. Cambridge, MA: MIT Press, 1055–1124.

Grover, Dorothy L. (1979). Prosentences and propositional quantification: A response to Zimmerman. *Philosophical Studies*, 35(3): 289–297.

Grover, Dorothy L., Joseph Camp, and Nuel Belnap (1975). *Philosophical Studies*, 27: 73–125.

Hacking, Ian (1967). Possibility. *Philosophical Review*, 76: 143–168.

Hales, Steven D. (1997a). A consistent relativism. *Mind*, 106: 33–52.

Hales, Steven D. (1997b). A reply to Shogenji on relativism. *Mind*, 106: 749–750.

Hamblin, C. L. (1973). Questions in Montague English. *Foundations of Language*, 10: 41–53.

Hare, R. M. (1967). Some alleged differences between imperatives and indicatives. *Mind*, 76: 309–326.

Hare, R. M. (1970). Meaning and speech acts. *Philosophical Review*, 79: 3–24.

Harman, Gilbert (1975). Moral relativism defended. *Philosophical Review*, 84: 3–22.

Hawthorne, John (2004). *Knowledge and Lotteries*. Oxford: Oxford University Press.

Hazen, Allen (1976). Expressive completeness in modal language. *Journal of Philosophical Logic*, 5: 25–46.

Heck, Jr. Richard G. (2006). MacFarlane on relative truth. *Philosophical Issues*, 16: 88–100.

Hintikka, Jaakko (1962). *Knowledge and Belief: An Introduction to the Logic of the Two Notions*. Ithaca: Cornell University Press.

Horn, Laurence R. (1989). *A Natural History of Negation*. Chicago: University of Chicago Press.

Horty, John F. (2011). Perspectival act utilitarianism. In *Dynamic Formal Epistemology*, cccli, ed. P. Girard, O. Roy, and M. Marion. Synthese Library, 197–221.

Horwich, Paul (1998). *Meaning*. Oxford: Basil Blackwell.

Horwich, Paul (2005). The Frege–Geach point. *Philosophical Issues*, 15: 78–93.

Husserl, Edmund (2001). *Logical Investigations*, i. New York: Routledge. Translated by J. N. Findlay.

Huvenes, Torfinn (2012). Varieties of disagreement and predicates of taste. *Australasian Journal of Philosophy*, 90: 167–181.

Jackson, Dennis E. (1917). An experimental investigation of the pharmacological action of nitrous oxid. *American Journal of Surgery*, 31: 70.

Jackson, Frank (1991). Decision-theoretic consequentialism and the nearest and dearest objection. *Ethics*, 101: 461–482.

Jackson, Frank and Philip Pettit (1998). A problem for expressivism. *Analysis*, 58: 239–251.

James, William (1909). *The Meaning of Truth*. Longmans, Green, and Co.

James, William (1978). *Pragmatism and The Meaning of Truth*. Cambridge, MA: Harvard University Press.

Kamp, Hans (1971). Formal properties of 'now'. *Theoria*, 37: 227–273.

Kaplan, David (1989). Demonstratives: An essay on the semantics, logic, metaphysics, and epistemology of demonstratives and other indexicals. In *Themes from Kaplan*, ed. J. Almog, J. Perry, and H. Wettstein. Oxford: Oxford University Press, 481–566.

Karttunen, Lauri (1977). Syntax and semantics of questions. *Linguistics and Philosophy*, 1: 3–44.

Kelly, Thomas (2010). Peer disagreement and higher-order evidence. In *Disagreement*, ed. R. Feldman and T. A. Warfield. Oxford: Oxford University Press.

Kennedy, Christopher (2007). Vagueness and grammar: the semantics of relative and absolute gradable adjectives. *Linguistics and Philosophy*, 30: 1–45.

King, Jeffrey C. (2003). Tense, modality, and semantic values. *Philosophical Perspectives*, 17: 195–245.

Kölbel, Max (2002). *Truth Without Objectivity*. London: Routledge.

Kölbel, Max (2004a). Faultless disagreement. *Proceedings of the Aristotelian Society*, 104: 53–73.

Kölbel, Max (2004b). Indexical relativism versus genuine relativism. *International Journal of Philosophical Studies*, 12: 297–313.

Kölbel, Max (2008a). Introduction: Motivations for relativism. In *Relative Truth*, ed. M. García-Carpintero and M. Kölbel. Oxford: Oxford University Press, 1–38.

Kölbel, Max (2008b). "True" as ambiguous. *Philosophy and Phenomenological Research*, 77: 359–384.

Kolodny, Niko and John MacFarlane (2010). Ifs and oughts. *Journal of Philosophy*, 107: 115–143.

Kompa, Nikola (2002). The context sensitivity of knowledge ascriptions. *Grazer Philosophische Studien*, 64: 79–96.

Kratzer, Angelika (1981a). Blurred conditionals. In *Crossing the Boundaries in Linguistics*, ed. W. Klein and W. Levelt. Dordrecht: Reidel, 201–209.

Kratzer, Angelika (1981b). The notional category of modality. In *Words, Worlds, and Contexts: New Approaches to Word Semantics*, ed. H. J. Eikmeyer and H. Rieser. Berlin: de Gruyter, 38–74.

Kratzer, Angelika (1986). Conditionals. *Proceedings of CLS 22.*

Kripke, Saul (1972). Naming and necessity. In *Semantics of Natural Languages*, ed. D. Davidson and G. Harman. Dordrecht: Reidel, 254–355.

Kruger, Justin and David Dunning (1999). Unskilled and unaware of it: How difficulties in recognizing one's own incompetence lead to inflated self-assessments. *Journal of Personality and Social Psychology*, 77: 1121–1135.

Künne, Wolfgang (2003). *Conceptions of Truth*. Oxford: Oxford University Press.

Lasersohn, Peter (2005). Context dependence, disagreement, and predicates of personal taste. *Linguistics and Philosophy*, 28: 643–686.

Lasersohn, Peter (2009). Relative truth, speaker commitment, and control of implicit arguments. *Synthese*, 166: 359–374.

Leslie, Sarah-Jane (2012). Generics. In *The Routledge Companion to Philosophy of Language*. New York: Routledge, 355–366.

Lewis, David (1970a). Anselm and actuality. *Noûs*, 4: 175–188.

Lewis, David (1970b). General semantics. *Synthese*, 22: 18–67.

Lewis, David (1979a). Attitudes de dicto and de se. *Philosophical Review*, 87: 513–545.

Lewis, David (1979b). Scorekeeping in a language game. *Journal of Philosophical Logic*, 8: 339–359.

Lewis, David (1980). Index, context, and content. In *Philosophy and Grammar*, ed. S. Kanger and S. Öhman. Dordrecht: Reidel, 79–100.

Lewis, David (1983). Languages and language. In *Philosophical Papers*, i, 163–188. Oxford: Oxford University Press.

Lewis, David (1986). *On the Plurality of Worlds*. Oxford: Blackwell.

Lewis, David (1988). Relevant implication. *Theoria*, 54: 161–174.

Lewis, David (1991). *Parts of Classes*. Oxford: Oxford University Press.

Lewis, David (1996). Elusive knowledge. *Australasian Journal of Philosophy*, 74: 549–567.

Lewis, David (1998). *Papers in Philosophical Logic*. Cambridge: Cambridge University Press.

Lockie, Robert (2003). Relativism and reflexivity. *International Journal of Philosophical Studies*, 11: 319–339.

Ludlow, Peter (2005). Contextualism and the new linguistic turn in epistemology. In *Contextualism in Philosophy: Knowledge, Meaning, and Truth*, ed. G. Preyer and G. Peter. Oxford: Oxford University Press, 11–50.

Łukasiewicz, Jan (1920). O logice trójwartościowej. *Ruch filozoficzny*, 5: 170–171.

Łukasiewicz, Jan (1967). On three-valued logic. In *Polish Logic*, ed. S. McCall. Oxford: Oxford University Press, 16–18.

Lycan, William (2001). *Real Conditionals*. Oxford: Oxford University Press.

MacFarlane, John (2003). Future contingents and relative truth. *Philosophical Quarterly*, 53(212): 321–336.

MacFarlane, John (2005a). The assessment sensitivity of knowledge attributions. *Oxford Studies in Epistemology*, 1: 197–233.

MacFarlane, John (2005b). Knowledge laundering: Testimony and sensitive invariantism. *Analysis*, 65: 132–138.

MacFarlane, John (2005c). Making sense of relative truth. *Proceedings of the Aristotelian Society*, 105: 321–339.

MacFarlane, John (2007a). Relativism and disagreement. *Philosophical Studies*, 132: 17–31.

MacFarlane, John (2007b). Semantic minimalism and nonindexical contextualism. In *Context-Sensitivity and Semantic Minimalism*, ed. G. Preyer and G. Peter. Oxford: Oxford University Press, 240–250.

MacFarlane, John (2008). Truth in the garden of forking paths. In *Relative Truth*, ed. M. García-Carpintero and M. Kölbel. Oxford: Oxford University Press.

MacFarlane, John (2009). Nonindexical contextualism. *Synthese*, 166: 231–50.

MacFarlane, John (2011a). Epistemic modals are assessment sensitive. In *Epistemic Modals*, ed. A. Egan and B. Weatherson. Oxford: Oxford University Press.

MacFarlane, John (2011b). What is assertion? In *Assertion*, ed. J. Brown and H. Cappelen. Oxford University Press, 79–96.

MacFarlane, John (2012). Richard on truth and commitment. *Philosophical Studies*, 160: 445–453.

Maclay, Kathleen (2001, October). UC Berkeley's Davitt Moroney shares abiding love of music through teaching and performing. UC Berkeley press release.

Margolis, Joseph (1991). *The Truth About Relativism*. Oxford: Blackwell.

McArthur, Robert P. (1974). Factuality and modality in the future tense. *Nous*, 8: 283–284.

McGee, Vann and Brian P. McLaughlin (2004). Logical commitment and semantic indeterminacy: A reply to Williamson. *Linguistics and Philosophy*, 27: 221–235.

Meiland, Jack (1977). Concepts of relative truth. *The Monist*, 60: 568–582.

Meiland, Jack and Michael Krausz (ed.) (1982). *Relativism: Cognitive and Moral*. Notre Dame: University of Notre Dame Press.

Mellor, D. H. (1981). *Real Time*. Cambridge: Cambridge University Press.

Moltmann, Friederike (2010). Relative truth and the first person. *Philosophical Studies*, 150: 187–220.

Montague, Richard (1974). Deterministic theories. In *Formal Philosophy*, ed. R. H. Thomason, 303–359. New Haven: Yale University Press.

Montminy, Martin (2009). Contextualism, relativism, and ordinary speakers' judgments. *Philosophical Studies*, 143: 341–356.

Moore, G. E. (1912). *Ethics*. Oxford: Oxford University Press.

Moore, G. E. (1962). *Commonplace Book, 1919–53*. London: Allen and Unwin.

Nagel, Jennifer (2011). The psychological basis of the Harman–Vogel paradox. *Philosopher's Imprint*, 11(5): 1–53.

Neale, Stephen (2001). *Facing Facts*. Oxford: Oxford University Press.

Newton-Smith, W. (1981). *The Rationality of Science*. New York: Routledge.

Newton-Smith, W. (1982). Relativism and the possibility of interpretation. In *Rationality and Relativism*, ed. M. Hollis and S. Lukes. Cambridge, MA: MIT Press.

Nozick, Robert (1981). *Philosophical Explanations*. Oxford: Clarendon Press.

Nozick, Robert (2001). *Invariances: The Structure of the Objective World*. Cambridge, MA: Harvard University Press.

Parfit, Derek (1984). *Reasons and Persons*. Oxford: Oxford University Press.

Parfit, Derek (1988). What we together do. Unpublished manuscript, Oxford.

Parfit, Derek (2011). *On What Matters*. Oxford: Oxford University Press.

Passmore, John (1961). *Philosophical Reasoning*. London: Duckworth.

Patterson, Douglas (2005). Deflationism and the truth conditional theory of meaning. *Philosophical Studies*, 124: 271–294.

Percival, Philip (1989). Indices of truth and temporal propositions. *Philosophical Quarterly*, 39: 190–199.

Percival, Philip (1994). Absolute truth. *Proceedings of the Aristotelian Society*, 94: 189–213.

Perry, John (1986). Thought without representation. *Proceedings of the Aristotelian Society*, 60: 137–166.

Perry, John (2001). *Reference and Reflexivity*. Stanford: CSLI.

Portner, Paul (2009). *Modality*. Oxford: Oxford University Press.

Predelli, Stefano (1998). I am not here now. *Analysis*, 58: 107–115.

Predelli, Stefano (2005). *Contexts: Meaning, Truth, and the Use of Language*. Oxford: Oxford University Press.

Preyer, Gerhard and Georg Peter (ed.) (2007). *Context-Sensitivity and Semantic Minimalism: New Essays on Semantics and Pragmatics*. Oxford: Oxford University Press.

Price, Huw (1983). Does 'probably' modify sense? *Australasian Journal of Philosophy*, 61: 396–408.

Price, Huw (1994). Semantic minimalism and the Frege point. In *Foundations of Speech Act Theory: Philosophical and Linguistic Perspectives*, ed. S. L. Tsohatzidis. Routledge, 132–155.

Prichard, H. A. (1949). Duty and ignorance of fact. In *Moral Obligation*, ed. W. D. Ross. Oxford: Clarendon Press, 18–39.

Prior, Arthur (1953). Three-valued logic and future contingents. *Philosophy Quarterly*, 3: 317–326.

Prior, Arthur (1957). *Time and Modality*. Westport, Connecticut: Greenwood Press.

Prior, Arthur (1967). *Past, Present and Future*. Oxford: Oxford University Press.

Prior, Arthur (2003). *Papers on Time and Tense* (new edn). Oxford: Oxford University Press.

Putnam, Hilary (1981). *Reason, Truth and History*. Cambridge: Cambridge University Press.

Ramsey, F. P. (2001). The nature of truth. In *The Nature of Truth*, ed. M. P. Lynch. Cambridge, MA: MIT Press, 433–446.

Recanati, François (2007). *Perspectival Thought: A Plea for (Moderate) Relativism*. Oxford: Oxford University Press.

Recanati, François (2008). Moderate relativism. In *Relative Truth*, ed. M. García-Carpintero and M. Kölbel. Oxford: Oxford University Press, 41–62.

Regan, Donald (1980). *Utilitarianism and Cooperation*. Oxford: Oxford University Press.

Richard, Mark (1980). Temporalism and eternalism. *Philosophical Studies*, 39: 1–13.

Richard, Mark (1982). Tense, propositions, and meanings. *Philosophical Studies*, 41: 337–351.

Richard, Mark (2003). Introduction to Part I. In *Time, Tense, and Reference*, ed. A. Jokić and Q. Smith. Cambridge, MA: MIT Press, 27–45.

Richard, Mark (2004). Contextualism and relativism. *Philosophical Studies*, 119: 215–242.

Richard, Mark (2008). *When Truth Gives Out*. Oxford: Oxford University Press.

Rorty, Richard (1998). *Truth and Progress: Philosophical Papers, Vol. 3*. Cambridge: Cambridge University Press.

Rosenberg, Jay F. (2002). *Thinking About Knowing*. Oxford University Press.

Ross, W. D. (1939). *Foundations of Ethics*. Oxford: Oxford University Press.

Routledge, Robert (1881). *Discoveries and Inventions of the Nineteenth Century*. London: G. Routledge.

Rysiew, Patrick (2001). The context-sensitivity of knowledge attributions. *Noûs*, 35(4): 477–514.

Salmon, Nathan (1986). *Frege's Puzzle*. Cambridge, MA: MIT Press.

Salmon, Nathan (2003). Tense and intension. In *Time, Tense, and Reference*, ed. A. Jokić and Q. Smith. Cambridge, MA: MIT Press, 109–154.

Scanlon, T. M. (2006). Reasons and decisions. *Philosophy and Phenomenological Research*, 72: 722–728.

Schaffer, Jonathan (2004). Skepticism, contextualism, and discrimination. *Philosophy and Phenomenological Research*, 69: 138–155.

Schaffer, Jonathan (2006). The irrelevance of the subject. *Philosophical Studies*, 127: 87–107.

Schaffer, Jonathan (2012). Necessitarian propositions. *Synthese*, 189: 119–162.

Schiffer, Stephen (1996). Contextualist solutions to scepticism. *Proceedings of the Aristotelian Society*, 96: 317–333.

Schlenker, Philippe (2003). A plea for monsters. *Linguistics and Philosophy*, 26: 29–120.

Schlenker, Philippe (2004). Context of thought and context of utterance (A note on free indirect discourse and the historical present). *Mind and Language*, 19: 279–304.

Schroeder, Mark (2008). *Being For: Evaluating the Semantic Program of Expressivism*. Oxford: Oxford University Press.

Schroeder, Mark (2011). *Ought*, agents, and actions. *Philosophical Review*, 120: 1–41.

Searle, John R. (1962). Meaning and speech acts. *Philosophical Review*, 71: 423–432.

Searle, John R. (1969). *Speech Acts*. Cambridge: Cambridge University Press.

Searle, John R. (1979). *Expression and Meaning*. Cambridge: Cambridge University Press.

Sellars, Wilfrid (1948). Concepts as involving laws, and inconceivable without them. *Philosophy of Science*, 15: 287–315.

Shissler, A. Holly (2003). *Between Two Empires: Ahmet Agaoglu and the New Turkey*. New York: I. B. Tauris.

Shogenji, Tomoji (1997). The consistency of global relativism. *Mind*, 106: 745–747.

Soames, Scott (2002). Replies. *Philosophy and Phenomenological Research*, 65: 429–452.

Sokal, Alan D. (1996a). A physicist experiments with cultural studies. *Lingua Franca*: 62–64.

Sokal, Alan D. (1996b). Transgressing the boundaries: Towards a transformational hermeneutics of quantum gravity. *Social Text*, 46/47: 217–252.

Stalnaker, Robert (1975). Indicative conditionals. *Philosophia*, 5: 269–286.

Stalnaker, Robert (1978). Assertion. In *Syntax and Semantics, Vol. 9: Pragmatics*, ed. P. Cole. New York: Academic Press.

Stalnaker, Robert (1987). *Inquiry*. Cambridge, MA: MIT Press.

Stalnaker, Robert (1999). *Context and Content: Essays on Intentionality in Speech and Thought*. Oxford: Oxford University Press.

Stanley, Jason (2000). Context and logical form. *Linguistics and Philosophy*, 23: 391–434.

Stanley, Jason (2005a). Fallibilism and concessive knowledge attributions. *Analysis*, 65: 126–131.

Stanley, Jason (2005b). *Knowledge and Practical Interests*. Oxford: Oxford University Press.

Stanley, Jason (2007). *Language in Context: Selected Essays*. Oxford: Oxford University Press.

Stephenson, Tamina (2007). Judge dependence, epistemic modals, and predicates of personal taste. *Linguistics and Philosophy*, 30: 487–525.

Stevenson, Charles L. (1963). *Facts and Values*. New Haven: Yale University Press.

Stevenson, Leslie (1988). Can truth be relativized to kinds of mind? *Mind*, 97: 281–284.

Strawson, P. F. (1950). Truth. *Proceedings of the Aristotelian Society*, s.v. 24: 129–156.

Sundell, Timothy (2011). Disagreements about taste. *Philosophical Studies*, 155: 267–288.

Swoyer, Chris (1982). True for. In *Relativism: Cognitive and Moral*, ed. J. Meiland and M. Krausz. Notre Dame: University of Notre Dame Press, 84–108.

Tarski, Alfred (1935). Der Wahrheitsbegriff in den formalisierten Sprachen. *Studia Philosophica*, 1: 261–405.

Tarski, Alfred (1983). The concept of truth in formalized languages. In *Logic, Semantics, Metamathematics*, ed. J. Corcoran, 152–278. Indianapolis: Hackett.

Teller, Paul (1972). Epistemic possibility. *Philosophia*, 2: 303–320.

Thomason, Richmond H. (1970). Indeterminist time and truth-value gaps. *Theoria*, 36: 264–281.

Thomson, Judith Jarvis (1986). Imposing risks. In *Rights, Restitution, and Risk*, ed. W. Parent. Cambridge, MA: Harvard University Press, 173–191.

Unger, Peter (1975). *Ignorance: A Case for Scepticism*. Oxford: Oxford University Press.

Unwin, Nicholas (1987). Beyond truth: Towards a new conception of knowledge and communication. *Mind*, 96: 299–317.

Vallicella, William F. (1984). Relativism, truth and the symmetry thesis. *The Monist*, 67: 452–456.

van Fraassen, Bas C. (1966). Singular terms, truth-value gaps, and free logic. *Journal of Philosophy*, 63: 481–495.

van Gelder, Tim (1995). What might cognition be, if not computation? *Journal of Philosophy*, 92: 345–381.

van Heijenoort, Jean (1967). *From Frege to Gödel: A Source Book in Mathematical Logic, 1879-1931*. Cambridge, MA: Harvard University Press.

Velleman, J. David (2000). *The Possibility of Practical reason*. Oxford: Oxford University Press.

von Fintel, Kai and Anthony S. Gillies (2008). CIA leaks. *Philosophical Review*, 117: 77–98.

von Fintel, Kai and Sabine Iatridou (2003). Epistemic containment. *Linguistic Inquiry*, 34: 173–198.

Weatherson, Brian (2009). Conditionals and indexical relativism. *Synthese*, 166: 333–357.

Wedgwood, Ralph (2002). The aim of belief. *Philosophical Perspectives*, 16: 267–297.

Wedgwood, Ralph (2003). Choosing rationally and choosing correctly. In *Weakness of Will and Practical Irrationality*, ed. S. Stroud and C. Toppolet. Oxford: Oxford University Press, 201–230.

Weiner, Matthew (2009). The (mostly harmless) inconsistency of knowledge attributions. *Philosopher's Imprint*, 9: 1–25.

White, F. C. (1986). On a proposed refutation of relativism. *Australasian Journal of Philosophy*, 64: 331–334.

Whyte, Jamie T. (1993). Relativism is absolutely false. *Cogito*, 7: 112–118.

Wiggins, David (1980). What would be a substantial theory of truth? In *Philosophical Subjects: Essays Presented to P. F. Strawson*, ed. Z. van Straaten. Oxford: Clarendon Press, 189–221.

Williams, J. R. G. (2010). Aristotelian indeterminacy and the open future. Unpublished manuscript.

Williams, Michael (1999). Meaning and deflationary truth. *Journal of Philosophy*, 96: 545–564.

Williamson, Timothy (1994). *Vagueness*. London: Routledge.

Williamson, Timothy (1996). Knowing and asserting. *Philosophical Review*, 105: 489–523.

Williamson, Timothy (2000). *Knowledge and Its Limits*. Oxford: Oxford University Press.

Wollheim, Richard (1980). *Art and Its Objects* (2nd edn). Cambridge: Cambridge University Press.

Wright, Crispin (2008). Fear of relativism? *Philosophical Studies*, 141: 379–390.

Yalcin, Seth (2007). Epistemic modals. *Mind*, 116: 983–1026.

Yalcin, Seth (2011). Nonfactualism about epistemic modality. In *Epistemic Modals*, ed. A. Egan and B. Weatherson. Oxford: Oxford University Press, 265–332.

Zimmerman, Aaron (2007). Against relativism. *Philosophical Studies*, 133: 313–348.

Zimmermann, Thomas Ede (2000). Free choice disjunction and epistemic possibility. *Natural Language Semantics*, 8: 255–290.

INDEX